Politics and the Social Sciences

Politics
and the Social Sciences

EDITED BY
SEYMOUR MARTIN LIPSET

New York
OXFORD UNIVERSITY PRESS
London 1969 Toronto

Contents

Politics and the Social Sciences: Introduction

SEYMOUR MARTIN LIPSET

The study of politics has fluctuated between two poles ever since men began to think about the nature of the polity. At one end were those who focused on the political institutions as key agencies of social control and social change. They regarded the behavior of the state, and the intentions of the prince as the most important aspects. Conversely, others stressed how much extra-political factors or conditions affected political events and institutions. In a real sense, these two emphases differed about whether society or the polity is primary. Since the study of non-political institutions ultimately constituted the content of various social science disciplines, anthropology, sociology, economics, and psychology, the issue of the relations between the study of politics and the other social sciences has existed from the start of intellectual interest in such matters.

Clearly, few if any writers, whose concern is the nature of political action, fall solely in one category or the other. Plato looked for a prince who would use political power to set up the ideal Republic; yet he also was sensitive to how the structure of the family, or how the nature of education affected the possibilities for varying forms of political action. Aristotle specified a causal relation between the distribution of wealth and status in communities, and the type of political regime they had. He also studied the contents of the constitutions of the Greek states to see how political systems varied. In more contemporary times, Marxism was a prime example of an approach to politics which located the primary source of political behavior in sociological factors, i.e., level of technological development and class structure. Yet leading Marxist theorists, such as Friedrich Engels and Leon Trotsky, pointed out that the causes of specific political events often lay in the internal dynamics of the political system, that the heads of states and political bureaucracies acted in ways designed to enhance their own power positions, which could be counter to the needs of the dominant social classes or the requirements of the economic system.

In the late nineteenth and twentieth centuries, as the social sciences emerged as separate though related disciplines, each concentrated on distinct aspects of human behavior. Each field came to be defined by the specific class of human behavior which it sought to explain, yet clearly no field has limited itself to its major area of concern. There is almost no form of behavior which is not treated, to some extent, by each of the social sciences. Each varies only in its primary area of interest. The economist is concerned with analyzing the factors which affect social behavior in the system of production. That is, he asks what affects decisions about the investment or use of economically relevant resources, primarily capital, labor, and goods. Since the value of these can be specified in monetary terms, economics, earlier than the other social sciences, has been able to define its theoretical conceptions in the language of mathematics. Yet the economist is continually forced to analyze the impact of "non-economic factors," cultural values, personality, political needs, status concerns, on economic behavior, i.e., decisions to invest, to take jobs, and the like. The psychologist is interested in learning why individuals vary in their behavior. Such concerns require him to understand the ways in which biochemical and physiological factors determine how humans behave, how these factors affect ability to perform various tasks, to interact with each other, and the like. Since one of the key sources of personality formation, and of individual behavior generally is response to participation in varying social situations, to interactions with others, the psychologist must also deal with social psychology, with the effects of different group involvements on the individual. The anthropologist is concerned with the varying ways in which men have organized their culture, the structured pattern of interrelationships which differentiate one society from another. To analyze culture requires not only specifying the basic values of different societies, but also looking at the ways in which satisfying basic material needs—food, clothing, and shelter, the definition of familial relationships (the kinship system), or the system of authority relationships including the polity—limit or affect other aspects of the culture. The sociologist concerned with how institutions, stabilized systems of expectations and actions, fulfill the varying needs of man in society, particularly complex society, includes within his domain almost every aspect of human behavior.

The study of politics, which is the oldest as well as the newest of the social sciences, has probably faced more difficulties in limiting its concern in analytic terms than any of the other fields. Like philosophy, it traces its intellectual origins and present concerns to the works of men who thought of the polity as the area in which men resolved their social relationships, their family systems, their ways of producing goods, within the society or culture as a unit. As Gabriel Almond has pointed out, "classical political theory is more a political sociology and psychology and a normative political theory than it is a theory of the political process. What goes on inside the black box of the political system and its consequences are inferred from the ways in which the social structure is represented in it. The Platonic, Aristotelian, and later Roman classifications of types of political systems are far more explicit on the consequences of varieties of social stratification and their representation in political systems for their forms and their performance than they are regarding the varieties of political decision-making processes. The bases of political classification are sociological rather than political. . . . The Greek and Roman theory of political development is a social-psychological theory, treating the pure forms of rule [monarchy, aristocracy, or democracy] as inherently unstable because of their susceptibility to corruption stemming from sociological and psychological processes."[1]

As the various social sciences emerged, they took over problems which had been treated as part of an interrelated whole by Aristotle, Plato, Locke, Hobbes, Hegel, Montesquieu, and the myriad of others who, concerned with the good society, with moral behavior, directed their attention to the ways in which men act in concert, therefore, politically.

The other social science fields as they separated from philosophy, and thus from the study of the polity, took on distinct methodological foci. Limiting both the independent (causal) and dependent (what they sought to explain) variables, they attempted to form a body of theory which specified the interrelationships among the factors which fell in their jurisdiction. As they specified such limited propositions about human behavior, they looked for methods of testing or validating their propositions.

The study of politics, however, long remained a general field which dealt with all aspects of human behavior. The polity inherently holds policy jurisdiction over everything man does. Therefore, students of politics tried for a long time to continue in the tradition of the ancient philosophers. Their concern was not the creation of empirically verifiable propositions derived from a theoretical system, limited to the variables appropriate to the discipline, but rather the explanation of political actions, using whatever knowledge and insights were available from all fields of human knowledge.

The term political science, which gradually emerged to describe a particular academic field of study, originally meant what we now call policy science: the application of knowledge to the concerns of the prince, of those who seek to foster the good society. One of the earliest appearances of the term in an American university catalogue was in the 1890's when the Columbia University graduate social science faculty was founded as the Faculty of Political Science. This faculty came to include departments such as economics, sociology, history, anthropology, statistics, and public law and government. The latter department was seen, not as covering political science, but rather as *one* of the political, i.e., policy, sciences.

As a policy science, a role which fitted in with the traditional normative concerns of the classic writings about politics, which came to be known as political theory, the field of government (or political science) drew on the other social sciences. Its early interests were normative, historical, or analytic in a policy sense. That is, it did not involve efforts at systematic generalization along the lines of the other social sciences. But while political science was emerging as a separate field, the other disciplines continued to exhibit considerable interest in politics. This was particularly true of the early sociologists, both in Europe and America. In their efforts to generalize about institutions and social behavior, they could not ignore as important a set of institutions as the political or the formation of attitudes and group norms in politics. Thus men like Max Weber, Robert Michels, Vilfredo Pareto, and Emile Durkheim, involved themselves in political analysis as part of their sociological concerns. In America, Arthur Bentley who was to become a major intellectual force in political science, was trained as a sociologist in Europe, and held his only academic appointment in the department of sociology at the University of Chicago. Franklin Giddings, one of the "fathers" of American sociology, encouraged his students to engage in empirical studies of voting behavior in the teens and early twenties. Psychologists, interested in the formation of attitudes, turned to examining political values and behavior. Interest in personality, particularly flowing from knowledge of Freudian psychoanalytic theory, also influenced political writing.

As Richard Jensen points out in the first chapter in this volume, the burgeoning field of political science began to turn toward these new behavioristic or social science approaches to political analysis during the 1920's. Some may question Jensen's conclusion that the behavioral or psychological approach took over the field during this period, but there can be little doubt of its influence. The twenties were characterized by a growing interest in interdisciplinary social science work, marked by the formation of the Social Science Research Council. The study of politics particularly reflected this development.

Although one can point to intellectual continuity in the field during the 1930's, this decade was marked more by a return to normative philosophical considerations than by the spread of social science behavioral concerns among political scientists. Jensen credits this to the considerable influence of major European emigré political theorists who brought their interest in political philosophy to American universities. It is ironic that while European intellectual emigrés pressed American political science toward normative and philosophical interests, sociology was spurred on by Paul Lazarsfeld, who had emigrated from Austria, to become more quantitative and behavioristic, in the sense of becoming more psychological. Lazarsfeld not only was interested in developing more rigorous research techniques, he expanded the academic study of voting behavior into a major sub-discipline by pressing further various topics first studied by Stuart Rice. The field of political sociology, defined as the effort to apply various concepts and methods of sociology to the study of political behavior and institutions, suddenly emerged as a major enterprise. Its practitioners not only sought to explain voting behavior, but they also applied the analyses of bureaucratic structures developed in the work of Max Weber and Robert Michels to a variety of institutional structures ranging from government agencies, to trade unions, political parties, and economic institutions. Economics also returned to an interest in political economy, seeing in the need of individuals and policy makers to make repetitive choices a further substantive area within which to elaborate their increasingly rigorous mathematical and statistical models. The political issues which dominated the thirties and forties, particularly the growth of totalitarian political movements, pressed other social scientists in psychology and anthropology to apply their concepts and methods to analyzing the sources of various forms of politically relevant phenomena. The *Authoritarian Personality* studies of the 1940's involved efforts to apply insights gained from psychoanalytic theory and social psychological methods to understanding extremist political appeals. As Arnold Rogow describes in his chapter, similar orientations influenced the work of Harold Lasswell and his disciples in their studies of the influence of psychological factors on the appeal of extremist movements, and of political behavior generally.

The post-war period has witnessed important changes in the work of political scientists. To a considerable extent, they gradually absorbed the theoretical and methodological approaches to political analysis of political sociology and psychology. Studies of voting behavior and of political attitudes have become commonplace as subjects for scholarly inquiry and doctoral dissertations. Community power studies pioneered by the work of sociologists such as Robert and Helen Lynd and W. Lloyd Warner have been furthered by political scientists in recent years. Most major political science departments now require their graduate students to take work in statistics and to gain familiarity with the techniques of survey research. The Survey Research Center of the University of Michigan, the principal center of voting research, has contributed greatly to this trend by sponsoring special courses in survey methods for political scientists. Concern for historical voting research has also increased the links between political scientists and historians. As Richard Jensen indicates in his chapter on voting research, some American historians, spurred on by the approaches of Frederick Jackson Turner, undertook quantitative analyses of voting behavior long before World War I. These efforts have re-emerged during the last decade, using more sophisticated statistical techniques and informed by the findings of survey studies of voting behavior.

Perhaps most important of all the forces which have pressed toward genuine cooperation among the social sciences has been the growth of the field of development: economic, social, and political. Clearly, interest in development reflects the sudden appearance of more than fifty "New Nations," particularly in Africa and Asia. Modern social science has been faced with the need to analyze the conditions under which societies are formed out of a complex of cultures placed under one political sovereignty. This field has had to deal with how new political systems acquire legitimacy and incorporate or "mobilize" a previously passive population within the polity. Finally, modern social science was forced to specify the conditions under which relatively impoverished agrarian societies advance economically, and to link all of these changes to the concomitant adjustments in various social relationships: e.g., kinship systems, social stratification, mechanisms of social control, and the like. Although each of the social sciences has focused on those aspects of development which fall within its general jurisdiction, it is obvious that any effort to treat development in economy, polity, and society as separate processes simply makes little sense.

The economist must be concerned with the ways in which governmental policies, degree of legitimacy and stability affect prospects for economic growth. He must also incorporate in his analysis the effect of diverse social values, or modal personality orientations, on economically relevant behavior. The sociologist, concerned with changes in values, shifts in class relations, effects of education, modifications in family systems from extended kinship structures to nuclear families, knows that these are greatly influenced by government policies, by the ideologies of political movements, and by the forms of political legitimacy which emerge in the societies he is studying. The value orientations of societies are sharply affected by the requirements of the economic system. Psychologists and anthropologists also have examined such processes from their own perspectives. The political scientist interested in political development has learned that he cannot treat this topic without looking for the conditions of social mobilization; men cannot become citizens in a political sense without changing their values and personality orientations. A key set of factors which determine the basis of political allegiance and cleavage in such societies are those inherent in the systems of inheritance and familial obligations. Politics will be different in caste and non-caste societies. It will vary among systems which have different concepts of kinship ties, and the nature of class and status relationships in various traditional societies will affect the possibilities for acceptance of a legal-rational political order.

The concern for development has forced the social sciences to think in terms of conceptual approaches which include the polity, economy, society, and personality. As a result, for the first time, there has been a real movement toward social science rather than the social sciences. Intellectually, this change has been reflected most in the growing influence of various related theoretical orientations which fall under the rubric of system theory. Such approaches, as their name implies, assume the fundamental interrelatedness of all forms of social behavior. Changes incorporated at any part of the "system," whether economic, political, social, or psychological, will have an impact on the other dimensions. To understand pressures toward either change or stability, it is necessary to have a concept of how the social system—all aspects of it—hangs together. Sociologists and anthropologists have been in the lead in formulating such conceptions, and as a result that form of system theory —functional analysis—which first emerged in these fields has had a considerable impact on the others. Durkheim, Malinowski, Parsons, Merton, Shils, Eisenstadt, and Levy have made influential contributions outside their own disciplines, particularly in political science. Political scientists, of course, have sought to elaborate system theory, giving particular emphasis to the role of the polity in affecting social development. Although this interest was fostered by concern with developing societies, the theoretical work now affects work on the developed states as well as international relations.

The emergence of system theory, largely derived from sociology has, in turn, found its critics and superceders among those looking to increase the scientific predictive powers of political science. Although it lends itself to carefully structured analyses of the relationships of the polity to other parts of society, and to describing the consequences of changes in the system on other aspects, some now see in system theory only another variant of a conceptual scheme whose basic utility is as an intellectual organizing framework but which in fact does not submit itself to the cardinal test of science—empirical verification. Some of the discontent with this general approach also reflects the shortcomings of many of the analyses of political development. The early literature about political development sought to generalize from the first few years or decades following independence of the various "new nations." Almost all of them have experienced subsequent sharp discontinuities in their political structures. Competitive party democratic regimes have collapsed, while a variety of autocratic structures, seemingly stabilized and legitimated by the charisma of their "founding father," have proved no more stable. Efforts to account for the absence of authoritarianism in various countries have fallen victim to the emergence of authoritarian patterns in the very countries whose system had been carefully analyzed. Conversely, the number of "charismatic" leaders now in exile or under "house-arrest" has challenged the conclusions drawn by studies of the functions of charismatic authority for new states.

The enthusiasm expressed for the economic and political potential of the underdeveloped world has gradually declined. Events have undermined the commitment of the United States to foreign aid programs, as well as the belief of social scientists that they could provide adequate analyses of the requirements of these systems for "development" or "modernization."

With this decline in intellectual self-confidence in sociological or system theory has appeared a new enthusiasm for the application of economic theory to politics. The chapters by Mancur Olson, Jr., and William Mitchell reflect this new theoretical orientation. And Mitchell exemplifies this change in his own work. He is the author of two books which elaborated the value of system theory for political science. One is a study of the relevance of Talcott Parsons' theory to political analysis, and the other is a systems analysis called *The American Polity*. Now Mitchell concludes that his confidence in sociological and system theory was misplaced, and he joins the ranks of those who see in the application of economic models to political problems the route to making political science a rigorous scientific discipline.

The revival of economic analysis in the study of politics may be credited to two factors. On the intellectual side is the increasing acceptance of the utility of mathematical or statistical models as the best way to formulate social science theory. Many social scientists have come to believe more and more that the social sciences must follow the lead of economics in defining their propositions in ways which can be specified in formal model terms. If social science seeks to be scientific, it must spell out its assumptions in clear-cut rigorous terms. But the growing acceptance of "political economy" among political scientists cannot be explained solely or primarily as a response to an intellectual development. The policy problems faced by the discipline have changed. Poverty, race, and the problems of urban government have taken over as the dominant domestic issues of the day. These involve efforts to decide how to allocate resources in an optimum way to attain certain agreed upon objectives within the system. Formulated in this way the problems are conducive to economic model analysis. Thus, the political scientist now turns to the key policy science—economics—to find a model for inquiry.

Any examination of the political science journals or books published in recent years will demonstrate that the field remains as heterogeneous as ever. Leading departments include political philosophers concerned with interpreting and elaborating normative theory, political historians whose work differs little from that of scholars located in history departments, political journalists concerned with detailed analyses of specific contemporary events, specialists on how politics takes place in different areas, regions, and governmental sub-units, political sociologists seeking to apply sociological generalizations to the analysis of political institutions, political psychologists drawing their intellectual sustenance from psychology and applying it to the study of political attitudes and behavior, and political economists analyzing the decision process in allocating resources such as votes, budgets, or other policy relevant resources.

The interrelationship of political science with its neighboring social science disciplines has complicated the task of scholars and students in the field. Much of the literature is replete with references to works, concepts, and methods which come from a variety of disciplines. A fledgling graduate student is often under pressure to learn traditional political theory, which includes ancient and modern political philosophy, and what has come to be known as empirical political theory, which treats the work of sociologists, psychologists, and economists. Sophisticated contemporary research in political science necessitates knowledge of statistics, the more the better, as demonstrated by the monographic presentation of Hayward Alker, Jr., in the final chapter.

This book is an outgrowth of an effort at the 1967 meetings of the American Political Science Association to assess the state of the links between political science and the other fields. Early drafts of a number of the chapters were discussed at panel sessions which I organized. When the suggestion was made to publish these as a book, I invited a number of other scholars to present papers which would make the treatment more comprehensive. While the approaches of the authors vary considerably, the different essays do add up to a comprehensive discussion of the values and liabilities of interdisciplinary collaboration for political scientists.

Clearly, as Ronald Cohen points out, efforts to bridge disciplines run the risk of encouraging dilettantism. The standard, often valid, critique by members of given fields to efforts by those in others who seek to apply their theories is that they misuse them, that those who have not been trained in a given field do not understand the subtleties or the complexities of its approach. Another constant source of difficulty in the relations between social science disciplines is resentment at efforts of "subsumesmanship." Practitioners of different fields try to subsume the problems of the others under their own theoretical framework. Given the aspiration of various sociologists, psychologists, anthropologists, and economists to include much, if not all, of social behavior within their specific theoretical orientations, it is not surprising that some scholars in each discipline see the extension of the scope of their own theory as the solution to the need for general social science theory, or for the specific analysis of the operation of the polity.

The effort to subsume political analysis within the theoretical orienta-

tion of other fields may be seen here in the chapters by Olson, an economist; Greenstein, a political scientist; and Greer, a sociologist. Olson, who is
primarily interested in social science collaboration to improve social
planning, considers the role of political science essentially through its
contribution to social engineering, in which it processes the information of
other social sciences, primarily economics and sociology. Political science
appears in his judgment to be more of a social insight *consuming*, than a
social insight *producing* discipline, drawing on the work of economists such
as Arrow, Downs, Tullock, Lindblom, Schelling, and Buchanan. Essentially government must be concerned with "utility maximization," the
concern of economics, or with "alienation minimization," the interest
of sociology.

Greenstein and Greer argue that there are basically only two theoretical
levels of social science analysis: the sociological and the psychological,
society and personality. The other disciplines, including political science
in Greenstein's judgment, exist not because they have a distinct theoretical
orientation but because they concentrate on the detailed study of specific
institutions. Political science, therefore, becomes the application of
sociological and psychological analyses to the study of the behavior of
government and other political structures. In making his argument,
however, Greenstein acknowledges that personality theory and other
branches of psychology have, as yet, made little effective contribution to
political analysis. He presents a prolegomena of how a more extensive
investigation of the impact of psychological variables on a variety of
political behaviors would contribute to a more thorough understanding of
politics. Rogow, in his chapter on psychiatry and politics, also points to
the possible contributions of personality theory. Both men indicate that
among the reasons psychological approaches have not been as influential
as they would wish on political analysis is the imprecision of theories of
personality, the fact that psychology itself has come to no agreement about
how to characterize personality, or how to resolve differences concerning
competing models.

Greer, in his chapter on sociology and political science, presents the
most coherent case for the existence of a general social science approach
or theory within which political science appears as the field which deals
with the political-governmental aspects of society. The existence of
different social sciences must be seen not as variations in basic epistomo-
logical strategies, but as functions of historically changing differentiating
actual social institutions. Thus, political economy arose in response to the

knowledge requirement of the monarchical mercantilist nation-state. It split into the two separate disciplines—political science and economics— as a result of the emergence of a market economy independent of the state. This separation between economy and polity, was a temporary one which already has been supplanted in the modern era. Sociology, therefore, reflects the growing recognition of the need for concern with social integration, including economy and polity. We are now at the point where all social science must operate with a common conceptual scheme and vocabulary. Greer points out that all social behavior occurs through groups, and, therefore, all social science involves an explication of the nature of group behavior, leadership, decisions, social control, et cetera. The existing common-sense historically determined basis of the division of labor among the social science fields involves, in his judgment, naïve phenomenologies and inappropriate obsolete institutional foci which must be abandoned in favor of cognate group oriented terminologies applicable within each discipline. Greer argues: "[The] social sciences are essentially one, in their units, men in aggregates, are the same; their explanatory theories, developed from the study of human groups, are cognate, and their utility for philosophy and action depends on our developing transitivity between them." Greer is the only exponent of system theory here. He defines the concern of political science as the study of the more or less conscious control mechanisms over society's efforts at direction and adaptation to the non-social, non-human environment.

Although all contributors to this volume are in principle committed to interdisciplinary cooperation between political science and the other social sciences, two, Mitchell and Sartori, as political scientists, point up the intellectual autonomy of the field by emphasizing how the political environment and political imputs, parties, governments, voting, and the like determine behavior. Mitchell and Sartori correctly point out that much of political sociology and political behaviorism have emphasized the impact of social factors or contexts, or psychological variables, on politics. If politics is treated as epiphenomena, as the dependent variable to be explained by factors existential to the political system itself, there is no real intellectual justification for an independent political science. Mitchell seeks to find a basis for the field in a political economy which treats rigorously the impact of government on the social enivironment. Almost all his examples, however, are from the field of public finance, an area which like economics itself can deal with easily quantifiable units of analysis—money. His level of analysis does not treat the problems raised by Ronald Cohen, who as an anthropologist is concerned with the outputs of the polity on various aspects of social structure in emerging polities.

Sartori argues effectively that the sociology of politics has underplayed politics as such, because in the past the sociologist has ignored political variables, constitutions, electoral systems, and ideological groupings, as sources of political and social behavior. He would move from the sociology of politics to political sociology, the latter meaning the fusion of the two sets of variables, rather than assuming as the sociologist does that the social structural variables are the independent factors, while the political variables are the dependent factors.

The criticism which Sartori levels against much of the work in the sociology of politics, that it has not been political, has of course been made by various political scientists in the past. V. O. Key, Jr., argued some years ago that much of voting decision research based on survey data was not concerned with politics. In his judgment, students of voting behavior in the Lazarsfeld–Berelson–Columbia tradition as well as in the Campbell–Michigan school deemphasized those aspects of the voting process which reflected the decision of political actors, i.e., parties and candidates, and the commitments of large segments of the electorate to parties or political perspectives. He also suggested that sociological and psychological perspectives tended to overemphasize irrational or non-rational factors, ignoring the extent to which the allegiances of diverse strata and areas to parties and candidates made rational sense.

Clearly, as Sartori suggests, recent developments in the field of electoral studies have restored the political dimension to its proper place in such research. He draws many of his negative and positive examples from work with which I have been associated, but it ought to be noted that the Michigan Survey Research Center has increasingly moved toward dealing with the effect of political structures and ideological tendencies on voting. As the editor of this book, I do not want to take undue advantage of having seen all the chapters before they went to press to correct any references to my own work or that of other political sociologists. I will, therefore, only note that Sartori's discussion of changes in my own work, in which he points to my analysis of the effect of electoral laws on the voting decision as progress from my supposedly earlier writing which placed a greater emphasis on existential social factors such as class, contains a minor error. The basic substance of my discussion of electoral systems is contained in two articles which appeared either before or contempor-

aneously with my book *Political Man*.[2] I would also note that my first
book, *Agrarian Socialism*, published in 1950, points up how purely political
factors differentiated the dominant political responses of three political
units, Saskatchewan, Alberta, and North Dakota, which were highly
similar from a sociological point of view.[3]

Although Sartori's criticism of the sociology of politics has considerable
validity, it is also important to note that the modern father of the field,
Max Weber, clearly specified the need for a political sociology as an
intellectual response to the process of structural differentiation discussed by
Olson. The sociologist has to treat politics as an independent variable
precisely because of the separation among society, economy, and polity.
Weber suggested to Robert Michels that he study the structure of the
German Social Democratic party in order to understand the impact of the
political parties created to mobilize the masses in electoral democracies on
the economic and social structures.

Clearly, the issues implicit in any effort to discuss the relations between
political science and the other social sciences are not resolved in the essays
in this volume. Whether political science can or should attempt to formulate an analytically distinct theoretical system remains an open question.
And although the concerns of the field increasingly overlap with the work
of other fields this should not be taken as a threat to the autonomy of the
discipline. Actually, the converse thesis could be argued. The political
in the form of concern with the decision-making process, with the distribution of power, with the nature of legitimate authority, with the place of
the state as the principal agency of collective action within society, with
the analogy between the behavior of the voter and the buyer in the market
place, has intruded into the work of the other social sciences. Economics
as a policy science finds that it cannot operate without making assumptions about and studying the actual operation of the polity. The age old
issue of the primacy of state or society, while no longer stated in these
terms, points up the concern of the sociologist for the political. The
anthropologist must view the societies he studies as political units and
consequently must introduce political concepts into his analyses. And
regardless of the overlap, the analysis of power relations within all
institutions, not simply the state, will remain as an analytically distinct
topic. It is probably true, as Smelser asserts, that as "formal theories of the
political system continue to develop in political science, they will undoubtedly come to resemble formal economic theories, insofar as they
will deal with the creation and exercise of power and will rest on a relatively

formal series of assumptions regarding the givens within which political processes occur."[4]

The concern with processes of social change, which has been reactivated by interest in the development process in third world nations as well as by the increasingly conscious efforts to reduce birth-right inequities in the more affluent nations, has also increased the significance of political science as the field concerned with the key set of social institutions, which constitute the legitimate mechanism for expressing society's will to attain commonly agreed upon objectives. Max Weber stressed the unique position of the state as the institution which has the legitimate monopoly of the instruments of force. But in societies committed more and more to a democratic legitimation of forms of authority, there is a growing assumption that the right to command, to exercise power over the wills of others, must come from the approval of the majority. Consequently, politically controlled institutions, rather than private ones such as religion or business, are the only institutions which have the moral right to command. Efforts fostering macroscopic social change must be approved by the political system. The differentiation between economy and polity, which characterized the early industrial society, has broken down, often with dire consequences for liberty. Hence, men who seek to maximize social utility while minimizing alienation, the two key "policy tasks" which Olson, correctly in my view, assigns to economics and sociology, must find a political solution. By posing the issues in this way, we return to the classic normative function of political theory. Perhaps the issue of bridging which should concern political science is not one of its place in the social sciences, but rather of its need to form the link between the normative aspirations of mankind which are expressed in their desire for the good society, and the efforts of the social sciences to understand the operations of society from a scientific perspective.

This task is clearly not a simple one. It is much more difficult now than in the past since it is no longer possible to imagine any consensus concerning the moral objectives of society. As S. N. Eisenstadt has pointed out, there has been "a growing awareness of the improbability that any single institutional arrangement could fully epitomize *the* best moral order or, indeed, represent any transcendental order at all adequately."[5] Conflict, instability, and change are inherent in all complex social systems. All important modern social analysts recognize that the social forces which make for integration and consensus, thus appearing to stabilize given social systems and polities, include aspects which are dysfunctional for some elements of the system, and hence they also make for conflict and change. As Hobbes pointed out, the study of social disorder is part of the study of order, and *vice versa*. The task of the political scientist includes generalizing about the ways in which the conscious actions of men affect the processes of social change. Political and social actors are continually making *non-random* decisions in which the moral order—conceptions of right and wrong—affects the outcomes. Although it becomes more and more clear that the effective arena in which such choices are made is the polity, our hypotheses concerning the determinants of action must come from the other social sciences.

Notes

1. Gabriel A. Almond, "Political Theory and Political Science," in Ithiel de Sola Pool, ed., *Contemporary Political Science: Toward Empirical Theory* (New York: McGraw-Hill, 1967), p. 5.

2. S. M. Lipset, "Democracy in Alberta," *The Canadian Forum* (November and December 1954), pp. 175–77, 196–98; "Party Systems and the representation of Social Groups," *European Journal of Sociology*, 1 (1960), pp. 50–85.

3. S. M. Lipset, *Agrarian Socialism* (Berkeley: University of California Press, 1950; expanded edition, Garden City: Doubleday and Co., 1968). I would also note that the emphasis on class as a determinant of voting behavior is modified in my article, "Religion and Politics in American History," in Robert Lee and Martin E. Marty, eds., *Religion and Social Conflict* (New York: Oxford University Press, 1964), pp. 69–126, also published in revised form in S. M. Lipset, *Revolution and Counterrevolution* (New York: Basic Books, 1968), pp. 246–303; see also Chapter 5, "Class, Politics and Religion in Modern Society," pp. 159–78 in *ibid*.

4. Neil J. Smelser, *Essays in Sociological Explanation* (Englewood Cliffs, N.J.: Prentice-Hall, 1968), p. 31.

5. S. N. Eisenstadt, "The Development of Sociological Thought," in David Sills, ed., *The International Encyclopedia of the Social Sciences*, 15 (New York: The Macmillan Company, 1968), p. 23.

Politics and the Social Sciences

I

History and the Political Scientist

RICHARD JENSEN

"History is past politics and politics present history" was the motto of the first generation of American political scientists. These men, particularly John Burgess and William Dunning at Columbia, Herbert Baxter Adams at Johns Hopkins, Woodrow Wilson at Princeton, and Albert Bushnell Hart at Harvard, were often more conversant with history than with government. They stressed the historical evolution of political institutions as the proper focus of political science. Succeeding generations of political scientists progressively abandoned the study and use of history until what began as a cognate field had become as distant as astrophysics. Counter-reaction was inevitable, and came in the 1960's as younger scholars turned increasingly to the record of the past for a broader data base on which to ground their theories of political behavior and development. This Chapter explores the rejection of history in terms of the internal dynamics of political science as an academic discipline in the United States, and considers the ways in which the contemporary generation of scholars may engage in interdisciplinary research.

The first generation of political scientists (1880–1900), inspired by dreams of a comprehensive science of man, recognized explicitly the necessity of basing their interpretation of the evolution of governmental forms upon historical research. To their students they stressed the importance of interdisciplinary approaches built around history. Many had been trained in history, especially in the famed seminars of the German professors whose ideas dominated the world of nineteenth-century scholarship. Besides the interdisciplinary range of topics outlined by the Germans the Americans worked under conditions which necessitated familiarity with all the social sciences. The American college and university faculties were so small in the late nineteenth century that one professor typically covered material that teams of scholars today could not handle. At Johns Hopkins, Herbert Baxter Adams trained dozens of scholars in the historical approach to social science he had learned from J. K. Bluntschli at Heidelberg. Adams taught economics to Thorstein Veblen, sociology to Albion Small, history to Frederick Jackson Turner, and political science to Arthur Bentley, Woodrow Wilson, the Willoughby brothers, and John Dewey. Succeeding generations of scholars increasingly differentiated the social sciences in the late nineteenth century and early twentieth century, forcing even Renaissance men to stay within the bounds of a single discipline.

Early in the twentieth century the second generation of political scientists (1900–1920) encountered an identity crisis regarding the proper place for the study of government among the increasingly differentiated social sciences. First was the problem of whether students of government should be academicians (like historians and economists), or become established in independent organizations, especially bureaus of government research (like the social workers and their settlement houses). Some of the leaders of the second generation, like Arthur Bentley, Charles McCarthy, and Charles Beard, were more comfortable outside than inside universities. However, the pull of the cognate social sciences and law schools and the prestige of Ph.D. training indicated the necessity of making university departments the major center of research for the new discipline. The founding of the American Political Science Association in 1903, and its *Review* three years later, put the academicians in firm control of the discipline. To differentiate political science from the work of lawyers, historians, and sociologists constituted the second challenge of the identity crisis. With respect to history the resolution involved the progressive abandonment of historical analysis of the development of institutions in favor of an emphasis on the description and evaluation of current institutions, in the manner of James Bryce's *The American Commonwealth* (1888), and A. Lawrence Lowell's *Governments and Parties in Continental Europe* (1896, 1897). Since few, if any, historians attempted to write about the recent past the separation from history was effected without a methodological crisis. Increasingly those scholars who tried to maintain good standing in both disciplines either wrote the political history of the recent past (Burgess, Dunning, Beard, Carl Becker, and Hart), or shifted toward the history of political thought (Dunning, Charles McIlwain, Becker). The latter arrangement was unsatisfactory. Studies of past ideas were placed in the framework of the intellectual currents of the time; no effort was made to distill the wisdom of past theorists, so empirical researchers found theory less and less useful or interesting.

The First World War turned the profession's attention away from its identity crisis and placed in its stead a legitimacy crisis over the goals and justifications for the study of government. No discipline has been more convulsed by war than political science. World War I, with its massive and unprecedented redirection of government activities toward tight control of domestic industry, agriculture, society, and thought, together with the horrors of destruction and the tragic aftermath of Versailles, could not fail to induce a radical rethinking of the nature of politics. First the utopian crusading reform impulse of the Progressive era disintegrated, forcing a more realistic and sober appraisal of the necessity for careful analysis, planning, and cooperation if social problems were to be solved. Second the optimistic belief in the inevitability of progress through gradual social evolution collapsed. The careful description of the historical evolution of legal and governmental institutions now seemed irrelevant for the historic world of prewar days was utterly dead. History no longer was important, for the tragedy of war and the opportunity for reconstruction had erased the past and focused all attention on the future. True understanding of the irrationality of man and of the power of government action for good or evil emerged as the proper goals for the research work of political scientists. Casting about for a new intellectual paradigm to guide their discipline in the modern age, political scientists fastened upon science—science as the key to planning, and the science of psychology as the key both to research methodology and to the nature of human behavior.

Charles Merriam, the dominant figure in the third generation (1920–40), typified and in many ways led his colleagues through the crisis of legitimacy. Trained in the historical method of Dunning and Burgess, imbued with confidence in the inevitability of progress, and prominent in Republican and Progressive politics in Chicago, Merriam was forced by the shock of the war to rethink radically all his premises. In 1919 his attempt to return to active politics was crushed; the old ways were dead, and Merriam used his energies and the immense resources of his Chicago department to grapple with the legitimacy crisis. "Allowing for the despondency following a catastrophic war", he told his colleagues, "we are in fact coming into a new world, with new social conditions and with new modes of thought and inquiry, and we may well inquire what direction and form our politics must take if it is to interpret and express these new tendencies of the new world."[1] Science, with its unbounded potential for rational planning and control of the human environment, was Merriam's key. His brother John, a prominent geologist, undoubtedly turned his attention to science, but the vividness of the wartime experience and a fresh reading of Graham Wallas's *Human Nature in Politics* (1908) heightened his awareness of the irrational forces in the affairs of men and turned his attention to psychology. *Public Opinion* (1922) by Wallas's star pupil Walter Lippmann convinced Merriam that political science could profit greatly by microscopic research into political behavior.

As he turned to psychology, Merriam rejected history. In several discussions of the role of other disciplines in political science, Merriam, while insisting that he was not altogether rejecting evidence from the past, argued that the work of historians was irrelevant. He complained that modern historians too much ignored the psychological, sociological, and economic factors in human affairs. Only Turner and Beard won any praise, and he considered these men lonely pioneers. "The historian could distinguish the genuine writing from the bogus," Merriam said, "or he could scour the world with immense enthusiasm and industry to uncover hidden manuscripts or archives hitherto unknown. In his critical analysis, however, he waited on the activities of other social studies. At their methods and results he was not infrequently prone to cavil and complain."[2] History might have some uses for studies of party politics, but Merriam felt that the traditional descriptive approach was an inadequate basis for what he sought—a new science of politics. Merriam was wrong about the historians. Turner and Beard were acknowledged leaders, not lonely pioneers, and in fact the best work in legislative and electoral analysis was being done by historians whose techniques would have repaid careful study by political scientists.

Merriam's odyssey from historical progressivism to psychological behaviorism paralleled that of the profession as a whole, with a short lead. Most of the leading professors and their brightest graduate students attended three special conferences on the "science of politics" in the summers of 1923, 1924, and 1925. There they thrashed out the basic goals and methods of political science with far more seriousness than ever was permitted at the regular annual conventions. The legitimacy crisis was the focus of attention, and at the second conference it was resolved. The first conference proved inconclusive, but Merriam and his colleague Leonard White arranged to hold the second at Chicago, where they brought in several of the most brilliant (but offbeat) scientific psychologists of the day, particularly L. L. Thurstone of Chicago and Floyd Allport of Syracuse.[3]

Thurstone and Allport seized the opportunity, and in five days in September 1924 revolutionized political science by converting virtually every leader of the profession to the behavioral persuasion. The *rapporteur* noted the agreement of the participants "to the genuine eagerness of the profession to advance scientific methods", and the realization that "the great obstacle to scientific progress is found in the lack of technique and method." Allowing that "there may always be some political questions that will elude any effort to reduce them to questions of fact, of objective treatment, or of precise quantitative measurement," the profession nonetheless agreed, *"there can be no doubt that much of our political experience is capable of accurate measurement and scientific generalization if we can only find the method."*[4]

To the scholars searching for method, Thurstone offered the paradigm of experimental psychometrics, and they eagerly adopted it. Every bona fide scientific problem, he explained, can be phrased in the form "what is the effect of A upon B?" The two variables should be expressed in quantitative terms by means of a common, universally accepted unit of basic measurement, and then experiments designed to obtain from observed behavioral patterns paired observations for A and B. Scientific analysis then involved the causal interpretation of the observed patterns of bivariate relationships. Since the scientific methodology of the day in psychology (and in most sciences) did not stress the analysis of mutual interaction of a number of variables and constraints within a unified system, Thurstone's formulation proved satisfactory to the political scientists. They now knew what the scientific method was all about, but the stumbling block was to designate a suitable basic unit of measurement analagous to money in economics.

Combining his own research interests with those of Merriam and of several other participants, Thurstone suggested *attitude* as the basic unit. Forty years later Heinz Eulau defined the concept of political behavior in terms of "those perceptual, motivational, and attitudinal components which made for man's political identifications, demands and expectations, and his systems of political beliefs, values, and goals."[5] Of course, Thurstone could not formulate such a neat definition on the first day of the revolution, but he was able to indicate the research strategy that much of political science followed for two generations. For Thurstone the concept "attitude" denoted "the sum total of a man's inclinations and feelings, prejudice or bias, preconceived notions, ideas, fears, threats, and convictions about a specific topic."[6] Attitudes could best be measured by scaling the opinions a person expressed in questionnaires. Thurstone's previous experience with political matters involved designing psychological tests for civil service personnel, and his horizon did not extend very far. Others, however, suggested that votes in elections, referenda, legislatures, and courts could serve in lieu of questionnaires and enable the political scientist to map the distribution of opinions and construct scales of attitudes.

The orientation Thurstone provided was wholly experimental. History could be dredged to provide hypotheses to test, and the classics of political thought could be scanned for the psychological generalizations they might contain, but the real work of the political scientist should be under quasi-experimental conditions. A number of pregnant research designs emerged from the conference. For example, someone suggested that "straw votes be taken on a selected group of individuals at intervals of three months between March and November in order to ascertain the changeability of public opinion in specified voting groups."[7] It is not clear whether this proposal was the original inspiration for the Erie and Elmyra studies of the 1940's, but it does suggest why political scientists later responded so favorably to panel studies of voters' attitudes. Another suggestion that bore fruit in the work of one young participant, Harold Lasswell, was the study of the psychological impact of political propaganda, using techniques such as content analysis of newspaper editorials. Given the experimental bias of the proposals to operationalize Thurstone's suggestions, and the near-unanimous opposition to purely descriptive studies, the anti-historical biases of the profession were strongly reinforced.

Charles Merriam summarized some of the spirit of the science of politics conferences in his *New Aspects of Politics* (1925). Much of the book had been written before the second conference, and therefore displays more confusion about methodology than persisted afterwards. Also Merriam hesitated at the widespread demand that statisticians be teamed with political scientists in future conferences and in research projects. To Merriam "statistics" denoted factual numerical information about the state of society that government experts could use for planning purposes. He did not fully comprehend the point of Thurstone and his new disciples that the generalizations of political science ought to be phrased in semi-mathematical form, and that statistical methods should be used more for testing hypotheses than for pure description. In any case, Merriam's book did not create the revolution, the conferences did that. The notion that mature scholars *read* somebody's new manifesto and changed their basic paradigms thereby is surely a fallacy. The personal interaction and unanimity of the leading professors at the conference, coupled with the strong feeling that the old historical-descriptive paradigm was obsolete, created the environment in which Thurstone, Allport, and Merriam could guide the outcome of the legitimacy crisis.

Nowhere was the new science of politics more avidly studied than at Chicago, home of Merriam, Thurstone, and a host of brilliant scholars committed to the new behavioral paradigm. Under Merriam's tireless entrepreneurial leadership, Leonard White, Harold Gosnell, Quincy Wright, Harold Lasswell, Frederick Schuman, Roscoe Martin, V. O. Key, Gabriel Almond, Avery Leiserson, C. Herman Pritchett, Herbert Simon, and David Truman turned their talent to scientific behavioral research, often of a quantitative cast. However, the first wave of enthusiasm for behavioralism did not change the tenor of publications and research in the discipline overnight, except perhaps at Chicago. A variety of institutional and technical factors slowed the transformation between old and new paradigms.

Even in the affluent 1920's money was a problem. The third conference held in 1925 was the last, and afterwards the funding and organizational skills of the leaders, especially Merriam, were channeled through the new Social Science Research Council. The SSRC gave money to political science, but shifted most of its funds to sociology, psychology, anthropology, statistics, economics, history, and interdisciplinary projects. The big money in the 1920's was available for planning projects, like President Hoover's commissions on recent economic changes and recent social trends. Not enough money was available for training programs to retool the profession, or at least its younger members, in the quantitative skills demanded by the new paradigm. Projects to collect, standardize, and disseminate the most important quantitative political data (such as election returns) languished for lack of funds. The availability of scholarships, fellowships, and grants was too uncertain to permit young scholars from venturing too far away from well-trodden paths, or too deeply into the unknown. Quincy Wright at Chicago did organize a massive interdisciplinary project on the causes of war (summarized in *A Study of War*, 2 vols. 1942) which brought material and students together in a search for the antecedents of international conflict—but the project was weak on its statistics, uncertain how to apply behavioral methodology, and quite hostile to the traditional historians who interpreted wars in terms of political, ideological, social, or economic, but not psychological causes.

More difficulties came when political scientists actually tried to use Thurstone's proposed techniques. At first the hope was that aggregate election statistics could be scaled, so that the opinions expressed by the voters could be reduced to basic attitudes. Quickly scholars discovered that social groupings, especially ethnic and religious ones, so dominated the voting returns that "public opinion," if such a creature existed, could not be measured. Instead of turning to an analysis of the social and religious factors underlying historical voting patterns, most of the political scientists hewed to the paradigm which implied that only psychological variables were important, and abandoned election analysis.[8] Legislative roll calls also received little attention, because preliminary analysis showed that party, geography, and social background accounted for most of the patterns, leaving little role for psychology.[9] The study of judicial voting patterns, on the other hand, was more amenable to psychological interpretation. The first reports of statistical analysis of judicial decisions came at the third conference in 1925, but not until Pritchett successfully tied voting analysis with Thurstone's methods in 1941 did the fledgling field of jurimetrics reach take-off stage. Since the role of precedent in American constitutional law cannot be overlooked, every scholar specializing in public law, including jurimetricians, has some training in and respect for historical approaches. Unfortunately constitutional history has never been integrated into the mainstream of historiography, so the interdisciplinary contacts between public law and history are too weak to treat at length here.[10]

Besides its inability to extract attitudinal information from aggregate data, Thurstone's approach had internal bugs. Thurstone was unable to derive a perfectly satisfactory method of scaling responses to questionnaires (he did not have Guttman's scalogram approach), and he decided the problem was that the basic attitudes were not unidimensional but multi-dimensional. After 1931 Thurstone therefore concentrated his efforts on the problem of multidimensional scaling, which he solved by means of factor analysis. Quickly the mathematical complications became far too difficult for political scientists to follow. Only one intrepid researcher, Harold Gosnell, experimented with factor analysis, and he abandoned it in 1937. By then, the failure of the political scientists of the middle 1920's to launch a crash program of statistical training meant that the profession no longer had an adequate number of men who could follow or even read the technical advances in statistical methodology that were being made in the 1930's. Not until the 1960's would methodological training for political science graduate students be adequate to enable them to carry out successful and sophisticated behavioral research projects on a routine basis.

The behavioral revolution completely swept political science in 1924. The unanimity of the leaders at the conferences guaranteed that no return to the old paradigm could succeed. The few articulate opponents of the "new science" criticized and protested to no avail; they realized they were in a hopeless minority, the spokesmen for a past generation. While the new paradigm was dominant in the sense that its standards for the significance of problems, data, and techniques were considered the best criteria against which all research had to be measured, it was not yet true that all or even most political science research followed the rules of the paradigm. The complete transformations of the research style of political science came only after World War II, when the younger scholars, influenced by those in the 1920's who had trained themselves in quantitative and interdisciplinary techniques took control of the leading departments. Before then, the requisite skills were not available for routine distribution to the average graduate student, and only the more talented were able to pick up statistics by themselves. The transformation could have come in the late 1930's, but then and during the war years most of the talented younger political scientists were working on urgent practical problems for the government. The conditions for transformation were met at Chicago in the 1920's and 1930's. No other department could boast the depth of young talent or the indomitable energy of a chairman like Merriam, committed to the new paradigm and unusually adept at organizing and funding team projects. After the war, the tenor of the Chicago department turned sharply anti-behaviorist under the leadership of two historically minded, European-trained scholars, Hans Morgenthau and Leo Strauss. Neither had participated in the exciting days of methodological revolution in the mid-1920's, and both opposed the behavioral resolution to the legitimacy crisis. That such men would so quickly dominate the Chicago department, even as Merriam still lived, is but one of the ironies of history.

In one aspect of the new science Merriam was eager to use history. That was in the psychological analysis of the character and leadership qualities of representative American statesmen. Merriam and his students prepared a number of character studies and "psychobiographies" in the 1920's, but interest quietly died out when it was realized that only trained historians could handle the biographical challenge well. Harold Lasswell became intrigued with the possibilities of a developmental analysis of the psychological history of the modern world, but more from a Freudian than Thurstonian viewpoint. "The attention of one who wishes to analyze social relationships," he maintained, "must play back and forth continually between the events that have receded into history, and to the future events destined to become history."[11] Although he used historical examples and analogies and even case histories extensively, most notably in his widely read *Politics: Who Gets What, When, How* (1936), Lasswell suffered from his lack of historical training. His efforts to psychoanalyze the past were quickly frustrated by his failure to do his own historical research. Nor did he train disciples who might have followed his lead with sound historical research.

The historian can only speculate about the possible paradigms that might have emerged if the conferences had invited economists or sociologists instead of psychologists. Economics was already a deductive science with an impressive record of achievement. However, very little of the quantitative economic theory of the day was applicable to observed or measured statistical data. Scientific economics was not at all empirical, and its models would not have been of any help to political science. If any economists had been invited they would have been empirical data-oriented "institutionalists" like Wesley Mitchell of business-cycle fame, or Paul Douglas, the leading investigator of labor statistics. Merriam was familiar with the work of both men, but was so committed to psychology that the possibilities of index construction, econometric analysis of time series, or the systematic search for historical trends, cycles, and stages in quantitative political phenomena did not occur to him. Several sociologists were interested in these problems, especially William F. Osborn, Stuart Rice, Stuart Chapin, and Pitirim Sorokin, but there was remarkably little communication between these men and the political scientists. If any sociologists had been invited, they probably would have been members of the Chicago school of urban ecology—not just because of their acquaintance with Merriam, but because their approach to the structure of cities meshed with the scientific planning that Merriam and other political scientists hoped to achieve. However, the Chicago sociologists had only a dim conception of the "scientific method," and surprisingly little interest in politics; they were therefore of little use in a legitimacy crisis.

For the interwar generation two lesser crises faced the political scientists. The first was a participation crisis involving the role of the profession in the training of citizens to understand and participate in a democratic government. The recent rapid expansion of the secondary school system in the country made the problem far more urgent than before, especially since the political parties and mass media no longer performed a major role in informing citizens about the work of government. The behavioral paradigm, being too difficult for most graduate students to master, was totally unsuited for adaptation to high school civics textbooks. Consequently the leading behaviorists, with the exception of Merriam, ignored the crisis, permitting the opponents of the new paradigm to move in and tackle the problem. The anti-behaviorists favored moralistic training in the virtues of democracy, and historical or descriptive accounts of the institutions of government. The civics textbooks that emerged were not congruent with the behaviorist research in political science, and to outsiders gave the field an image as the most moralistic and least scientific social science. Historical description of the rise and role of political parties filled a substantial part of these textbooks long after serious research in this topic had been abandoned by political scientists. The history was an old-fashioned rehash of the conclusions of earlier writers, and further discredited the potentials of history in the minds of behaviorists. The second minor crisis of the third generation was the penetration crisis, regarding the relationship of mature scholars in their role as experts with the actual administration of government. The resolution came in the late 1930's when, led again by Merriam, a substantial number of leading younger scholars went to work for the New Deal. During World War II, virtually everyone worked for the war effort, especially in administrative positions in superagencies, like the Bureau of the Budget, the War Production Board, or the Office of Price Administration. The result was a temporary suspension of basic research, a long-run impact as a result of greater familiarity with the actual working of bureaucracies, and, even more important, a fruitful exchange of ideas with economists and sociologists that greatly broadened the horizons of political scientists.

The impact of the identity and legitimacy crises on those scholars who attempted to be both political scientists and historians was disastrous, as exemplified in the career of Charles Beard. Before World War I, Beard had firmly established his reputation in the forefront of both American history and public administration. He responded to the identity crisis by carefully segregating his two disciplinary interests. Beard's major history books betrayed not at all his status as a leading specialist in municipal government. His popular college textbook on *American Government and Politics* (1910 and nine subsequent editions) contained detailed discussions on the writing and contents of the Constitution, but never once borrowed ideas from his spectacularly successful *history* book, *An Economic Interpretation of the Constitution* (1913). In each revision of the textbook Beard made room for more detail on state and local government by progressively abbreviating or removing the introductory historical sections. Beard may have been uneasy about the compromises he made to meet the identity crisis, but he retained enough balance to be elected president of the American Political Science Association for 1926, and president of the American Historical Association for 1933.

The compromise that worked during the second generation proved inadequate during the third generation; the legitimacy crisis baffled Beard. He was willing to delete history from his political science, but he was fundamentally hostile to the new science of politics. Social and economic factors, he felt, were much more important than psychology, and were unduly neglected in the new paradigm. More important, the lessons of the past, the moral content of politics, were incompatible in his mind with the value free scientific methodology of Thurstone. In his 1926 presidential address, Beard indicated his belief that no "science" of politics was possible, or if possible, desirable:

> Research under scientific formulas in things mathematically measurable or logically describable leaves untouched a vast array of driving social forces for which such words as conviction, faith, hope, loyalty, and destiny are pale symbols—yielding to the analysis of no systematists.[12]

By ignoring history, Beard felt, political science was missing the crux of politics, and was veering from the proper goals of the study of government. Beard's arguments were not well received. Outside the less important municipal research bureaus no scholar any longer paid attention to him, and no student became his disciple. Realizing that he was on the losing side in the crisis of legitimacy Beard threw his efforts into the crisis of participation. Since few of his behavioral colleagues much cared, Beard played a major role in shaping the content and direction of civics training in the 1930's and beyond. After 1928 Beard rarely attempted research in political science. He continued to advise governments (mostly in foreign lands) and educators (mostly in teachers' colleges), but he undertook no more research in political science. Beard's crisis as a historian came a little later, when he attacked the critics of his economic interpretation by protesting that history cannot be objective at all, let alone scientific. "History as it actually was," he concluded, "is not known and cannot be known."[13] From 1928 to his death twenty years later Beard's writings consisted of secondary textbooks, discussions of current events (from a historical perspective), some undistinguished political theory and philosophy of the social sciences, and increasingly bitter polemics on the course of the New Deal and the "betrayal" that brought American entry into World War II.

In the fourth generation (1940–60) behaviorism finally became the dominant research style in political science. Its legitimacy for a while was the subject of heated dispute, but the remaining "traditionalists" could not agree whether their criticism was that behaviorism was not sufficiently rigorous and scientific, or whether its fault lay in its neglect of certain traditional values. History entered the debate to the extent that the traditionalists thought that human values could be extracted from the study of the past, something twentieth-century historians had been unable to do themselves. On the other hand the more aggressive behaviorists crusaded for a "truth" they were certain they possessed, and looked askance at history because of all disciplines history was at once the closest and the most anti-scientific. The debate was not entirely a sham—it did decide who got what, when, and how, in terms of prestige, promotion, and foundation grants. Usually the behaviorists emerged victors on every battlefield—for the war had been over twenty-five years.

Behaviorism in the style of Thurstone was, however, inadequate as a fundamental paradigm for a major social science. Its conception of the scientific method was too narrow, especially in its failure to include systems approaches. Its choice of attitude as the fundamental unit reflected a narrow approach to psychology and proved unsatisfactory to scholars who felt that power, role, socialization, value allocation, or communications, among other concepts, were claimants to the all-important title of political atom. No academic discipline in the postwar period engaged in more controversy about its methodological principles, and all the manifestos called for more interdisciplinary studies. History, however, was rarely mentioned when pathmarkers coaxed the profession to greener pastures. Most of the leaders of the fourth generation did not use any data more than twenty years old, and thus avoided confrontation with historical problems. V. O. Key was a notable exception; almost alone he stressed the use of long-run time series for the understanding of contemporary voting patterns. His books were widely admired, but with the exception of an unusually small number of men who became his disciples, few researchers followed his lead. Karl Deutsch was a more influential user of historical data in the fourth generation, especially in his emphasis on the need to study historical trends of political mobilization and international transactions. Deutsch had more influence on the fifth generation than Key, because the general movement was toward quantitative models of international behavior and comparative development, and away from studies of American elections, the latter field being preempted by survey research groups.

While the behaviorists of the fourth generation did not endorse historical approaches, they did hold out for admiration the work of sociologists with a historical orientation, especially Alexis de Tocqueville, Moisei Ostrogorski, Gaetano Mosca, Max Weber, Talcott Parsons, Robert Merton, Barrington Moore, and Seymour Lipset. Thus the influence of sociologists who applied systemic analysis to historical structures finally pointed the fifth generation (1960–   ) toward a new appreciation of the possibilities of historical inquiry. The broadening of research into the past was most notable in election studies,[14] international relations,[15] and comparative development.[16]

The fifth generation wanted above all to develop empirical theory, and needed the wealth of data that only the past could provide to underpin its models. They worked with a scientific methodology much broader than Thurstone's simple two-variable causality schemes. Systems approaches were in favor, and called for the mapping of all the boundaries, norms, functions, and development patterns of the complex institutional framework in which the actors (either persons or states) moved.[17] The first step in comparing systems is the construction of a taxonomic scheme that displays the various possible and actual types of configurations. It is a short step from constructing a taxonomy to asking what developmental sequences are possible, and which have actually occurred.[18] But as the fifth generation discovered it needed historical materials, it also found itself inadequately trained in historical research. Even very simple questions about the state of the world in 1914, say, are very difficult to answer if the scholar does not know where to look for information. But the problem of the relationship between the fifth generation of political scientists and history goes much deeper than matters of bibliography, and the second part of this chapter considers some of the problems and possibilities of future interdisciplinary cooperation.

History is unimportant—such is the attitude of many political scientists, especially those who believe that sociology, economics, anthropology, or psychology is important. The typical political scientist does not find the works of historians useful in his own research. In large part this attitude can be explained by the fact that the bulk of political science research involves case studies of contemporary events and institutions, and that few professional historians come within twenty-five years of the period under study. Political scientists who ransack history books for suggestions about hypotheses, discussions of trends, or even descriptions of major events, engage in a frustrating search. The researcher discovers he has to be his own historian, pulling together information from interviews, newspapers, and government documents to discern the general shape of recent events in a particular country or area. His colleagues in the next building may specialize in the same country, but they have published little to help. Indeed, historians have written very little about events since the end of World War II, the major research site for the great majority of political scientists. The neglect stems not from lack of interest, but from lack of evidence. True, most of the major events are matters of public record, and more documentary and autobiographical records exist for recent events than for many past periods. But the availability of documentary evidence does not provide the historian with what he needs most, adequate criteria for judging the overall significance of conditions, trends, and events. These criteria consist primarily in the future consequences of the events which have not yet unfolded. Thus the historian does not write about the Cold War because he does not know what it will lead to, and the significance of events like the Korean War cannot be evaluated without knowing whether there will be a World War III. The political scientist, who is actively concerned with preventing another world war, will obviously be spurred, not inhibited, by this fact. Doubtless much of the attraction the Middle Ages or the American colonies have for brilliant historians lies in the fact that most, if not all the consequences of those events have appeared and can be used as a basis of evaluation.

On the other hand, to consider the historian to be a journalist interviewing dead people is a fallacy.[19] A good journalist combines reporting of today's happenings with a stiff dose of speculation and projection about tomorrow, and tomorrow he may well change his tune. Political scientists making case studies act the role of journalists, but tone down the speculation in favor of closer analysis of recent trends. Unlike the journalist who implicitly relies upon some forgotten theorist and is forced to dramatize the spectacular in order to attract readers, the political scientist pays special attention to his sophisticated methodology and theory, and focuses solely on those patterns that his theory says are important and his methods allow him to handle. Neither dramatization nor even good style is a prime consideration of the format of the final report. Historians pay a good deal more attention to writing style than other social scientists, but they also hew closely to the theoretical and methodological foundations of their research.

The fallacy of seeing the historian as a sophisticated journalist of the past is a naïve version of a more widespread misinterpretation of the nature of historiography. Many philosophical outsiders have categorized history as the study of the unique and the particular aspects of past events. This view ascribes to "science" the contrasting role of finding the general laws of the universe, and to social science the role of finding general laws of human behavior. Philosophers thereupon debate whether history is the application of general laws to particular episodes, or whether the multiplicity of unique conditions surrounding complex events makes general laws useless. Unfortunately, no one has managed to show that general laws of human behavior in real situations do in fact exist, nor indicated what such laws would look like when found. In any case, the debate among philosophers ignores the actual behavior of historians. Each historian works within the framework of a particular paradigm which specifies what factors and types of events are significant, and which types of particular conditions are "accidental" or irrelevant to a broader sweep of events.

The historian is not a mere chronicler of events, like the compiler of the *New York Times Index*. He is not primarily interested in describing what happened in the past—too many things happened!—but rather in the analysis of the important structures of a society or in the explication of how significant factors interacted with the decisions of men with power to produce important events. Most historians couch their final results in a narrative style, the livelier the better. Perhaps the style misleads political scientists into thinking historians are "just" describing events. In any case, narrative is not absolutely essential to history (Turner, and Lewis Namier, for example, seldom told stories), but it is considered the best medium for conveying the spirit and complexity of events and for allowing the reader to share vicariously in the experiences recorded, and thus understand them more fully. The narrative style is not the best for scientific analysis of models or for hypothesis testing, and many historians abandon it in favor of analytic description of the social, political, or intellectual structure of a given society. Analytic history resembles analytic political science, but usually lacks explicit discussion of underlying theoretical assumptions.

Since Merriam, most political scientists have failed to understand that historians strive to transcend entertaining description with analytic and even scientific study of intellectual, political, social, and economic development. Even biographers dealing with the uniqueness of a single career try to put their subject in perspective by relating his thoughts and actions to a wider context of his times. Research in history for nearly a century has been guided by a handful of paradigms that resemble the theoretical models or systems in political science, although the statement of the paradigm often does not appear explicitly in the final history book. Generalizations about historians' paradigms are somewhat difficult since the field has not experienced a single legitimacy crisis, and there exists no discipline-wide strain toward methodological unity. History is divided into a number of autonomous subdisciplines, each focusing on a historical unity defined by geographical extension and temporal duration. Within each subdiscipline historians tend to specialize in one or several aspects of the material, such as social, intellectual, diplomatic, economic, or political history. Cultural, artistic, or literary history is usually handled by scholars in other departments, while military, geneological, and antiquarian interests are rare among professional scholars.

Although the history profession nationwide is quite large, any one sub-discipline on any one campus will be represented by only two or three scholars. In contrast to a political science department in which each man can understand and evaluate the work of nearly all his colleagues, historians are competent to appreciate the research of only a few departmental colleagues. A specialist on the American Revolution, for example, is not familiar with the theoretical orientation, the primary sources, or even the language of the documents studied by a colleague in medieval history. The variety of paradigms expounded in any single history department produces a tolerance of widely divergent approaches. There has never been, nor is there likely to occur, intradepartmental methodological crises of the sort that has proven nasty in the social sciences. The various historical subdisciplines are led by a handful of eminent scholars in the United States and Europe, men somewhat older than the leaders of political science. Tolerance and maturity of leadership have given history a composure, if not complacency, toward its legitimacy.

Some subdisciplines have been remarkably receptive to new ideas and approaches emanating from other disciplines. American colonial history, to cite one prominent example, has incorporated an approach to intellectual history derived from literary critics, and more recently has proven highly receptive to quantitative methods and behavioral models from political science, economics, and sociology. The historical profession as a whole has paid considerable attention to the social sciences; it is ready to use new approaches, whether derived from literary criticism, psychology, or statistics. Behavioral approaches have their advocates, who are listened to respectfully, though with some skepticism. The skepticism doubtless stems from the experience of having seen too many revolutionary manifestos that promised a brave new historiography, but which never produced the solid scholarship necessary to command respect.[20]

Historians do not think of themselves as obsolete guardians of an obsolescent field. They know the material they deal with concerns the most important happenings known to man, and look askance at scholars who think that laboratory experiments on rats, pigeons, or sophomores will tell very much about how a society in crisis behaves. Historians are thus not likely to abandon their methodological principles when confronted with braggadocio about the "true" scientific method, especially when the achievements of that method in the social sciences leaves a great deal to be desired. The central principle of most, if not all working historians is the integrity of past cultures. The notion, stemming from Hegelian idealism via Ranke, holds that any period must be understood in its own terms, and not forced into some taxonomy or system devised to answer different questions about different cultures. Scholars often haggle about the boundaries of, or even the validity of, proposed historical units (e.g. when and where did the "Renaissance" occur, if there was one), but in the very act of research the historian must be satisfied in his own mind that there is a unity and a reality about the particular set of events he studies. To be more specific, the historian is not likely to scrap his paradigm of, say, early American national development when confronted with a model of development based solely on recent African experience. The historian instead would inquire why the political scientist does not try to fit the African experience to a model of eighteenth-century development—after all, more is known about the Thirteen Colonies than about practically any new African country. This is not to insist that conceptual insights about the functioning of government and the prerequisites for nationhood are not of interest to the historian, only that the exchange of insights must be two-way if it is to avoid cross-sterilization.

Since World War II, historians have become increasingly uncomfortable with the realization that the principle of historical uniqueness, coupled with the old-fashioned role of the historian as the creator of the myths of national unity, tends to induce parochialism and excessive intellectual inbreeding within each subdiscipline. Leading historians have been trying to break away from this parochialism either by closer attention to ideas from other disciplines, or by fitting their research into a more comparative framework. Great national crises, such as revolutions and civil wars, have already been fitted into comparative frameworks, as evidenced by the studies of Crane Brinton on *The Anatomy of Revolution* (1938) and Robert Palmer on the *Age of Democratic Revolution* (1959, 1964). Historians studying economic development have explicitly used comparative approaches, and the comparative study of social upheaval by Barrington Moore's *Social Origins of Dictatorship and Democracy* (1966) has won wide acclaim among historians. Cyril Black has turned to the historical aspects of *The Dynamics of Modernization* (1966), and C. Vann Woodward has gathered a fascinating collection of essays by leading historians on *The Comparative Approach to American History* (1968). The comparative historical sociology of Moore, Lipset, Rokkan, Dahl, Rustow, Key, Deutsch and others does not differ so drastically from the approach of Mosse, Cochran, Palmer, McNeil, Thrupp, Chambers, Handlin, Black, Brinton, or Woodward that cooperation is impossible or cross-fertilization unlikely.

If the fifth generation of political scientists does open lines of intellectual exchange with historians, the first contacts are likely to prove frustrating to both sides. Differences of terminology and methodology will prove frustrating. Historians will object to useless and inpenetrable jargon, while political scientists will counterreact by insisting on the need for a precise and scientific vocabulary. The historians' uncanny ability to extract hidden meaning from documents and speeches will surprise the political scientists, who eventually will complain that the historians' efforts to try to read everything are a waste of time, and should be abandoned in favor of a content analysis of a sample of documents. Historians are not too familiar with quantitative content analysis, but once they understand the dictionaries and counting process used, they will probably not object to the approach as a supplement, not a replacement for enlightened reading. Reading, they will observe, permits the continuous adjustment and refinement of theory, while content analysis methods are relatively inflexible once the theoretical decisions are made. Historians will probably be nervous about the use of small samples to reduce unmanageable data files to reasonable size, fearing that a 2% random sample of documents is likely to miss 98% of the important material. The historians' intuitive fear of sampling perhaps stems from an awareness that *new* information can only be found by searching mountains of records. The fear is misguided when the task is to find the patterns and distributions of attitudes, rhetorical usages, or activities; for a good deal of important analysis can be done by studying distributions in the total population by sampling that cannot be found by the intensive analysis of a few major documents.

Scholars from both disciplines will set up taxonomic schemes to sort the data into a small number of basic types, but there will be conflicting approaches. Political scientists have a stronger propensity to order cases along a linear continuum, say liberal to conservative, developed to underdeveloped, or authoritarian to democratic. Conceptually, linear continua are easy to handle, and they lend themselves to simple statistical methods, but to the historian they appear to work too much injustice on the complexity of the patterns. Historians tend to use complex discrete taxonomies, often without a single unifying theory, and thus have difficulty generalizing on the basis of their classifications. They also will want to incorporate so many different factors and dimensions in a single model that the methods of statistical analysis known to political scientists, including even factor analysis, become very difficult. The greater statistical sophistication of the political scientists, if coupled with the historians' strong intuitive sensitivity for historical linkages, hopefully will yield better taxonomies and models than either group could produce alone.

Although historians may prove confused about statistics, they will have some useful insights about the processes of evolutionary development across time that may not be familiar to political scientists. Most political science training and research in the fourth and fifth generations involved cross-sectional data in which long-run changes over time were ignored. The consequence of moving from cross-sectional data to longitudinal data may be a tendency to deduce longitudinal patterns from cross-sectional information. For example, the fact that blue-collar workers in America today, both young and old, tend to vote heavily Democratic, may suggest to the political scientist that sixty years ago, when the proportion of blue-collar workers in the cities was much greater, the Democrats must have enjoyed even larger electoral majorities in the big cities. Actually, blue-collar workers were much more Republican in those days than now. The historian would probably perceive the point, and note that partisanship cannot be mechanically projected backwards; he would emphasize that societies from time to time encounter crises, critical junctures with alternative paths. As Lipset and Rokkan have noted, societies

> are typically faced with choices among historically given "packages" of programs, commitments, outlooks, and, sometimes, *Weltanschauungen*, and their current behavior cannot be understood without some knowledge of the sequences of events and the combinations of forces that produced these "packages."[21]

The study of this sequence of events and challenges constitutes the unique study of a society, and is the major concern of historians. Projections backward that attempt to leap over these crises are preposterous; the duty of the social scientist, as Dankwart Rustow has argued, is "to ascertain the margin of choice offered by man's social condition and to clarify the choices in that margin."[22]

The convergence of research interests in both disciplines on the problem of historical crises presents a fruitful area for cooperation. Some frustration is inevitable when team members discover that their colleagues from the other discipline have very different ideas about what factors should be studied in explaining crises. Historians generally deal with three types of factors. First come long-run demographic and economic changes that upset the equilibrium established in an earlier period and lead to the emergence of disruptive or dysfunctional activities, and a perceived imbalance in social norms. Since political scientists do not commonly deal with long-run demographic or economic changes, they will have to acquaint themselves with the relevant studies by historians, economists, and sociologists. Second, historians look for the conflicts between various social groups (aristocracy vs. middle classes, agrarian vs. trade interests, different religions), with an eye to discovering how imbalances caused by long-run economic or social changes are reflected in the struggle for power. As part of the heritage of the behavioral emphasis on psychology, political scientists are surprisingly backward in asking who governed, and who constituted the opposition. Political scientists who never shared the psychological orientation of the Chicago school, Robert Dahl for example, have started to ask these questions, but historians have worried about the problem for many years. Third, and most important, the basic motivating forces that interest historians are either reduced to or summarized by trends in the intellectual climate of opinion, which includes the myths and ideologies of the different groups in society. Before the 1960's, political scientists paid little attention to the role of prevailing myth or ideology, save in the analysis of totalitarian systems. When these political scientists studied democracy, they looked at suffrage requirements and the competitiveness of parties. Historians of democracy have turned more to asking questions about the prevailing patterns of deference, fears of corruption or oppression, and the relationship of democratic ideals to religious and other cultural forces. The role of climate of opinion is invariably greater in historians' paradigms than in those of political scientists, but recently the nature of belief systems has become a major research topic in political science, as exemplified by the emphasis in David Easton's *A Systems Analysis of Political Life* (1965). Team projects would have to agree at an early stage on the causal role to be assigned to myths and ideas, or else communication will become progressively more difficult. Perhaps the assistance of anthropologists will help produce a satisfactory compromise.

Interdisciplinary cooperation can range from full scale team projects down to instances of political scientists requesting information about specific facts. Cooperation is not likely to be achieved by the political scientist plunging into history books and journal articles for help, for he is likely to become confused and trapped by the implicit historical paradigm. Every historian has file cabinets crammed with facts, and he selects a very small number of them for final publication, ignoring a large number that a political scientists, or indeed another historian, would consider of great importance. The facts finally presented are those judged "significant" in terms of the historian's theoretical framework; this includes both facts relating to causally important events as well as facts that have no great intrinsic importance but which yield deep insight into the nature of important forces, institutions, or belief systems. Thus the historian is certain to discuss a civil war, but may also discuss an obscure speech that in itself had no impact but which clearly indicates the alignment of forces the historian considers important. Events that contemporaries considered important may escape mention, like natural disasters, while subtle events no one noticed at the time may be studied for the information they contain about social structure. Political scientists who find that historians have written a great deal about a specific movement, American Populism for example, may confuse the two criteria of significance and think that Populism is important because of the impact it had on political events. Actually the Populists had very little impact, but historians write about them because their behavior and beliefs are thought to reflect certain basic social or intellectual strains, either agrarian vs. industrial, urban vs. rural, east vs. west, or parochial vs. cosmopolitan. "Study the historian before you begin to study the facts," E. H. Carr recommends, or else one will not know what kinds of facts the historian has chosen to write about.[23]

Interdisciplinary team research, if and when it does come about, will focus on certain types of crises, developmental sequences, or institutions that play important roles in the paradigms of the participants from both disciplines. Obvious candidates include the study of revolutionary social or political crises,[24] and the evolution of political parties and voting patterns. The institutions most likely to be studied are those whose basic characteristics are invariant over time or across cultures, and which can be studied from the documentary traces that historians can locate. Bureaucracy is a leading example, and individual researchers have already published a number of major books on the historical development of bureaucracies and their impact on the political system. Prominent examples are Leonard White's four volumes on the administrative history of the United States government from 1789 to 1901, S. N. Eisenstadt's widely ranging study of The Political Systems of Empires (1963), and Karl Wittfogel's theory of hydraulic societies presented in Oriental Despotism (1957). Other institutions (using the term in its broadest sense) that seem to be amenable to interdisciplinary study include political parties, legislatures, military establishments, patterns of international conflict and cooperation, internal wars, and networks of economic transactions and communicaᐧons.

Quantitative interdisciplinary studies are likely to become fashionable because of the inherent lure of precise numbers, and more specifically because the statistical patterns inherent in documentary data are relatively robust, i.e. meaningful in terms of a great variety of paradigms. That is, scholars of different disciplines, with differing paradigms, and biases, can all agree on the numerical value of a well-defined index, like growth rate of GNP, even though each scholar uses and interprets the value in different ways. It is tempting to think that scholars who agree on little else can work together establishing commonly accepted values for specific indices. Consequently the establishment in the 1960's of data banks for time series of political, social, and economic indicators will provide the institutional locus for cooperative research. The Inter-University Consortium for Political Research, which has built the largest data archives, began methodological training programs for political scientists and historians in the mid-1960's, and has become one of the leading centers for inter-disciplinary work.

Unfortunately the availability of quantitative data archives alone will not guarantee successful cooperation. Statistical manipulation of files of numbers will not produce results unless guided by an explicit theory of what patterns to look for and an understanding of the historical context in which the raw data were generated. The historical voting studies of scholars with big statistical guns hunting at random for patterns, or concerned only with testing a narrowly conceived hypothesis, are not likely to be fruitful. Some of the chapters in Stuart Rice's *Quantitative Methods in Politics* fell prey to the dangers of theory-less research, while V. O. Key's election studies were always informed by a greater concern for insight and understanding than for a display of mathematical prowess. The world is full of competent mathematicians; it is short of men with a deep understanding of politics, and no discipline, least of all political science, will profit by improving its mathematics at the expense of its insight.

Historians cooperating with political scientists will emphasize the desir-ability of using a multiplicity of sources to derive estimates for indices, drawing upon archival, manuscript, and newspaper sources that are largely unfamiliar to social scientists. Historians will recognize that documentary sources are inferior to recorded behavioral patterns in the analysis of the distribution of important attributes. For example the letters, diaries, memoirs, and speeches of a period are not likely to reveal the opinions of more than a fraction of legislature members on current political issues, while the roll call record can be scaled to derive good approximations to attitudinal positions. However the historian will not be satisfied that attitudinal scales constructed by a statistical algorithm are congruent with the actual structure of attitudes, unless independent confirmation can be secured from traditional documentary sources. Recently jurimetricians have tended to read too much into their statistical roll call analyses about the attitudes of judges. A reading of letters and diaries of judges high-lights the give-and-take, the uncertainties, hesitations, and confusions inherent in any small group decision-making process, and warns against any rigid conclusions based on partial evidence.[25] Similarly, historians will react against misplaced determinism that depicts intelligent actors as Turing machines grinding out predictable behavioral patterns on the basis of their attitudes and environment. The decisions that lead to actions in the political world cannot all be predictable any more (any less?) than the intellectual decisions of scholars. There is room for a limited amount of *aggregate level* determinism in the social sciences—the most successful paradigm of the century, Keynes's theory of the relationship between aggregate income, investment, consumption, and deficits was, after all, highly deterministic. But paradigms that attempt to predict which choice an *individual* will choose when confronted with an important decision, will not be favorably received by historians. Even the economists, who once favored such deterministic models, have come to emphasize stochastic decision processes in which chance and uncertainty play large enough roles to keep historians happy and busy.

True cooperation between historians and fifth generation political scientists is likely to come only when both sides understand each other, and have selected a problem and an approach amenable to each other's paradigm. Historians alone will gradually pick up ideas, theories, and methods from political scientists, but only a few can be expected to abandon the paradigms they were trained in, leap the fence, and devote themselves to testing political science theories on past data. Such men will probably sever their links with historians as quickly and gracefully as possible, and regard themselves as "historical political sociologists" or some such. The small band of eminent political scientists who were trained in the European interdisciplinary tradition, thus escaping the direct influence of the behavioral revolution of 1924, will gradually dwindle in number. A majority of them, who fled to America in the 1930's in the great intellectual migration, have already exerted the bulk of their influence.[26] Most of the political scientists who are fond of citing historical examples all the time—Carl Friedrich, Hans Morgenthau, Leo Strauss, Sigmund Neumann, Otto Kirchheimer, Denis Brogan, François Goguel, Bertrand de Jouvenel, Giovanni Sartori, David Butler, Arnold Brecht, Herman Finer, Maurice Duverger, Karl Deutsch, and Stein Rokkan, to cite the most prominent—are Europeans trained originally in law or history. Political scientists who seek to go beyond the citation of historical events and to generalize across time must remember that history is more treacherous than it appears in encyclopedias, and more complex than the problems for which giant electronic computers were built. Karl Deutsch, keenly aware of the promise and difficulty of cooperation, has admonished his colleagues that "we need history not as a handmaiden of the social sciences, but as their full-fledged partner, guide, and friend."[27]

Notes

1. Charles E. Merriam, *New Aspects of Politics* (Chicago, 1925), 2. Merriam discussed many of the current trends in political science, and the preface to the second edition (1931) covered the later 1920's. For another interpretation, see Albert Somit and Joseph Tanenhaus, *The Development of American Political Science: From Burgess to Behavioralism* (Boston, 1967). Brief biographies of most of the pioneers appear in the *International Encyclopedia of the Social Sciences* (New York, 1968).

2. Merriam, *New Aspects*, 31.

3. Thurstone was trained originally in electrical engineering, and his work was largely confined to technical problems of scaling. Thurstone's research showed little interest in broader psychological problems. Floyd Allport (not to be confused with his much more important brother, Gordon) was an extreme behaviorist of the John B. Watson school.

4. The conference reports appear in the *American Political Science Review*, Vols. 18, 19, 20 (1924, 1925, 1926). The quote, without the italics, appears in Vol. 19, p. 106.

5. Heinz Eulau, "Segments of Political Science Most Susceptible to Behavioristic Treatment," in James Charlesworth (ed.), *Contemporary Political Analysis* (New York, 1967), 35. Note that the term "behavioral" gained currency only in the 1950's.

6. L. L. Thurstone, "Attitudes Can Be Measured," *American Journal of Sociology* (1928) 33: 520.

7. *American Political Science Review* (1925) 19: 120.

8. Arthur Holcombe, Gosnell, Key and a few others acquainted with Turnerian quantitative election analysis continued to work with voting statistics, usually emphasizing historical, social, and economic forces to the exclusion of psychological factors. For further details see the author's chapter, "American Election Analysis: A Case History of Methodological Innovation and Diffusion," pp. 226–243 in this volume.

9. Stuart Rice reinvigorated roll-call analysis in *Farmers and Workers in American Politics* (New York, 1924), and *Quantitative Methods in Politics* (New York, 1928). Rice was a sociologist looking for group cohesion patterns in roll calls, not revealed psychological attitudes. Hence his statistical methods were not adopted by behavioral political scientists, at least not until the 1950's.

10. See Glendon Schubert (ed.), *Judicial Behavior* (Chicago, 1964), 306–18, for a brief history of jurimetrics.

11. From a 1933 essay quoted by Robert Horwitz, "Scientific Propaganda: Harold D. Lasswell," in Herbert J. Storing (ed.), *Essays on the Scientific Study of Politics* (New York, 1962), 245.

12. *American Political Science Review* (1927) 21: 9; see also Somit and Tanenhaus, *Development of Political Science*, 117–22.

13. Charles Beard, *The Discussion of Human Affairs* (New York, 1935), 87. Carl Becker, another dual-discipline scholar of the second generation, adopted a similar, but less extreme position with respect to both disciplines.

14. Especially in William N. Chambers and Walter Dean Burnham (eds),. *The American Party Systems: Stages of Political Development* (New York, 1967); Seymour M. Lipset and Stein Rokkan (eds.), *Party Systems and Voter Alignments: Cross National Perspectives* (New York, 1967); Joseph LaPalombara and Myron Weiner (eds.), *Political Parties and Political Development* (Princeton, 1966); Angus Campbell *et al.*, *Elections and the Political Order* (New York, 1966); Robert Dahl (ed.), *Political Order* (New York, 1966); Robert Dahl (ed.), *Political Opposition in Western Democracies* (New Haven, 1966).

15. Especially J. David Singer (ed.), *Quantitative International Politics* (New York, 1968); and Karl Deutsch, *The Analysis of International Relations* (Englewood Cliffs, 1968).

16. Especially Leonard Binder (ed.), *Crises in Political Development* (Princeton, 1969); Gabriel Almond and G. Bingham Powell, *Comparative Politics: A Developmental Approach* (Boston, 1966); and Karl Deutsch *et al.*, *Political Community and the North Atlantic Area* (Princeton, 1957).

17. See Oran Young, *Systems of Political Science* (Englewood Cliffs, 1968), for a concise review of recent paradigms.

18. See S. N. Eisenstadt, "Social Institutions," In *International Encyclopedia of the Social Sciences* (1968) 14: 409–29, and "Evolution: Social Evolution," *ibid.*, 5: 228–34; cf. J. H. Hexter, "Historiography" in *ibid.*, 6: 387. For broader theoretical discussions of time and evolution, see S. N. Eisenstadt, "Social Change, Differentiation and Evolution," *American Sociological Review* (1964) 29: 375–86; and Max Heirich, "The Use of Time in the Study of Social Change," *ibid.* 29: 386–397.

19. For an example of this fallacy expressed by a political scientist who specializes in the prompt reporting of British elections, see D. E. Butler, *The Study of Political Behavior* (London, 1958), 40–42.

20. On behavioral history see Allan B. Bogue, "United States: The 'New' Political History," in Walter Laquer and George Mosse (eds.), *The New History* (New York, 1967), 185–207. On the attitude of historians towards social science, see C. Van Woodward, "History and the Third Culture," *Journal of Contemporary History* (April, 1968) 3: 23–35.

21. Seymour Lipset and Stein Rokkan, "Cleavage Structures, Party Systems, and Voter Alignments: An Introduction," in Lipset and Rokkan, *Party Systems*, 2–3.

22. Dankwart Rustow, *A World of Nations* (Washington, 1967), 17.

23. E. H. Carr, *What Is History?* (New York, 1961), 26.

24. For a political scientist's imaginative use of history, see Otto Kirchheimer, "Confining Conditions and Revolutionary Breakthroughs," *American Political Science Review* (1965) 59: 964–74; for a historian's appraisal of social

science models, see Lawrence Stone, "Theories of Revolution," *World Politics* (1966) 18: 159–76. A century ago the great Swiss historian Jacob Burckhardt studied the "Crises of History" in a comparative framework that is still of value; see his *Force and Freedom* (New York, 1943), 257–92.

25. See J. Woodford Howard, Jr. "On the Fluidity of Judicial Choice," *American Political Science Review* (1968) 62: 43–56, for an excellent example of the revision of jurimetric results based on manuscript discoveries.

26. See Laura Fermi, *Illustrious Immigrants* (Chicago, 1968), 348–51.

27. Karl Deutsch, "The Limits of Common Sense," (1959), reprinted in Nelson Polsby, Robert Dentler, and Paul Smith (eds.), *Politics and Social Life* (Boston, 1963), 57.

2

Anthropology and Political Science: Courtship or Marriage?

RONALD COHEN

Introduction: The Courtship

When disciplines begin exchanging materials, one may say that they are attracted to one another; and if this behavior continues the situation may well develop into a full courtship. In this case consistent references to one another become quite common and concepts from the one discipline may be widely accepted by the other. However such proto-unions are, in my view, not fully consummated until an area of overlap begins to emerge as a new subfield between the two original fields. Thus physical chemistry, social psychology, even political sociology, are today accepted areas of research and teaching that overlap into neighboring disciplines. In general the stimulus for such development comes from some theory, some research, and some faith, that utilizing a mixture of the two disciplines can provide insights and explanations that were hitherto unavailable. The question then becomes: where in this process of marital and premarital relations can we place anthropology and political science and what are the prospects for such a union?

Although my own knowledge is severely limited to African research and my experiences to membership of one department of political science, I will try to assess the situation and make some prognostications about whether there is a blossoming love affair developing that has any real contributions to make to both of the disciplines concerned.

In a recent article on new nations and their contributions to the development of political theory, Lucien Pye[1] borrows a number of terms that have a familiar ring to the anthropologist. Cultural relativism, social evolution, cultural diffusion, and acculturation—all seem to be concepts that Pye is able to use in order to focus on processes of nation building. As he says, theories developed from Western nation states cannot do the job of describing something as different as the new national entities of the non-Western world. On the anthropologist's side, terms such as regime, inputs and outputs (as these have been used in recent political theory) are now becoming quite common especially among American anthropologists interested in political phenomena. The fact that Pye does not feel it is necessary to define his terms, and that a number of terms from political theory are now commonly used in anthropology indicate that a readership has developed that is becoming familiar enough with these terms so that definitions are unnecessary. From the scope of citations, it is becoming, again, commonplace to see political scientists quoting anthropologists and vice versa. However, the emphasis is still strongly rooted in one discipline or the other. Thus Glickman[2] in his review article of political science in Africa refers to 173 separate works by political scientists and 29 by anthropologists. A recent book on political anthropology, where only authors trained in anthropology were invited to contribute, does exactly the reverse.

Furthermore, unlike physical chemistry, social psychology, or political sociology, I know of only one appointment (my own) at the university level which allows either an anthropologist or a political scientist to join actively in the work of both departments and have formal access to graduate students in both fields. In some ways then, it would be difficult to assess the present situation as one of marriage. However there does seem to be enough mutual attraction going on so that a number of people in both disciplines can now honestly say of each other: "Some of my best friends are . . . !"

The Role of the Interdisciplinarian

Because there is as yet no established subfield unifying political science and anthropology, the role of the person who attempts to create such linkages is a particularly difficult one. Training is thoroughly rooted in one or the other of the disciplines and a great deal of this training may, at least in the short run, seem inapplicable. Depending upon the types of problems, the background of the colleagues and students with whom interaction is taking place, the time of day, and several other factors having to do with the personalities involved, the interdisciplinarian is either a pioneer or a fraud. As a pioneer, he sees complexities and opportunities in an original and often stimulating way usually because very few students have actually viewed things from this vantage point. As a fraud, he is a person who may have recourse to special knowledge beyond that of his critics in each of his "fields," thus arming himself with extra defense against criticism, and an extra set of barbs among his own critical arrows. In other words it is not unthinkable that a person of fairly weak talents in several disciplines could survive nicely by straddling all.

Nonetheless, as I shall try to show, the need for interdisciplinary work between anthropology and political science does exist. The possible danger exists, however, that in pioneering such interstitial positions we can create areas of refuge for the incompetent, or at least until recognizable demands of training and background become more standardized. This leads to the conclusion that for the persons involved in interdisciplinary work, there is a commitment to gain some definite measures of competence in all of the fields he is attempting to fuse or straddle. The ideal in this regard is well-nigh impossible, so that in practice the would-be interdisciplinarian generally hovers between the poles of pioneering and fraud hoping that the goals of the game are, in the end, worth the strain. Whether such goals are in fact worthwhile depends upon the issues that have stimulated the courtship and whether a combined effort using the energies and resources of both disciplines has anything creative and worthwhile to contribute to problems being raised within each discipline.

The Issues: (1) Political Science

As political science has expanded its field of interests beyond that of the formally instituted governmental system, it has come more and more to appreciate and study the socio-cultural milieu of political life. Pressure groups, voting behavior, social movements, and political socialization are just a few of the directions that have given political scientists a more general social science orientation. In doing so, political science has turned to sister disciplines, especially sociology and psychology. These disciplines were already equipped with a body of theory and techniques directed at the new variables that came more and more to be included within the purvue of political science research. Thus in terms of actual empirical research, political scientists have in the past two decades widened their conception of what is politically relevant to include a large number of factors related to the formal structure of government, and how the activities of the political system are related to both internal and environmental conditions. This move into society and culture using empirical research has created a mood of receptivity and openness among political scientists that serves as a background within which other developments have taken place.

Along with this development has come an increase in variance occasioned primarily by the rise of new nations over the last ten to fifteen years. With a plethora of new states to be studied, the variance in political phenomena has increased in a sudden spurt and stimulated interest in the functional approach to political systems such that particular and novel societal structures can be viewed as adaptations to universal requirements of political life. Such claims to universality, however, require broad testing. Many of the new nations are made up of traditional non-Western societies whose local political organization is often not that of the nation state. Do the so-called universal categories of political activity apply to these societies as entities in and of themselves, or only as subunits of the larger nation state whose political life is the main focus of the political scientists? Theoretically if such an entity as *the* political system exists, political theory should be applicable to all societies no matter how simple or complex they happen to be. If, for example, political activity is an aspect of all human social action, and "interest articulation" is a universal function of all systems—then how is this function performed among a small isolated hunting band in the high Arctic? In other words the gambit of societies known to the anthropologists represents a highly various set of polities for which political theory should be applicable if such ideas lay claim to universality. The data of the anthropologists' basic descriptions of non-Western societies around the world provide a wide spectrum of behavior against which political theory should be tested.

It is naïve, however, to think such testing is easy. With some students I have tried to apply Almond and Coleman's ideas as well as those of Easton's concerning the political system to a variety of non-Western polities. In general I think that such work has taught us that applying a complex set of categories to a very simple political system constantly involves the danger that one behavior, or set of role activities, can easily become an indicator for several variables in the political theory model. Thus, if an Eskimo band articulates interest at the time a decision is to be made, the activity of decision-making and of interest articulation are fused into one behavior, which taking each variable means measuring the same behavior twice in order to make a correlation. On the other hand, the application of theory from political science to anthropological data can point out weaknesses in the anthropological materials. Thus one student in trying to apply some of Riker's ideas on coalitions to a very simple island society in the Pacific found that the requisite data there were unavailable. There were wide areas of relevant political activities simply not reported by the ethnographer.

For the political scientist the presence of the anthropological literature is not only a stimulus to theory-testing but forms a basis for understanding local political situations as well. Coleman realized this when he said "traditional political systems have largely shaped the political perspectives, orientation to politics and attitudes towards authority of all but a small fraction . . . of Africans involved in modern political activity."[3] Certainly a number of individual case studies have taken this approach to heart. Young and Fosbrooke[4] have looked at local political organizations in analyzing the effect of a modernizing program in Tanzania, and Apter[5] utilized such materials in attempting to understand the Buganda contribution to Uganda political development. However, systematic work along these lines is still quite rare.[6] John Paden and his colleagues at Northwestern have begun a study of internal stability and national integration in Africa. Through the use of aggregate data they hope to outline some of the major variables which are related to stability and instability among modern African states. Their approach involves taking into account the major traditional political systems within each country, so that the characteristics of these traditional societies will be able to compete with each other as variables in assessing what is related to the differences between more and less stable systems. In order to carry out the study, of course, the researchers have had to utilize the ethnographic materials on major tribal societies in each country.

At both the substantive and theoretical levels, the most important reason why there is a coming together of anthropological and political science research interests stems, I believe, from the relative weakness of the so-called country study among the new nations. By country study I mean that many of the earlier field investigations by political scientists in places like Africa focused on national elites, colonialism, the growth of nationalism and independence, central government policies, and other national data such as constitutional history, national elections, and party politics. When local politics are mentioned they are generally summarized quickly or typed according to indigenous political features that might have an effect on the national scene. In some cases we are left in doubt as to what the traditional system is and only the most meagre data are presented for quite abstract generalizations about local populations. Thus Kilson[7] in his work on Sierra Leone characterizes peasant disturbances from the 1930's to the mid-1950's as a political awakening of this group. We are not told, except through references to colonial reports and comparative interpretations by researchers from elsewhere in Africa, why in fact the peasants were causing disturbances, except that it seemed to be related to taxation. Was taxation felt to be excessive? Was it never accepted in its Western form? Were the peasants attempting to destroy the traditional authority as Kilson[8] claims? Or were they trying to restore an older pre-colonial situation of relationship between themselves and their leaders? Unfortunately the research emphasis is from the point of view of the central government—not the peasants; therefore there are no data from peasants themselves to substantiate one of several possible interpretations for their rioting. However, since the general trend of change in the country as a whole, and especially in the cities, has been away from tradition, the researcher feels justified in assuming that a peasant riot must be in the same direction, that is, away from tradition. But given the method of argument the generalization still remains an assumption rather than a validated conclusion. Country studies are nevertheless important as first steps, since they have helped us to map out and describe the variety of national units that make up the new nations. However, the very nature of such studies has tended to reinforce theoretical developments in political science that embody the weaknesses of such a research approach.

Let me explain. If the political scientist working in a new nation has to comprehend the entire national entity and its sub-parts, it is simpler to classify the entire national entity as being of a particular type. This classification is then assumed to have causal power which determines the way that social change and political developments are taking place. Supporting data for such a position come from an analysis of the elite who are assumed to have ultimate power and authority in the new nation. Thus Pye claims that "in these systems [the new countries] the source of dynamic change often resides largely with the small governing elite who control the formal structures of government which in turn do not represent the institutionalization of indigenous cultural patterns but rather foreign importations."[9] A concrete example of such theorizing is given by Professor Apter who has recently attempted to characterize modernizing nations. Out of his experience with various approaches in political theory and his rich understanding of new nations, he sets up ideal categories for the modernizing countries. The implied assumption here is that the characterization of a whole unit—the new nation and its government—will allow us to predict and understand, its parts and their development—the institutional infrastructure and the attitudes of the people. Thus a "modernizing" state is doing one set of things which have some effect throughout the entire nation, while a "reconciliation" state is doing something quite different.

Although characterizing whole nations this way may in fact give quite an accurate account of a national policy through the efforts and activities of central government agencies, is it an accurate picture of what is really going on inside the nations? And how deterministic is such a characterization? Is a "mobilizing" state that much different from a "reconciliation" one over time or are there sets of internal determinants such as traditional political systems and their interrelationships, the natural resource base, population pressures, etc., that predict to developmental paths more accurately than the apparent structural and ideological characterization of the whole nation?[10] Put in other terms, can we say Russia and the United States, which are both modern industrial nations, have reached similar or different societal results because they have different political structures and ideological features?[11] Can we trace out the similarities and differences and explain them by simply analyzing each society as a whole?[12] Obviously research on the internal features of such societies is required before we answer such questions; and research on the local areas and among institutions of the new nations brings the political scientist and the anthropologist into the same area treating the same populations and many of the same behaviors. In many parts of the non-Western world, local political systems are heavily dependent on forms of sociopolitical structures that are still strongly influenced by their traditional cultures. To say that these are "traditional" or "primitive" hides the fact that there is a bewildering array of such systems and the means by which they are articulated with and are becoming incorporated into larger systems is as yet poorly known and many of the results we have are often contradictory. Thus we have hypotheses to suggest that traditional state-like societies adapt more easily to incorporation within a larger modern state than do acephalous tribal societies in East Africa,[13] while others working close by in Central Africa claim just the reverse.[14] Each different variety of traditional political systems has its own means of recruitment to office, its own structures for making decisions, and there are, probably, different varieties of political culture and attitudes toward authority that go along with such systems.[15]

Besides the type of traditional political system that is being incorporated there are the differential effects of modernization itself on the population at large. Terms like "development," "modernization," and "national immigration," mean that processes of change are operating at both the institutional and the individual behavioral level. We can describe and analyze changes in national and local institutions often by using documents alone. However, the effects of these changes on the people and their behavior in both political and nonpolitical roles can only be achieved through field work. Urbanization, labor unions, Western education, agricultural developments, new industry, and new forms of political participation must be studied among local segments of the population to gauge their effects. In such studies ethnicity is a variable besides the traditional socio-political structure. Thus Southall[16] points out that urbanities from acephalous ethnic groups in Kampala have many more voluntary associations and more official office holders per organization than those from ethnic groups organized traditionally into centralized polities. In my own work, secondary school students from noncentralized tribes in Northern Nigeria report that their future marriage and family relations will be more independent of those around them than people from more traditional state societies, who see themselves as having a marriage and family unit embedded into larger groupings to which they will defer for many of their decisions. The research strategy here is a well-developed one in anthropology. Each of these studies focuses on a modern situation and then asks what effect traditional cultural variables have in determining the paths of change. Thus to be precise about the actual direction of development, research at the local level is essential—and only when such work is carried out can we assess whether or not national policies, or local contingencies, or what combination of both decide the direction of national development.

In the spheres of methodology and techniques, political science has moved very quickly in recent times toward a hard science approach so that research design and quantitative measurement have become heavily emphasized. Anthropology has been much slower to adapt such techniques, although changes are evident. Research at a local level in developing areas presents the political scientists with field work conditions not unlike those the anthropologist has been facing for years. It is these conditions, and not the conservatism of anthropologists, that have slowed down the growth of more rigorous research techniques in anthropology; and because that is so the political scientist must face up to many of the same problems.

The problems are complex but can be summarized. First, the language of almost all but a few of the local people is not English and meaningful research must be carried on through an interpreter or by learning the language or a combination of both; second, there is often a vast difference between the standard of living of the researcher and that of his informants; and third, the cultural milieu of his informants is, to an unknown degree, different.

To solve such problems many anthropologists try to learn the language; they are all trained within a mystique from their own disciplinary past which preaches that endurance of physical hardship in field work is somehow enobling and fruitful with respect to the goals of science. The assumed (but not yet rigorously tested) rationale here is that being able to cope with, and appreciate, differences in living standards enables the field worker to interact on a daily basis with members of another culture while remaining within his own Western living standard produces a shield between the researcher and those whom he seeks to understand. Thus differences in standards of living are often not only expected but welcomed by the doctoral candidate as part of the initiation into full professional status, and by the experienced field worker as a validation of his professional abilities. To collect data in a strange culture, anthropology has developed participant observation using both directed and nondirected interviews, as well as living among and observing on a full day-to-day basis the behavior of people acting out their local roles in their local institutions. The essence or fundamental assumption of this anthropological field technique is easily stated but not so easily learned. In any non-Western situation an anthropologist assumes that all behavior, all representations, and manifestations by other people are not fully understandable unless placed in their own context. Thus a spoon may not be just a spoon as we know it, or a leader and his follower may conceive of their relationship in terms that are totally unfamiliar but which make sense, given the full understanding of the local ideology of leader-follower relationships. For such work, the personality of the investigator, his patience, continual curiosity, and ability to systematize everyday life into some set of meaningful categories for data analysis, are the essentials for what has become a highly sensitive technique. Certainly it is not the only method available for studying local political activity in non-Western areas and both anthropology and political science will use many techniques in local areas in the coming years. However, some use of this traditional anthropological approach is probably essential for any social scientist who wishes to obtain an intelligent basis for more restrictive and focused data collection having to do with a well-developed research design in a non-Western area.

At the level of theory construction, it has been suggested that anthropology (along with sociology and general systems theory) has stimulated an emphasis on functionalism in political science.[17] This is probably true, although I suspect it would have happened anyway with or without anthropology. I say this because requisite functional theory is one of the few and perhaps the most efficient way of handling a sudden burst of variance, which is what happened to political phenomena once the plethora of new nations arrived on the scene. However, just as in anthropology such "theory" has contributed to the description of variety, so too in political science requisite functions such as "rule-making" or "political demands" are no more than descriptive categories that allow for unknown amounts of variety in the structures that express such theoretically universal functions. Much still remains to be done within the new nations. But once the variety has been mapped there is still the much more essential job of explaining why such variety exists. In anthropology, knowing about widely varying forms of kinship, marriage, religion, and politics has been only an initial step in "explaining" why such variety has occurred and what factors condition its change over time. The reason requisite functional models seem appropriate at the present time in political science is that older typologies in comparative politics simply have not been applicable to the wide variety now available for study. Using a structural approach to theory construction is in effect complementary to functionalism. As political anthropologists have recently tried to show,[18] such an approach still provides a fruitful way of building theories and designing research once the range of variance has been dealt with. Thus functionalism can answer the question: How is a certain purpose performed? Structuralism then takes over and directs our attention toward explaining why certain forms differ from one another and how they change over time.[19]

Another theoretical contribution related to functionalism which anthropology is making to political science, is the evolutionary aspect.[20] Explicitly or implicitly, anthropologists have almost always ordered the societies they study into an evolutionary framework. Theories that discuss how societies change from simple to complex and from one type to another are viewed as evolutionary, although they may not always meet the conditions that such studies demand.[21] However, by attempting to see a large variety of societies from the same point of view as that of biology, the anthropologist assumes that developmental direction is a natural quality of his comparative material and as a theorist he arranges material in order to ask what creates the changes or differences as one set of systems develops into another. In large-scale comparative work, evolution involves property differentiation as a constituent. This approaches a Guttman scale, since each "higher" or more evolved system contains, theoretically, many of the same elements as the "lower" or less evolved ones, plus new aspects not present in the earlier, less differentiated systems. Such evolutionary analyses can help us to develop typological character-izations of new nations based on empirical data, and structural analyses can procede to guide research toward an understanding of why societies differ at higher and lower ends of the scale. In effect this is what Adelman[22] and her colleagues have been doing by dividing a large sample of underde-veloped countries into low, middle, and high groupings based on GNP per capita, and then attempting to analyze them through factor analysis and dis-criminant function analysis in order to see just what social, political, and economic variables are associated with these different levels of development.

Another possible realm of theoretical and empirical interchange between anthropology and political science is international relations. If we assume that theoretical work in international relations is intended to create generalizations about the way in which independent polities interact across political boundaries, then such theories, to be truly general, should help to explain interaction between pre-industrial polities as well. In turn, such comparative data can help stimulate new insights into the nature of international interaction. However, such work must, if it is to be seriously approached, use the full range of interpolity relations found among non-Western peoples. To create a comparative model of inter-national relations by examining one type of system, such as the segmentary lineage societies (which vary among themselves), is to avoid the very quality that anthropological data have to offer—the ability to extend and increase variance such that we are in fact talking of the political life of mankind. Here anthropology has been somewhat remiss in developing comparative analyses and theoretical schemas. However, there is available in the literature a respectable amount of material on inter-tribal relations. How such phenomena as blood brotherhood, joking relations between tribes, intercommunity alliances through marriage and trade, clan alliances, cooperative economic activities, hostages, and warfare, all fit together is still virtually an unworked area of comparative analysis within anthropology. What we need are functional categories that systematize the nature of interpolity relations, which can then be directed at pre-industrial societies. Only when such work has been done will we have a fully comparative basis for the study of international relations.

The Issues: (2) Anthropology

In my view anthropology has experienced two major stimuli in the last half century, each of which has seriously changed the direction of its development. The first was a field work revolution that had its roots in natural history prior to the twentieth century, but which as a method provided a new thrust away from the somewhat simplistic evolutionism of the latter nineteenth century. How the field work tradition played itself out as "normal" research in England, the United States, France, and elsewhere was a function of local academic conditions and the particular areas of the world where each national group did most of its field work. Out of this research came the holistic approach, social structural studies, psychological anthropology, acculturation studies, and, above all, a unit—the tribe or ethnic group. Anthropologists became identifiable as "those chaps who knew about the Bongo Bongo" and in so doing they achieved an academic nitch in the universities as well as an identifiable role in the overseas colonies of the imperial powers. As long as the groups studied by anthropologists remained isolated or semi-isolated, field work rested on something mildly real; these groups had some meaningful integrity as wholes and thus the interrelationships of their parts and the comparisons of these relationships across a number of such ethnic units were methodologically appropriate, defensible, and enriching to the general social science community.

The second major change in anthropology began with the end of World War II. During the last two and a half decades, with ever quickening pace, the tribal societies have come more and more to play a role in modern nation states whose leaders envisage rapid social change as a basic assumption in any ideology they expound for their country as a unit. Thus in a flash, as it were, the older unit of anthropology—the ethnic group—has lost much of its wholeness because one of its most significant features is its belonging to a larger national state. In some instances[23] where the ethnic group maintains its corporate identity, politically and economically, we have been able to study how the national and local systems intermesh, what the effect of role conflict is in the intermediate role, and how each system effects the other. But many local community activities are new and emergent. Trade unions, neighborhood and ward organizations in cities, political party organizations at the local ward level, student organizations, attitudes to modern vs. traditional ways of doing things—all of these are interesting and vital features of contemporary social life in the new nations. However there is one major difference from the traditional field situation of the anthropologist. In modern situations ethnicity is only one among many properties of local community life and thus it becomes one variable in the new research situation.

This is the stimulus to change that has provided the anthropologist with a new research orientation; indeed it forces these orientations upon the field worker. By looking at the field situation in these ways new kinds of data emerge which are derived from different sources and from the use of different techniques. Furthermore, whereas twenty years ago the anthropologist was almost alone in his interest in the social, cultural, economic, and psychological behavior on non-Western man, today he has been joined by many others all of whom, from their various disciplinary orientations as well as their interest in new nations, are studying specific aspects of behavior among non-Western peoples. The anthropologist then has to choose which particular problem he wishes to study, he is no longer an expert on everything. As one of my African colleagues commenting on this point suggested; he could see no reason whatsoever for any anthropologist's trying, under contemporary conditions, to write a book that attempted to describe all of Yoruba culture or all of Buganda culture; to do so he claims would be to remain superficial in a scholarly sense and probably condescending in a normative one.

Rapid change is taking place all over the underdeveloped world. Urbanization, Western education, nationalism, and other forces are producing wide variations in attitudes and behavior. To simply gather data using participant observation techniques means that one must attempt to assess a pattern that is some kind of central tendency or give some estimate of the ranges of variation using some independent variables as a means of grouping the population. Thus in speaking of political participation the writer may note what overall differences there are according to sex, age, class, and rural urban residence, in terms of the observations he has made on each of the categories of people through using participant observation techniques. Obviously to be precise such generalizations require some quantitative measures of the variances involved and this requirement again forces the anthropological researcher to limit the scope of his problem. This means that in the future general ethnographic techniques will probably be used to understand the local context, while more precise social science techniques will become common in order to gather data on specific problems.

In overall terms, what these developments mean for social and cultural anthropology as a discipline is that the foundation of its unity—the study of a whole ethnic group (often through intensive work in only a few settlements)— is proving to be less durable than anyone twenty years ago would have believed. It also means that some specialties within anthropology, such as economic anthropology, political anthropology, and psychological anthropology are developing and moving out toward other social sciences such that a regrouping of interests across disciplinary boundaries is taking place. This can be seen at Northwestern where the Anthropology Department has six out of nine faculty members with joint appointments in other social science departments. Although this situation is probably extreme, I suspect that it represents a trend not just toward the breaking down of disciplinary boundaries in the social sciences, but toward a reshaping of these boundaries based on the common interests of the people concerned.

In the realm of theory, anthropologists have traditionally had an over-simplified view of what the political system is and what kinds of categories of behavior must be observed in order to report fully on the political life of the people. Through the study of contemporary theorists much more adequate conceptionalization of politics is being diffused into anthropology.[24]

Perhaps the best example of such interchange is in the area of conflict theory. Many anthropologists with their traditional interests in understanding how exotic systems work have tended to ask functional questions and create interpretations of data, including conflict, in terms of the contributions such activities make to the ongoing system. Political scientists have more often used conflict as a causal force to explain adjustments, social and political movements, and change in general. Although it is always important to assume that conflict may have positive as well as negative effects given a rapidly changing social milieu, I suspect that anthropologists will become progressively interested in conflict as a stimulus to change, both in terms of role conflict, class conflict, and in terms of social or inter-ethnic rivalries and interregional ones and so on.

Here political science abounds in hypotheses and theories that could be meaningfully tested by anthropologists working at the local level in the new nations. For example, Karl Deutsch has developed a theory[25] that a polity which includes sharply differentiated living standards should also have an intensity of nationalistic feelings (a) inversely proportional to mobility between classes and regions, (b) directly proportional to the barriers against cultural assimilation, and (c) directly proportional to the extent of economic and prestige differences between culture, classes, and regions.

What Deutsch is suggesting here is that inequalities produce tensions and frustrations while nationalism provides a social and political catharsis or channel through which collective aggressions may be expressed. This may be true, at least for the modern world, but it needs testing in local areas; and I suspect it needs refinement in terms of types of the traditional systems it is applied to. Thus I would suspect the hypothesis to produce very different sets of results for India as compared with Eastern Nigeria. In the latter case people have practically no sharp class distinctions traditionally and N-achievement has been described as relatively high, at least in relation to other Nigerian groups.[26] The hypothesis might be strongly validated in Eastern Nigeria where economic and prestige differentiation can be theorized to be a new and frustrating characteristic of the modernizing situation. However, India with its ancient and locally developed inequities of class status and economic positions must have already developed in its traditional life non-nationalistic modes of adaptation to these same conflicts and these could be utilized, at least partially, in the modern situation as well.

In terms of method, the behavioral techniques being developed in both political science and sociology are also being carried over into anthropology, although this movement can be seen most clearly among cross-cultural surveys of large samples of societies. Nevertheless, within the next ten years I expect that training in research design, questionnaire construction, statistical techniques, and computer analysis will become much more common in social anthropology than it is at the moment; on the other hand, the relativism of anthropology will be expressed in a strong emphasis on the use of culturally specific indicators for theoretically derived variables. This means that the traditional emphasis on understanding the local cultural context will not be given up, but rather used as a building block or stepping stone to the more restrictive problems derived from comparative research and theory.

Conclusions: The Result of Courtship and the Promise of Consummation

As I have already pointed out the relations between anthropology and political science have gone beyond the point of dalliance to a real courtship. However marriage is not yet, indeed may never be consummated because social science itself is moving toward group marriage. A number of things are clear.

1. For the political scientists, anthropological data provide an increase in variance such that theory may be tested on wider samples of political systems. In order to accomplish this, political scientists should have courses and texts available to them in political anthropology and such materials should introduce the student to the range of political variety known to the anthropologist. A start has been made in this direction and will expand in the future.[27]

2. For research purposes political scientists should be made aware of aggregate data sources in anthropology, such as the Human Relations Area Files, and research must be designed at the local level in the new nations.[28] This latter feature is well advanced already and seems to be a growing trend in political science research in foreign areas.

3. Anthropology can aid political science in the analysis of ethnicity and in preparing researchers for the use of participant observation techniques in the field.

4. Anthropology has a great deal to gain from political science in terms of theory and more precise behavioral methods which at this point in its development the discipline sorely needs.

The overall conclusion toward which all of these statements point is that, outside the milieu of the industrialized Western nations in particular, and for comparative purposes in general, anthropology and political science are both facing issues and specific research problems that must eventually bring them closer together. However such convergence is not simply a matter of each discipline reaching over into the other's bailiwick and grabbing for a solution. The issues raised here call for new and different kinds of work in both disciplines in order that something constructive come out of their mutual attraction. Unfortunately, work already completed can only partially solve new problems for which such research was not intended.

Let me illustrate this point with a problem that is plaguing some of us at Northwestern—the definition of local units. To say, as many do these days, that new nation research must move to the local or micro-political level is one thing, but it begs a number of difficult operational and research design problems. As of now there are a number of studies going on at the local level among the African nations. But in order to coordinate and systematize such research, we need to know what are the significant units of study at the local level: Are they the ethnic groups? The towns? Local institutions such as trade unions, local government or combinations of these? Unfortunately, much of the best traditional ethnography in Africa is concerned with small, often isolated groups while larger more complex and variegated "tribes" are often less well studied. Furthermore, such ethnographic accounts are often time-bound such that they describe conditions at the time the research was carried out. How then can a researcher use this literature to characterize the ethnic properties of a new African nation. Ethnicity may also not be a stable entity. So-called ethnic groups can coalesce and subdivide over time and in the face of different situations. Indeed one anthropologist[29] has suggested that the sense of ethnic identification is a reaction formation that results from the nature of a wider political unit of which the ethnic group is a part. Thus "easterner" and "northerner" may be an emergent ethnic group in Nigeria, but if these areas were to become separate political entities, then subdivisions within them such as Hausa, Fulani, Ibo, or Ijaw would become more important politically. Choosing local ethnic units may be somewhat arbitrary. Zolberg[30] has tried to work out "culture centers" for the Ivory Coast and John Paden is working with the idea of constructing local ethnic entities that are politically relevant in the modern era. The question can then be posed whether these units have any significant effect on national developments and if so, then we must ask what is it about these groupings that produces such results. Another way of solving the same problem may be to devise some means for isolating "natural" developmental units or regions within or even across the new nations. Such units could be isolated, hopefully, through the objective measurement and analysis of various kinds of transaction flows, such as telephone calls, trade, use of natural resources, road use, migration patterns, etc. Then, traditional ethnicity, local political structures, traditional authority patterns, attitudes towards national policy goals, and other socio-cultural and political variables could be studied in relation to these units.

Whether these solutions are the "right" ones or not is not as important as the fact that the problem exists and neither political science nor anthropology has a simple answer already worked out. And this is only one example. As already noted, work in international relations involving non-Western polities requires that data in anthropology be organized with this particular purpose in mind, i.e. that of cross-cultural comparisons, because adequate categories of data analysis do not exist as yet. Thus a convergence of goals in anthropology and political science means that some significant restructuring of both field research and their comparative foci must be accomplished before common interests can be pursued. Marriage often results from courtship, but unless it results from complete self-deception it creates as many new problems as it solves.

Notes

1. Lucien Pye, "Democracy, Modernization, and Nation Building." *In* J. R. Pennock (ed.), *Self-Government in Modernizing Nations*. Englewood Cliffs, N.J.: Prentice-Hall, 1964, pp. 6–25.
2. H. Glickman, "Political Science." In R. A. Lystad (ed.), *The African World: A Survey of Social Research*. New York: Praeger, 1965.
3. James S. Coleman, "The Politics of Sub-Saharan Africa." In G. A. Almond and J. S. Coleman (eds.), *The Politics of the Developing Areas*. Princeton: Princeton University Press, 1960, pp. 247–368, especially p. 258.
4. R. Young, and H. A. Fosbrooke, *Smoke in the Hills: Political Tension in the Morogogo District of Tanganyika*. Evanston: Northwestern University Press, 1960.
5. David E. Apter, *The Political Kingdom in Uganda*. Princeton: Princeton University Press, 1961.
6. A. Zolberg, *Creating Political Order: The Party States of West Africa*. New York: Rand-McNally, 1966, p. 153.
7. Martin Kilson, *Political Change in a West African State: A Study of the Modernization Process in Sierra Leone*. Cambridge: Harvard University Press, 1966.
8. Ibid. p. 61.
9. Lucien Pye, *Self-Government in Modernizing Nations*, p. 7.
10. A. Zolberg, *Creating Political Order*.
11. John K. Galbraith, *The New Industrial State*. Boston: Houghton Mifflin, 1967.
12. I wrote this before reading Professor Zolberg's interesting and useful account of the West African party states. He too questions the usefulness of such characterizations as "reconciliation" and "mobilization" because they do not take account of changes in such states over time in which reconciliation and mobilization are simply aspects of state politics. He then builds up an alternate configuration (viz. the party state). My criticism can however also be leveled at his typological analysis as he readily admits, since we still know very little, if anything, about the micro-politics of these new nations and much of these

characterizations are based on analyses of national elites and nationally based ideological developments.

13. L. A. Fallers, *Bantu Bureaucracy*. London: Routlege and Kegan Paul, 1955.

14. Introduction to R. Apthorpe (ed.), *From Tribal Rule to Modern Government*, the 13th Conference Proceedings of the Rhodes–Livingston Institute, 1959.

15. R. A. Levine, *Dreams and Deeds: Achievement Motivation in Nigeria*. Chicago: University of Chicago Press, 1966.

16. A. Southall, "Voluntary Societies in Pampala." Paper delivered at African Studies Association Meeting, 1965.

17. H. Glickman, "Political Science." In R. A. Lystad (ed.), *The African World: A Survey of Social Research*. New York: Praeger, 1965, pp. 131–165, especially p. 149.

18. R. Cohen, "Political Anthropology: The Future of a Pioneer." *Anthropological Quarterly*, 38 (1965), 117–131; and R. Cohen and J. Middleton, *Comparative Political Systems: Studies in the Politics of Pre-Industrial Societies*. New York: Natural History Press, 1967; and M. G. Smith, "A Structural Approach to Comparative Politics." In D. Easton (ed.), *Varieties of Political Theory*. Englewood Cliffs, N.J.: Prentice-Hall, 1966, pp. 113–129.

19. Functionalism is concerned with the contribution a partial activity makes to the total activity of which it is a part. Structuralism is concerned with the relations of parts to one another and the conditions which are correlated with such relations to effect their change and/or stability.

20. Cf. H. R. Barringer, G. I. Blanksten, and R. W. Mack, *Social Change in Developing Areas*. Boston: Schankman, 1965.

21. R. Cohen "The Strategy of Social Evolution." *Anthropologica*, 1962, 4: 321–348.

22. Irma Adelman, *Society, Politics, and Economic Development: A Quantitative Approach*. Baltimore: Johns Hopkins Press, 1967.

23. L. A. Fallers, *Bantu Bureaucracy*; and R. Cohen, "Conflict and Change in a Northern Nigerian Emirate." In G. K. Zollschan and W. Hirsch (eds.), *Explorations in Social Change*. Boston: Houghton Mifflin, 1963, pp. 495–521.

24. D. Easton, "Political Anthropology." In B. Siegel (ed.), *Biennial Review of Anthropology*. Stanford: Stanford University Press, 1959, pp. 210–263; D. Easton (ed.), *Varieties of Political Theory*. Englewood Cliffs, N. J.: Prentice-Hall, 1966; and G. A. Almond, and G. B. Powell, Jr., *Comparative Politics: A Developmental Approach*. Boston: Little, Brown, 1966.

25. Karl Deutsch, "The Growth of Nations: Some Recurrent Patterns of Political and Cultural Integration." *World Politics* (1953), 179–180.

26. Levine, *Dreams and Deeds*.

27. Isaac Schapera, *Government and Politics in Tribal Societies*. New York: Humanities Press, 1956; L. Mair, *Primitive Government*. Penguin, 1962; Max Gluckman, *Politics Low and Ritual in Tribal Society*. Chicago: Aldine, 1965; M. Swartz, A. Turner, and A. Tuden (eds.), *Political Anthropology*.

Chicago: Aldine, 1966; Almond and Powell, *Comparative Politics*; Cohen and Middleton, *Comparative Political Systems*; also see *Rural Africana: Research Notes on Local Politics and Political Anthropology*, edited by Norman Miller, Michigan State University, 1968–.

28. A. Zolberg, *Creating Political Order*.

29. M. H. Fried, "On the Concept of 'Tribe' and 'Tribal Society.' " *Transactions of the New York Academy of Sciences*, Ser. II, 1966, 28, 4, 527–540.

30. Aristide R. Zolberg, *One Party Government in the Ivory Coast*. Princeton: Princeton University Press, 1964.

3
Sociology and Political Science

SCOTT GREER

In looking at the actual, possible, and appropriate relationships between sociology and political science, it is necessary to remember our common origins. Neither discipline emerged out of enlightened thought applied to the affairs of mankind. Both owed a great deal to an old tradition of intellection, the medieval European university and its synthesis of thought and value.

A philosophy of history, originally bent on justifying God's ways to man, later intent upon making sense of what was known or thought to be known in terms of the Christian mythology, led to a growing concern with fact. The power of kings and popes and the proper relations between them, their governance by natural and sacred law, the order of the universe supplied by a God who, to paraphrase Whitehead, was orderly, created order, and implied order for man, all imposed a putative structure upon history.[1] And by history was meant the career of the human race upon earth.

Then, with the increasing separation of the polity from the agrarian society and the growth of nations, came the dominance of the monarch. His concerns became concerns of state and the intellectuals followed in the wake of power and symbolic splendor (as they usually do.) Thus we have the development, out of the philosophy of history, of the interventionist science—statecraft. How shall a monarch rule so that his state be legitimate and successful? What is the nature of society as viewed through glasses which separate polity and society?

The result was the discipline of political economy. We might pay close attention to it, for it is the origin of empirical sociology, economics, and political science. Focused upon the practical problems of statecraft, it viewed all aspects of society as subordinate to the monarch who was, in a germinal sense, the state. (We can, of course, reverse it and speak of the nation state as the culmination of the idea of a monarch.)

Now paralleling this shift of attention was the development of the university, a growing structure administering the development of thought, science, ideology, skills, and superstition. Its growth corresponded to the growing scale of society, increasing differentiation, and the importance of urban control centers. In short, there was a market for a wide variety of specialists in the emerging "genteel professions." These included law, an increasingly important force as feudal law, civil law, and canon law met in an inextricable and profitable can of worms. There was a career to be made in merely knowing the esoteric artifacts of a legal structure created by men who were, in many cases, semi-literate but knowledgeable of the world and, in other cases, literate but ignorant of life. The law was a happy hunting ground for the literate opportunists, and many did well.

Along with the law came the emergence of the sciences. They were, first of all, the moral and natural sciences. The first meant theology—useful to the large and growing professional cadres of the religious bureaucracy. But it led to philosophy and the development of "humanists" who were, to say the least, suspect as religious bureaucrats. Closely allied to the moral scientists were, in the early years, those who endeavored to say something about the empirical nature of human society; it is important to note, however, that what they said usually had a moral attached. It had to do with the proper life for mankind, the good state, the aperture into heaven.

And the natural sciences were not all that separate. They too leaned heavily upon moral and theological precept. Lewis, in *The Splendid Century*, gives us some notion of just how ideological was medicine under the reign of the Sun King, and we know how much Newton valued his works on theology.[2] But the truth was, men neither emphasized nor valued such distinctions; in a basic sense, they were all philosophers.

Then we can look at the differentiation of knowledge that went on as the society proliferated, the disciplines differentiated. We can see the efforts to make sense of canon law, natural law, and feudal law as the origin of a more important synthesis: national law. And we can see, over time, the translation of this into the effort to make a science of government as the notion of "statecraft" became dominant. Such is the interrelation of thought and action, idea and power. Later, when the science of government lost its province as statecraft, we see the emergence of something called political science, but that is to get ahead of the story.

Another aspect of statecraft was the development of political economy. This was, preeminently, a system of thought which aimed to maximize the profitability of the nation for the use of the monarch; if the people were his sheep, he did well to understand the conditions for their waxing fat and wooly. Political economy emerged during the commercial revolution that resulted from the improved use of sail; its earliest form was mercantilism—the nation viewed as a small farmer or business man. Now it is true that the approach had its limits; it paid little attention to consumers at home, and much to the national power abroad—it encouraged the use of domestic surplus for the financing of wars among the monarchs and their kinfolk. But it embodied the notion of empirical understanding and control of the national economy.[3]

These managed economies, then, preceded the Industrial Revolution. They rested upon extractive industries and crafted articles; the aim was to get the best price for your wool, improve the balance of trade, and "beggar my neighbor." However, the increase in scale resulting from the expanding networks of trade stimulated an increase in scale at home; work was increasingly rational in goal and means, and the size of the productive organization increased with the importance of surplus, as against mere subsistence. Thus the agricultural revolution, together with the various components of the factory system, resulted from the commercial revolution—preparing the way for the age of steam.

In such a context Adam Smith, a pivotal intellectual figure, developed his ideas on the wealth of nations. Unconcerned with the older project of aggrandizing the monarch, he looked instead at the importance of the division of labor, the utility of the marketplace as distributor, the intrinsically *economic* aspects of the political economy. And, viewing certain disastrous results of the efforts of the government to control the economy, he leaned toward the notion that the economy could, in most respects, govern itself better than could the state.[4]

Such were the germinal notions of economic "liberalism." They were further elaborated by many lesser thinkers and became, particularly in England, the "utopia" used against the "ideology" of the older system.[5] The new way of thinking was, in short, congruent with the interests of the rising bourgeoisie; it focused upon factors of production and exchange, not upon land, lineage, and traditional national power. It was an insidious intellectual solvent.

Its growth was intertwined with the second great energy revolution, the discovery of techniques for releasing the stored energy in fossil fuels. With coal and steam power the energy surplus was many times greater than ever before, and human wealth increased fantastically. Economic liberalism provided a rationale and a moral reason for the uncontrolled exploitation of every technological discovery and invention, including the use of mass labor in factories. In short, the economy was virtually freed from control by the public interest and economic power was accumulated, by certain groups, at a great rate.[6]

This separation of government and economy in fact was reflected in a comparable separation in thought. Economics developed around the notion of the self-regulating system of production distribution, consumption, and saving. Government, in this scheme, kept the public peace and enforced contracts. There was order in the economic system and it was sufficiently codifiable that modern economics could develop rapidly during the nineteenth century.

The same cannot be said of political science, or what was left when economics was subtracted from political economy. It became a specialty emphasizing the theory of the good state, constitutionalism, and the law. Its data were the codified charters and the gross histories of nations.

It could be argued that Marx recombined the study of polity and economy. Certainly the political implications of Marxism are drastic. But in fact, Marxism tended to encourage apolitical thought about politics and political action about just anything that excited its communicants. Marx was, in his convictions concerning the primacy and autonomy of the economic system, a direct descendant of Adam Smith; they were much closer to each other in basic perspective than either was to the older tradition, or the one which emerged after the collapse of economic liberalism.

The separation of political economy into two specialties left a great deal of social behavior out of the picture. Further, it left no real bridge between these two aspects of human life. From this peculiar situation came the impulse to create a more general framework for the study of society— sociology. Indeed, sociology owes much of its intellectual vigour to its developing critique of the older specialties. Thus Weber's work depended for much of its intellectual penetration and drive upon his interest in Marx, while Durkheim, educated as a philosopher, was intrigued by the creative possibilities in Adam Smith's ideas concerning the division of labor.[7] He was also worried by the atomistic view of social life which it assumed.

In their critiques of the economic determinists and political formalists, the fathers of sociology were implicitly or explicitly arguing for a study of society as a whole. The seeds are to be seen in the grand speculations of a Comte: the blossoming is still far from complete. But, given the hiatus between economics and politics, sociology became the study of that something more which made possible the functioning of the two. This included the study of substantive problems—social groups, organizations, and aggregates. It included also the development, slowly at first but accelerating with time, of a general systematic theory of human social structures regardless of their "content."[8]

Thus sociology cannot afford to allow the phrase, "the economic, political, and social aspects of. . . ." Sociologists must be concerned with economic and political behavior, since these are powerful limits and determinants of human actions and the destinies of social groups. And, as they are social phenomena, these areas of organization should be amenable to the same tools of analysis as the kinship system, community, or tribe. Sociology is, intrinsically and inescapably, an integrative force among the social sciences; it demands, and to some degree provides, a common vocabulary.

The situation which produced the separation of economy and polity was a transitory one. As Polanyi notes at length, it was a "freak" in human history.[9] But the freakish intellectual results still linger in our disciplinary pride and prejudice, as in the administrative structure of our university. Just as we have separate schools for the written word and the spoken word, so we have separate departments studying man as political actor, economic actor, and as actor in general. To be sure, there is some payoff from specialization: intellectual asceticism, specific work norms, continuity in focus. But too frequently we are specialists by default; it is not that we know much about our subject, we are just ignorant of everything outside it.

How then should we delimit a field of inquiry?[10] There seem to be two major approaches; the first we will call the naïve phenomenological, the second, the analytical. In the naïve phenomenological approach, we look at the problem as defined in our folk thought; we look at regularities in terms of the received vocabulary and we try to explain and predict in such terms. Thus we have a science of apples, a sociology of blue-eyed people or criminals. In studying the political, we study everything that is called "political" and that is the way our science is bounded. We are then, of course, at the mercy of the folk language which defined our problem for us.

That language is not always clear. Politics refers to many things; official, governmental actions and reactions on one hand, maneuvers for advancement and control on the other. In short, it is very difficult to draw any boundary around the political if we take the folk definitions. On the other hand there is an advantage; if the folk have found some type of event important enough to name, there is a high probability that it is (1) empirically accessible, observable, and (2) of some importance to somebody. Thus we have a crude empirical control and a criterion of significance.

The alternative method of delimiting a field is one derived from the analytical theory that we use. This is closely bound up with the unit of study (apples, criminals) but the critical point is that the units do not define the field—they are selected by a theory which postulates them. They become, so to speak, examples and research sites for general variables and the interrelations among them. Thus a theory of social organization might be applied to a problem of politics simply because the given events seemed amenable to such analysis, while a psychoanalyst's interest in Napoleon might have little to do with his importance for political change in Europe.

If one adopts the naïve phenomenological approach to the political, he is then free to use any kind of explanation that he pleases. His aim is to explain completely, predict completely; if he has to combine meteorology, sociology, and a measure of sugar in the blood, that is perfectly permissible. In short, his work norm is clear—complete prediction. Linear programming, factor analysis, multiple regression, are examples of techniques devised to do just this. The difficulty with them, however, is that while one may predict he does not know why he can; he has no structure among his variables.

If, on the other hand, we use the analytical-theoretical to delimit our field of study, we are quite clear about what counts and what does not. Much is disregarded for, lying outside the particular abstractions we use in our business, our explanatory theory has nothing at all to say about it. Thus we have clarity about the theoretical enterprise but prices are exacted. For one thing, if you know that yours is a partial analysis of a phenomenon—say your only interest is in organizationally directed and controlled behaviors—how do you know what proportion of the variation should be explained by your theory? In short, what is your work norm? Empirically this may have serious consequences; your partial analysis may have omitted considerations critical for your predictions and those who use them may suffer failure.

Political science today is best described as delimited by naïve phenomenology. Using official and other folk definitions of the political, it is collectively a random search for the appropriate theoretical approach. Individual and social psychology, sociology, cultural anthropology, and economics have all been tried as tools to explain the political, by individuals teaching and publishing as political scientists.

Thus a psychosomatic condition has been used to illuminate the career of Cermak, one-time mayor of Chicago, while failure to vote has been examined through the use of such concepts as apathy, privatization, alienation, and the like.[11] Such sociological tools as organizational analysis have been used in the study of administration, while anthropology with its heavy emphasis on culture has been exploited in the study of political modernization[12] Economic analysis, as latecomer to the game, is going well with game theory applied to international politics, exchange theory to city government, and so on.[13]

This raises the question: Is it possible for political science to be delimited by analytical theory? And if so, is it desirable? On the whole it seems to me the answer to both questions is "No." Those who have tried to delimit "the political" and make a science of it have never been able to develop an explanatory theory which did not essentially turn out to be an application of notions from other disciplines. The most noble efforts hinge upon the terms "power" and "influence." They are not particularly convincing, however, and have had little effect upon the empirical research of political scientists; this is not the only test of an approach, to be sure, but it is an important one.[14]

And political science is not alone in this predicament. My reasons for rejecting the desirability of a separate analytical approach hinge on this fact: all of the social sciences are eclectic among themselves in approaching empirical problems because the analytical theories of each are partial and incomplete. The fragmentation of political economy is still with us.

In short, I would propose that there are really only two basic analytical schemes in the study of human behavior—the psychological and the sociological. I would go further and say that the social sciences are essentially one, in that their units, men in aggregates, are the same; their explanatory theories, developed from the study of social groups, are cognate, and their utility for philosophy and action depends upon our developing transitivity between them.

There are, of course, differences of focus and information, and these lead to different discoveries of regularity, inventions of theory. But all share in common the concern with social aggregates, patterns of behavior arising in them, group structures and their impact upon each other. Political science focuses primarily upon the formal organizations of the public control system and their interaction with the relevant environment. As such it provides a needed corrective to economic determinism, on one hand, and an apolitical study of organizational evolution and societal trends on the other. (Recently one of the "Students of the Future" explained that he had predicted America in the year A.D. 2,000 but had omitted consideration of political developments, as politics is too unpredictable. Maybe not Hamlet, but at least his stepfather, is missing.) One might say that each of the specialties within social science is a lobbyist for the significance of one or the other organizational segments of the society: political science speaks for governance, the contention for control.

As such, political science has contributed a great deal to sociology. Indeed, the source of most theory in political sociology is an adaptation and acclimatization of ideas first promulgated by political scientists and political economists. Aristotle and Machiavelli certainly, but also Maine, Mosca, Michels, James Marsh, and Herbert Simon, are all contributors to general social science. Their work leads, ineluctably, to the development of organizational analysis—to my mind the central armature of sociology. Of course the political is not autonomous and self-explanatory; it is still supported by a larger social system, its legitimacy resting upon culture and its organization upon the stratification system, neither completely accounted for by the polity. But the polity's consequences for that system, in turn, merit a greater concentration of intellectual energy than they receive. It is well enough to speak of, say, suburban growth as a result of preference patterns of households, but it is important to realize that this growth was underwritten by government finance policies hammered out in the halls of Congress.[15] (It is also important to realize that changes in transportation have shifted the use value of central locations versus peripheral locations for commerce and industry; economic analysis is also required.)

Let us look then at social science as a total enterprise, an evolving general theory of human societies. Its first concern is with the system in its relationship with the environment, the way the patterning of behavior relates to the relevant other aspects of *homo sapiens*, to other species, and to the nonliving universe. Its second concern is with the impact of innovation, accident, breakdown, change, upon these social systems. A third concern lies in the analysis of the systems, particularly those aspects which are concerned with self-correction (of breakdowns) and with innovation. These may be called the integrative and the directive structures of the society. They range from the role of the male leader among the little bands of Brazilian Indians described so poignantly by Levy-Strauss, to the government of the United States: in short, they encompass the political.[16]

In looking at the relationships between systems and environment, the social sciences have tended toward a concern with *energy turnover*. One can see the beginnings of this thinking in Spencer, its development in Leslie White, and its continued presence in ecology, social geography, and physical anthropology. It is perhaps best exemplified in the work of a little known (to political scientists) political scientist, Fred Cottrell. By turns political scientist, sociologist, economist, geographer, and demographer, he presents in his volume, *Energy and Society*, one of the most challenging integrated theories of society as a system that I have come across. Looking at the transactions between man and environment, with physical and social technologies as mediators, he considers the ways in which institutions (including the political) inhibit, encourage, and are affected by the changing rate of energy surplus a society produces. Substituting energy surplus for surplus value, he out-Marxes the Marxist and provides the basis for a genuinely culture-free science of political economy.[17]

But he is only one among many who insist upon looking at human society as a man-machine system in a nonhuman world. The general systems approach encourages and, indeed, demands such a view. From Bertalanffy to Easton, Parsons, and Levy, we are dealing with a theory, however partial its explication, which requires that we understand the interrelations within the structure as a response to the structure's ecological niche in a much wider environment.[18] The emphasis varies, from an obsession with inner order and small concern with the external, to the opposite which sees the inner order as a dependent variable and the external as the cause of it all. There are heuristic reasons for such differences in emphasis: they may lead to new insights. Pragmatically, it is clear that we have an interactive relationship with at least two major terms: system, environment.

Another concern of social science is the study of innovation, accident, and change. Whether one is most concerned with the purposive change (innovation), the random result of lack of fit between organization and problem (accident), or simply structural variation over time, it is necessary to note the rate and direction of social change.[19] We have studies of innovation, ranging from concern with the conditions under which individuals deviate and invent to a focus upon the conditions under which social organizations accept: all are at one in positing that all institutions within societies, and all societies, are in a continual state of tension between change and stability.

We might note that Marx emphasized such an approach. Instead of beginning with an Aristotelian view, that bodies at rest remain so until disturbed by an outside force, he tended to adopt the Galilean view — indeed extending it—all bodies are in motion and will continue so in a given direction unless deflected by a contrary force.

Thus the proper view of change is one which emphasizes the *rate of change*, one which sees structural-functional regularities as not strictly repetitive and reiterative but as varying, in some degree, with each cycle of the system. It then leads us to look at the mechanisms for variation, from those which are brought about by error to those which are (or are thought to be) purposive. The political is, in this view, continually subject to reinspection. Legal realism is an example of an application to political theory; it leads us to look at the system as having four dimensions. It moves over time, no stage is ever repeated exactly, and our concern is with regularities over time and variation in detail; we may be concerned with radical structural shifts (revolution) or with the accumulating effects of quite small changes.

Finally we turn to the analyses of systems, the central focus of the social sciences until recently. Such analyses look to the general coercive effect of the common culture in the society, the specific concrete organizations, the interrelations among them, and the interstices where no specific organization controls human behavior yet aggregates congregate and act. At the simplest level we speak of ecological relations, essentially relationships based upon interdependence but not accompanied by communication and the ordering of behavior within a larger scheme of order. Thus "nature's half acre" summarizes much of the systemic but nonorganizational aspects of human society.[20]

But there is order within the organized groups, across groups in the generalized norms enforced by spatial community and culminating in the nation state, and in the accommodations worked out between organized groups. On the other hand, there is nothing foreordained about such order and it is frequently problematic, sometimes precarious, occasionally impossible. Under such circumstances we must look at the emerging structures which profit from order, whose tasks are, essentially, integrative and directive. These are the specialized organizational segments, within the society, whose job is to maintain accommodation among organized groups and unorganized aggregates, and to do so within a larger general system. This system is one which has a monitoring and directing task for the society as a whole: it is the system of political governance.

It is, notably, a two-term phrase. It is political in the sense that there are differentiated and bounded social groups with varying interests contending for power—in any society. As societies become more complex, it becomes necessary to have another differentiated and bounded social group with another set of interests whose job is, specifically, accommodating the other groups within a framework which allows some degree of direction for the society as a whole. This latter group is government. It exists only as an outrider for the general society of groups, but it is necessary as an outrigger, cobbled up when the existing symbiotic system fails to work.

Such being the case, what can a general social science say about the understanding of politics? Most important, perhaps, is the application of organizational theory to politics: the study of government as a separate concrete group (or congeries of groups) with perfectly regular internal structures as easily studied as any factory or street-corner gang. Such an approach would emphasize the existing system, its interdependencies and strains, and its ways of processing the external world: that is, we would look at a governmental group as a circular energy processing system, paying attention to the requirements for survival. These are (1) access to the necessary resources, human and nonhuman energy (action and materials), (2) the orderly processing of resources through the actions of the system which permit (3) the trading of such output for the resources necessary to continue the system.

Secondly, we would look at government as a manipulable system of human action. We might be concerned with function, ranging from a concern with the minimal requirements of persistence (functional pre-requisites) to concern with maximizing given values to, finally, optimizing a total array of values. The first aim, minimal requirements, is usually about as far as the "structural-functionalist" approach ever goes. The last, optimizing, is a major job for politics, since it requires that we be concerned with side-effects, unintended consequences, and the opportunity costs of one type of investment versus others. It is, of course, a preeminently *political* approach, and one might say that a democratic polity is one which has for its assignment the optimizing of the vital interests of the society as a whole. Its failures result in the frustration of vital interests and, possibly, breakdown of the working consensus with a consequent loss of governmental controls. As for maximizing, this seems to be a characteristic of the controlled economy, the monarch or the dictator seeking to increase national power, racial purity, doctrinal rectitude, or what have you.

A third way of viewing social organization is one which emphasizes the processual. Organization is a continual process which relates, more or less adequately for the task at hand, the action of aggregates over time and space. Thus one could view disorganization, unorganization, reorganization, as aspects of a flow, a stream which meets obstacles and reintegrates or, in some instances, dissipates its substance into desert or savannah. One would not, however, expect to find the disappearance of the stream. Organization is, in this view, coterminous with social life, and biological individuals are dependent upon this collection of their kind. Thus the Aristotelian problem is solved; what persists is not a specific form of state but the principle that adamantly requires a modicum of social organization. This may vary in scale from the small band to the massive nation state; that variance in form is the real problem.

Another way in which a general social science can help us in the study of politics is through the notion of cultural-organizational tension. As the culture is the belief system and normative structure of a population at any given point in time, it is also inadequate to the problems that population faces. For it rests upon accumulated knowledge, wisdom, preferences, superstitions, formed by others under other conditions. Its viability in the present is always problematic; if the present reiterates the past in all respects, it will probably fit. But this of course does not occur. Thus one is forever being catapulted into situations where action is demanded but its exact nature is unclear. Under such conditions we have innovation, the application of new rules or the distortion of old rules to fit new situations.

Such a development is clear in the emergence of labor unions, a phenomenon common to all industrializing nations. The union amounts to a surrogate for many unusable cultural prescriptions; it is also, of course, a new thing under the sun and its emergence, in turn, presents problems for others, including the economic and political leadership of the society. But the labor union is part of a larger process, the increasing internal inclusiveness of the society.[21] For as the scale of organization in the society increases, interdependence among the constituent parts increases *pari passu*. With such interdependence comes the activation of hitherto isolated and stable (or stagnant) populations, together with increasing vulnerability for the system as a whole. Vulnerability, in turn, allows the generation of social power, political and otherwise. Thus we see the progressive inclusion of workers, through the universal franchise, universal free education, and, lately, the norm of "full employment" and minimal welfare. We see a parallel development in the inclusion of the ethnic minorities, women, and to a degree children, in the larger "adult" world. Finally, as the society spins off new social segments, we can predict an unending process of creation of new groups—out of the discrepancy between culture and organization falls a stream of new culture complexes.[22]

Finally, social science should be useful for political analysis because it can place the political problem in its more general social context. Thus the gradual, but massive, shifts in the composition of the population are a clue to the burdens which government will have to assume. The increase in the proportion of United States population made up of the elderly, their propensity to vote proportionally to their numbers, their disadvantaged positions *vis à vis* the productive population, indicate a source of political discontent and, quite likely, of organization. The trends in the society indicate, in fact, the possibility of an "age politics" to go with those emerging from division by race and class.

Population trends are only one sort of social fact which produces problems for the polity. Important also are technological change and economic development. Each can be influenced by the polity, yet not completely controlled, with the consequence that awareness and prediction of each are important for the student of politics; as a gross example we need only consider the Industrial Revolution and its consequences for the polity. It is quite likely that the newest phase of revolution, the "cybernetics" revolution, will have equally drastic results. Already the workforce of the United States is over 50 per cent white collar in composition, and the labor force predictions would have it more like two-thirds by the turn of the century. Labor union organization, devised to give power to manual laborers, does not seem to be the effective way of binding white-collar workers into the society and some interesting new devices are emerging.

In short, we have cultural expansion following the increasing richness and differentiation, complexity and scale of the existential society. Such expansion is not necessarily adequate, in either timing or form, and there is always the possibility of a disastrous lag between what the situation demands and what we know and want to do. Our politics may, in fact, be viewed as lagging behind our problems; with such a view one would analyze the political culture, its form frozen by charters and constitutions and its very existence contributory to cooperation among groups uninterested in protecting it but concerned with a given balance, a game which they can win by existing rules.

Most of what I have written can be summarized in a few brief propositions. Political science is the application of general social science to the political-governmental aspects of society. It can best be viewed, not as a competitor with sociology, but as a focus of research attention, an aspect of human behavior of critical importance in its own right, and a fascinating site in which to study contention for control and the evolving mechanisms of control. Its fascination lies, in part, in the continually problematic nature of political events; they call forth, in turn, not only our most intransigent conservatism, but some of our most ingenious experimentation. As such, they illuminate the receding limits of what is possible for man as a self-conscious actor in a society increasingly well understood.

Notes

1. Alfred North Whitehead, *Science and the Modern World* (New York: Macmillan & Co., 1925), Chap. 1.
2. Warren Hamilton Lewis, *The Splendid Century, Some Aspects of French Life in the Reign of Louis XIV* (London: Eyre and Spottiswoode, 1953).
3. Ibid.
4. See Karl Polanyi, *The Great Transformation* (New York: Rinehart & Co., 1944), for a discussion of Smith's thought as expressed in *The Wealth of Nations*, compared to the ways it was used as ideology.
5. Herbert Spencer's "evolutionary" social philosophy, expressed in his *System of Synthetic Philosophy*, and its American translation by Sumner, were among the more important scholarly products of, and creators of, this utopia. Utopia here is, of course, conceived of in Mannheim's sense as a fighting weapon of an emerging social class. See *Sumner Today, Selected Essays of William Graham Sumner with Comments by American Leaders*, edited by Maurice R. Davie (New Haven: Yale University Press, 1940). Karl Mannheim, *Ideology and Utopia*, translated from the German by Louis Wirth and Edward Shils, International Library of Psychology, Philosophy and Scientific Method (New York: Harcourt Brace, 1955).

6. See Richard Henry Tawney, *Religion and the Rise of Capitalism* (London: J. Murray, 1933).

7. From *Max Weber: Essays in Sociology*, translated by Hans Gerth and C. Wright Mills (Glencoe: The Free Press, 1949), particularly the translators' introduction; Emile Durkheim, *The Division of Labor in Society* (New York: The Free Press of Glencoe, 1964). Durkheim's concern for the potential atomization of society is well stated in the "Preface to the Second Edition."

8. For an effort to separate form and content, see *The Sociology of Georg Simmel*, translated, edited and with an introduction by Kurt H. Wolff (Glencoe: The Free Press, 1950). The introduction gives a brief, admiring, but critically aware, precis of Simmel's efforts.

9. Polanyi, *Great Transformation*.

10. For a full discussion see Scott Greer, *The Logic of Social Inquiry* (Chicago: Aldine Press, 1969).

11. Murray Burton Levin, *The Alienated Voter* (New York: Holt, Rinehart and Winston, 1960); Edward M. Levine, *The Irish and Irish Politics, A Study of Cultural and Social Alienation* (Notre Dame: University of Notre Dame Press, 1966).

12. Herbert A. Simon, *Administrative Behavior* (New York: The MacMillan Company, 1957, second edition). See especially, Almond in the Readings.

13. Harold Steere Guetzkow, *Simulation in International Relations* (Englewood Cliffs, N.J.: Prentice-Hall, 1963); Anthony Downs, *An Economic Theory of Democracy* (New York: Harper and Brothers, 1957).

14. Harold Lasswell and Abraham Kaplan, *Power and Society* (New Haven: Yale University Press, 1950). See David Truman, *The Political System* (New York: Alfred A. Knopf, 1953), for another approach.

15. Scott Greer, *Urban Renewal and American Cities* (Indianapolis: The Bobbs-Merrill Company, 1965).

16. Claude Levy-Strauss, *Tristes Tropique*, Chicago: Univ. of Chicago Press, 1966.

17. Fred Cottrell, *Energy and Society* (New York: McGraw-Hill, 1955).

18. Ludwig Von Bertalanffy, *Problems of Life* (London: C. A. Watts and Co., 1952); "An Approach to the Analysis of Political Systems," David Easton, *World Politics*, vol. 9, pp. 383-400, reprinted in S. Sidney Ulmer, *Readings in Political Behavior* (Chicago: Rand-McNally & Co., 1961), pp. 136-146; Talcott Parsons, *The Social System* (Glencoe: The Free Press, 1951); J. Marion Levy Jr., *The Structure of Society* (Princeton: Princeton University Press, 1952).

19. For innovation see H. G. Barnett, *Innovation, The Basis of Cultural Change* (New York: McGraw-Hill, 1953); for conflict between organization and culture see Scott Greer, *Social Organization* (New York: Random House, 1955).

20. See Norton Long, "The Local Community as an Ecology of Games," in *The Polity* (Chicago: Rand-McNally and Co., 1962).

21. See *The Democratic Revolution in the West Indies*, edited by Wendell Bell

(Cambridge: Schenkman Publishing Company, Inc., 1967), especially "Epilogue" by Bell, for a concise application of this proposition to a set of emerging nations.

22. The same evidence may be evaluated very differently by various observers; thus the controversy over the meaning of "mass society." It is both the collapse of older order and the emergence of new order, as is clear in such collections as *America as a Mass Society*, edited by David Olsen (New York: Free Press of Glencoe, 1963).

4

From the Sociology of Politics
to Political Sociology

GIOVANNI SARTORI

1. The Issue

The phrase "sociology of politics" unmistakably indicates a sub-field, a subdivision of the overall field of sociology—like the sociology of religion, sociology of leisure, and the like. By saying sociology of politics we make clear that the framework, the approach, or the focus of the inquiry is sociological.

The phrase "political sociology" is on the other hand unclear. It may be used as a synonym for the sociology of politics, but it may mean something else. When using the term political sociology, the focus or the approach of the inquiry generally remains unspecified. Since political phenomena are a concern for many disciplines, this ambiguity turns out to be a serious drawback. This is particularly apparent in Europe, where many scholars share Maurice Duverger's view that "in a general way the two labels [political sociology and political science] are synonymous."[1] This view is very convenient,[2] and is particularly prevalent among European sociologists eager to expand to the detriment of political scientists; for this very reason it goes a long way toward explaining the persistent lag of political science in Europe. Nonetheless the view that political sociology and political science largely coincide hardly applies after the time of Michels and Pareto.

This is an expanded and revised draft of a paper delivered at the Berlin conference of the Committee of Political Sociology of the International Sociological Association, held under the auspices of the *Institut für Politische Wissenschaft*, January 16–20, 1968.

One may complain about the excessive compartmentalization among the social sciences, but it can hardly be denied that the scientific progress of the social sciences follows from their proliferation and specialization. The reason for this is fairly obvious. To borrow from Smelser's perceptive analysis, the initial picture in the study of man is one of an enormous *multiplicity* of conditions, a *compounding* of their influence, and an *indeterminacy* regarding the effect of any one condition or several conditions in combination.[3] The scientific picture is, instead, a picture in which "givens," variables, and parameters obtain some order in this bewildering maze.

Givens are diffuse factors which are left in a twilight zone under a variety of assumptions: the *coeteris paribus* clause, i.e. that the givens are constant; that the givens are implicitly incorporated in the formulation of the problem at hand; and that, in any case, givens exert a "distal," not a proximate, influence. In practice this is the basis of the division of labor among the social sciences. Whatever is a "problem" for one discipline becomes an "assumption" or given, an external factor, for the neighboring disciplines. For instance, economists assume the culture and the institutions to be given. Likewise, sociologists assume political structures to be given. In a similar vein, political scientists assume social structures to be given. Each discipline throws light on a set of variables precisely because other factors are assumed to be external, distal, and equal.

Variables are factors, conditions, or determinants which have been adequately specified and isolated from one another. In practice the scientific advance of each discipline hinges on its ability to select and isolate a manageable set of variables. However, the identification and selection of the relevant variables require each discipline to make parameters out of variables. Parameters are variables which are held constant. The distinction is as follows:

> Parameters are determinants that are known or suspected to influence a dependent variable, but, in the investigation at hand are made or assumed not to vary. Operative variables are conditions that are known or suspected to influence a dependent variable and, in the investigation, are made or allowed to vary, so that the operation of one or a few conditions may be isolated and examined.[4]

Givens and the interplay between parameters and variables highlight, then, the extent to which the strategy of the social sciences consists of successive steps of drastic simplifications. A first set of diffuse sources of variation are eliminated by assuming a number of factors to be "givens." This is the division of labor strategy. Then other specific sources of variation are frozen by turning variables into parameters. At this point each discipline is confronted with the problem of constructing models out of numerous explanatory variables, each related, in turn, to a variety of schools and conceptual frameworks.

If this is so, there is little point in claiming that there is but one social science with politics as one of its topics. There is even less payoff in claiming that one of the social sciences is the "master science." And while nobody denies that the social system, the economic system, and the political system are interdependent, surely the problem of establishing some unity among the social sciences cannot be solved by denying the division of labor strategy, or by advocating pure and simple mergers among neighboring disciplines. In either case we would simply reintroduce chaos where some clarity has been painfully obtained. Clearly, the "integration" among the social sciences presupposes their "specialization." Hence, the problem is to combine gains in specialization with gains in cross-fertilization. There are many ways of attacking the problem. One is simply to import concepts and models from other disciplines. Another is "interpenetration," which presumably means that the barriers between the various disciplines are broken down. But the solution that recommends itself because of its more systematic (or less haphazard) nature, is to build connecting bridges, i.e. interdisciplinary hybrids, across the various boundaries. This solution recommends itself also in that it destroys barriers without canceling the boundaries, i.e. without implying loss of identity.

Having placed the issue in perspective, the first question is: How are we to draw the dividing line between sociology and political science? If, as Smelser suggests, "the focus of a scientific discipline . . . can be specified by listing the dependent and independent variables that preoccupy its investigators,"[5] sociology can be defined as the discipline that "tends to opt for social-structural conditions as explanatory variables."[6] Symmetrically, political science can be defined as the discipline that opts for political-structural conditions as explanatory variables.[7] One may equally say that the independent variables—causes, determinants, or factors—of the sociologist are, basically, *social* structures, while the independent variables—causes, determinants, or factors—of the political scientist are, basically, *political* structures.

The retort could be that this demarcation is neat in principle but hardly applicable to the current state of political science. There is a widespread feeling, in fact, that while sociology has emerged as a core social science discipline, political science is in a serious plight. I shall explain later why I do not share this view. But two points should be clarified from the outset: First, which is the pertinent confrontation between the two disciplines; second, where are we to search for the distinguishing traits.

With reference to the first point, the performance of political science may be compared with the overall performance of sociology, or the science of politics may be contrasted more specifically with the sociology of politics. I submit that, *for the purpose of evaluation*, the first comparison just falls short of meaninglessness. It may well be that sociologists are doing nicely with their analyses of the family, urbanization, education, and the like. The relevant issue, however, is whether sociologists are performing better than political scientists in dealing with *politics*, in the understanding of political phenomena. This will be the major discussion throughout this chapter.

Concerning the second point, care must be taken to note the difference between the formalized level of a discipline, i.e. its theoretical frameworks and explanatory models on the one hand, and its research methods on the other hand. It makes little sense to search for the demarcation between sociology and political science—indeed between any of the social sciences —at the research level, that is, with reference to the methods employed for the verification of statements. The research methods are largely decided by the kind of evidence which is available for the units and the kind of problems with which one deals. In principle, all the social sciences are perfectly willing to employ all the known methods of scientific inquiry and validation. In practice, the experimental method is within easy reach of the psychologist, but hardly available to the sociologist beyond the range of small group experimentation. Statistical manipulation is largely adopted, with varying degrees of mathematical sophistication, by a number of disciplines, and depends on the availability of quantitative or quantifiable data—and so forth. Hence the fact that the behavioral persuasion in politics[8] has taught political scientists to draw heavily on the research methods of the sociologists, cannot prove that political science lacks identity at the formalized level.

In attempting to spell out the essential conceptualizations of sociological thinking, Nisbet indicates the following terms as the "unit-ideas" of sociology: community, authority, status, the sacred, and alienation.[9] It is immediately apparent that these are not the unit-ideas of political science. To be sure, one may be unhappy with Nisbet and draw, for instance, from Talcott Parsons. But I would equally argue that the Parsonian-type models are of little use to political science.[10] Indeed, the incessant efforts at "reconceptualization", which characterize the discipline, testify in no small part to the frustration of the behavioral political scientist *vis à vis* the categories of the sociologist.[11]

The point is, then, that if the demarcation between sociology and political science is sought—as it should be—at the level of their respective conceptual frameworks, it soon appears that the formal theory of the social system leaves off where the formal theory of the political system begins. Granted there are many reasons for asking where political science stands; but, as Almond puts it, "confusion, even loss, of identity is inevitably associated with professional growth".[12] The theoretical ferment in the discipline is undeniable.[13] If one is alerted, moreover, to the developmental logic of the social sciences outlined above, one should expect that the need for mutual articulation between sociology and political science will grow, and that "the relations between sociology and political science will come to resemble more those that now obtain between sociology and economics."[14]

Having drawn the dividing line between political science and sociology, the question turns on how to bridge the gap between them—the problem of building inter-disciplinary bridges. *Political sociology* is one of these connecting bridges—under the strict condition, however, that political sociology is *not* considered a synonym for sociology of politics. I propose, in fact, to use the two labels in contradistinction. Political sociology is an *interdisciplinary hybrid* attempting to combine social and political explanatory variables, i.e. the inputs suggested by the sociologist with the inputs suggested by the political scientist. The sociology of politics is instead a *sociological reduction* of politics.

Admittedly the proposed definition of political sociology is largely normative. That is to say, the establishment of political sociology as a real interdisciplinary approach, as a balanced cross-fertilization between sociologists and political scientists, is more a task for the future than a current achievement. In actuality much of what goes under the misnomer of "political sociology" is nothing more than a sociology of politics ignorant of political science; in substance, an exploration of the polity that sets aside as "givens" the variables of the political scientist. My argument is, then, that if we are interested in interdisciplinary achievements, we must drop the view that political sociology is a sub-field of sociology thereby separating political sociology from the sociology of politics.

2. The Sociology of Parties

It is both unfeasible and unnecessary to review the whole range of political topics investigated by the sociologist.[15] I shall select, therefore, a major stream in the sociology of politics, namely, the stream that investigates the imprint of social classes and stratification upon political behavior. While the investigation can be carried out at various levels—the electoral level, the party level, and the elite level—the various threads are amenable to the general heading of "sociology of parties." For the question "do parties represent classes?" presupposes, on the one hand, that we inquire about class voting, and is conducive, on the other, to the sociology of elite studies. It should be stressed, however, that the sociology of parties will be used here as an emblematic device. It would be fool-hardy to say that the sociology of politics can be reduced, in its major substantive achievements, to the sociology of parties. But one may safely generalize—I suggest—from this particular body of literature to certain overall characteristics of the sociology of politics as such.

Since the study of parties is equally a concern of the political scientist, let us first draw the boundary. As already implied, the political scientist is likely to consider parties and party systems as explanatory variables, whereas the sociologist tends to perceive parties and party systems as dependent variables—that which is to be explained. With the boundary drawn, I now propose to examine the sociology of parties on its own grounds and merits. That is, I shall not be concerned with whatever the political scientist might have to say from his point of view. My position is that the sociologist *should* proceed according to his own disciplinary focus. Indeed the distinctive contribution of the sociologist to the study of parties *is* to investigate to what extent parties and party systems are a response to, and a reflection of, social stratification, the solidarity structure of the society, its socio-economic and socio-cultural cleavages, its degree of heterogeneity and of integration, its level of economic growth, and the like.[16]

The classic formulation of this approach is concisely presented in Lipset's *Political Man* as follows: "In every democracy conflict among different groups is expressed through political parties which basically represent a 'democratic translation of the class struggle.' Even though many parties renounce the principle of class conflict or loyalty, an analysis of their *appeals* and their *support* suggests that they do *represent the interests* of different classes."[17] To be sure, Lipset makes the point that "there have been important exceptions to these generalizations . . . and class is only one of the structural divisions in society which is related to party support." Nevertheless it is clear that Lipset's thread is, in *Political Man*, the class thread. "More than anything else," he goes on to say, "the party struggle is a conflict among classes, and the most impressive single fact about political party support is that in virtually every economically developed country the lower-income groups vote mainly for parties of the left, while the higher-income groups vote mainly for parties of the right."[18]

It is unnecessary to stress that these views display a familiar Marxist ring. In their 1957 perceptive review of the state of the art, Bendix and Lipset themselves acknowledge that the chief impetus in the voting behavior studies "stems from an 'interest theory' of political behavior and goes back ultimately to the Marxian theory of class consciousness."[19] Given the fact that the sociology of parties relies heavily on correlations with voting behavior, the statement is equally true for the party topic: the chief impetus of the sociology of parties also goes back, ultimately, to Marxist assumptions.

A comment should be added, however, with reference to the interest theory of politics; and I would rather say the "interest terminology" inspired by, and derived from, Arthur Bentley. The interest terminology is a convenient dilution of Marxism, but hardly offers a substantial alternative. In the Bentleian school, "interest" is a synonym for "activity," and when Bentley says that there can be no activity without interest he says merely that there can be no activity without motivation. Nothing could be more patently true, but to use "interest" in this sense is both superfluous and equivocal. It follows that the interest terminology either leads to fuzzy theorizing, or acquires its substance from the more or less covert assumption that interest generally is "economic interest". It is not surprising, therefore, that the refinement of the interest theory has made much less headway than the refinement of Marxist theory. This also suggests that the Bentleian aspect may be safely set aside.

The problem, as Lipset points out, has three sides: i) a class-type *appeal*, ii) a *support* based on class loyalties, iii) the actual *representation* of class interests. It is superfluous to warn that these features may, or may not, hang together. It is more interesting to illustrate, on these premises, four possible ways of arguing the case.

a) The class appeal is played down to a point of invisibility precisely because the support of class loyalties is firm (e.g. when the appeal is directed to cross-class floating voters).

b) Conversely the class appeal is very visible and explicit precisely because class support is low (or class loyalty dwindles).

Since the foregoing suggests that class *appeal* is an equivocal indicator, we are left with the indicator provided by a class *support*, and the rest of the argument can be developed according to the two following possibilities:

c) Class support is beyond question, and yet class interests are misrepresented: in actuality, the party betrays class interests.

d) No class support is apparent, and yet the party is an inter-class disguise for representing and serving class interests.

The first three arguments suggest, then, that neither class appeal, nor class support, can show that class interests are actually represented. And the fourth argument shows that there is no way of pinning down a true believer: under any and all circumstances he can maintain that politics is class politics. This is tantamount to saying that the theory winds up at a formulation that escapes empirical verification. When we come to the notion of "representation of class interests", we are deferring to a conjecture that is beyond proof and cannot be falsified.

The thorny point is, then, the *representation of class interests*. Lipset is very cautious on this matter, but one finds only too often, in the literature, the assertion that "parties act as representatives of different class interests"; that "political parties have developed largely as instruments of various class interests," and "historically have come to represent specific coalitions of class interest."[20] Given the fact that statements of this sort are delivered by many sociologists as if they were self-evident, let me present the view that I find them obscure, historically incorrect, and scientifically unacceptable.

The first question is: What is the assumption? Surely we are referred, more or less implicitly, to a *general theory of politics*, according to which politics is ultimately a struggle between classes pursuing their class interests. However, this reply does not suffice to clarify the assumption. The interest of a class can either conflict or coincide with the interests of other classes. More technically, inter-class relations may be zero-sum but may also be positive-sum; and, clearly, a zero-sum class theory is radically different from a positive-sum class theory. Yet the sociology of politics is seemingly unaware of the distinction. As a result, we are left to wonder what the theory of class interest and conflict is supposed to mean, and what each author is actually trying to say.

If the general assumption remains obscure, the same conclusion applies to a second, more specific question, namely, what is *class interest*?

Assuming that interest means economic interest, an economic-minded orientation may be imputed to an actor without being consciously held by the actor himself, or pursued by the actor according to his perception of self-interest. In the first case both the interest and the class are "reconstructed": we are saying only that all the people to whom the observer attributes the same economic interest can be placed in a same categorical class. And the fantastic distance between these "reconstructions" and the real world of politics hardly needs underlining. It is only in the second case, then, that economic interests may lead to class voting, class parties, and so called class politics. If so, the thesis applies to *some*, not *all* parties; and can be applied only, historically, to the post-enfranchisement developments of party systems.

The third, and even more crucial question, is: What do we mean by *representation*. Once more, we are confronted with an astonishing lack of sophistication, for it appears that representation is conceived as a pure and simple *projection*. The argument seems to run as follows: since individuals have a "class position" which is reflected in their "class behavior," it follows that millions of such individuals will be represented by thousands of other individuals on account of similar social origins. If one is reminded, however, that not even *individual* representational behavior can be safely inferred from class origin and position, one is bound to be dazzled by the transplantation of such a naïve projective logic at the level of entire collectivities.

The fantastic irreality of the argument that an entire "class" is being "represented" (in some meaningful sense of the term) by such a complex organization as a mass party, has been recently spelled out in a very cogent manner by Mancur Olson. As he suggests, it is contradictory to assume that individuals are motivated by material self-interest, and that individuals so motivated will seek to achieve their common or group interests. In other terms, the more individuals pursue their self-interest, and the more numerous these individuals, the less their interests can be represented by large-scale organizations—for this reason, "if the members of a large group rationally seek to maximise their personal welfare, they will *not* act to advance their common or group objectives."[21]

In conclusion, the theoretical status of the class sociology of parties is poor. In the first place, the concept of representation is patently abused. Projectively speaking we are only permitted to say that parties *reflect*, or may reflect, social classes. This means that one may find "class resemblance" between party voters on the one hand, and the party personnel on the other hand. From this finding one may infer that voters and leaders are linked by a state of socio-psychological *empathy*—but one cannot infer more. The difference between empathy and representation is abysmal, as for some 20 centuries jurists, constitutional thinkers, and, in everyday experience, anyone involved in representational dealings have known. Empathy facilitates understanding; representation poses the intricate problem of replacing one or more persons with another person in such a way that the representative acts in the interest of the represented. Hence it is entirely gratuitous to assert that parties "represent" classes. In fact, we can only verify, on sociological grounds, whether parties "reflect" classes. It would be much to the advantage of clarity, therefore, to drop the notion of representation altogether, both with reference to "class" and to "interest". For no scientific progress is in the offing whenever a highly technical concept is brought back to the year zero, i.e. to a generic common nonsense meaning.[22]

The theoretical status of our subject matter is equally unsatisfactory with regard to the notion of conflict. In this respect the problem is how classes relate to one another. Most of us seem to abide by a "conflict model". However, the class theory of conflict is radically different from the pluralistic theory of conflict. In his philosophical writings Marx is unquestionably manichean.[23] Therefore conflict, i.e. the class stuggle, is only a temporary necessity, and is necessary only insofar as it is conducive to the victory of the (good) slave over the (bad) master.[24] This is clearly shown by the fact that his end-state—the classless society—is imagined as a conflictless monocromatic society. Contrariwise, in the pluralistic approach, conflict—or antagonisms, contestations and dissent—is positively valued not only because all parties may stand to gain, but especially because conflict results from variety, and variety is per se seminal.

Clearly Marxists and pluralists are not speaking of a same conflict. The word has a very different descriptive and evaluative meaning in the two approaches; whereas much of the current sociology of politics muddles a class conflict with a pluralistic conflict. This is not only to say that the notion of conflict remains hopelessly cross-contaminated, but also to suggest that by testing whether social conflicts are zero-sum or positive-sum, we would also be in a position to decide which of our conflict models applies—the Marxist or the pluralistic.

Finally, the theoretical poverty of the class sociology of parties (and politics) is particularly striking with regard to the very notion of "class," which is also hopelessly cross-contaminated—as we shall suggest later—with the notion of "status." Meanwhile let the caution simply be—in the words of Raymond Aron—that we are "at the same time obsessed by the notion of class and incapable of defining it."[25]

3. Class Voting

Whatever the theoretical failings, what are the empirical findings? Research has been heavily concentrated on "class voting," under the assumption that class voting reveals to what extent party systems reflect socio-economic cleavages, and particularly the class structure of the society. Alford's comparative survey of the Anglo-American democracies can be taken as an illustration of the standard approach, that is, of the statistical method of correlating occupation and class position with voting behavior.[26]

The overall finding of Alford's *Party and Society* is that England, and to a lesser degree Australia, are class-polarized polities, while the United States and Canada belong to the less class-polarized systems. More precisely, Alford's index of class voting shows, for the period 1952-62, a mean of 40 in Great Britain, 33 in Australia, 16 in the United States, and 6 in Canada. These and other findings are of great interest precisely because they replace commonplaces with figures. However, when one reads Alford's conclusion that "Great Britain . . . has a relatively 'pure' class politics",[27] one cannot help wondering how this conclusion relates to the figures. According to what standard are we to assess a situation of a relatively *pure* class *politics*? Apparently Alford had decided that this was the case with England long before assembling his evidence. For the figures warrant only the conclusion that England displays *relatively more* class *voting* than the other three countries—which is indeed a very different conclusion. The difference between relatively "pure" and relatively "more" is highlighted by the estimate of R. T. McKenzie and Allan Silver "that at most elections (from 1884) the Conservatives have won about one-third of the working class vote, and that this working class element has constituted about one-half of the party's total electoral support."[28] And if one bears in mind that over the last seventy years, from 1896 to 1966, the English "Labor party has obtained only twice a sufficient governing majority, and that since 1922 ... it has been in power for 15 years only,"[29] one might well conclude that England displays *relatively little* class *politics*.

If one inspects, furthermore, the comparative evidence, nothing supports the contention that class is the major single determinant of voting behavior. Indeed, a reviewer could well subtitle Alford's book as bearing on *non-class voting* in the Anglo-American democracies. Alford develops his argument as if religious, regional, and ethnic factors were intervening variables. Nonetheless, his actual data indicate that this is contrary to fact in two out of four cases. Let it be added that a comparative assessment also weakens the significance of the English case. The reason that class appears prominent in Britain may well be, in fact, that all the other dimensions of cleavage have withered away. If so, one may well argue that even under the most favorable conditions (the absence of counter-vailing cleavages) the class imprint is very poorly—indeed impurely—reflected in the English voting behavior.[30]

However that may be, the overall evidence offered by Alford warrants only the following hypothesis: class is the major determinant of voting behavior *only if* no other cleavage happens to be salient. Thus the correct formulation of the problem is: Given a multiplicity of cleavages, can it be shown that there is a hierarchy of cleavages according to which the class cleavage tends to prevail?

As a matter of fact, the thesis that parties reflect, roughly, social classes is buttressed by Continental Europe far better than by the English-speaking world. Mattei Dogan has compared the voting behavior of industrial workers in ten European countries and, according to his estimates, class voting in Europe finds its peak in Finland, where 80 per cent of the industrial workers are supposed to vote either Communist (45 per cent) or Socialist (35 per cent). Finland is followed by Norway (75 per cent), Sweden, Denmark, Italy, France, and seventh, England.[31] This evidence is *prima facie* rather impressive, but we should not lose sight to begin with, of the fact that the foregoing percentages leave aside half, or more than half, of the total voting population. Sweden, Norway, England, and Finland are the countries in which the Socialist and/or Communist left gains roughly half of the total returns; in Italy and France the working class parties are at a 40 per cent level; and in Holland and Western Germany the proportion is still lower. Now, if half and often more than half of the total vote is given to parties which in terms of class politics should be largely outnumbered, how can this discrepancy be explained? Surely the proportion between the well-to-do and the have-less is equal nowhere, no matter how these categories are apportioned.

Even if we restrict the problem to the class voting of the working class, the evidence appears far less impressive when we come to the breakdowns. For one thing, the data aggregate the Socialist and Communist turnout, an easy thing to do in statistics, but a more difficult thing to understand in politics. If the assumption is that voting behavior basically follows class patterns, then the problem presented by the evidence of Finland, Italy, and France is not class voting, but class splitting. From the point of view of the sociology of politics the question is: Can class splitting, and the correlative choice between a Socialist and a Communist allegiance, be explained by socio-economic factors? As for the countries with no significant class splitting, the puzzling evidence is that three of the four countries having the highest proportion of the working class in their adult population (England, Belgium, and Western Germany) are at the same time the countries in which the workers are less likely to vote Socialist, i.e. to follow class loyalties. Of course the cases of England Belgium, and Western Germany can be explained, but hardly in terms of a theory of class politics.[32]

The problem can be attacked, then, from two sides. One is to explain why most workers *do* vote for "their party." The other is to explain *class splitting* and/or *class deviants*. I submit that the first approach leaves the issue at a trivial stage of explanation.

Whether or not a party should be considered a class party is usually decided by ascertaining which parties do obtain a class support on the basis of a class appeal. The class appeal says: vote for the party that will augment your wages, diminish your working load, and shift the balance of power from your class enemies to yourself. In short, vote for the party that discriminates in your favor. This is like having a bank that offers to pay an interest of 15 per cent while the other banks offer only 3 per cent. To be sure, an observer may be terribly interested in discovering why a majority of depositors does switch to the 15 per cent bank; but my guess is that economists would want to explain why a substantial portion of depositors does not switch.

According to the analogy, the non-trivial problem is posed by the "working class Tories",[33] by the fact that a substantial portion of workers fails to respond to the class appeal. As Dogan puts it, the problem is why so many workers do *not* vote left.[34] Both in England and in France one-third of the working class vote is not given to working class parties; in Western Germany until 1957 almost one worker out of two had voted for the Christian-Democratic party; in Italy almost 20 per cent of the working class vote is retained by parties which are neither Communist nor Socialist; and even in the countries which are led by social-democratic majorities—Sweden, Norway, and Denmark—one-fourth of the working class still votes for the bourgeois parties. Why so?

In addition to class deviants and class splitting, a third difficulty is posed by *non-class voting*, I mean, by those countries in which no class parties can be said to exist. Some, if not all these difficulties are apparently overcome if we merely speak of *left*—as when we assert that workers tend to vote left, or that the world goes left, and the like. But what does "left" mean? The usual way of getting around the problem is to say that "left" *includes* Communist, Socialist, and labor parties, plus whatever exists more-on-the-left than on-the-right wherever the former parties do not exist. This is hardly a reply, however. The question hinges precisely on which criterion, or criteria, these parties are included, and other parties are excluded, from the "left" categorization.

One criterion is clear enough: property rights. According to this, the left is critical of private property or advocates collective property, while the right opposes collective property and defends private property. But the criterion has two shortcomings. One is that it leaves out of a number of countries in which the left does not believe in collective property and is not particularly obsessed by the problem of private property (e.g. the United States). The second, and major, shortcoming is that to explain the *economic* meaning of left does not explain the *political* meaning of left. Hence the critical question is: What is "left" in political matters? Aside from the decisions affecting private property or the distribution of wealth and income, how is one to behave leftwards in all the other areas of decision?

Here we are at a loss, at least if one is to judge by the extravagance or the fuzziness of a number of proposed definitions.[35] Choosing from the sensible interpretations, I would still adhere to the suggestion of Goguel: left means, politically, "more change," the attitude of moving ahead faster and of opposing the *status quo*.[36] This yardstick is, however, too loose and somewhat too relativistic. Obviously enough, the politics of the left is to oppose the *status quo* of the non-left; in victory, however, the left opposes the changes proposed by its opponents and upholds its own *status quo*. Accordingly the Soviet Communist party should be reclassified by now as a conservative force, and it would be hard to explain in what sense the British trade unions remain a progressive force.

It is not sufficient to say, then, that left is "more change"; we are required to qualify the statement by adding: change in favor of the under-privileged. Even so we are still in trouble. For it is hard to understand why, according to this criterion, Fascism, Nazism, Peronism, and the like should be excluded from "left." These movements advocated change (and eventually did produce change); they certainly had large working class support, and possibly took as much care of the underprivileged as many Communist parties in power have done so far. On the other hand, it would not do to say that "left" cannot be a dictatorship: Communist regimes surely are dictatorships.

It would seem, therefore, that "left" is actually defined—no matter how unconsciously—by the following three stipulations: first, that Marxist parties and voters are left by definition; second, that if no such parties exist we may have recourse to a supplementary criterion, i.e. discrimination in favor of the underprivileged; third, that the second criterion does not apply to the parties which propound an anti-Marxist philosophy, even if they advocate change and express a protest of the lower strata. If so, the "left lumping" is little more than a weird ideological aggregate. Whatever its ideological validity, its scientific validity is highly dubious. Granted that "left" may be used as a convenient short-hand, it does not follow that such an aggregate helps our understanding— rather, it obscures our understanding.

Why is it that the worker's allegiance largely goes, in some countries, to Communist parties, in other countries to Socialist parties, in some other countries to both, and still in other countries to neither? Conversely (at least according to the convention that Fascism is, by definition, a "right"), under what conditions does, or can, the protest of the underprivileged be expressed on the right? Finally, why is it that in some countries—not necessarily the wealthy ones—no real left has yet materialized? These are the problems that need investigation—and these are precisely the problems beheaded *a priori* by the "left lumping."

All in all, and to sum up, class voting studies cannot warrant a class theory of politics—nor a class theory of parties—unless these studies lead to the formulation of a "law" of class voting which incorporates and explains non-class voting (or cross-class voting). This is how political scientists are required to demonstrate the effects of electoral systems on electoral behavior; and the same requirements apply to any demonstration of the effects of class on electoral behavior. Why should the standard be lowered for the sociologist? That is, why should "sociological laws" be exempt from the test required of "politological laws"?

One is entitled meanwhile to conclude that the average performance of the statistical line of inquiry has been largely trivial. Given the fact that one can always find socio-economic data, the field has largely developed as a by-product, as an outgrowth of the data. If one is reminded, however, that "data is empirical information processed and refined so as to measure theoretical concepts,"[37] the point remains that the data in question are seldom theory relevant.

These conclusions are hardly surprising if one reflects on the theoretical misgivings spelled out in the previous paragraph. I take it, in fact, that if the conceptual framework is poor, the findings will follow suit. And we still have to discuss the central concept. So far I have reviewed the sociology of voting as if the meaning of "class" at least was clear. But I am afraid that also much of the evidence collected under the class rubric is hopelessly confused and confusing.

4. The Hypothesis Reversed

Even though social scientists tend to neglect, or are unable to account for, subjective class identifications whenever they come to cross-national comparisons, yet it is generally acknowledged that there is a difference between "subjective" and "objective" class. Only *prima facie*, however, does this distinction clarify the problem: because "subjective class" takes on two very different meanings, and even the notion of "objective class" is far from being unequivocal.

When we speak of subjective class, it is seldom clear whether we mean *status self-perception* or *class consciousness*, or both. In any case, more often than not the distinction is inadequately underpinned.[38] Status applies to a problem of ranking, i.e. to the fact that individuals are able to locate themselves on a stratification scale. We thus obtain a set of "prestige levels" and a prestige hierarchy. Does status awareness correspond to some kind of "class awareness"? This inference is, at best, permissible, but only if we make clear that the slices of a stratification system do not correspond to the slices of a class system, neither in number nor in kind.[39] Furthermore, it should be equally clear that "class awareness"—the fact that class is perceived—is by no means the same as "class consciousness," which is a far more serious matter bearing on the belief system.[40]

Class consciousness meant to Marx, still means to much of the European reality and literature, and can be increasingly expected to mean in many underdeveloped areas, a sense of "belonging" to a socio-economic class. That is to say that the notion of class consciousness points to class-minded individuals, to class devotees who actually live a *class ideology*. The first implication is that "stratification" is irrelevant to a "class identifier." He neither perceives nor follows the whole line from soldier to general; he simply dichotomizes between "we" and "they," the class enemies.[41] Another implication is that class consciousness confronts us with a "living reality," that is, with a subjective class which is also, in some sense, an objective reality. In Aron's wording, this class exists as a "collective reality," as a "real totality."[42]

If properly underpinned, then, status awareness on the one hand, and class consciousness on the other, are not even within shouting distance. To perceive one's position on a stratification scale is one thing, to be class minded is quite another thing. At most, status sensitivity may lead to "status polarization";[43] but even a situation of status polarization is hardly conducive to a class-type conflict. Every society is a "stratarchy"; but relatively few societies are "class polarized." In particular, a system of status stratification is far removed from *class action*.

As for the objective notion of class, we need not get entangled in the controversy about the "reality" of collective nouns. Whether class consciousness and action are also an objective reality is immaterial for the present discussion, since both Marxists and non-Marxists agree that the objective starting point is provided by class conditions. It will be sufficient, therefore, to retain the notion of "class conditions," with the understanding that we are referring to an index of objective measures. The notion is surely objective but merely denotes a statistical category, a categorical class.

Bearing these distinctions in mind, let us take a fresh look at the matter. Given the fact that the various class approaches tend to argue the case with reference to class voting, the preliminary query is: What does class voting indicate?

Most people would reply that class voting is an indicator of class consciousness. But we have seen that this is by no means sure. In some countries so-called class voting may simply reflect status polarization; in other countries it may reflect a combination of both, status sensitivity as well as class consciousness. Moreover, as I shall suggest shortly, class voting may well be an indicator of something else. The trouble is that the discriminating power of the indicator "class voting" is almost nil. For one thing, voting is more *act* than *action*, or rather voting reflects a single very discontinuous and superficial layer of behavior. This is also to say that class voting does not suffice to detect class action—unless we are satisfied with the tautology that class action merely signifies class voting. But I would rather say that class action and class voting point to very different stages or levels of *activation*. Hence class action comprises class voting, but not vice versa. In the second place, and more especially, class voting does not suffice to detect "class consciousness"—unless we are satisfied, once again, with the tautology that class consciousness merely signifies class voting.

Whether or not class voting flows from class consciousness, from adherence to a class ideology, can be ascertained via interviewing. But here we pay the price for the theoretical poverty of the category. For the information supplied by the interviews is generally indicative of status self-perception (or of status estimation, if one uses the reputational method), but often inadequate for the purpose of identifying class consciousness. Granted that it is easier to elicit responses about status than about ideology, yet research can be so designed as to capture both kinds of information in their distinctiveness. However, if status and class are conceptually muddled, the research design and the research findings will be equally muddled. If so, we are left to wonder if so-called class voting is *real* class voting, i.e. whether we are dealing with class consciousness or not.

We are thus left to confront directly the crucial issue: namely, how do we pass from class conditions to class consciousness and action? As Max Weber already pointed out, "no differentiation of life opportunities, no matter how deep, produces by itself 'class action,' that is, a common [collective] action of those belonging to the class."[44] This is unquestionably the crux of the matter. Yet, surprisingly enough, the issue is generally dismissed. Let us try to understand why with the help of the four breakdowns recapitulated in Figure 1.

If the problem is formulated by asking "how does objective class relate to subjective class?" we may either envisage the passage from quadrant I to quadrant II, or the passage from quadrant I to quadrant III. Hence, if the

I Class conditions	II Status awareness
III Class consciousness	IV Class action

FIGURE I

Breakdowns of "Class"

notion of "subjective class" remains undeveloped, it is only too easy to confuse the step from I to II with the step from II to III. And precisely this *quid pro quo* goes a long way toward explaining why the crucial point has been sidestepped.

We have discovered, in fact, that an index of class measures tends to correspond fairly well with status self-perception. But this is hardly surprising, given the fact that our respondents have been taught to rate their status precisely on the basis of education, occupation, and income. As is only to be expected, therefore, quadrants I and II are likely to vary, across Western nations, along a semantic dimension more than any other, i.e. depending on whether "worker" and "middle-class" are good or bad words. Thus the European polling data eventually reveal an inflation of workers whereas the American interview data often reveal an inflation of middle-class.

So far, so good. But the interchangeability between I and II—between objective occupational level and self-rated status—does not imply in the least that I or II are equally interchangeable with III. As a matter of fact, the problem of how class conditions relate to class consciousness has not even been touched upon. And we have already seen that status awareness has little, if anything, to do with class consciousness. Hence the question is once again: How do we pass from quadrant I to quadrant III, and ultimately to quadrant IV? In the final analysis, how do we know that class conditions are *the cause* of class consciousness and action?

According to the foregoing analysis, the reply is, very simply, that we do *not* know. This is to say that between class conditions on the one hand, and class action on the other hand, there is a wide gap, a major missing link. Presumably, therefore, we must search for an *intervening variable*.

In the course of his argument Alford notes in passing that "it seems probable that the relative strength of labor unionism is both a cause and a consequence of class politics."[45] Admittedly Alford is justified in leaving the argument at its bifurcation, for correlations cannot warrant a causal relation. Nonetheless the point is crucial. Further probing has revealed, in fact, that while the English class vote is highly correlated with trade-union affiliation, no class vote can be said to exist for the non-union members of the working class, who actually split their vote at random between the Labor and the Conservative parties.[46]

Now, suppose that a country by country probe confirmed that class voting correlates significantly with trade-union affiliation (not with non-union members). Suppose, furthermore, that the research design included an *organizational variable*—a systematic mapping of "networks" implemented by indexes of organizational coverage and pressure—and that the findings did support the hypothesis that a thoroughgoing organizational network is a necessary condition of class consciousness and behavior, for the latter varies with, and follows the density of, the organization.[47] More specifically, suppose that the countries in which the Communist parties outweigh the Socialist parties are found to be the countries in which the Communists were the first to establish the "apparatus mass party"; or the first, with the downfall of a regime, to seize the pre-existing strategic networks and control positions;[48] and suppose, therefore, that the lasting success of Communism was found to coincide systematically with the occupancy of an organizational void, rather than with objective conditions of deprivation.

If these conjectures were adequately tested and buttressed, the conclusion would be that what we are really investigating, via class behavior, is the impact of an organizational variable: *the influence of party and trade-union control*. Class conditions are only a facilitating condition.[49] To put it bluntly, it is not the "objective" class (class conditions) that creates the party, but the party that creates the "subjective" class (class consciousness). More carefully put, whenever parties reflect social classes, this signifies *more* about the party end than about the class end of the interaction. The party is not a "consequence" of the class. Rather, and before, it is the class that receives its identity from the party. Hence class behavior presupposes a party that not only feeds, incessantly, the "class image," but also a party that provides the structural cement of "class reality."[50]

The point can be restated from the angle of my former assertion that *class is an ideology.*[51] Classes materialize in the real world in close correspondence with belief systems in which "class" becomes the central idea-element; and only the ideology of class obtains "class action." If so the question becomes, how do ideologies take hold? And to this effect I would unreservedly subscribe to the statement that "no idea has ever made much headway without an organization behind it. . . . Wherever ideologies seem to be important in politics they have a firm organizational basis."[52] In sum, large collectivities become class structured only if they are class persuaded; and the most likely and apt "persuader" is the party (or the union) playing on class-appeal. In any case, ideological persuasion requires a powerfully organized network of communications.[53]

Let me repeat that these are only conjectures. However, if the assumption that "class conditions" are the prime mover had been seriously probed, there would be no room for such conjectures—they would have long been disproven. Hence the fact that alternative hypotheses have hardly been put to test goes to show to what extent the causal explanation of the sociologist has been taken for granted not only much too readily, but in the most uncritical fashion.[54]

It is interesting to wonder why the sociologist's naïve class explanation finds audiences of predisposed believers with so much ease. I am not satisfied by the reply that the sociologist tends to be more or less a subconscious Marxist, in the sense that Marxism implicitly privileges a science of society. For the question turns on the lasting success—in scientific quarters—of a nineteenth-century derivation of Hegelian philosophy; and to this question I would reply that precisely in scientific quarters we are the victims of a naïve quest for "ultimate objectivity." It is this crude objectivism—which belongs to our inferiority complexes *vis à vis* the physical sciences—that helps to explain, in turn, the lasting popularity not only of Marx but also of social Darwinism, i.e. the idea that man is a creature of his environment.[55]

The reason that we are predisposed to believe in the causal explanation of the sociologist is, then, that we are the victims of an *objectivist bias*. The underlying argument goes something like this: the polity (and politics) is an "artifact," whereas in the society we find the "facts." To be sure the argument is generally rephrased in less crude fashion, e.g. saying that the political scientist deals with short range predictions, whereas socio-economic indicators detect long range trends. But also in this form the argument reflects an objectivist superstition. For the long range validity attributed to socio-economic forecasts (in political matters) represents another instance—I will suggest at the end—of belief accepted without evidence.

To say that our credulity reflects a crude objectivism is to say that whenever a thesis is accepted uncritically we are likely to discover, in the background, an objectivist discrimination. This discrimination can be illustrated with reference to the unequal treatment given, respectively, to "religion" and to "class." Why is it, in fact, that religion is seldom presented as a prime mover, but far more often is presented as an intervening (if not disturbing) variable?

If one inspects the evidence with an unbiased mind, the striking fact is precisely the extent to which religion remains important in spite of the pace of secularization, if not of de-christianization. Thus wherever one finds different religions, one finds that denominational cleavages relate to political behavior just as much, or even more, than class cleavages. This is the case, for example, with the Netherlands and the United States. And the case is presumably not very different with all-Catholic countries such as France, Austria, and Italy. In France, for instance, it is the Catholic influence that explains—according to Dogan—"the absence of a relationship between the importance of the working class and the electoral strength of the parties which call upon such class."[56] In a similar vein, Converse notes that "even in current France one can predict with greater accuracy whether a citizen will be a partisan of the 'left' or of the 'right' by knowing his position on the clerical question than by knowing his position on the more central issues typically associated with the left-right distinction."[57]

Let us note first this difference: Converse is merely suggesting that the clerical question is a parsimonious predictor and, as such, a good indicator —he is not committing himself to the view that religion motivates political behavior. There is a striking difference, then, between our caution in handling the religious factor, as against the lack of caution with which we accept the assumption that class motivates political behavior. Why so? According to my interpretation, the religious factor is "weighed less"—no matter how unwittingly—on two counts: 1) because we can forget that class is subjective, but not that religion refers us to a subjective belief, and 2) because the hold of religion is obviously related to Church, i.e. to an organizational backing, and this is not, again, objective enough: it leaves us with "superstructures." The discrimination is evident: religion is "too subjective" to be a prime mover— hence we have to fall back on class.[58]

Let there be no misunderstanding. I do not deny that, in politics, class may be, or become, more important than religion. I am saying, instead, that the causal factors involved are, in both cases, the same: the relative strength of the *organizational support* of each belief system. In other words, whenever the class appeal outweighs the religious appeal, this is not because class is an "objective reality"; rather, this is because the ideology of class wins the "belief battle," in conjunction with the prevalence of a new organizer, the mass party, over the former organizer, the Church.

Toward Political Sociology

Thus far I have reviewed a major stream of the sociology of politics, properly called. It is with exclusive reference, then, to the sociological approach that I have noted an impressive disproportion between assumptions and findings, between ambitions and accomplishments. It would be unfair, therefore, to conclude the review at this point. In fact, a fundamental and most promising reorientation is underway, as is shown by Lipset and Rokkan's introductory chapter in *Party Systems and Voter Alignments—Cross National Perspectives*,[59] which represents, in my view, a landmark. In the Lipset–Rokkan approach the question which *is* conducive to causal explanations and does grapple with the real problems is: How are conflicts and cleavages translated into a party system?

The first advantage of this approach is that it gives equal attention to *any kind* of conflict and cleavage. Race and ethnicity, region and locality, culture and tradition, religion and ideology, all point to dimensions of cleavage which may be as important as its class dimension. In other terms, conflicts are not only economic and related to the class stucture, but also regional, ethnic, linguistic, religious, and ideological. To assume that these latter sources of conflict are destined, in the long run, to give way to "objective" economic factors amounts to a naïve view of the complexity of human nature, at least in politics. The second advantage is that the inquiry is now correctly focused on the real problem—*translation*. This is indeed the crucial consideration, as a couple of reminders will help to underline.

Racial cleavages would appear *prima facie* the more irreducible source of conflict. However, they are not "translated," for instance, in the party system of the United States; in other words, so far they remain below the threshold of the North American political culture. On the other hand, we are often confronted with conflicts and cleavages which appear, at least *prima facie*, far less deep-rooted, and yet prove to be irreducible. The Irish question was settled only by secession; the French-speaking Canadians are currently more bitter than they were in the past; the cleavage between Flemish and Walloons in Belgium has grown deeper and the conflict is more acute in the 'sixties than it has ever been. Now, surely these conflicts could be managed better if we knew more about them, and particularly if political sociology explained how they become, and why they may not become, "translated" into a party system.

So far we have been content with saying that when cleavages are cross-cutting, or overlapping, they are likely to neutralize one another, at least on a global scale, whereas they otherwise tend to be cumulative and hence to reinforce one another. However, as Dahl rightly points out, the assumption that cross-cutting cleavages encourage conciliation does not hold "if all the cleavages are felt with equal intensity"; it holds only under the condition that "some cleavages are less significant than others."[60] Moreover, if the notion of translation is taken seriously—as it should be— it points to an additional important question: whether cleavages are deviated and domesticated, or instead intensified and exasperated precisely by *translation handling*. And here politics enters.

This is another novelty that equally deserves to be highlighted. To most sociologists, politics is little more than a *projection*. To be sure, Lipset and a number of other sociologists have always refused to reduce politics to an epiphenomenon. Yet if one compares the earlier with the current Lipset, it is apparent that the "weight of politics" is no longer the same. In the 1957 Lipset–Bendix *Essay and Bibliography*, what cannot be explained by social and economic status merely is "the competing strategies of the political struggle": the peculiar essence of politics is reduced to the "strategy" of conflict management.[61] It is only on account of this element that politics is weighed on its own right, as an independent variable. In the 1967 Lipset–Rokkan *Introduction*, however, politics emerges as a major independent factor. No small part of the inquiry is focused, in fact, on the following variables: 1) traditions and rules of decision-making (e.g. conciliar or autocratic); 2) channels for expression and mobilization of protest; 3) opportunities, payoffs, and costs of alliances; 4) limitations and safeguards against direct majority power.[62]

The foregoing may well appear to be an analytical breakdown of what Lipset had in mind when speaking of "strategies." But now a mere chapter heading has been followed-up, and stands as a chapter. Furthermore, a source of political alignments is traced back to the *"we" versus "they" interaction*. Here we reach to the very roots of alignment-making in terms of a strictly political factor of alignments.[63] All in all, then, the Lipset–Rokkan approach represents a momentous rebalancing of the discipline.[64] In my terminology, Lipset and Rokkan definitely surpass the old-style sociology of politics and unquestionably inaugurate the new political sociology. Politics is no longer a mere projection.

The turning point having been turned, let me go on to force the Lipset–Rokkan text, hopefully in accord with their intentions. The problem is not only that "cleavages do not translate themselves into party oppositions as a matter of course."[65] The problem is also that some cleavages are *not translated* at all. Furthermore, the importance of the notion of translation lies in the implication that translation calls for *translators*, thereby focusing attention on translation handling and/or mishandling. As long as we take for granted that cleavages are *reflected in*, not *produced by*, the political system itself, we necessarily neglect to ask to what extent conflicts and cleavages may either be channeled, deflected, and repressed or, vice versa, activated and reinforced, precisely by the operations and operators of the political system. But now we are required to wonder whether "translation mishandling" may largely contribute to the cleavage structure that one finds in the polities characterized by low coincidence of opinion. And one may even wonder whether we can have a translation of socio-economic cleavages into party cleavages without having elites bent on attaching rewards and deprivations to class divisions.

Another important breakthrough of the Lipset–Rokkan *Introduction* lies in the importance given to the historical dimension. In their own words, "to understand the current alignments of voters behind each of the parties, we have to map variations in the *sequences of alternatives* set for the . . . citizens. . . . In single-nation studies we need not always take this history into account. . . . But as soon as we move into comparative analysis we have to add an historical dimension. We simply cannot make sense of variations in current alignments without detailed data on differences in the sequences of party formation. . . ."[66] The accomplishment is superb, and the gains in depth and perspective are invaluable. On the other hand, the historical treatment acquires an overwhelming importance. The emphasis is constantly on the side of historical explanation, and this implies that some inherent limitations should also be noted.

History leads to the understanding of the origins and of whatever follows from the take-off matrix, to the extent that the explanation can proceed from antecedent to consequence on the basis of a same propelling force. However, at a certain point Lipset and Rokkan are struck and intrigued by the "freezing" of party systems (and of voter alignments), i.e. by the fact that, in spite of the tremendous rate of socio-economic change, the "party systems of the 1960's reflect, with few but significant exceptions, the cleavage structures of the 1920's".[67]

In my terminology this freezing represents the stage of "structural consolidation" of a party system. With the freezing the cycle of the origins ends, and another cycle begins: either the propellent is no longer the same, or the original propellent is exhausted. Therefore, in my interpretation, the 1920 freezing of party systems and alignments is intriguing only as long as we persist in understanding party systems as dependent variables. It is not intriguing, however, if we realize that a freezed party system is simply a party system that intervenes in the political process as an independent *system of channelment*, propelled and maintained by its own laws of inertia.[68] This is the same as saying that the stage of structural consolidation of party systems confronts us at the point where genetic explanations leave off.[69]

Clearly, then, my suggestion is that the final establishment of political sociology *proprie dicta* still requires another step. In the Lipset–Rokkan approach, politics enters basically via the historical reconstruction. But politics should enter from another door as well. The final step on our future agenda is the full recognition of the programming of the managers.

The sociology of politics deals with the consumer and ignores the producer. According to the analogy, this is like explaining an economic system as if there could be buyers without sellers. Political sociology is required, instead, to follow all the cycle from both ends, from the producer's no less than from the consumer's end. In principle, the producer's market does not matter less than the consumer's market. Hence, in the perspective of political sociology a party system is not only a response to consumer's demands, but is equally a feedback of producer's options. In practice, moreover, the political entrepreneur exerts a greater persuasive influence on the voter than does the economic entrepreneur on the buyer.

To be sure, in terms of "reconstructed explanations" a sociology of politics can recount the whole story without accounting for the initiative of the managers. But this does not even begin to prove that the *reconstruction* accounts for the *actual construction*. There are almost infinite ways of regressing *ex post facto* from consequences to causes. When the outcome is given, nothing is easier than to adjust the alleged cause to its (known) effect. And my contention is that the reconstructed explanation of the sociologist, the pure sociologist, does not account for the actual construction.[70]

This is also, I suspect, a reason why the performance of the sociology of politics on predictive grounds borders on failure. Take the cleavage thread, the assumption that party systems reflect socio-economic cleavages. Under this premise it is fairly obvious, in the first place, that we shall detect past, not emerging cleavages. It is fairly obvious, that is, that we shall obtain not only a static, but also an eminently retrospective picture. In the second place, if we start from societal cleavages it is equally clear that we shall miss all the conflicts which have a non-cleavage origin. These are not only the *issue-conflicts*—e.g. a crisis of legitimacy and the issue about the regime itself—but also the *within-elite* conflicts which remain important even if they escape visibility. In the third place, the sociology of politics is likely to miss the fact that "objective cleavages" can be largely manipulated, that is, used as *resources*, and thereby over- or under-played according to alignment and coalition strategies.

If we turn to the class thread, its predictive implausibility can be highlighted on similar grounds. With reference to the United States, Converse makes the point that "if we take as a goal the explanation of political *changes* . . . as opposed to questions of more static political structure, then the explanatory utility of the social-class thread is almost nil."[71] Now, if we cannot explain change we are even less likely to cope with forecasting. And there are good reasons for assuming that the conclusion of Converse applies to many other countries.

Assuming that the class thread is actually supplied by an index of class conditions, we are confronted with this dilemma. If we construct a "soft index" it will not register interesting variations, and hence will predict perpetuation rather than change; whereas if we construct a "hard index" it will account for variations which may not affect in the least the political system. In any case the trouble is that we are confronted with *distal causation*, that is, with distal effects that cannot be predicted, almost by definition, with any useful degree of accuracy. Hence, objective class conditions may change and the polity may not—or may react rather than reflect.

The sociologist may concede the foregoing points and yet argue that his socio-economic indicators are more powerful, in the long run, than the more subjective indicators utilized by political scientists. But the "long run" argument is a convenient alibi for anyone, for the political scientist no less than for the sociologist. In long run terms there is always an ulterior future—beyond the future that has already deceived us—to which the verification of our predications can be deferred. Therefore, either we indicate "how long" the run is supposed to be, or we enter an entirely futile debate. For the sake of the argument, let it be assumed that we agree to a deadline of fifty years. If so, I find no convincing evidence in favor of the contention that the sociologist detects long range trends, while the political scientist is confined by his subjectivism to short range predictions.[72] Surely the sociological forecast is more complicated than the forecast demanded of the demographer. Yet even the record of demographic predictions is a record of persistent miscalculations—and this before the advent of birth control techniques.

I would thus rejoin my general point that the widely spread belief that socio-economic indicators have a higher predictive potentiality than any other indicator actually represents another instance of the "objectivist superstition." An unbiased, if impressionistic view suggests, in fact, that the pros and cons are more or less evenly distributed. Socio-economic indicators are advantaged by the fact that they are quantifiable; but they are handicapped (let alone their reliability and crudity) by their "distal" nature. On the other hand, the indicators used by political scientists may be handicapped by their nonmeasurability, but are at an advantage because of their "proximal" nature.

To recapitulate on the route traveled thus far, my major points could be summed up as follows:

1) Political sociology is often a misnomer, for what goes under its name often is a "sociological reduction" of politics. This approach is as legitimate as any other, but should be called for what it is, namely *sociology of politics.*[73]

2) Political sociology is only born when the sociological and "politological" approaches are combined at their point of intersection. If the "sociology of politics deals with the *nonpolitical* reasons why people act the way they do in political life,"[74] political sociology should include also the *political* reasons why people act the way they do. A real *political sociology* is, then, a cross-disciplinary breakthrough seeking enlarged models which reintroduce as variables the "givens" of each component source.

3) The need for a real political sociology has been obscured by the apparent headway of the sociology of politics. This is, however, an optical

illusion which draws on a false appraisal. The optical illusion magnifies the technical sophistication of the research methods of the sociologist to the point of losing sight of the poverty of his conceptual framework—a poverty revealed by the correct appraisal, i.e. by comparing political science with the performance of the sociologist *in the field of politics*.

4) The encounter that gives rise to a real political sociology is hindered by two major obstacles: an objectivist superstition, and poor causal reasoning. With regard to the first fallacy, the sociologist should take stock of the fact that he deals with artifacts just as much as the political scientist does. With regard to the second fallacy, the sociologist should realize that he cannot cover the whole way from the society to the polity by extrapolation, i.e. with crude projective techniques. A fundamental condition of causal inference is that the effect must be contiguous, or contiguous enough, to the cause. Hence *distal effects* cannot be demonstrated as if they were *proximal effects*.

5) With specific reference to the party topic, a real political sociology calls for a simultaneous exploration of how parties are conditioned by the society *and* the society is conditioned by the party system. To say that a party system is a response to a given socio-economic environment is to present half of the picture as if it were the complete picture. The complete picture requires, instead, a joint assessment of the extent to which parties are dependent variables reflecting social stratification and cleavages and, vice versa, of the extent to which these cleavages are picked out as a resource by elite decision, and thereby come to reflect the channeling imprint of a structured party system.

These points run flatly counter to the Bendix–Lipset agenda of ten years ago, namely, that in the long run we should look forward to establishing "a theoretical framework for political sociology as an integral part of sociology *sans phrase*."[75] In my opinion it is fortunate that the suggestion has been disregarded.

A final comment by way of conclusion. We live in an ever more politicized world. This does not merely mean that political participation and/or political mobilization are becoming worldwide phenomena. This means above all that the *power of power* is growing at a tremendous pace—almost with the pace of technology—both with reference to the manipulative and coercive capability of state power and, at the other extreme, with reference to the explosive potentialities of state power vacuums. Now, the greater the range of politics, the smaller the role of "objective factors." All our *objective certainties* are increasingly exposed to, and conditioned by, *political uncertainty.* If so, it is an extraordinary paradox that the social sciences should be ever more prompted to explain politics by going *beyond* politics, by developing a fetishism for the "invisible hand." The foregoing is predicated upon the opposite assumption, namely, that the sociologist should catch up with the hazardous uncertainties of politics.

Notes

1. *Sociologie Politique*, Paris: Presses Universitaires, 2nd ed., 1967, p. 24. Duverger has been delivering this view for the last 20 years. Already in his 1951 *Political Parties* one finds that the laws concerning the influence of electoral systems—indeed the most manipulative instrument of politics—are presented as an instance of "sociological laws." Along similar confusing lines see, W. G. Runciman, *Social Sciences and Political Theory*, Cambridge: Cambridge University Press, 1963; many national reports collected in *Politische Forschung*, Vol. 17 of the "Schriften des Instituts für Politische Wissenschaft," Köln: Westdeutscher Verlag, 1960; and E. Pennati, *Elementi di Sociologia Politica*, Milano: Comunità, 1961.

2. For instance, it enables Duverger to publish the same volume (with irrelevant variations) under two different titles, *Méthodes de la Science Politique* in 1954, and *Méthodes des Sciences Sociales* in 1959.

3. See Neil J. Smelser, "Sociology and the Other Social Sciences", in P. F. Lazarsfeld *et al.* (eds.), *The Uses of Sociology*, New York: Basic Books, 1967, p. 11. This section is largely indebted to the analytical clarity of Smelser's presentation.

4. *Ibid.* p. 15.

5. *Ibid.* p. 5. More exactly, the criteria proposed by Smelser are four: dependent variables, independent variables, logical ordering (cause-effect relationships, models, and theoretical framework), and research methods.

6. Smelser, "Sociology and the Other Social Sciences," p. 12.

7. This is by no means an original demarcation. Bendix and Lipset make the same point (in less technical fashion) by saying that "political science starts with the state and examines how it affects society, while political sociology starts with society and examines how it affects the state." "Political Sociology: An Essay and Bibliography" in *Current Sociology*, Vol. VI, Paris: Unesco, 1957, N. 2, p. 87.

8. This is the felicitous wording of Heinz Eulau, *The Behavioral Persuasion in Politics*, New York: Random House, 1963.

9. R. A. Nisbet, *The Sociological Tradition*, New York: Basic Books, 1966, pp. 4–6. Society, power, and class are also mentioned as related "unit-ideas."

10. I am confirmed in this judgment in spite of William C. Mitchell, *Sociological*

Analysis and Politics: The Theories of Talcott Parsons, Englewood Cliffs: Prentice-Hall, 1967, esp. chaps. V–VIII.

11. This is not to deny that in the last 20 years political science has largely profited from models and theories that have originated outside of the field. My argument is that the more rewarding imports have not originated for sociology. The excellent collective volume, edited by David Easton, *Varieties of Political Theory*, Englewood Cliffs: Prentice-Hall, 1966, is very much to the point.

12. This is Almond's presidential address at the 1966 convention of the APSA, now in *Contemporary Political Science*, p. 17. Actually the statement should be imputed to the comparative expansion of political science into the developing areas, not to most other segments of the discipline. It should also be noted that Almond immediately goes on to say that "political science is not science in general and not social science."

13. See the recent, excellent symposium edited by Ithiel de Sola Pool, *Contemporary Political Science—Toward Empirical Theory*, New York: McGraw-Hill, 1967. James C. Charlesworth (ed.), *Contemporary Political Analysis*, New York: Free Press, 1967, equally testifies to this intellectual ferment.

14. Smelser, "Sociology and the Other Social Sciences," p. 28.

15. Seymour M. Lipset has contributed more than any other author to this task. See "Political Sociology 1945–55," in H. L. Zetterberg (ed.), *Sociology in the United States*, Paris: Unesco, 1956, pp. 43–55; "Political Sociology: An Essay and Bibliography" (together with R. Bendix) in *Current Sociology*, Paris: Unesco, Vol. VI, N. 2, 1957; "Political Sociology," in R. K. Merton *et al.* (eds.), *Sociology Today*, New York: Basic Books, 1959; *Political Man*, Garden City: Doubleday, 1960, chap. 1; "Sociology and Political Science: a Bibliographical Note," in *American Sociological Review*, October 1964, pp. 730–734.

16. This is not to say that the sociologist does not have other interests, but rather to sort out the most distinctive concern. Other subjects, such as the problem of inner-party democracy, are of great interest to the sociologist, but are not particularly distinctive, for the political scientist is equally interested.

17. S. M. Lipset, *Political Man*, p. 220 (italics mine). These are the opening lines of Chapter 7.

18. Ibid. pp. 221 and 223–24. I underline that this is the case in *Political Man*, for the emphasis is very different in Lipset's later writings, as indicated in the last section and Note 64.

19. "Political Sociology: An Essay and Bibliography," in *Current Sociology*, p. 80. But see Note 55.

20. R. R. Alford, in Lipset and Rokkan (eds.), *Party Systems and Voter Alignments*, New York: Free Press, 1967, p. 69. I am not discussing, however, a particular author; the quotations are merely for the sake of illustration.

21. Mancur Olson Jr., *The Logic of Collective Action—Public Goods and the Theory of Groups*, Cambridge: Harvard University Press, 1965, p. 2 *et passim*. The italics are in the original.

22. For a summary overview of the technical complexity of the concept, see e.g. my article "Representational Systems" in the *International Encyclopedia of the Social Sciences*, New York: Macmillan Free Press, 1968, Vol. 13, 465–474.

23. The specification is necessary because in his more circumstantial writings—especially historical essays or occasional pamphlets, such as *The Eighteenth Brumaire of Louis Bonaparte*—Marx is more concerned with empirical details. But the *Weltanschauung* of Marx refers us to his historical materialism, or his dialectical materialism, which is outlined in his philosophical writings. In my opinion, the best introduction to the understanding of the philosophy of Marx remains Karl Löwith, *Von Hegel bis Nietzsche*, Zürich: Europa Verlag, 1940.

24. This is to remind one of the patent derivation of Marx from Hegel's *Phänomenologie des Geistes*, and particularly from the "dialectics between master and slave" (Section A, chap. 4). A classic analysis is Alexandre Kojève, *Introduction à la Lecture de Hegel—Leçons sur la Phénomenologie de l'Esprit*, Paris: Gallimard, 1947.

25. *La Lutte de Classes*, Paris: Gallimard, 1964, p. 87.

26. See *passim* Robert R. Alford, *Party and Society—The Anglo-American Democracies*, Chicago: Rand-McNally, 1963.

27. Ibid. pp. 289–290.

28. In *Party Systems and Voter Alignments*, p. 117. Cf. R. T. McKenzie and A. Silver, *Angels in Marble*, Chicago: University of Chicago Press, 1968.

29. Richard Rose, "Classes Sociales et Partis Politiques en Grande-Bretagne dans une Perspective Historique," in *Revue Française de Sociologie*, N.ro Special, 1966, p. 643.

30. This conclusion is reinforced by noting that the British Liberal party survives, in spite of the coercive impact of a single-member district system, without having "a strong class base any more than a sectional one." Leon D. Epstein, *Political Parties in Western Democracies*, New York: Praeger, 1967, p. 64.

31. "Il Voto Operaio in Europa Occidentale," in *Il Mulino*, N. 94, pp. 250–275; also in *Revue Française de Sociologie*, I, 1960. The percentages are purely indicative and should be accepted with caution, for in a number of cases—e.g. Italy and Germany—a large portion of the respondents refused to divulge their party affiliation.

32. The closest explanation in line with the class assumption is that the three countries in question have a high vertical mobility which favors cross-class coalitions. However, this argument displaces the emphasis from social cleavages to social mobility, and is not entirely convincing either. As section 4 indicates, religion explains far more, at least in the French case; whereas in Belgium the major factor is ethnicity and language. As for England, I have suggested above that it is not a convincing case.

33. This is also the title of a book by Eric A. Nordlinger, London: MacGibbon & Kee, 1967.

34. This is not only the thread of the article cited *supra*, but also a persistent theme of all the writings of Dogan, which emphasize over and over again the "feeble relationship" between the size of the working class and the electoral turnout of the working class parties. Among his more recent writings see: "Le Vote Ouvrier en France: Analyse Ecologique des Elections de 1962," and "Comportement Politique et Condition Sociale en Italie," both in *Revue Française de Sociologie*, VI, 1965, pp. 435–471, and VII, 1966, pp. 700–734; and esp. Dogan's chapter "Political Change and Social Stratification in France and Italy," (in the cited Lipset–Rokkan volume), pp. 129–195. With regard to the problems discussed in this section one should note the growing sophistication of ecological analysis. A recent instance is Giorgio Galli (ed.), *Il Comportamento Elettorale in Italia*, Bologna: Il Mulino, 1968.

35. Both qualities are combined, for example, in the following clarification: "[Left is] structural criticism and reportage and theories of society, which at some point are focussed politically as demands and programmes. . . . To be "Left" means to connect up cultural with political criticism. . . ." C. Wright Mills, *Power, Politics and People*, New York: Oxford University Press, 1962, p. 253.

36. His distinction actually is between "movement" and "established order." See F. Goguel, *Geographie des Elections Françaises 1870–1951*, Paris: Colin, 1951, p. 9.

37. H. A. Alker Jr., "The Comparison of Aggregate Political and Social Data," in S. Rokkan (ed.), *Comparative Social Science Research*, Gravenhage: Mouton, 1968.

38. In his article "Political Sociology" for the *International Encyclopedia of the Social Sciences*, Vol. 12, p. 300, Morris Janowitz observes that the studies on the social basis of political cleavage and consensus "are mainly derived from a social stratification theory of politics [derived in turn from Marx] and have been characterized by a progressive refinement of categories of analysis from broad concerns with class and occupation to much more refined measures of social status." Since this is a fair representation of the general development of the discipline, my point can be reformulated by noting, first, that Marx has been misread, and, second, that "class" and "measures of social status" do not belong to the same continuum.

39. If the notion of class system is taken seriously, as it should, we are referred— in Apter's terminology—to a "bounded class" with relatively fixed boundaries. Conversely, a class system breaks up whenever we find "multibonded classes" (in which attributes of membership derive from many factors that are no longer conducive to solidarity), and is definitely surpassed by the "functional status systems" based on status clusters primarily organized around instrumental ends. See David E. Apter, "Notes for a Theory of Non-Democratic Representation," in J. W. Chapman and J. R. Pennock (eds.), *Representation*, New York: Atherton Press, 1968.

40. *Contra* Joseph A. Kahl, *The American Class Structure*, New York: Rinehart,

1953, p. 9: "The degree which people, at a given stratification level . . . are explicitly aware of themselves as a distinctive social grouping is called their degree of *class consciousness.*" This is a fairly representative sentence.

41. This is what S. Ossowski calls the dichotomous perception of social stratification, "La Vision Dichotomique de la Stratification Sociale," in *Cahiers Internationaux de Sociologie,* 1956, pp. 15–29.

42. *La Lutte de Classes,* pp. 67–69. This is also very much the emphasis of Georges Gurvitch, *Etudes sur les Classes Sociales,* Paris: Gonthier, 1966.

43. The "status polarization" conceptualization represents a distinctive contribution of the Michigan Survey Center group, and correctly implies that a status-polarized society is not the same as a class-polarized society. See Angus Campbell and associates, *The American Voter,* New York: Wiley, 1960.

44. Max Weber, *Economia e Societa',* Milano: Comunità, 1961, vol. II, p. 231 (*Wirtschaft und Gesellschaft,* VIII, sect. 6) my translation.

45. *Party and Society,* p. 292.

46. According to a 1964 Gallup poll the proportion of union workers voting for the Labor party is 4 to 1. See also Martin Harrison, *Trade Unions and the Labor Party since 1945,* London: Allen & Unwin, 1960; and Jean Blondel, *Voters, Parties and Leaders—The Social Fabric of British Politics,* London: Penguin Books, 1963 (with reference to the 1958 general elections.)

47. What happened for instance to the class consciousness of the Italian workers under Fascism? Or to the class consciousness of the German workers under Hitler, in spite of a long tradition of class action?

48. This was definitely the case in the aftermath of World War II in Italy; to a lesser extent in France; and (for different reasons) in Finland; while exactly the opposite happened in West Germany. As far as the Italians are concerned, it is a fact that the Communist apparat managed to take over from the Allied Military Government an exceedingly high number of control positions as soon as they were returned to civilian rule. Had the Socialists or the Catholics been equally organized, it is my conjecture that Italy would not currently have the strongest Communist party of Western Europe.

49. This is not to deny the relevance of the ecological conditions. I am suggesting, however, that the explanatory power of the "organizational hypothesis" is greater (especially in communication and cybernetic terms) than the explanatory power of ecological analysis.

50. An empirical analysis in line with the conclusion is Heinz Eulau, *Class and Party in the Eisenhower Years,* New York: Free Press, 1962. However, American parties represent the feeblest conceivable instance of party organizational incapsulation. When Lenin made the point he had in mind a very different party.

51. From this point of view one may well conceive students to be a "class," as the student revolt goes to show—however, an ephemeral class if no organizational backing follows.

52. Samuel H. Barnes, "Ideology and the Organization of Conflict," *The Journal of Politics*, 28 (1966), p. 522.

53. Naturally the foregoing applies to "class," not to "status." This points again to the importance of the distinction.

54. One may suggest that the organizational hypothesis can be tested via multiple regression analysis, i.e. by treating the impact of the organizational network as a residual variable. But regression analysis merely brings out variations across electoral districts of the organizational strength of each party, and thus does not even begin to meet the new hypothesis.

55. On the impact of "social Darwinism" see, e.g., David C. McClelland, *The Achieving Society*, Princeton: Van Nostrand, 1961, p. 391. This also concurs with Lipset's view that "some of those who uphold the single attribute position are far from being Marxists. They do not believe that position in the economic structure determines all other aspects of status; rather, they would suggest that statistical analysis suggests the presence of a basic common factor." *Revolution and Counterrevolution*, New York: Basic Books, 1968, p. 149. My point equally applies, however, to statistical analysis, for an underlying objectivist bias facilitates our acceptance of appallingly crude data.

56. "Le Vote Ouvrier en France," p. 466.

57. Philip E. Converse "The Nature of Belief Systems in Mass Publics," in D. E. Apter (ed.), *Ideology and Discontent*, Glencoe, Ill.: The Free Press of Glencoe, 1964, p. 248. The findings are in Converse and Dupeux, "Politicization of the Electorate in France and the United States," *Public Opinion Quarterly*, Spring, 1962.

58. Needless to say, the causal factor "race" would do just as well, or even better. But race raises unpleasant associations, while class points to a progressive attitude, that is, to a positively valued ideology.

59. Pp. 1–64. As the editors of the volume indicate, their introductory chapter "was undertaken *after* most of the articles were completed" (p. xii). Therefore, in spite of other magnificent chapters (e.g. the two chapters by Juan Linz, or the one of Allardt and Pesonen on Finland), the Lipset-Rokkan Introduction stands alone. The assertion that "the introduction represents an effort to synthesize the knowledge . . . presented by the chapter authors" testifies more than anything else to the modesty of the authors.

60. In R. H. Dahl (ed.), *Political Oppositions in Western Democracies*, New Haven: Yale University Press, 1966, p. 378.

61. In *Current Sociology*, pp. 85 and 83.

62. See *Party Systems and Voter Alignments*, esp. pp. 26–33.

63. Ibid. p. 3. The authors draw the inference that "parties themselves might . . . produce their own alignments independently." But the suggestion is not really followed up.

64. With Lipset this evolution is already very evident if one compares *Political Man* with *The First New Nation*, New York: Basic Books, 1963; Anchor Books ed., Garden City: Doubleday, 1967. In the 1963 volume, Lipset writes

that "sociologists tend to see party cleavages as reflections of an underlying structure," thereby putting forward an image of social systems "at odds with the view of many political scientists. . . . An examination of comparative politics suggests that the political scientists are right, in that electoral laws determine the nature of the party system as much as any other structural variable" (pp. 335–36, 1967 ed.).

65. *Party Systems and Voter Alignments*, p. 26.

66. Ibid. p. 2.

67. Ibid. p. 50.

68. This notion of "structural consolidation," as well as the focus on party systems *qua* "channeling systems," is clarified in my volume, *Parties and Party Systems* (Harper and Row, forthcoming). See also my article "Political Development and Political Engineering," in *Public Policy*, vol. XVII, Cambridge: Harvard University Press, 1968, pp. 261 ff.

69. It seems to me, therefore, that Lipset and Rokkan evade the problem when they conclude the discussion on the "freezing of political alternatives" by saying that "to understand the current alignments . . . it is not enough to analyze . . . the contemporary sociocultural structure; it is even more important to go back to the initial formation of party alternatives . . ." (p. 54). The argument goes around in circles by missing the limits of the genetic type of historical explanation.

70. As Spiro forcibly puts it, the theories that require first development of the substantive substructure, and then assume that politics will be a reflection, "reverse the actual sequence of events. In virtually every historical instance, substantive change in economy, society, culture, or elsewhere was brought about by political action." Herbert J. Spiro, "The Primacy of Political Development," in *Africa, The Primacy of Politics*, New York: Random House, 1966, p. 152.

71. In *Ideology and Discontent*, p. 260, Note 44.

72. This is, for example, the criticism leveled against the concern of the authors of *The American Voter* with the "perception" of conflict. Among others, Alford argues that this "subjective" concern only affects "short range change." *Party and Society*, p. 87.

73. In his already cited *Encyclopedia* article, Vol. 12, p. 299, Janowitz holds that along with the stratification approach there has always been an "institutional approach" to political sociology stemming from the influence of Weber, in which "political institutions emerge as . . . independent sources of societal change." Without denying the influence of Weber, I would rather say that it counteracts on a more sophisticated level the influence of Marx, hardly that the "institutional approach" belongs to the inner logic of development of the sociological focus.

74. Nathan Glazer, "The Ideological Uses of Sociology," in *The Uses of Sociology*, p. 75.

75. In *Current Sociology*, p. 87.

5
The Shape of Political Theory To Come:
From Political Sociology to Political Economy

WILLIAM C. MITCHELL

Political science has only recently undergone a revolution of sorts in the definition of its mission, problems, and methods; that revolution has been aptly termed "The Behavioral Persuasion" by one of its key figures, Heinz Eulau,[1] and deemed a "successful protest" by Robert A. Dahl.[2] No doubt the claims and achievements of that doughty band of revolutionists have been exaggerated by friend and foe and no doubt we will soon agree that the changes it introduced were not only necessary, but that they were hardly as momentous as the original foes feared and behaviorists hoped. In any event, as we emerge from one revolution we seem to be headed into another—not a counterrevolution but a totally new one, one which may be far more reaching in its implications. Interestingly, as in real revolutions, some of the old revolutionists will be swallowed up by subsequent events and a few, in response, become reactionaries.

The past fifteen years of internecine warfare over behavioralism was accompanied and indeed implemented by the remarkable growth of political sociology. That field has, in some ways, dominated political analysis with its questions, concepts, findings, and theories. Many of the most prominent practitioners of modern political analysis are leading sociologists, including Lipset, Greer, Inkeles, Moore, Kornhauser, Mills, Horowitz, Hunter, Janowitz, Lazarsfeld, Eisenstadt, Selznick, Rokkan, Dahrendorf, Gusfield, and MacRae.

It will be the central theme of this chapter that political sociology has made and will continue to make enormous contributions but that its questions and modes of analysis are rapidly being challenged as a basic framework for political analysis. In its place will come new questions from a new breed of investigators with radically different training, questions, styles of analysis. I should like to call this approach "The New Political Economy."[3]

The Shape of Political Sociology

Political sociology consists of, of course, whatever political sociologists do and/or claim they are doing. Lipset, for example, has stated, "If the stability of society is a central issue for sociology as a whole, the stability of a specific institutional structure or political regime—the *social conditions of democracy*—is the prime concern of political sociology."[4] Elsewhere, Lipset and Bendix have asserted that political sociology studies 1) voting behavior in communities and in the nation (attitude and opinion research); 2) concentration of economic power and political decision-making (documentary evidence and mathematical models); 3) ideologies of political movements and interest groups (documentary evidence, content and analysis); 4) political parties, voluntary associations, the problems of oligarchy and psychological correlates of political behavior (documentary evidence, attitude and opinion research, psychological testing, etc.); 5) government and the problem of bureaucracy (documentary evidence, attitude and opinion research, etc.).[5]

Several years later Greer and Orleans wrote of political sociology as being mainly concerned with "explanation of the peculiar social structure called the state."[6] More specifically, they claimed that political sociology has been mainly concerned with the following items: 1) the structure of the state; 2) the nature and conditions of legitimacy; 3) the nature of the monopoly of force and its use by the state; 4) the nature of the subunits and their contention with the state.[7] This agenda of research and theory is subsequently translated by the authors as "consensus and legitimacy, participation and representation, and the relationships between economic development and political change."[8] These three surveys or accounts of the concerns of political sociology seem fairly complete and thorough and, given the eminence of their authors, may be accepted as the most authoritative description of the field.

The above agendum of research have been implemented by a number of highly talented and sensitive analysts, but they have proceeded for the most part, as Bendix and Lipset have recognized, without an explicit conceptual framework.[9] While the latter is no logical or practical obstacle to fine empirical work on particular problems, it does have limitations in directing research, systematizing ever-growing amounts of data, rationalizing inquiries and the development of general theories. Political sociology has surely enlightened us on the power structure of states, problems of system maintenance, participation, control and authority, but it has done so at a great cost. To tackle one problem usually, although not always, imposes real costs in the sacrifice of other problems. The sociologist's concern over social structure has led him to ignore formal governments, decision- or policy-making at the collective level, choice processes at the individual level, certain types of outcomes of collective decision-making institutions or mechanisms, and a variety of system processes including political competition, coalition building and maintenance, and exchange through log-rolling and compromise. Furthermore, most political sociologists have been extraordinarily reluctant to consider and design formal normative theory or policy and strategic prescriptions for both the individual political actor and public policy.

Political economy, on the other hand, has not been as thoroughly surveyed nor criticized for the simple reason that it has not existed for nearly as long as political sociology. With the volume of publications rapidly increasing, however, we can now begin to discern the emerging outlines of a new area of inquiry—one embracing political science and economics. As sociologists have defined the issues in political sociology, economists are now defining the basic issues of the new political analysis. For some reason or other, political scientists have played lesser roles in both developments.[10.] Very nearly all the work done in the new political economy is being done by economists in the pages of the economics journals. Whereas political sociology was carved out by Weber, de Tocqueville, and Michels, and further developed by such luminaries as Lipset, Dahrendorf, Greer, Kornhauser, Heberle, Bell, Berelson, Rokkan, Lazarsfeld, Gusfield, Hunter, Inkeles, Janowitz, we now find politics the object of such noted economists as Downs, Buchanan, Tullock, Musgrave, Arrow, Lindblom, Black, Bamoul, Davis, Rothenberg, Harsanyi, McKean, Olson, and several others. I must confess some professional embarrassment at the paucity of political scientists in these two interdisciplinary fields but continue to have high hopes.

The New Political Economy

Political sociology has not, according to Bendix and Lipset, developed a theoretical framework but simply a set of tacit agreements about certain general areas of inquiry including social order, legitimacy, and consensus.[11] I must also be fair and indicate that the new political economy has not as yet self-consciously elaborated its own theoretical framework but the outlines of one are becoming clearer and more precise than has been the case with political sociology. In any event, I see a set of questions—rather precise and highly interdependent questions—emerging as distinct parallels to the basic questions of economics about the functioning of an economy. For convenience the questions are listed in Table 1. I will attempt to relate political sociology to these questions as we proceed.

TABLE I

Basic Questions of Economics	Basic Questions of Political Economy
1. What is the general level of economic activity, or the volume of goods and services, and employment?	1. What is the size of the public budget, or the volume of public goods and services?
2. To what uses are resources put?	2. Composition of public budget, or which goods are produced, in what quantities?
3. How are goods produced? Problem of economic organization.	3. How is the political division of labor organized?
4. How is the final product distributed? Problem of income distribution.	4. How are public goods and services distributed and income redistributed?

As economic systems produce "solutions" to the above problems so, too, polities provide solutions or make decisions and choices through time and are constrained by uncertainty in response to the universal necessities of employing scarce resources among competing goals. How various political systems arrive at their choices through non-market institutions is the central question of the new political economy. Political sociology and political science have not seen fit to define their missions in these terms. Since I am inclined to view the functioning of entire polities as the crux of analysis, I am also inclined to view the work of political economists with favor.

Before reviewing each of these problems in detail, it may be useful to outline the basic conception of politics found in the new political economy and contrast it with that predominant in political sociology. As may be inferred from the above questions, these two approaches differ in substantial ways. There are trends within sociology, however, which are more compatible with the economists' work; I have in mind the recent writings of Blau, Homans, Parsons, and Coleman.[12]

Paradigm of the New Political Economy: Exchange Models

Underlying these questions is a fundamental conception of politics as essentially an *exchange* phenomenon not totally different from economic exchange.[13] In this view of politics, the economists are inclined to emphasize *rational choice* on the part of *individuals* and *organizations* as they engage in various types of exchange among themselves and with political parties and governments in pursuit of their *subjective self-interests*. The action and the choices are made under varying degrees of *uncertainty* concerning the specific *goals of others*, their *strategies*, and the *rules of the game*. While the individual is considered as the basic analytical unit and is self-interested, he does engage in *cooperative* as well as *competitive* behavior. Thus, he seeks allies to increase his bargaining strength but he also competes with his allies and opponents over the terms of the bargains. Governments want support, compliance, and resources while the individual citizen wants to improve his share of the benefits and/or reduce costs. All these individual choices and activity are products of *interdependent choices*, since one person's choice must take the uncertain choices of others into account.

If this summary is accurate, we note the distinct outlines of economics and economic behavior in the basic model of politics. Then, too, we may quickly observe that the new political economists are primarily concerned with the politics of democracy just as economists have historically been mostly interested in private market economies. Such a concern is understandable but it may pose severe limitations on research since most of the polities of the world are non-democratic. But, if economists can apply exchange models to non-competitive and only partially competitive markets as well as bureaucracies, I see no inherent reason why exchange models cannot be expanded to include the less competitive political systems.[14] After all, both Hobbes and Rousseau constructed exchange models of what many regard as highly autocratic systems. In any case, economists have begun their work on democracies; how long they will concentrate on them remains to be seen.

The position of the new political economist should be contrasted with that of the conventional economist who confines himself to economic matters. The latter tends to limit himself to a consideration of the economic impacts or consequences of public policies, with policies being taken as givens. Only, incidentally, does he involve himself with the political determinants of policy or the political consequences of economic policies.

Typically, he relies upon clichés and second-hand political science to explain the political aspects. The new political economist, on the other hand, takes the political elements—whether as dependent variables or as explanations of economic policy—as his major concerns. But like his colleagues, he employs economic tools of analysis. These divergent concerns are depicted in Figures 1 and 2. The conventional economist deals with the feedbacks of public policy on the economic behavior of the actor in the market (Figure 1), while the political economist concentrates on the remaining components of the diagram. In Figure 2 we see a representation of the exchange model employed by political economists. Here the emphasis is placed upon a complex circular.flow of exchanges including resources, demands, support, benefits (income, status, opportunities), controls, and actual public goods and services. Questions to be raised obviously include the varying levels and rates of the flows, equilibrium conditions, the roles of individual choice in their determination, and disequilibrium. Other questions less apparent in the diagrams and in the new political economy relate to problems of change in institutional structures, choices and outputs of the entire system. Such matters are, at present, the least developed areas within political economy.

Political sociologists, of course, come in various types. Still, I doubt that many, whether of the older conflict school or the newer consensus type, would construct exchange models or diagrams such as Figures 1 and 2. As Lipset has observed, "the intellectual and ideological heritage of political sociology, its identification with the concerns of the political left, has led to a strong tendency to emphasize concerns with conflict and cleavage and to neglect the implications of consensus and cohesion."[15] More recent political sociology has followed the lead of Lipset, Parsons, and Kornhauser in emphasizing consensus. In so doing they have furnished a potential linkage with the new political economy which I hope both schools will perceive and develop to their mutual profit.

An older tradition of political sociology under the influence of Mosca, Marx, Pareto, Weber, and Michels still informs sociology and political science. Its lesson has been to emphasize inequality, controls, struggles, superordination, subordination, irreconcilable interests, and all the tougher and seamier sides or "dysfunctions" of political life. The impression of politics left in most sociology textbooks is an unpleasant one, at best. Much of politics is regarded as epiphenomenon—the product of social forces and nonrational responses to them in the political arena. The new political economy, however, treats political behavior as essentially

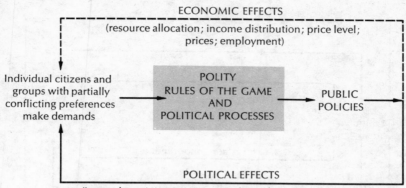

FIGURE I

The Political System

rational adaptation and/or attempts at control on the part of individuals who are not "overly socialized" into passivity. Whereas political economy sees rationally calculating individuals and organizations, including governments, the political sociologist has typically populated his systems and books with "social movements" based on mass appeals, having irrational latent motivations, and not very conscious of making strategic choices in the pursuit of their interests.[16] Governments hardly enter the picture. Public policy determination is a total void as are its consequences for the citizenry. These omissions are also largely true of the Lipset school of political sociology which emphasizes consensus and order and their conditions. In neither branch do we find a concern with the types of questions put forth in Table 1, questions to which we now turn our attention.

With a conceptual framework derived from an economic analysis of markets, the political economist proceeds to ask analogous questions about the functioning of collective decision-making institutions. Questions concerning resource allocation, the distribution of benefits and costs, control mechanisms for adaptation, growth and stabilization are standard fare. The system which provides solutions to these problems is a "public economy" differing from the market economy because of its internal processes of collective choice.

The polity as a formal analogue to the economy allows the use of standard

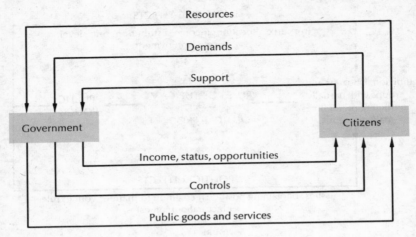

FIGURE 2

Exchange Model of the Polity

economic tools, but the substantive behavioral propositions differ precisely because the conditions of choice confronting the voter are different from those confronting the consumer. The same is true for the analogous roles of producer and politician. Political man is not a derivative of economic man but the same person faced with divergent conditions of choice. Decision rules differ, not human nature. That is why the political economist feels he can use economic analysis on political behavior. But, let us return to the questions noted in Table 1 since they provide the areas of research and the core of theoretical propositions now in the process of development. I might add, that as these questions become distinct focal points the political science curriculum will change; instead of a potpourri of courses we may be teaching seminars on "resource allocation," "the distribution of benefits," the "allocation of costs," etc.

RESOURCE ALLOCATION

Political theory must provide us with explanations of the choices both individuals and entire political systems make with regard to the allocation of their scarce resources among competing objectives. In short, nations have budgets which allocate resources. These budgets are political documents, arrived at through collective or political decision-making processes

TABLE 2

Percentage Distribution of Government Expenditures (Excluding Expenditures for Defense and Social Security) by Function, Selected Countries, 1956

Country	Total	Education and Culture	Justice and Police	General Administration	Transport and Communications	Subsidies	Housing	Public Debt Management	Other
All levels of government									
France	100.0	21.2	6.7	11.5	(19.4)	(11.3)	12.3	(7.3)	10.3
United Kingdom	100.0	22.6	4.6	9.5	16.0	10.8	12.4	24.1	—
Germany	100.0	25.8	10.2	14.1	14.5	(2.4)	15.5	8.8	8.7
Norway	100.0	20.3	3.4	10.4	20.8	23.3	4.7	(6.4)	10.7
Switzerland	100.0	23.4	8.2	16.2	14.9	(12.1)	11.9	13.3	—
Central government only									
Austria	100.0	19.9	9.8	26.9	27.5	10.0	1.5	(4.4)	—
Belgium	100.0	19.1	3.6	9.0	12.3	7.9	2.8	21.5	23.8
Finland	100.0	28.1	4.2	13.9	24.6	(25.8)	—	(3.4)	—
Luxembourg	100.0	14.6	4.2	16.7	25.0	16.7	2.1	14.6	6.1
Netherlands	100.0	16.1	6.1	9.2	13.4	14.4	5.6	13.4	21.8
Sweden	100.0	35.0	(6.8)	(12.0)	19.9	13.5	—	10.8	2.0

Source: J. Frederic Dewhurst, et al., *Europe's Needs and Resources* (New York: Twentieth Century Fund, 1961), p. 420.

and the subject of great dispute in all countries. Resource allocations such as presented in Table 2 should be a basic set of data in all beginning and advanced textbooks in political science. At present they are seldom found as fundamental questions in either political science or political sociology. If political systems directly allocate from one-fifth to one-third of the GNP and indirectly affect the remainder as they do in Western democratic nations (and even more in totalitarian states), we must include such decisions and their determinants within political theory. The new political economy makes such as effort, although mostly on American budgets at the state and local levels.[17] Eventually cross-national comparisons will become more feasible.

A theory of resource allocation must emphasize then at least three different choices: (1) the proportion of the national product to be administered by government; (2) choices among public goods and services; and (3) time preferences concerning the choice between present consumption and investment for future consumption. This set of possibilities is depicted in the "production possibility" or "transformation" curves of Figure 3.

The production possibility curves of Figure 3 depict society's alternative choices given scarcities of resources having alternative uses. They indicate what can be done given the resources; they do not indicate preferences of individual citizens nor the collective preferences however revealed. In order to illustrate these latter considerations we can make use of the economist's well-known "indifference curves." Indifference curves summarize choice or preference ratios among whatever goods or alternatives are being considered. In Figure 4 are placed a parallel set of indifference curves for each of the production possibility curves of Figure 3.

FIGURE 3
Resource Allocation Alternatives

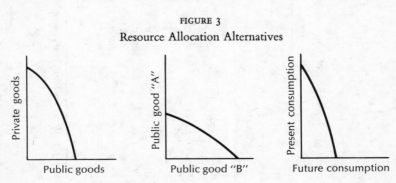

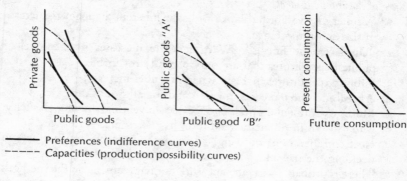

Preferences (indifference curves)
Capacities (production possibility curves)

FIGURE 4
Preferences in Resource Use

By superimposing the two sets, we can depict what a society wants and what it can accomplish and presumably point to optimal choices at the tangencies of the highest production and indifference curves.

A theory of resource allocation requires empirical theories to account for the demand and supply of public goods. Neither political sociologists nor political scientists have elaborated a systematic theory to account for these phenomena at the individual or systems levels. A variety of *ad hoc* factors are occasionally pointed to as determinants, but neither formalization nor testing has been conducted until recently and most of that by economists. Students of public finance including Bowen, Musgrave, Buchanan, Siegel, Tiebout, Williams, Breton, Samuelson, primarily, have elaborated models of the demand for public goods.[18] Birdsall has been among the few to empirically test such models.[19]

Propositions about resource allocation are found for the most part in textbooks on public finance and scattered about in the literature of the new political economy. Many of these generalizations appear to have been derived from observations about American practices, although some are found in studies of public finance in European countries. While I have not made a systematic effort to inventory such statements (a much needed task), I have included a sample of the types of propositions one is apt to find concerning both citizen preferences and policy outcomes for all three sub-choices in allocation, i.e. on the size of the budget, the distribution of or choices among public goods, and time preferences.

Size of the Public Budget
1. Wagner's Law: The public sector has an inherent tendency to increase in size and importance.
2. "Displacement Effects": Wars generate increases in the level of public expenditures that are only partially reversible.
3. Public expenditures increase when revenues increase.
4. As real income increases, the demand for all goods increases.
5. Most governmental goods and services have a high income elasticity.
6. The growth in public expenditures has taken place "stepwise."
7. Cost considerations outweigh ideas about desirable expenditures in deciding the size and rate of growth of the budget.
8. There is probably a greater measure of disagreement on the methods of raising taxes than on the size of the budget.

Allocations among Public Goods and Services
1. The allocation of resources to military consumption among nations varies far more than does the size of the civilian share.
2. Governments do not have a specified revenue sum to allocate among various uses.
3. While the desire for extended governmental services is pronounced in all income groups, there are distinct differences in kinds of services which are desired.
4. Social security programs are most preferred among lower income groups, while public works projects receive widest support among middle and upper income groups.
5. Party identification has only a weak relationship to fiscal policy attitudes.
6. Voters attempt to judge fiscal programs from the point of view of both national and immediate personal benefit.
7. Public goods which are complementary to private goods are more likely to be chosen than those which are not or are competitive.
8. Goods produced under conditions of decreasing marginal costs are most apt to be produced by governments.
9. Interest groups prefer improvements involving added benefits rather than decreased burdens.

Time Preferences
1. Present consumption expenditures are preferred by voters and governments over deferred consumption or the promise of uncertain investments.

2. People do not judge fiscal policies in terms of long-term general benefit.

3. Short-run, incremental gains are sought by budgeting agencies.

The empirical foundations of these generalizations are not impressive and in some cases they may be logically incompatible, as is the case with Downs claiming that uncertainty (ignorance) leads to smaller public budgets than would be the instance with complete information, while Buchanan maintains that ignorance of costs produces larger budgets than would be enacted if the actors had more information. Whatever the status of these particular observations, they illustrate the economist's approach to the political system on issues and processes of resource allocation. I expect these propositions to be refined and tested on a cross-national basis during the next decade of theory building. Hopefully, political scientists will insist that political variables be included in the analyses.

The new political economy attempts not only to deal with problems of societal resource use but individual resource employment as persons or groups go about being citizens, politicians, bureaucrats, or as interest organizations. In this case, the concern is with the ways in which the political actor chooses to employ whatever limited resources of power or influence he may have at his command. Happily, a number of political scientists, including Banfield, Dahl, Sayre and Kaufmann, Wildavsky, and Kramer have made significant contributions to the theory of individual resource management.[20] But the basic formulations are those of Downs, and Buchanan and Tullock.[21] Outside of, perhaps, Michels, few political sociologists have shown much interest in problems of resource use and/or the mechanisms by which individual and collective decision on resources are made. Even in studies of community power structures—an area where one might expect such concerns—we find sociologists eschewing conceptualizations which enable research to focus on choice in nonmarket resource use. In fact, most sociological models of power are based on nonchoice variables. Political sociologists can make a contribution; what that contribution is will be suggested, below.

A concern over individual or organizational uses of their influence resources inevitably raises questions of strategic choice. Whenever alternative means are available and one's choice of means is partially dependent upon the choices of competitors, strategic choices are posed. Most of what we know about conflicting interdependent choices appears to have been derived from games theory and relatively little from "non-game" sources. Political scientists and sociologists have done little to explore the uses of games theory in explaining the behavior of candidates, political parties, legislators, voters, and interest groups. Political scientists have, however, made some use of game notions in describing international politics. The allocation of resources and choices in strategy are often implicit in such works as Truman's *The Governmental Process* and Gross's *The Legislative Struggle*, but they are seldom systematized to the extent of predicting choices. For the most part the analyst is content to categorize alternative courses of action and occasionally relate them to certain situational features. But little effort is made to explicate the actual situation of choice and the eventual choices, themselves. The new political economy is less likely to permit this lacuna to persist.

DISTRIBUTION OF BENEFITS: INCOME, STATUS, OPPORTUNITIES, ETC.

Political scientists label their activities with such fashionable terms as Lasswell's "who gets what, when, how," or Easton's "authoritative allocation of values," but it is little less than amazing how little research and theory are actually directed to these notable and universal choices and events. While a great deal of writing describes the "how," very little identifies and measures the *incidence of benefits* which governments create and distribute. Measures of incidence among benefits or public goods will be still more difficult to construct than incidence with respect to burdens because governments do not keep as meaningful records as they do with taxes. And, some public goods are, by definition, impossible to measure in distributive terms. But the significance of the distributive patterns cannot be questioned. We must be able to explain *who* gets *what*, *when*, *how*, and *why*. As tables of budgetary data become basic data for resource allocation analysis so, too, such illustrative tables as 3, 4, and 5 on subsidies and various other expenditures will become basic material in identifying the recipients of benefits or utilities. No doubt the measurement of income will prove more tractable than measurements of status, indirect market opportunities, and symbolic benefits, but optimism seems in order.

One reason for measuring received benefits is to resolve the "power attribution" dilemmas we have experienced in recent years; perhaps it is more useful and easier to determine power structures by who gets what and how much of the output than to identify power by who governs. Let us try defining power not as one who makes decisions but as who gets how much from the system. Those who acquire the largest shares of the goods, services, status, and opportunities are those who have the most power. If this be the case, new techniques of power attribution (e.g. budgetary analysis) will complement the conventional interview schedules. Instead of drawing power pyramids we will construct Lorenz curves and calculate Gini coefficients to summarize the distribution of public goods.

TABLE 3

Federal Grants to State and Local Governments and Estimated Burden of Federal Grants: Four Highest and Lowest Recipients (1962)

States	Amount Paid for Every Dollar of Aid Received
Delaware	$2.25
New Jersey	2.11
Connecticut	2.00
Indiana	1.70
.	
.	
.	
Wyoming	.45
Louisiana	.44
Vermont	.35
Alaska	.19

Source: *Allocating the Federal Tax Burden by State*, Research Aid No. 3 Revised (New York: Tax Foundation, Inc., 1964), p. 30.

TABLE 4

Subsidy Programs of the Federal Government (1955 and 1965)

Group	1955 (millions of dollars)	1965
Agriculture	$1,074	$5,600
Business	741	1,466
Labor	269	465

Adapted from *Statistical Abstract of the United States, 1966* (Washington, D.C.: U.S. Bureau of the Census, 1966), p. 394.

Our illustrative tables on the distribution of subsidies and various other Federal expenditures point up the need for more such data for more countries. They also raise the ultimate empirical and normative questions of explanation: Why these particular distributive patterns and not some other? While economists have evolved a very sophisticated theory of functional income distribution in private market economies, neither they nor the political sociologists have devised an equally sophisticated theory of distribution by various political systems. Several presumably crucial variables have been pointed out by David Truman,[22] Robert Dahl,[23] and Floyd Hunter,[24] but few of these have been subjected to tests which match

TABLE 5

Regional Shares of Population, Income, and Selected Federal Expenditure Programs, 1963 Percentage Distributions

Region	Population	Personal income	Defense	Composite nondefense	NASA	Reclamation	Highways	Veterans	Public assistance	Corps of Engineers	Education*	Farm subsidies
Low income	29.7	22.9	17.8	36.2	21.8	22.4	31.1	32.8	37.1	38.7	45.1	52.9
Southeast	21.7	16.1	11.2	24.6	18.8	—	21.8	23.9	26.2	21.4	34.6	30.9
Southwest	8.0	6.8	6.6	11.6	3.0	22.4	9.3	8.9	10.9	17.3	10.5	22.0
Average income	36.3	37.7	32.1	33.9	15.8	43.2	39.9	35.4	31.9	28.6	28.0	42.5
Rocky Mountain	2.4	2.3	4.2	3.2	.4	35.4	5.8	2.5	2.8	.3	1.8	1.6
Plains	8.3	7.9	6.3	13.8	9.0	12.8	9.5	8.9	8.7	21.1	8.9	31.7
Great Lakes	19.8	21.0	12.6	13.0	3.3	—	19.6	17.2	14.5	5.8	14.2	9.2
New England	5.8	6.5	9.0	3.9	2.5	—	5.0	6.8	5.9	1.4	3.1	(†)
High income	34.0	39.4	50.1	29.9	62.4	29.4	29.0	31.8	31.0	32.7	26.9	4.6
Mideast	21.4	24.6	22.0	12.9	11.3	—	15.1	20.1	15.9	10.1	17.6	.3
Far West	12.6	14.8	23.1	17.0	50.0	29.4	13.9	11.7	15.1	22.6	9.3	4.3

* Program for fiscal year 1966.   † Less than 0.005 percent.

Source: "U.S. Economic Growth to 1975: Potentials and Problems," Joint Economic Committee 87th Congress, 2nd Session, 1966.

distributive outcomes against the resource bases these theorists have advanced as significant determinants.

In addition to producing raw tabular data on distribution, generalizations are apt to appear about who gets what, when, how, in specific polities as well as categories of systems. Perhaps these generalizations will resemble some of the following:

1. Governments can do but little to affect the basic distribution of income in society.
2. Democratic governments tend to favor the producers more than the consumers.
3. To the extent that redistribution takes place it is from the rich to the poor.
4. Projects which benefit minorities will be awarded disproportionate shares of the public budget.
5. No one gets all he wants, but neither is anyone excluded.
6. Decisions are more favorable to the *status quo* than to innovators.
7. Neither party in a two-party system can afford to make excessive concessions to any given pressure group.

ALLOCATION OF BURDENS

When resources are allocated and benefits distributed, burdens are incurred by a society. When benefits are distributed in private enterprise economies, burdens are simultaneously levied on those who presumably enjoy the use of the goods. The market, in other words, coordinates the functions of resource allocation and income distribution and does so through the more or less automatic and decentralized operations of a price mechanism. In political systems such decisions are not made simultaneously nor are they necessarily governed by distributing benefits to those who produce and pay.[25] The incidences of benefits and burdens are seldom if ever identical. Some receive more than they pay in while others pay in more than they receive. What little we presently know about these matters has been accumulated by economists not political scientists, nor, to any great extent, by political sociologists. It is interesting to note, parenthetically, that very few political science case studies of politics deal with tax or revenue issues.[26] Yet, the newspapers are continually filled with items about intense daily debates and bargaining over alternative governmental financing of public activities. Voting studies rarely inquire into voter preferences on public finance and economic policies more generally.[27]

Political theory of the future will make the allocation of burdens or costs, material as well as psychic, direct as well as external, a major theoretical question and area of research. Crucial questions will center about *who pays, how much, how, when, and with what political consequences for citizens and governments.* In short, individual, party, and governmental choices with respect to governmental financing (inflation, borrowing, taxing, seizure, user-fees, etc.), will become focal points of political analysis. On the basis of what we now know we may expect considerable variations in personal revenue preferences and actual system choices and therefore in the total tax bills and incidence of costs among the polities of the world. Variation in the mix of financing methods and types of taxes, in particular, are considerable even within the same geographical areas of the world and among similar types of political systems.[28] Determinants of these revenue patterns is a primary inquiry of political economy. So, too, is the incidence of whatever tax system is used.

From such inquiries as these will emerge propositions of a type not typically encountered in political sociology, such as:

1. The more democratic a system, the greater the reliance on direct taxes.
2. The more democratic a system, the greater the reliance on progressive income taxes.
3. Governments prefer inflation to taxation as a means of financing their operations.
4. Governments prefer increasing the rates of established taxes to imposing new taxes.
5. Ignorance or uncertainty causes governments to enact budgets smaller than the ones they would enact if both electorates and governments possessed complete information.
6. Democratic governments will prefer hidden to open taxes, regardless of their incidence.
7. Public expenditures tend to rise more rapidly than the increases in population and per capita income.

The above generalizations are illustrative of those one finds scattered about in the traditional literature of public finance; the new political economy, I hazard to predict, will inventory, systematize, and test them on a much wider and more rigorous scale than has heretofore been the case. Perhaps we will begin to produce a fairly tight body of genuinely comparative quantitative propositions about the inputs of resources into political systems based on budgetary data.

BURDENS/BENEFITS RATIOS OF THE CITIZEN

As we learn more about the distribution of benefits and burdens, we will also learn more about those peculiar individual exchange relationships with government. In fact, we may learn how to calculate individual "balance sheets" as suggested in Downs's theory of voter behavior. Such balance sheets may resemble those in Figure 5, depicting the percentage of total income, governmental benefits, and tax burdens shared by different income classes in the United States during 1961.

The significance of burden/benefit ratios is usually assumed in political science and sociology but in general terms concerning the distribution of loyalty or support for political institutions and democratic rules in particular. Perhaps this new information will assist in clarifying which groups in society are most inclined to be cynical, revolutionary, or indifferent. In any case, the growing importance of governments in the lives of individual citizens makes these ratios assume greater import for the investigator. If the data of Figure 5 are valid and reliable[29] we are led to an interesting observation about American voting behavior; namely, that those whose voting participation is greatest are those who not only have the highest incomes but also experience adverse or net losses in their exchanges with the government. Regardless of the causal relationships involved, the apparent connections or correlations are curious. One might additionally speculate that it is an interesting political situation when the "power elites" permit the lower income groups to have more favorable or net balances with the government, while they incur deficits. My point is not that we have discovered some new and revealing facts, but that data such as these raise some exceedingly interesting questions which have not been handled well, if at all, by political science and sociology.

POLITICAL DIVISION OF LABOR

Both the new political economist and the sociologist are mightily concerned with what I call the "political division of labor," but concerned in different ways because they ask different questions. The political sociologist tends to view a political system as a place of *struggle* for power or influence while the economist tends to see it as an essentially *cooperative* division of labor within which various forms and degrees of competition may take place for the various roles and rewards that constitute the system. Both approaches are subject to abuse if pursued too far; the economist's

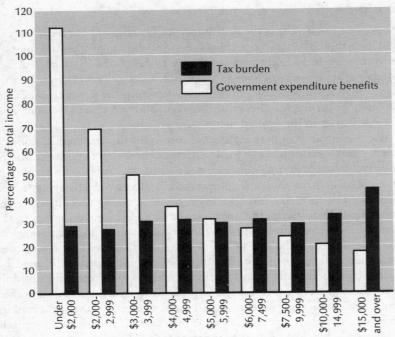

FIGURE 5

Total Tax Burden and Expenditure Benefits as a Percent of Total Income by
Income Class (All Families—1961)

Source: Allocating Tax Burdens and Government Benefits by Income Class (New
York: Tax Foundation, Inc., 1967), p. 3.

perspective could lead to a Platonic conception of harmony while the
sociological view could see little but struggle and dominance.

All societies, including the most primitive, have various divisions of
labor; some persons make collective decisions while others do economic
chores and still others perform religious functions. And, within every
major subsystem such as the economy and polity, a further segmentation
and differentiation take place. The economist is rightly concerned over the
structure of this division of labor and both he and the political sociologist are

rightly concerned with the allocation of persons to fill these roles, i.e. with the recruitment or allocative processes. Political sociologists have made signal contributions to our understanding of who attains which roles because of their concern with social background variables. But, I suspect that some have not much understood the essentially cooperative nature of divisions of political labor. Perhaps the tough-minded traditions of Pareto, Mosca, and Michels have left this imprint of struggle rather than complementarity. In any event, political sociologists have devoted much effort to studying authority, power, elites, and inequality generally. Complementary political services and exchange have not been focal points of structural recruitment studies.

It seems to me that the economist's conception is theoretically superior while that of the sociologist has certain normative advantages. Perhaps, in the new theory we can integrate these varying conceptions for our mutual advantage. One element to which economists might well make substantial contributions has to do with the efficiency evaluation of different divisions of labor. Given certain goals such as maximal citizen participation, cost reduction, coordination, speed of decision-making, or others, which division of labor will best achieve the stated goals? Political sociologists have not to my knowledge dealt with the problem.

A normative interest in the division of labor leads into an interest in the actual processes by which the division of labor is activated and made to function. One of the curious facts, here, is that few sociologists have followed the Burgess and Park, or the von Wiese tradition in dealing with certain types of collective processes including competition, conflict, cooperation, and command. Not until quite recent years has there been much concern for these basic processes, except in the case of bureaucracy.[30] Few political sociologists have explored such typical political processes as bargaining, coalitions, and competition in the depth or with the technical facility of the economists. Even sociologists who work with systems analysis tend to ignore the internal political processes of a polity to concentrate instead upon boundary exchanges with the remaining subsystems. On the other hand, much of the best political theory has been produced on precisely these matters by the new political economists including Chamberlain, Schelling, Lindblom, Buchanan. Polanyi's remarkable examination of the consequences of the size or number of persons involved in a decision-process may be a sign of things to come;[31] and so, too, will the critical debate which has taken place over the relative efficiencies of socialist and capitalist forms of collective economic choice. Perhaps, the debate over the relative virtues and shortcomings of various political systems will be elevated by economic theory. Surely, the debate between Downs and Tullock has already increased our theoretical appreciation of the rules of the game (simple majorities, plurality, and extra-majority rules).[32] And, surely, the controversy between Riker and Pennock on the effects of federalism is among the more remarkable critical exchanges in political science literature.[33] Political sociologists have not contributed much along these lines.

Once more we can illustrate the theoretical questions with some sample empirical generalizations concerning divisions of labor and political processes. The wealth of propositions in this case is unusual but is very scattered and lacking in rigorous formulation. I would expect the political economists to attempt some improvement in this regard. The generalizations follow:

1. Clusters of decision-areas exist, each with its own distinct group of participants.
2. Crises are of extreme importance in encouraging experimentation in policy and institutions.
3. Processes of office-seeking and policy-making tend to be more distinct in democracies than autocratic systems.
4. Competition in the Soviet Union tends to magnify policy differences between contestants while in the United States it tends to moderate them.
5. Government is normally passive, waiting for issues to come to its attention.
6. Government gravitates toward decisions with immediate payoffs, avoiding those which produce mainly long-run effects.
7. The restriction of decision-making to small and cohesive groups promotes speed and agreement.
8. Once innovations in policy are made, they are seldom reversed.
9. Policy changes tend to be incremental.
10. If plans are radical, they seldom survive; if they survive, they seldom work major changes in a going system.

CONTROL MECHANISMS

Collective decisions on distribution and resource allocation must of course be implemented if objectives are to be realized. The new political theory will have need for developing analytical theory to account for the types of controls employed in different societies, in different policy areas, and their relative success or efficiency in operation. At present we lack such theory except in the general area of economic planning and policy. Political science as well as sociology has tended to ignore the formulation of propositions about control mechanisms and their effects. If one wishes to know how to prevent and control race violence, achieve integrated housing or education, he will find many proposals but relatively little advice that is as substantially based as are the control mechanisms for fiscal and monetary policy in economics. The latter are cast as highly systematized alternatives of public policy with reasonably clear and determinant consequences; in fact, one can learn about them simply by consulting almost any elementary economics textbook. The same cannot be said with respect to sociology and political science.

In brief, we need propositions about the range of control mechanisms available in any given society, their relative effectiveness, time lags in implementation, costs and possible returns. There is much in the literature of social control and public administration that can be organized into potentially useful generalizations. We should want to know why some systems pursue certain combinations of controls in certain policy areas while others rely upon different combinations. A great deal of evidence has been documented on these choices among Western democracies with respect to economic policies. Perhaps these studies can be supplemented with similar ones for other areas of public control. One highly suggestive and interesting study in public economic policy-making is Hirschman's *Journeys Toward Progress*.[34] Another, far more quantitative and comparative, is the three-volume work of Kirschen and colleagues on *Economic Policy in Our Time*,[35] dealing with the western European democracies and the United States. Finally, I cannot close this section without reference to that modern classic of political economy, Dahl and Lindblom's *Politics, Economics and Welfare*, a veritable compendium of information and theory on controls.

ADAPTATION AND STABILIZATION

Another focus for the new political economy will be system adaptation and stabilization. At present, I am forced to conclude that it is the least developed area of theory and research, although some isolated aspects have been explored.

By adaptation and stabilization I mean the efforts of a political system to deal with its somewhat uncertain and uncontrollable environment. Systems, through the intended and unintended efforts of their leaders and others, usually attempt to adapt themselves to the situational givens and to stabilize those elements within their control from disturbances. In general, we can reduce these attempts at survival in an uncertain environment to those which concern the *institutional* aspects of the system and *policy* changes having to do with particular activities within society. Let us consider them in the same order.

The institutional structure of the polity is of particular importance because it shapes the public policy-making process, determining which issues and problems are accorded what order of priority, and in part the actual outcomes of policy. When the rules of the game are drastically changed these choices are also affected. This being the case, the institutional structure of a system is of paramount importance in political life. Political scientists and sociologists have recognized this for a long time but have not managed to provide the order I believe desirable and possible. James March has defined the problem in the way I think it must be if a fruitful beginning is to be made in systematizing whatever we think we know.[36] He has suggested a "table of probabilities" which contains the possibilities of any given system being converted into each of the other given alternatives. Figure 6 depicts the approach but with empty cells since we do not know the probabilities even in ordinal terms. Consider Plato's system types.

Political sociologists with their historical inquiries have shed some light on the problem, but so far as I know neither they nor the political economists have made any statistical efforts to trace the rise and fall of various systems.[37] Such a task will be heroic since the necessities of system classification conflict with the infinite diversity of institutional arrangements and combinations. Still, we ought to conceptualize in such terms in order to make sense of change through time. The actual paths from one system to another, from one state of the system to another will necessarily be less precise and neat than the actual outcomes which can be counted. However, we may learn from the experience of economists dealing with dynamic problems involving the growth of firms, business cycles, the "cobweb theorem," and comparative statics of markets.

In addition to structural changes we must account for overall performances of whatever institutional arrangements are employed; that means policymaking for the most part. If political sociologists have largely ignored policy-processes, the political scientists have treated them in far too purely descriptive terms. Countless case studies have been made but few efforts to synthesize or translate them into abstract and general propositions. Some useful work could be done in terms of policy changes. Before Lindblom's theory of "disjointed incrementalism" becomes a cliché, we ought to press studies which empirically test the extent of policy alterations through time in a variety of policy areas and in varying systems. Brzezinski and Huntington have provided some interesting but highly impressionistic leads in the cases of the United States and the Soviet Union.[38] Policy changes in the USSR do not sound very incremental by their descriptions. The *Congressional Quarterly* survey of Federal economic policy during the 1945–65 period lists at least twelve major changes in taxation alone.[39] What of foreign policy? or defense?

A concern for policy-making is but a part of a more general concern with the capacities of a political system, or its parallel in economics—the concern to explain the general level of activity or performance. Some systems generate greater power and adapt themselves to a changing environment more efficiently and rapidly. The new political economists are developing measures of governmental productivity and benefits.[40] They have not, however, delved into the political correlates of varying levels of productivity, an area in which political scientists might well contribute; nor have they looked into social determinants, an area particularly appropriate for the political sociologist. Policy-making and system capabilities under varying conditions should provide a useful focus for studies in adaptation and stabilization.

FIGURE 6

Probabilities of System Changes

	Ideocracy	Timocracy	Oligarchy	Democracy	Tyranny
Ideocracy					
Timocracy					
Oligarchy					
Democracy					
Tyranny					

Normative Theory: Policy and Strategic Criteria

While historians of political philosophy and others have long maintained that values and norms are important and that political scientists ought to and, indeed, cannot avoid making value judgments, it is strange that they should have produced so small a body of systematic, explicit normative propositions that can be taught students and others interested in receiving such advice. Political sociologists have been even more remiss in providing policy criteria and political strategies for those anxious to improve their distributions of benefits and allocations of costs. The inventories of political sociology mentioned, above, do not make reference to deliberate normative theorizing. I predict that the new political theory, under the influence of economics, will fill this gap if we do not. They have already made a powerful beginning in welfare economics and in the development of such tools as "cost-benefit analysis," "systems theory," "program budgeting," and economic theory more generally. In fact, so busy have the economists been that Aaron Wildavsky warns us that they will "swallow up political rationality . . . if political rationality continues to lack trained and adept defenders."[41] Unhappily, many regularly trained political scientists and political sociologists have hardly heard of welfare economics and the tools of efficiency which Wildavsky evaluates with skill and perception.

Political scientists and sociologists have not developed generalized criteria for the evaluation of political systems and their products—public policies. Welfare economics, in spite of its controversial status among economists, has at least come forward with criteria for discussion. I have in mind criteria for resource allocation including the well-known marginal conditions for optimal production and distribution—in other words optimal social welfare.[42] Given an assumed scarcity of resources, the policy-maker must take into account both the relative and conflicting urgency of demands for them and their relative costs of production. The relevance of this problem for politics and political theory ought to be apparent: the factual behavioral problems we have discussed are simply translated into "ought" questions of policy. Thus,

1. What is the most optimal combination of private and public goods?
2. What is the most optimal combination of public goods?
3. What is the most optimal allocation of public costs?
4. What is the most optimal distribution of benefits?
5. How can we most efficiently attain these optima?

In answer to these questions, welfare economists have elaborated a number of generalizations including those of "Pareto's optimality," the "Kaldor–Hicks criterion," and Scitovsky's further refinements concerning the "compensation principle" and Bergson's "welfare function."[43] More specific recommendations of more direct relevance to political theory include a variety of proposals from Samuelson, Bowen, Lindahl, and others on the size and composition of the public budget and the pricing of public goods and services.[44] Policy recommendations on public expenditures and revenues, of course, are one of the lasting contributions of Keynes and his followers. Specific social and political problems involving education, urban renewal, transportation, use of natural resources, housing, air pollution, farm problems, poverty, and national defense have also come within the purview of the economists during recent years. They seem to have more to say on these pressing issues than most political scientists and sociologists. Given a surplus of problems and a scarcity of resources the economist is bound to be interested. And, given the facts of conflicting preferences and the nature of collective decision-making institutions which must aggregate conflicting preferences into authoritative public policies applying to all, it is not unexpected that some economists have turned their attentions to the analysis of these institutions and their efficiency in aggregation problems. Some have concluded, like Kenneth Arrow, in what must be regarded as one of the greatest contributions ever made to political theory, that it is impossible to produce public policies which are consistent with all the expressed preferences of voters.[45] Others have suggested a way out of this dismal conclusion for democracy by relaxing the stringent but reasonable if unrealistic standards of democratic rules originally proposed by Arrow.[46] In any case, a considerable literature has been spawned around this basic political issue but little, if any, has come from political theorists or sociologists. Mention must also be made of the significant contributions in this general connection of the consequences of various democratic institutions and rules advanced by James Buchanan, student of public finance.[47] Relationships among individual citizens, rules of the game and public policies form the crux of political theory, but it has been given a more rigorous and insightful formulation by economists than many other social scientists. While the economists have concentrated upon the logical dilemmas, political scientists and sociologists have focused on the actual empirical conditions, of collective decision-making. Interestingly, many political sociologists have, since Pareto and Michels, tended to agree with Arrow about the possibilities of democracy but for quite different reasons and by quite distinct methods. But that is another story.

What should be done in the way of public policy is not the end of the problem; interested political actors must also work for their attainment. Once more, resource limitations and alternative courses of action produce decisional dilemmas of strategy. A President wants to expedite a bill through Congress in the most efficient manner; an interest group wishes to increase its share of income or reduce its tax bills; a political party desires to win an up-coming election; a reformer wants to alter the governmental structure; a revolutionist plots to overthrow an entire polity and a Secretary of State wants to outmaneuver some foreign power. How can these goals be best achieved? Such is the other normative dimension of the new political economy and the emerging political theory. Mobilizing scarce resources and selecting the optimal strategy in conflict situations has hardly been touched by political sociologists, although their findings could be employed to shed light on the conditions of conflict. But for those who wish more economical means of advice, it is probably better to read Hirschman, Lindblom, Neustadt, Wildavsky, Schelling, and the game theorists on problems of strategy. Presidents are not likely to gain astute strategic advice from political sociology although, of course, individual sociologists may be most clever. Still, presidents tend to hire more economists than either political scientists or sociologists as advisers. None of what I have said should be construed to mean or imply that the economists and game theorists are agreed upon the most appropriate strategic choices; they most definitely are not. But they pose the problem and they do propose ingenious solutions, neither of which is done by many other social scientists.

Normative theory in the hands of economists has its virtues but they do not always include a consideration of fundamental value positions. Efficiency is the chief goal and criterion. How a person or society should rank efficiency against other values is something many economists would rather not confront. Here the political scientist and, to a lesser extent, the political sociologist may take heart for many of them have raised that broader and more difficult problem. Economists seem to prefer taking tastes or preferences for granted, as givens in the analysis. Political scientists and sociologists cannot in the long run. Still, political scientists will have to handle policy problems in which preferences are givens so that a useful dialogue can be established. In any event, normative theory—like the positive or behavioral theory outlined earlier—will be shaped by the new political economist whether we like it or not. Let us hope that the "political" in the new discipline will receive as much emphasis as the "economy." And it will, if we learn to meet the economists on their grounds as well as our own.

Methods of Analysis

As the questions of political theory change, so too will the methods. Political sociology has raised questions which seemingly required the more commonplace tools of historical analysis and current survey research. Most of political sociology has relied upon description and relatively simple statistical analysis. It certainly has not relied upon the tools of the economist—mathematics and deductive model-building. One need only contrast a copy of *The American Economic Review*, not to mention *Econometrica*, and *The American Sociological Review*; or, contrast Arrow's *Social Choice and Individual Values* with Parsons's *The Social System*! Theory will become increasingly logical, deductive, and mathematical. In terms of its content we will make increasing use of economic theory, game theory, decision theory, welfare economics, and public finance. Models of political systems analogous to types of economies and markets will proliferate. As economists began with the extreme opposites of perfect competition and monopoly, so political theorists will proceed from models of democracy and dictatorship to admixtures analogous to monopolistic competition, duopoly, oligopoly. At first, the models will be constructed in the absence of empirical data as they were in economics; then a generation of general critics and "political econometricians" will come along to test the fits. In fact this has already begun in the work of Otto Davis in particular.[48] Statistical testing of models involving election results and governmental budgets, will become a major enterprise. Perhaps less sophisticated methods will also be employed to generate and test predictions about the consequences of formal political institutions or rules of the game. In any event, formal rules—derided for a decade by behaviorists and some political sociologists—will be rediscovered, but in a different way from that of the traditional political scientist. Logical consequences of, say, majority rule, à la Buchanan and Tullock, will be debated in terms quite different from those of traditional students. Federalism, will be analyzed with the statistical tools of a Riker or Pennock, or Grodzins.[49]

One thing to which sociologists and behaviorists in political science will need to adapt and even master is the construction of formal models based on seemingly unrealistic axioms. For sometime we shall be able to make do with verbal, geometric, and algebraic models, but eventually the economists will overwhelm with higher-level mathematical statements. Some of the axioms political scientists and sociologists will encounter include:

1. Individuals seek a multitude of goods (public and private).
2. Each individual prefers more to fewer goods.
3. Each good is subject to diminishing marginal utility.
4. That the resources of society are scarce and have alternative uses.
5. That individuals place different valuations on goods.
6. That exchange is possible among individuals placing different valuations on goods.
7. That the future is uncertain.
8. That all choices entail costs.

On the basis of these relatively simple postulates economists have constructed a magnificent edifice of theory; I see the possibilities of transferring some of this theory to political decision-making and nonmarket choice more generally. Regardless, political sociologists have not employed models as tools and, given their strong historical-empirical tradition, are likely to remain highly skeptical. Models may be ends in themselves but some highly respectable empirical testing of formal models in politics has been accomplished by Otto Davis, his colleagues, and others.[50] Much of this work has been done on governmental expenditures but one of the most fascinating, if least known, efforts is that of Wolf on revolutionary conditions.[51]

The willingness to employ models raises a critical problem of choice: the optimal combination of "realism" and "simplicity" in analysis. Having more of both is preferable but normally we cannot have more of one without some sacrifice of the other. In such cases, a second-best choice is one which allows the same level of return from, say, realism but permits greater simplicity. Or, one might prefer the opposite combination. In any case, I suspect that in future debates we will find the sociologists preferring greater realism while the political economists will reveal a preference for more simplicity. Consider it as a choice between two "commodities" with a given level of resources to achieve the preferred positions as in Figure 7. The student has a choice to make between realism and simplicity; an optimal selection will be dependent upon his

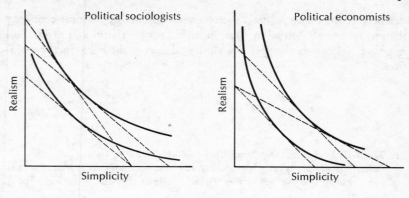

FIGURE 7

preferences and his resources of time, energy, abilities, and money (dotted lines in Figure 7). The more resources he has, the more of each commodity he can acquire; in other words he can reach higher indifference curves. A change in the "price" of one or both commodities produces changes in the attainable ratio of realism and simplicity. With the same resources and prices in effect, political sociologists will opt for more realism and less simplicity while the economists usually place more value on greater simplicity. Their marginal rates of substitution, that is, the rates at which each discipline will exchange realism for simplicity, are also apt to be considerably different. The political sociologist generally wants a great deal more simplicity for any small sacrifice of realism while the economist will give up a great deal of realism to attain a small increment of simplicity. This is depicted in Figure 7 by the relative slopes of the indifference curves.

As we have debated behavioralism during the past decade, now we will engage in debates concerning the utility of model-building. I hope it will be less costly. In any event, the new political economy has made its appearance and I predict a long life. While I expect the new political economy to provide our theoretical orientations, political sociology will continue to shed light on some problems for which economics is poorly prepared to consider. Such problems include the maintenance of systems and their growth. We would be foolish, indeed, to ignore such questions and the brilliant scholars that political sociology has produced during the post-World War II period. Still, I believe that it is better, from a theoretical perspective, to make political sociology an adjunct of political economy than to reverse the situation. But, in making these claims and proposals I hope we can reduce the costs we all shared during the behavioral revolution.

Notes

1. *The Behavioral Persuasion*. New York: Random House, 1963.
2. "The Behavioral Approach in Political Science: Epitaph for a Monument to a Successful Protest," *American Political Science Review*, 55 (Dec., 1961), 763–772.
3. The label has some misleading characteristics in that it may suggest a political interpretation of the economy. The "old political economists," including most of the American Institutionists, did offer political explanations of the economy. The new political economists concentrate on the polity and unlike the old group use the conventional tools of analysis. Veblen, Mitchell, and Commons rejected these tools.
4. "Political Sociology," in Robert K. Merton, *et al.* (eds.), *Sociology Today*. New York: Basic Books, Inc., 1959, pp. 91–92.
5. "The Field of Political Sociology," in Lewis A. Coser (ed.), *Political Sociology*. New York: Harper & Row, 1966, p. 10.
6. "Political Sociology," in Robert E. L. Faris (ed.), *Handbook of Modern Sociology*. Chicago: Rand-McNally & Co., 1964, p. 810.
7. *Ibid.*
8. *Ibid.*
9. Bendix and Lipset, "The Field of Political Sociology," p. 15.
10. Among those who have contributed are Dahl, Banfield, Riker, J. Q. Wilson. Wildavsky, and I would add the often-forgotten name of George E. G. Catlin—whose advocacy of economic models and conceptions in political science goes back to *The Science and Method of Politics*. George Allen & Unwin, Ltd., 1927; *A Study of the Principles of Politics*. London: George Allen & Unwin, Ltd., 1930; and, most recently in his *Systematic Politics*. Toronto: University of Toronto Press, 1962.
11. Bendix and Lipset, "The Field of Political Sociology," p. 15.
12. Peter M. Blau, *Exchange and Power in Social Life*. New York: John Wiley, 1964; George Homans, *Social Behavior: Its Elementary Forms*. New York: Harcourt, Brace & World, 1961; Talcott Parsons, *Sociological Theory and Modern Society*. New York: The Free Press, 1967; J. S. Coleman, "Foundations for a Theory of Collective Decisions," *American Journal of Sociology*, LXX (May, 1966), 615–629.

13. Perhaps, the best single statement by economists of their version of the political system is that of James Buchanan and Gordon Tullock, *The Calculus of Consent*. Ann Arbor: University of Michigan Press, 1962, Part I.

14. See Gordon Tullock, for an imaginative application of economic analysis to restrictions on political competition; "Entry Barriers In Politics," *American Economic Review, Papers and Proceedings*, LV (May, 1965), 458–466.

15. Lipset, "Political Sociology," p. 113.

16. The reaction against the working class as the standard-bearer of democracy takes the rather interesting form of a somewhat psychoanalytic attack on their political perceptions and actions. The quest for symbolic benefits and social status is treated as less than rational by most of those who contributed to Daniel Bell (ed.). *The New American Right*. New York: Criterion Books, 1955; a later edition is entitled *The Radical Right*. Garden City, N.Y.: Doubleday & Co., 1963.

17. The citations are too numerous to mention all. But a representative sample might include: Harvey Brazer, *City Expenditures in the United States*. New York: National Bureau of Economic Research, 1959; Glen Fisher, "Determinants of State and Local Government Expenditures: A Preliminary Analysis," *National Tax Journal*, XIV (Dec., 1961), 349–355; Glen Fisher, "Interstate Variations in State and Local Government Expenditure," *National Tax Journal*, XVII (Mar., 1964), 57–74. Some recent studies by political scientists include Richard E. Dawson and James A. Robinson, "Inter-Party Competition, Economic Variables, and Welfare Policies in the American States," *Journal of Politics*, XXV (May, 1963), 265–289; Neil S. Wright, *Trends and Variations in Local Finances: The Case of Iowa Counties*. Iowa City: Institute of Public Affairs, The University of Iowa Press, 1965; and Thomas R. Dye, *Politics, Economics, and the Public: Policy Outcomes in the American States*. Chicago: Rand-McNally & Co., 1966.

18. Howard R. Bowen, *Toward Social Economy*. New York: Rinehart & Co., 1948, Ch. 18; Richard A. Musgrave, *The Theory of Public Finance*. New York: McGraw-Hill, 1959; James M. Buchanan and M. Z. Kafoglis, "A Note on Public Goods Supply," *The American Economic Review*, LIII (June, 1963), 403–414; Albert Breton, "A Theory of the Demand for Public Goods," *The Canadian Journal of Economics and Political Science*, XXXII (Nov., 1966), 455–467; Paul A. Samuelson, "Diagrammatic Exposition of a Theory of Public Expenditure," *Review of Economics and Statistics*, 32 (Nov., 1955), 350–356; C. H. Tiebout, "A Pure Theory of Local Expenditure," *Journal of Political Economy*, LXIV (Oct., 1956), 416–24; Barry N. Siegel, "On the Positive Theory of State and Local Expenditures," in Paul Kleinsorge (ed.), *Public Finance and Welfare*. Eugene, Oregon: University of Oregon Press, 1966, pp. 171–186; Alan Williams, "The Optimal Provision of Public Goods in a System of Local Governments," *Journal of Political Economy*, LXXIV (Feb., 1966), 18–33; James M. Buchanan, *The Demand and Supply of Public Goods*.

Chicago: Rand-McNally & Co., 1968, is the first full-length book treatment of the problem.

19. William C. Birdsall, "A Study of the Demand for Public Goods," in R. A. Musgrave (ed.), *Essays in Fiscal Federalism*. Washington, D.C.: The Brookings Institution, 1965, pp. 235–294.

20. Edward C. Banfield and Martin Myerson, *Politics, Planning, & the Public Interest*. New York: The Free Press, 1955; Edward C. Banfield, *Political Influence*. New York: The Free Press, 1961; Robert A. Dahl, *Who Governs?* New Haven: Yale University Press, 1961; Wallace Sayre and Herbert Kaufmann, *Governing New York City*. New York: Russell Sage Foundation, 1960; Gerald Kramer, "A Decision-Theoretic Analysis of a Problem in Political Campaigning," in J. L. Bernd (ed.), *Mathematical Applications in Political Science, II*. Dallas: The Arnold Foundation, 1966, pp. 137–162; Aaron Wildavsky, *The Politics of The Budgetary Process*. Boston: Little, Brown & Co., 1964.

21. Anthony Downs, *An Economy Theory of Democracy*. New York: Harper & Brothers, 1957; J. M. Buchanan and G. Tullock, *Calculus of Consent*. More recently, Downs published *Inside Bureaucracy*. Boston: Little, Brown & Co., 1967, while Tullock expressed his views earlier in *The Politics of Bureaucracy*. Washington, D.C.: Public Affairs Press, 1965.

22. *The Governmental Process*. New York: Alfred A. Knopf, 1955. Truman's independent variables appear to include such group resources as cohesion, monetary strength, leadership, and status.

23. *Who Governs?* The crucial variables include available resources such as those enumerated by Truman but qualified by the idea that they may be badly employed or invested.

24. *Community Power Structure*. Chapel Hill: University of North Carolina Press, 1959.

25. James M. Buchanan uses this divergence to critically reflect on political processes in "Individual Choice in Voting and the Market," in the author's *Fiscal Theory and Political Economy*. Chapel Hill: University of North Carolina Press, 1960, pp. 90–104. The problem of distributing benefits and allocating costs in the polity has long been a major one in public finance. The argument has been phrased in normative terms concerning the appropriate criteria: "the benefits approach" vs. "the ability to pay approach." See Musgrave, *Essays in Fiscal Federalism*, Chs. 4–5.

26. Taxation is mentioned but three times in the Index of Truman's *The Governmental Process*. Robert A. Dahl devotes about six pages in *Who Governs?* to tax issues, a major issue in most local communities; see pp. 79–84.

27. The term "taxation" is not to be found in Berelson, *et al.*, *Voting*. Chicago: University of Chicago Press, 1954, and it is only briefly mentioned in Campbell, *et al.*, *The American Voter*. New York: John Wiley & Sons, 1960, pp. 174, 182, 195–197. Economists have, however, looked into individual perceptions and attitudes toward fiscal and monetary policies. See Eva Mueller, "Public

Attitudes Toward Fiscal Programs," *Quarterly Journal of Economics*, 77 (May, 1963), pp. 210–35; B. L. Gensemer, Jane A. Lean, and W. B. Neenan, "Awareness of Marginal Income Tax Rates Among High-Income Taxpayers," *National Tax Journal* (Sept., 1965), pp. 258–67; and Robin Barlow, Harvey Brazer and James N. Morgan, *Economic Behavior of the Affluent.* Washington, D.C.: The Brookings Institution, 1966, Ch. XI on "Tax Consciousness"; Birdsall, in Note 19. More generally on these and cognate economic policies see George Katona, *Psychological Analysis of Economic Behavior.* New York: McGraw-Hill, 1951, especially Chapter 14, and *The Powerful Consumer.* New York: McGraw-Hill, 1960, Chs. 11–13.

28. See E. S. Kirschen, *et al., Economic Policy in Our Time*, Vol. I. Chicago: Rand-McNally & Co., 1964; Joint Tax Program OAS/IDB/ECLA, *Problems of Tax Administration in Latin America.* Baltimore: Johns Hopkins Press, 1965.

29. A note is not the place to decide a highly technical matter. Suffice it to say that roughly the same conclusions have been drawn by another student, W. Irwin Gillespie, for the year 1960; "Effect of Public Expenditures on the Distribution of Income," in Musgrave, *Essays in Fiscal Federalism*, pp. 122–186.

30. See Note 12 for citations.

31. Michael Polanyi, *The Logic of Liberty.* Chicago: University of Chicago Press, 1951.

32. Gordon Tullock, "Problems of Majority Voting," *Journal of Political Economy*, LXVII (Dec., 1959), 571–79; Anthony Downs, "In Defense of Majority Voting," *Journal of Political Economy*, LXIX (April, 1961), 192–199; Gordon Tullock, "Reply to a Traditionalist," ibid., 200–203.

33. William Riker and Ronald Schaps, "Disharmony in Federal Government," *Behavioral Science*, 2 (1957), 276–90; Roland Pennock, "Federal and Unitary Government—Disharmony and Frustrations," *Behavioral Science*, IV (April, 1959), 147–57.

34. *Journeys Toward Progress.* New York: Twentieth Century Fund Inc., 1963.

35. *Economic Policy in Our Time.* Chicago: Rand-McNally & Co., 1964, 3 volumes.

36. "Some Observations on Political Theory," in Lynton K. Caldwell (ed.), *Politics and Public Affairs.* Bloomington: Indiana University Press, 1962, pp. 134–136.

37. S. N. Eisenstadt, *The Political Systems of Empires.* New York: The Free Press, 1963, might be considered an exception.

38. *Political Power: USA/USSR.* New York: The Viking Press, 1963.

39. *Federal Economic Policy, 1945–1965.* Washington, D.C.: Congressional Quarterly Service, 1966, p. 9.

40. See *Measuring Productivity of Federal Government Organizations.* Washington, D.C.: Bureau of the Budget, 1964; and, Robert Dorfman (ed.), *Measuring Benefits of Government Investments.* Washington, D.C.: The Brookings Institution, 1965. For a more purely theoretical analysis consult Roland N. McKean *Efficiency in Government Through Systems Analysis.* New York: John Wiley, 1958.

41. "The Political Economy of Efficiency: Cost-Benefit Analysis, Systems Analysis, and Program Budgeting," *Public Administration Review*, XXVI (Dec., 1966), 310.

42. A succinct statement of these conditions is contained in William J. Baumol, *Economic Theory and Operations Analysis*, 2nd ed. Englewood Cliffs: Prentice-Hall, Inc., 1965, pp. 356–363.

43. Ibid., pp. 375–380. More extended and detailed analyses may be found in Jerome Rothenberg, *The Measurement of Social Welfare*. Englewood Cliffs: Prentice-Hall, Inc., 1961, and E. J. Mishan, *Welfare Economics*. New York: Random House, 1964. The latter volume has an excellent bibliography of welfare economics.

44. See Note 18 for relevant citations.

45. *Social Choice and Individual Values*, 3rd ed. New York: John Wiley, 1963.

46. Arrow cites the criticisms and answers them in Chapter VIII of the 2nd edition of his book, ibid., pp. 92–120. Also, consult William Riker, "Voting and the Summation of Preferences: An Interpretative Bibliographic Review of Selected Developments During the Last Decade," *American Political Science Review*, 55 (Dec., 1961), 900–911.

47. *Public Finance in Democratic Process*. Chapel Hill: University of North Carolina Press, 1967.

48. Otto Davis, M. A. H. Dempster, and Aaron Wildavsky, "A Theory of the Budgetary Process," *American Political Science Review*, LX (Sept., 1966), 529–547; Otto Davis, "Empirical Evidence of Political Influences upon the Expenditure Policies of Public Schools," in Julius Margolis (ed.), *The Public Economy of Urban Communities*. Washington, D.C.: Resources for the Future, Inc., 1965, pp. 92–111; James Q. Wilson and Edward C. Banfield, "Voter Behavior on Municipal Public Expenditures: A Study in Rationality and Self-Interest," ibid., pp. 74–91.

49. The Riker and Pennock investigations are cited in Note 33. Jacob Cohen and Morton Grodzins, "How Much Economic Sharing in American Federalism?" *American Political Science Review*, LVII (March, 1963), 5–23.

50. See Note 48.

51. Charles Wolf, Jr., *Foreign Aid: Theory and Practice in Southern Asia*. Princeton: Princeton University Press, 1960, Chs. 8 and 9.

6

The Relationship Between Economics and the Other Social Sciences: The Province of a "Social Report"

MANCUR OLSON, JR.

My primary purpose is to discuss the relationships between my own discipline of economics and some other social sciences, especially when these relationships seem to me to be of particular relevance to the political scientist. It is natural in these circumstances to begin by asking what basic differences distinguish the various social sciences from one another. Distinguishing the social science disciplines may seem trivially easy, but some good studies could as well be put under the rubric of one discipline as of another, and the essential or defining traits of each are by no means obvious.

This question is made more timely because an increasing number of studies are coming to be accepted as belonging to two or more disciplines. A variety of examples involving all of the social sciences could be given, but since I know most about what fellow economists have done, I will merely mention the names of a few economists whose work has made an impression in political science as well as in their own field, namely, Kenneth Arrow, Duncan Black, Kenneth Boulding, James Buchanan, Anthony Downs, John Harsanyi, Albert Hirschman, Charles Lindblom, Jerome Rothenberg, Thomas Schelling, and Gordon Tullock. The relevance of the work such men have done for political science is indicated by Professor William Mitchell's contribution to the present volume. Mitchell suggests that work by economists such as those mentioned will probably set the pattern for the advance of political science in the coming

The author was Deputy Assistant Secretary (Social Indicators) in the Department of Health, Education, and Welfare when this paper was written, but the argument of this paper does not reflect official views or policy in any way.

decades. The fact that not only work by economists but also studies by men in other disciplines can have a multidisciplinary impact is also illustrated by Mitchell's chapter, for he argues that the pattern for some of the most important work in political science in the recent past has been set by the theories of sociologists. Similarly, political scientists have done work which has come to be accepted as part of the heritage of other disciplines; the importance of Herbert Simon's work for economics is a particularly striking example. The overlap between economics and political science is perhaps best illustrated by the Public Choice Society (formerly the Committee on Nonmarket Decisions), an organization created to encourage the use of the economist's methods for the study of political and social institutions.

The question of how the provinces of the various social sciences should be distinguished has been raised, not only by scholarly efforts of the kind just cited, but also in debates about current public policy. Two recent innovations in the United States government have provoked disputes about what roles different social sciences should play in the policy-making process. One of these innovations was the Presidential directive in 1965 requiring that the Planning-Programming-Budgeting System, which is an outgrowth of economic analysis, should be used in all departments of the Federal government. This prompted disagreement about whether an economic approach is the most appropriate for dealing with the "social" programs of government, or suited to an inevitably political environment.

The other innovation was the effort to develop social indicators and social reporting in the Department of Health, Education, and Welfare. This effort grew out of the conviction that the nation needs statistics and other information on its social condition analogous to that which the Economic Report of the President's Council of Economic Advisers, and the statistics it contains, provide about the market economy. It led to the publication of *Toward A Social Report*,[1] the first across-the-board attempt to discuss the performance of a society in a systematic way. Since I had the immediate responsibility for the preparation of this report, I inevitably came up against the need to define what was "social," and the problem of deciding which social science disciplines and tools were appropriate to which problems. (This experience has, of course, had some influence on what I shall say here.)

The same questions have arisen on the legislative side of the government. Senator Walter Mondale and about a score of other Senators have sponsored the "Full Opportunity and Social Accounting Act." This bill, if passed, would establish a Council of Social Advisers, which would advise the President on social policy and issue an annual Social Report on the state of the nation. The hearings on this bill have elicited testimony from a wide variety of scholars and public officials.

Inevitably these hearings, and other discussions of the bill, have dealt in part with the division of labor among the social science disciplines. Several of those who testified on the Mondale bill wondered whether it might not be better to create a combined Council of Economic and Social Advisers than two separate councils. And there has been no agreement about how the "economic" and "social" spheres could be distinguished, so that there could be a clear allocation of responsibilities between the Council of Economic Advisers and any new Council of Social Advisers. Proponents of the Mondale bill are especially anxious that the President get more advice about the problems of the poor and the disadvantaged. The problems of these groups certainly are "social" problems, and the counsel of the best sociologists, psychologists, and political scientists should of course be available to the policy makers who deal with them. But, if poverty is not an "economic" problem, then nothing is. Moreover, social programs require scarce resources and that is what economics is all about. No consensus is emerging on what the respective roles of the different social sciences should be.

The diverse classifications of the work of particular scholars and the practical problems entailed in a social report may not seem to be of fundamental intellectual or theoretical interest. But they do at least suggest that the problem of distinguishing the basic features and spheres of responsibility of the various social sciences has not been resolved, and that there is a need to think it through. It can in fact be resolved only through a look at some of the most profound problems and theories in social science.

II

Why, then, are the fundamental features and respective spheres of the various social sciences so far from being delineated? The social sciences have not been adequately distinguished from one another largely because it has not usually been understood that the basic differences between the social sciences involve not the subjects they study, but rather preconceptions they have inherited, the methods they use, and the conclusions they reach. To distinguish their defining features, we must look at the ways in which scholars in various disciplines work rather than at the nature of the phenomena that they study.

This point can be better illustrated with examples from economics and sociology than with instances from political science. This is because, as I shall attempt to show, economics and sociology are at the opposite extremes of a conceptual continuum, whereas many political scientists are in somewhat a middle position along this continuum. As such, political science is probably less troubled by the extreme models ascribed to economics and sociology, and perhaps more engrossed with its substantive "subject." What is said may, however, have more relevance to political science than to any other discipline, for some controversies in political science can be best understood in terms of the economic-sociological differences I hope to make clear.

The most significant reason why the social science disciplines must be distinguished by their preconceptions, methods, and conclusions rather than primarily in terms of the objects studied, is that the theories or tools of thought of the social science disciplines are so general that each discipline's theory encompasses objects or problems that convention puts in the reservation of some other discipline. This comprehensiveness, which is manifest most clearly in economics and sociology, is not generally understood. It will therefore be necessary to consider the degree of generality of some of the basic theories of social science in more detail.

III

The general applicability of economic theory has not usually been understood by laymen, and indeed many of the older generation of economists also interpret economics too narrowly. This is probably due in large part to the special historical circumstances in which economic theory first came to have coherence. The great economists of the late eighteenth and nineteenth centuries, like many major theorists, were often inspired to intellectual innovation by immediate practical problems. They were for the most part caught up in the political controversies of their time and were sometimes passionate ideologues. Most of them, at least in Great Britain, were advocates for the rising middle classes and the mercantile and industrial interests. They were usually utilitarians, democrats, internationalists, and passionate advocates of *laissez faire*. Indeed, in nineteenth-century Britain, the word economist was often taken to *mean* an advocate of *laissez faire* in general and free trade in particular. The belief that economic theory is applicable only to goods that fetch a price in the markets of "capitalist" economies of the kind the classical economists admired has survived to the present day.

In fact, economic theory not only is, but (if it is to avoid arbitrariness and error) *must be*, so general that it also applies to "goods" that are *not* traded in markets—and also to traditional and communistic societies. If an economist is studying the housing market, he cannot ignore the fact that some locations have more prestige than others, are in areas occupied by different races or social groups, are in different political jurisdictions, and have different aesthetic attributes. Obviously any of these factors can affect the satisfaction an owner would get from a house, and the market price of that house, as much as its material characteristics. Thus none can be ignored in any complete and nonarbitrary economic analysis of the housing market.

Indeed, it is in general *not* possible to give an entirely accurate explanation of economic behavior in a situation unless *all* of the perceived advantages of a given alternative, to the actor being studied or advised, are counted as "returns," and all of the disadvantages of that alternative, as perceived by the relevant actor, as "costs." The economist will frequently—but by no means always—predict that the actor being studied will tend to choose the alternative that promises the largest excess of returns over costs, which is by definition the most advantageous in terms of the actor's values.

Of course, the actor may lack the intelligence, information, or detachment needed to choose the alternative that is best in terms of his own preferences. He might be a "satisficer" rather than a maximizer, or operate according to an erroneous traditional rule, or let biases distort his perception of the facts. In such a case the economist can take comfort from the fact that the actor being studied may be in the market for a consultant! In any event, economic theory will have relevance, if not always in a positive, at least in a normative way.

Economic theory is, indeed, relevant whenever actors have determinate wants or objectives but at the same time do not have so much of the means needed to achieve these ends that all of their desires are satiated. The ends in question may be social status or political power, and the means will be anything that is in fact conducive to the attainment of the ends, whether or not these means can bring a price in the market. *This makes it clear that economic (more precisely micro-economic) theory is in a fundamental sense more nearly a theory of rational behavior than a theory of material goods.*

To be sure, economic theory in its most general form can be as vacuous or trivial as it is broad. Many situations are so difficult, or so simple, that no formal method of thinking will be of any practical help. Economics, moreover, has not got very far with the problems of uncertainty, of strategic interaction (in the game theory sense), of acquiring or getting along without information, not to mention other problems we need to understand better before we can have anything like a complete or adequate theory of rational behavior. And where economic theory is not in itself deficient, economists often are: they sometimes lack the fullness of mind, the judgment, and (above all) the imagination needed to apply economic theory to problems outside their traditional purview. In any event, the purpose here is not to glorify or belittle economics, but rather to argue that some of the basic theories of social science, including economic theory, are limited, not so mch in terms of the objects they can be used to study as in other ways.

The generality of economic theory with respect to the objects of study is illustrated not only by the politically or sociologically relevant work of men such as those named earlier, but also by other recent developments. The output of the U.S. Department of Defense is not sold for money, yet the economic approach inherent in the Planning-Programming-Budgeting System has proved most helpful there. This system has even shown great promise in departments which deal in such obscure intangibles as health and education, and which are relatively far removed from the marketplace. In international relations, too, one finds that insights of economic theory have sometimes been decidedly relevant, as the work of Kenneth Boulding and Thomas Schelling shows; yet these men have dealt with the political-military, rather than the material, wants of nations, and often ignored the market sector in their models. The nations of eastern Europe have an institutional environment vastly different from that which the classical economists knew or wanted, yet many economists there are beginning to use the same economic theory we know in the West, and sometimes find it helpful in suggesting ways in which their *existing* Marxist-inspired institutions might be made to work more efficiently. (Indeed, economic theory has escaped the original ideological limitations on its generality to such an extent that I have read some interesting work by economists who, as I later learned, were avowed Communists, but whose work had led me to assume they were typical

Western intellectuals, if not *laissez-faire* enthusiasts.) Finally, the developing areas of the world, different and diverse as their cultures and conditions may be, have nonetheless proved to be about as amenable to ordinary economic analysis as the Western democracies.

IV

The fact that economic theory has no unique application to material goods, but deals with any objectives that people value in conditions of scarcity, cannot be adequately documented in any brief discussion. But it may nonetheless be useful to mention one basic idea that has an important, if in many respects trivially simple, application to political science. This is the notion of "Pareto-optimality," which is defined as a situation such that no individual in the group at issue can be made better off without someone else being made worse off. This idea is normally used to describe resource allocations that are efficient and ideal in the sense that they satisfy individual wants to the maximum possible degree, given the available resources, the state of technology, and the distribution of income. If someone could get more without anyone having less, that would mean a way had been found to get more utility from the available resources. Pareto-optimality means a little more than that aggregate income is a maximum, for the income or value of the goods and services produced depends on relative prices, which in turn depend on the income distribution in the group.

The generalization to politics comes from the fact that when we say a Pareto-optimal situation is one in which no one can be made better off without someone else being made worse off, we are not defining "better off" or "worse off" in terms of material goods alone. Indeed, if we consider only these so-called "economic" wants of the individuals concerned, *the whole analysis could be invalid*, for the only relevant measure of value in this context is that of the individuals concerned; if someone values a given degree of social status or political power more highly at the margin than some material good, he will be "worse off" if he has to give up that degree of social status or political power in exchange for the material good. An attempt to "sub-optimize" by considering only material objectives could be meaningless, for a step that seemed efficient because it increased the output of material goods might in fact be inefficient because the social or political goods that had to be sacrificed were worth more than the material goods gained. There is thus no way of defining a situation as Pareto-optimal without taking all of the things people value into account.

When "better off" and "worse off" are understood as they must be, it becomes clear that Pareto-optimality is a condition of political equilibrium in democratic societies. (I use the word "equilibrium," which I realize is the object of much controversy in political science, with the same meaning it has in economics.) If there is some step or combination of steps that will make one or more individuals better off, without making anyone worse off, there is always the possibility some political or administrative entrepreneur will respond to the incentive inherent in the situation and organize a change in policy. This is, to be sure, only one of a vast variety of necessary conditions of political equilibrium, and perhaps a rather weak one. But can we conceive of a complete theory of political change, or of the politics of consensus, that would leave it out? It is surely time for someone to think through the rich relationship between Pareto-optimality and political equilibrium and to study it empirically.

Some of the other political insights that can be got from the notion of Pareto-optimality have, however, been explored. The Swedish economist, Knut Wicksell, pointed out more than a half-century ago that optimal measures should be able to command something approaching unanimous support, since by definition there will be some possible distribution of the benefits and costs such that everyone would have an incentive to favor such measures. (This would not be the case under a complete unanimity rule, where an individual might withhold his then indispensable vote in an attempt to extort a large share of the total gains from the measure.) More recently, Professors James Buchanan and Gordon Tullock have, in their important book *The Calculus of Consent*, argued that reasoning of this sort shows that the majority rule principle is in certain respects arbitrary and unsatisfactory, and that the bicameralism, two-thirds rules, and general checks and balances of the American system have unsuspected virtues. A preoccupation with Pareto-optimality can, of course, sometimes support a classical-liberal opposition to the coercive redistribution of income. Redistribution, however desirable, cannot be expected to obtain unanimous support.

But there is nothing inherently conservative in the political use of Pareto-optimality. I have, for example, argued elsewhere that there may sometimes be a tendency toward what has been called public squalor in the midst of private affluence, since many Pareto-optimal measures for local areas may not be able to get majority support in the national government. Though the gains from a Pareto-optimal measure are by definition greater than the costs, the number of gainers will be smaller than the number of losers, when the benefits are local and the taxes are national. Fortunately, log-rolling may make it possible for a number of Pareto-optimal measures to pass as a package. (Log-rolling thus does not necessarily deserve its evil popular reputation.) But log-rolling requires complex and costly bargains and accordingly often will not occur.

V

What I have tried to argue as true of economic theory is just as true of sociological thought. The perspective of the sociologist has important implications for both economics and political science.

In attempting to illustrate this argument about sociological theory, I am handicapped in three ways: First, as an economist, I do not know the sociological literature as well as I would like to. The argument must therefore be based on what at best is a random sample of that literature. But for all the shortcomings of my knowledge of sociological thought, the major generalizations I will make about this literature will still almost certainly be correct; my sample could hardly be so untypical as to make me wrong about some of the great themes of this major intellectual tradition.

My second handicap stems from the fact that sociological thought is more pluralistic than economic thought: it is not a single, well-defined, almost monolithic entity like economic theory, but rather a collection of diverse and often independent theories. When I refer to "sociological theory," I will be speaking not of sociological thought as a whole, but of one particular sociological theory. That is the one associated with the tradition in which Professor Talcott Parsons has been the dominant contemporary figure. This is unfair to the *many* sociologists who use entirely different conceptions. It will also be unfair to Professor Parsons, whose views should properly be distinguished from the views of those who share only some of this thought.

The third handicap results from the particular nature of Parsonian theory. This theory is not, like economic theory, a logically elaborate yet unified hypothetico-deductive system susceptible to succinct, or even mathematical, description. Indeed, it is not theory in the sense in which that word is used in some other disciplines. It is rather an uncommonly rich and varied style of thought, replete with special insights, distinctions, and definitions, which makes *any* short summary insufficient and unfair. There is no alternative here, then, to a *Reader's Digest* level of over-simplification, and this will naturally prove offensive to the connoisseur of Parsonian sociological literature.

Even the most casual glance at sociological theory of the Parsonian type reveals that it is very general and that it includes the traditional domains of economics and political science, and parts of the fields of psychology and anthropology as well. Parsons explicitly makes both economic theory and political science a special case of his General Theory of Action. This unusual emphasis on generality has been criticized, but I do not think the criticism is justified. Right or wrong, Parsonian theories are general, and have to be.

The necessity of this generality stems largely from the basic role this theory (like many other sociological theories) gives to the process of socialization. The central preconception of this type of theory is that people do what they are brought up to do. It holds in effect that the hand that rocks the cradle does indeed rule the world. Even when particular individuals fail to be true to the values and norms they were taught, they are still subject to the sentiments society passes on from generation to generation, since societies tend to set up mechanisms of social control, ranging from informal social pressure to the sanctions of the legal system which enforce the patterns of behavior that they were brought up to believe were right.

The theory at issue holds that through socialization people acquire not only general attitudes relating to society as a whole or its major groupings, but also conceptions of particular "roles," such as husband, wife, business-man, priest, doctor, and soldier. The person who is born in a particular society is educated to expect that people with particular roles will act in certain ways—that mothers will care for their children, that doctors will care for the sick, and that businessmen will seek profits. In a well-developed and stable society, there is "institutional integration", i.e. laws, organiza-tions, and popular attitudes (as well as other mechanisms to insure con-formity) which are extensive, elaborate, and in harmony with one another. Mutual role expectations tend to be consistent. This reduces the amount of stress and alienation and strengthens the tendency to follow the pattern of behavior inculcated by the processes of socialization. There is a pro-nounced tendency in this tradition to regard extensive and consistent institutionalization as desirable for the health and stability of society, partly on the grounds that it minimizes alienation.

The Parsonian sociologist's emphasis on socialization by common beliefs and conceptions of roles through families, religions, schools, and other institutions inevitably forces him to encompass many "economic," "political," and "psychological" aspects of reality. For the same processes and institutions that give an individual his social values also inculcate attitudes about economic and political life, and influence his whole personality. The same family that teaches a child social usage passes on occupational aspirations and political ideologies. The churches, schools, media of information, and other agencies of socialization are similarly comprehensive. And often the values, ideologies, and religions passed on are themselves so general that they influence diverse aspects of life. It is thus not surprising that probably the most famous work in the sociological tradition at issue—or rather, one of the sources of that tradition—is Max Weber's *The Protestant Ethic and the Spirit of Capitalism*. Though much subsequent research has tended to discredit Weber's substantive hypothesis his heroic attempt to explain the singularity of the early modern European economy in terms of the Calvinistic religious ideas which many Europeans were taught, remains a magnificent example of the style of sociology I have described, and of the fact that the sociological perspective is inevitably relevant to economic behavior.

VI

It is now possible to see the closest thing there is to a basis for a distinction between sociology and economics in terms of the object studied. It we define sociology as the discipline that studies the formation and transmission of wants or beliefs of all kinds, and economics as the discipline that studies the ways in which people strive to obtain whatever it is that they want, we would be much closer to the truth than those who think of sociology as the study of life in groups, and economics as the study of material gain in the marketplace.

Still, it won't quite do to say that economists specialize in the study of satisfying wants and sociologists in the ways they were formed. There are a number of reasons for this. One is that they tend to use different methods, the economists relying on a nontrivially deductive theory, emphasizing quantification, and using simultaneous-equation techniques, the Parsonian sociologist using a less deductive method, relying occasionally on the case study, and often bringing a fuller knowledge of the history and context of a problem to bear. There are also differences of preconception, with some economists almost assuming that rationality is universal in the human animal, while some sociologists almost treat rationality as a cultural peculiarity of those with the Protestant, capitalistic ethic.

The economist and sociologist also often differ in the substantive conclusions they draw about the same problems. For example, when economists are asked to explain the choices about work and savings made by those who receive public assistance, they will often deplore the traditional 100 per cent tax on any wages or savings beyond a trivial minimum, and argue that recipients of welfare checks be allowed to work without sacrificing their claim to virtually all assistance. Some sociologists and social workers, on the other hand, seem to assume that the habits and attitudes people form are more or less independent of the incentives they face, and that larger amounts of public assistance to those not working would best provide the basis for the development of middle-class values. Another difference of conclusion typical of the two diciplines is that some Parsonian sociologists explain the choices a society makes in terms of what it needs (the "functions" that need to be performed) or in terms of what its people want. The economist, on the other hand, will not consider the statement that something exists because it has a function in a society a meaningful explanation, but will emphasize that the relation between wants and social outcomes may be complex and even paradoxical (so that, for example, when everyone wants and tries to save more, they may all end up saving less).

VII

The differences in method, preconception, and conclusion that distinguish Parsonian sociology and modern economics are perhaps best illustrated by considering the question of what holds societies and nations together or allows them to collapse. The stability of a society is perhaps as central as any concern in sociology, and has an inescapable importance in political science as well. This problem is important in its own right, and draws added interest from the recent urban riots and student demonstrations. It is obviously also relevant to any attempt at a social report, for one guide to the health of a society is its degree of unity and the probability that it will hold together.

This is not the place (and I am not the writer) to go into the manifold sociological controversies about the determinants of the stability of societies. But many sociologists of the tradition considered here have built their explanations of the coherence of societies around the existence of common processes of socialization. They contend that it is mainly the similarity of values, norms, collective attitudes, and role expectations that holds a society together. If people are brought up to want and believe in the same things, they won't need to fight each other. There must in any event be consensus about the most important things that will keep any divergencies and conflicts within tolerable bounds. Differences in culture, religion, family patterns, or educational systems so great that they inculcate basically different patterns of beliefs and wants, are then held to be inimical to the stability of a society.

Economists do not often explicitly consider the question of what holds a whole society together, but they do consider some of the factors that favor the survival of an economic union. And this is enough to reveal that Parsonian sociologists and orthodox economists operate with preconceptions and methods so different that they lead to drastically opposed conclusions about the determinants of a society's coherence and unity. The economist who is asked whether a group of nations should form a common market will usually argue that the more diverse the cultures and natural resources of these countries are, the greater the advantage of a common market, other things equal. The more diverse the resources, technologies, and tastes of the nations, the greater the gains from trade among them. Expecting nations that are practically identical to gain vast amounts from a common market, is about as realistic as expecting to maximize motherhood by bringing women together. A rough index of the gains from trade would be the differences in the relative prices of different tradeable goods in the different countries in the absence of trade. In general, the larger these differences in relative prices, the greater the gains from selling what has been relatively cheap in one country in return for something that would be expensive if produced at home, but which is not expensive in the country with a comparative advantage in producing it. Many economists would assume that the greater the gains from trade, and therefore the incentive to trade, the greater the interest in preserving the common market or other institutions that allow the mutually advantageous trade to take place.

If the logic of this argument about economic unions is generalized and applied to states and societies, it provides a perspective different from that of most Parsonian sociology or political science (though not altogether different from that of Durkheim's concept of "organic solidarity"). To see the general applicability of the economic approach, imagine a society where everyone thought that all vacations should be in August and at the beach. That society would tend to suffer congestion and conflict at its beach resorts in August, and a lack of essential services at home for those who couldn't squeeze in. (This is not an altogether unrealistic example: the French have been concerned about the need for policies to reduce the number of August vacations.) If, on the other hand, some of the people in the society have been brought up to prefer a skiing vacation, or a summer cabin in the mountains, there will be less to fight about, and everyone can get what he wants for less. To take another example, suppose a common culture and a common process of socialization mean that in a given culture everyone is brought up to strive to be a leader. Life in such a society will be a constant struggle for power and the society may therefore collapse. But if some of the people in the society should prefer to follow, there would be mutually advantageous relationships between leaders and followers which they would wish to preserve, along with the society that made these advantageous relationships possible. The use of the economist's method and preconceptions therefore seems to suggest that the more diverse the backgrounds and beliefs of a people, the greater the incentive they will have to continue their association.

It is in cases such as these, where different disciplinary methods and preconceptions lead to apparently opposing conclusions, that the lack of serious, detailed communication between economics and the other social sciences is most tragic. A lack of mutual intellectual esteem is often evident in the references some economists and sociologists make to each other's discipline, but this is no substitute for extended confrontations based on continuing research. Disciplinary specialization, though obviously beneficial on balance, is partly responsible. As I see it, there is today some effective censorship of extended interdisciplinary confrontations, not because of any desire to still debate, but because disciplinary parochialism prevents the use of the methods of one social science for the substantive problems supposedly in the province of another. The absence of constructive communication between economics and sociology is suggested by the ease with which new insights are gained when particular positions of the two disciplines are compared. This can be illustrated with the problem of social cohesion just considered.

In order to do this we will first have to draw a distinction between collective and noncollective (or, as they are more'often, but less precisely called, public and private) goods. Leaving some definitional niceties aside,[2] a collective good can be described as a good such that nonpurchasers cannot feasibly be excluded from its consumption. Defense is the classic example of such a good, since it is not practically possible to exclude anyone living in a country from the benefits (or dangers) of a nation's defense system. To a great degree, the benefits provided by the police and the system of justice are also collective goods. A constitutional monarch is a particularly neat example of a collective good; the benefits of his reign reach all of his subjects, from those who are more royalist than the king to those who are republicans. Noncollective or private goods are by contrast goods such that nonpurchasers can be kept from consuming them. Thus, if an individual buys bread, or a car, others can be and usually are excluded from the consumption of what he has bought. There is, in other words, no joint or communal consumption of a noncollective good.

Now that the distinction between collective and noncollective goods has been drawn, the opposition between the economic and sociological views can be resolved, and the outlines of an argument developed that is apparently better than either. The conclusion of that argument is that *a society will, other things being equal, be more likely to cohere if people are socialized to have diverse wants with respect to private goods and similar wants with respect to collective goods.* A "good" in this language is not of course necessarily a material good, but anything that people value. So what has been said means simply that, where individuals have objectives that they can consume or enjoy without others having to participate in this consumption, they will tend to cohere better if they have different tastes and productive capabilities, because this will maximize the gains from exchanges among them. On the other hand, where individuals have objectives such that if they are achieved for some, they are automatically also achieved for others, the greater the similarity in their tastes and situations the easier it will be for them to agree on a common policy. Thus, in a marriage it is helpful for one spouse to like fat and the other lean, but a danger if they want different numbers of children or different types of houses. Any gains from a comprehensive Middle Eastern common market would be increased by the fact that the Israelis and Arabs have different cultures and skills, but a common regional government with a single established religion would (to put it mildly) not be increased by the fact that the peoples of the Middle East have experienced different processes of socialization.

To be sure, many Parsonian sociologists seem to have sensed (as Durkheim[3] did long ago) that some differences in wants and value systems could somehow enhance unity, and almost every economist must have realized (if he had ever considered this question) that in certain areas divergencies of wants could disrupt a society. A point as obvious and important as this could hardly be altogether novel. Still, most discussions of the question of social cohesion are thoroughly misleading, if not largely wrong, because they do not either make the distinction between collective and noncollective goods or compare the perspectives of economics and sociology.

VIII

The divergences in methodology, presupposition, and conclusion that differentiate modern economics and Parsonian sociology can also be illustrated by contrasting their "ideal" states of society. The contrasting conceptions of the "ideal society" held by each of these intellectual traditions have considerable practical importance, for they help to determine what advice scholars of different disciplinary backgrounds offer to policy makers. They also influence a great deal of work in political science. They are, finally, absolutely fundamental to any possible Social Report, for they provide alternative standards by which to gauge a nation's advance or decline.

My use of the words "ideal society" may, however, create some misunderstandings. Neither economists nor Parsonian sociologists are normally utopians; they do not necessarily believe that their "ideal societies" can be achieved. The purposes these ideal conceptions serve are entirely different from those of, say, the utopian socialists, or of Plato's vision of an ideally just state run by a philosopher-king. They serve, not usually as visions of what we can and should obtain, but rather as intellectual models that can clarify and help to indicate whether a given policy leads in a desirable or undesirable direction. Some misunderstanding may also be caused by the fact that, while the economist's conception of the "ideal society" is at times almost explicit, the particular sociological conception I have in mind receives only tacit recognition. But this difference in the degree of explicitness of the ideal conception does not mean that the one ideal is necessarily more influential or important than the other; we must therefore strip these two ideal conceptions of their very different clothing and then set them out in a way that will facilitate explicit comparison.

One part of the economic ideal has already been set out in the literature of welfare economics, which describes the necessary conditions for an "efficient" and "optimal" allocation of resources, so there is no need for a rigorous statement of it here. Roughly speaking, a society with given resources and state of technology can be described as efficient if it is at the frontier of every production possibility function, which means that no more of any good can be obtained without giving up some amount of some other good (including leisure and future consumption as goods, to subsume the possibility that more resources would be devoted to production). Efficiency says nothing about whether the goods that are produced are those that would provide the most satisfaction, so it is not a sufficient condition for optimality. A necessary condition for an optimal allocation of resources is that no reallocation could be made which would make anyone better off without making someone else worse off. The standard of optimality is then the concept of Pareto-optimality mentioned earlier and this is not achieved unless the society is also efficient. The society will not, of course, be economically ideal unless the distribution of income is right; yet the "just" distribution of income cannot be scientifically determined. The constructs of welfare economics nonetheless can claim general interest, for they describe necessary conditions that would have to prevail if an economy were to be optimal, whatever the ideal distribution of income might be. The necessary conditions for Pareto-optimality in a society are stated principally in terms of a series of marginal conditions. These marginal conditions, and the many shortcomings in this sort of analysis, will not be discussed here, since this paragraph is meant to be only impressionistic, and because the welfare economics texts that set out this analysis more carefully are easily accessible.[4]

Welfare economics is static in that it leaves innovation and the advance of technology out of account. Economists have done a great deal of work lately on innovation and the economics of education and research, but this has not usually been explicitly tied in with welfare economics. In the rough and ready fashion in which we are operating at the moment, this can perhaps be done. In essence, the economically ideal society would maintain a Pareto-optimal allocation of resources at every moment in time *and* at the same time continually change to the best attainable production functions as knowledge advances. The rate of accumulation of productive knowledge and other forms of capital would be the maximum consistent with the society's rate of discount of future versus present consumption. This statement, alas, brushes over a number of profound complexities, such as the possible Schumpeterian conflict between short-run allocative efficiency and long-run innovation, and many unsettled issues involving what economists call "golden rules" or "optimal growth" theory.

But it is to be hoped that the subsequent discussion will reveal that these complications are not so important for the particular purpose of the moment. That purpose is to suggest that most economists have some fairly clear but incomplete models from welfare economics, and some vaguer notions about the importance of rapid innovation, which can be taken together to represent something in the nature of a vision of an economically ideal or optimal society. This vision derives from the elemental goal of maximum income, which demands an optimal allocation of resources at each moment in time plus a dynamic technology. This vision is an ideal in the sense that (vexing problems of "second best" solutions notwithstanding) it serves as a standard which economists use to help them judge practical policies.

The school of sociology considered here does not contain any models of "optimality" that parallel the constructs of welfare economics. But there is probably implicit in it a vision of something like an ideal society, which ideal would serve heuristic purposes and influence judgments about public policy. This implicit ideal might be more easily evident in the literature on "mass movements" than in Professor Parsons's own writings, but to some degree it exists in his works. The sort of sociological ideal at issue is, moreover, far too complex and comprehensive to be susceptible to brief summary. It is the result not only of extensive theoretical writing, but also of subtle insights emerging from many lifetimes of empirical research.

But perhaps the most basic dimension in that ideal can be mentioned, if not here precisely defined. That dimension is "alienation." However much they differ in other respects, a whole family of sociological studies unite in treating alienation, or some related psychological estrangement, as the principal sociological pathology. To say that the minimization of alienation plays a role in many sociological studies not unlike the maximization of satisfaction (or utility) in economics is to enunciate a half-truth— a statement that makes those who believe in the other half angry. Yet it is a half-truth that, because it refers to a part of the truth that has been neglected, should now be emphasized.

Though the minimization of alienation (in the broad sense in which that word is used here) is the most fundamental variable in this particular sociological ideal, it is perhaps not the most important, or at any event the most often discussed in the theoretical literature. The degree of "integration" of a society is probably even more central and ideally should be maximized. The degree of integration, or "institutional integration," as it is more carefully called, is important not only because it affects the amount of alienation, but also because it affects the chances that the society will cohere. This is because alienation affects the chances for stability and probably for other reasons as well.

The degree of integration tends to increase with the extent to which a set of individuals forms a "community," and would be nil in a situation in which a set of individuals had no social structure, common values, or institutions. It would be high in a situation in which everyone in a society was tied into the social order by bonds to a wide variety of associations, in which social structure was elaborate, in which common values, norms, and institutions were cherished, where individual roles were well understood, and where mechanisms of social control were well developed. The number and degree of group associations and affiliations, and the degree to which behavior is institutionalized, or organized, structured, and regularized, tend to be at a very high, if not indeed at a maximum level, in this ideal society. It is not only the extent of group association and institutionalization that is emphasized, but also its mutual consistency and stability. If the demands or values of different groups or associations with overlapping memberships or objectives are incompatible and different people have conflicting expectations about what people with particular roles should do, then the degree of integration is limited and the possibility of societal disintegration increased.

It may be possible to give an impression of this ideal with some examples. Many of the sociologists whom Parsons has influenced give a great deal of emphasis to "voluntary" association and other "intermediate" groups (organizations smaller than the state). This is especially true of the literature on the causes of what sociologists call "mass movements," and Professor Parsons has aptly said this literature constitutes a "new pluralism." There are many relevant types of intermediate groups, but the professional association, the labor union, and the organized pressure group are the leading examples. The professional association is perhaps most important of all. Some of these who share the Parsonian perspective think all types of economic life should be organized the way professions like medicine are organized, with a powerful guild organization and a pervasive occupational ethic controlling each industry. To be sure, this idea got most of its strongest support before the Parsonian school began—it was urged by Emile Durkheim, R. H. Tawney, the guild sociologists, some syndicalists, and by some advocates of a corporate or Fascist state. But the systematic conceptions needed to justify a system of economic organization modeled on the professions was developed by Professor Parsons, and he has repeatedly emphasized the functions of professional ethics, institutions, and associations.

The labor union and the organized pressure groups have also received special attention. One of the most interesting assertions in this literature is that labor unions, and perhaps even Marxian labor unions, may reduce the chances of a revolution in a modern society, because the labor union, however radical its ideology may initially have been, will provide a source of group participation for many workers, and the sense of belonging or group involvement that results may reduce alienation and thereby the desire to overthrow the social order. There is a tendency to emphasize the sense of group identity and the feeling of participation fostered by a pressure group more than its practical impact in the political system. For the Parsonian sociologist (and for many political scientists as well) it would probably be a necessary condition for an ideal society that there be many groups of the sort we have just discussed.

There will be objections that this ideal is unsatisfactory on its own terms, quite apart from the merits of other types of ideal societies that may be imagined. Many people—probably even some of those who have contributed to the dissemination of this ideal—would say that they personally prefer unstructured and mainly unorganized, if not disorganized, societies. Many of us love ill-defined roles and feel confined by extensive associational networks. A new generation of sociologists, mindful of Marx, emphasizes the inevitability, or even desirability, of social conflict, and thus has only contempt for the Parsonian prediction of consensus. Many people who look at the literature on group participation would agree that more attention ought to be given to the *impact* or share of power organizational membership can bring, and less to the fact of belonging *per se*. But the disadvantages of the sociological ideal described, and the impressionism and injustice of this brief and selective description of it, are not so important for the special purpose of the moment, which is to show how economic theory and a prevalent type of sociological theory can lead to conflicting conclusions.

IX

The economic and sociological ideals described are not only different, but polar opposites: if either one were attained, the society would be a nightmare in terms of the other. There are no doubt many social arrangements so inept that society is inside what the economist would call the production possibility frontier; that is, in a situation where it could get closer to either the economic or the sociological ideal without getting farther from the other. An example of this would be a society with total anarchy, in which a step taken to promote integration, such as the establishment of a government that created law and order, would bring both the economic and the sociological ideals nearer. But those positions that are "dominated," or inferior by both standards, are not very interesting. The important question is how much of the one ideal to give up in order to get more of the other when you can't get more of both. This is an important matter, for in terms of the values of most people I know (whatever their disciplinary backgrounds), there is profound merit in both ideals. The economic and sociological ideals, far from being destroyed by contradicting one another, are in fact expressions of the most fundamental alternatives human societies face. The fact that most of us want to choose compromise positions between these polar ideals does not negate their value as intellectual constructs that can give us a clearer understanding of the implications of a marginal move in one direction or another.

The fundamental character of the conflict between these two ideals may not however be immediately evident, so we must first show how one ideal prevents the achievement of the other. The economic ideal required that there be an optimal allocation of resources at any moment in time and rapid innovation over time. An optimal allocation of resources requires that a series of marginal conditions be satisfied throughout the society; the marginal rates of substitution of any two factors of production must be proportional to the ratio of their prices and the same in all employments, and so on. But if there is rapid growth, the demands for different goods, the methods of production, the location of production, and the marginal products of particular factors of production will change incessantly. A Pareto-optimal allocation of resources will therefore require *constant reallocations of resources*. This will mean that factors of production, including labor, must frequently move from firm to firm, industry to industry, and place to place.[5] Since methods of production are rapidly changing, the same *combinations* of labor and other resources won't be needed very long: new *groupings* of workers are needed as the economy changes. This means that individual mobility is normally required and this in turn means that the rewards of the incentive system must be offered on an individual basis. Rapid change and growth in an economy mean great gains in one area and vast losses in another, for incentives are needed to induce the needed mobility of labor and capital, and the changing pattern of incentives means many *nouveaux riches* and *nouveaux pauvres*. Both social and geographical mobility are at an extreme level in the economically "ideal" society, and there can be few if any stable group relationships, apart from those in a nuclear family in which *only one* member is in the labor force. There can be no group loyalties or organizational constraints that limit individual mobility in response to changing incentives. There can be no organizations or other mechanisms that give those whose legitimate expectations are frustrated by the pattern of change the power to defend their interests, for this will (except where normally infeasible "lump sum" transfers can be arranged) pervert the pattern of incentives needed to bring about the necessary resource reallocations. No group with a role in the productive process can restrict mobility by regulating entry, giving privilege for seniority, or featherbedding.

I have discussed some aspects of the relationship between rapid economic growth and social and political stability in more detail elsewhere,[6] so there should be no need to spell out the argument here. It should in any event already be apparent that the society enjoying the benefits of the economic ideal will, because of the magnitude of social and geographic mobility and the dearth of stable group relationships, be the very one in which individuals are constantly uprooted and in which alienation is probably at a maximum. The rapid change will also work against stable institutions and ethical norms. Moreover, the plurality of intermediate organizations, such as professional associations, labor unions, cartels, and lobbying organizations, which the sociological ideal cherishes, cannot be allowed; for such organizations, by defending the *group* interests of their clients through the political system, by limiting entry or exit, or by preventing the adoption of new methods of production, would prevent the maximum growth which the economically ideal system will by definition achieve.

It should similarly be obvious that, when the particular sociological ideal at issue has been achieved, the society will tend to become economically stagnant. The guild-like institutional integration and regulation inherent in the sociological ideal tends to prevent change and growth (just as the medieval guilds did). The "professionalization" of economic life that Durkheim and Tawney wanted would be one of the surest ways to prevent economic growth. The familiar argument that the Parsonian sociological tradition has a conservative bias turns out to be a heroic understatement when the economic aspect is considered, for the minimization of stress, alienation, and the elaboration and integration of institutions that it involves will tend to prevent economic even more than political change, and opposition even to economic change is indeed conservative. But this ideal must nonetheless not be belittled—its importance is evident whenever we examine the implications of its opposite.

At the most general level, what has been said is that *the typical individual's need for some degree of stability in group relationships, and therefore also some institutional stability, can in a wide range of situations work against the maximum attainment of other individual objectives.* To put it another way, the continuous reallocations and rearrangements needed to satisfy all of our other individual wants (be they material or not) to the maximum, are not usually consistent with the stable or enduring interpersonal relationships that most people apparently value and need. The ideal situation, interpersonal relationships aside, has been set forth, in part explicitly, by economists. A set of ideal arrangements for group interaction has been described, albeit implicitly, by sociologists. There are many ambiguities and shortcomings in both of these ideals, and even greater failings in my hurried vulgarizations of them, but it surely cannot be denied that it is often important to keep something like both of these polar cases in mind.[7]

These polar cases are not, however, always kept in mind in scholarly discussions, for each of them is monopolized by a different discipline. This has greatly hindered intellectual advance in the study of such topics as the labor union or foreign aid. It has also made it more difficult to develop methods for helping the country answer questions such as "What is the socially optimal rate of migration of Negroes from the rural South to the urban North?" It also presents a special challenge for social reporting, since a Social Report which keeps only one or the other of these ideals in mind could mislead a nation about some of its profound problems. The choice of a position along the continuum between the economic and the sociological ideals must, of course, be made by the political system. But scholars fail to do their duty if they do not help a society understand the implications of alternative choices.

X

All of these arguments bring us back to the original thesis: it is futile and harmful to attempt to determine the division of labor between social science disciplines in terms of the objects they are supposed to consider. Reality cannot be divided into departments the way universities are, and no logically defensible division of subject matters is possible. The various disciplines are, however, distinguished by their prejudices and their methods. Economics, sociology, and political science must therefore be whatever economists, sociologists, or political scientists do, or rather what they do best. But that can't be definitely determined before each discipline has tried to solve whatever problem is at issue. Therefore we should hope for a great deal of disciplinary overlap so that every problem that might benefit will, if the available resources permit, get the attention of scholars with different attitudes and methodologies.

If the spheres of the separate social sciences cannot properly be defined in terms of the nature of the reality studied, we can also conclude that a government should not in general seek advice about one segment of reality from only one discipline, and advice about some other segment of reality only from another discipline. We should not be surprised that the economic approach embodied in the Planning-Programming-Budgeting System can improve social programs. We should not be surprised when sociologists, psychologists, and political scientists contribute to the study of poverty, or business organization, or labor unions.

Above all, we should conceive of social reporting in multidisciplinary terms: all of the social science disciplines must be exploited (as they were in *Toward A Social Report*) if this innovation is to achieve its full potential. The division of emphasis between economic and social reports might pragmatically be determined in accordance with the Council of Economic Advisers' traditional and proper preoccupation with "macro-economic" questions—the problems of recession and inflation, or the fluctuation of the market sector as a whole. "Micro-economic" questions—those that relate to particular sectors and groups—and "social" problems have not been given much attention in the Economic Report. There is accordingly a continuing need for the systematic public assessment of these problems, which suggests that periodic multidisciplinary social reports could make a major contribution. If such reports also serve as a focus for interdisciplinary communication, they will be twice blessed.

Political science has a special role to play in this process of interdisciplinary communication. Political science not only has scholars with an approach unique to that discipline, but also includes many who share the presuppositions and theories of the sociologist, and still others who share the prejudices and tools of the economist. All that I have said about economics and sociology could have been said of particular scholars and works in political science. Political science may also be the discipline that comes closest to having men who are intimately familiar with the habits of thought and skills of both economics and sociology. And if for a moment we can identify government as the object of interest of political science (though ultimately we cannot, for there is "politics" in the corporation, the university, and the family as well), we can say that the customary object of interest for political science is one which, perhaps above all, demands an economic and a sociological and a political approach (not to mention anthropology, history, or psychology). The government allocates vast amounts of resources in pursuit of determinate ends. At the same time it expresses the culture and reflects the patterns of socialization of a people. And, most immediately, it is a complex political institution. I therefore hope and expect that political science will see important syntheses of diverse disciplinary approaches in the coming decades.

Notes

1. U.S. Department of Health, Education, and Welfare, *Toward A Social Report*. Washington, D.C.: Government Printing Office, 1969. See also the articles by Daniel Bell and myself on the history, plan, and purpose of this document in *The Public Interest*, No. 15 (Spring, 1969).

2. These definitional problems are dealt with more carefully in my book on *The Logic of Collective Action: Public Goods and the Theory of Groups*, Cambridge: Harvard University Press, 1965, and in Olson and Zeckhauser, "An Economic Theory of Alliances," *Review of Economics and Statistics* (August 1966).

3. Emile Durkheim distinguished "organic solidarity" resulting from the division of labor, and "mechanical solidarity" due to similar sentiments. Durkheim drew this distinction in the last century, but did not, of course, know the distinction between collective and noncollective goods, so his analysis on this point is accordingly wrong in many respects. Nonetheless, it is far superior to most modern treatments of the subject. Significantly, Parsons has repeatedly belittled Durkheim's notion of organic solidarity, subordinated it to an elaborated conception of mechanical solidarity, and failed to develop anything like the needed distinction between collective and noncollective

goods. See Parsons's fascinating but flawed article on "Durkheim's Contribution to the Theory of Integration of Social Systems" in Kurt H. Wolff, Ed., *Essays in Sociology and Philosophy*, New York: Harper Torchbooks, 1964, pp. 118–153, especially where he distinguishes values, differentiated norms, collective attitudes, and roles. See also his *Structure of Social Action*, 2d ed. New York: Free Press, 1949, pp. 301–342, and Emile Durkheim, *The Division of Labor in Society*, trans. George Simpson. Glencoe, Ill.: The Free Press, 1947.

4. See, for example, J. de V. Graaff, *Theoretical Welfare Economics*. Cambridge: Cambridge University Press, 1957; I. M. D. Little, *A Critique of Welfare Economics*. Oxford: Clarendon Press, 1950; Paul A. Samuelson, *Foundations of Economic Analysis*. Cambridge: Harvard University Press, 1958, Ch. 8, pp. 203–253.

5. It is logically possible that reallocations of resources could be ubiquitous, but that the rate of reallocation might still be so slow that social costs were small. Only those with a wanderlust, or the young adults who are leaving their parents' homes anyway, would then have to move. Rates of economic growth that are rapid by modern standards could, however, require much faster reallocations than could be handled in this way if the marginal conditions necessary for complete economic efficiency are to be satisfied at all times.

6. "Rapid Growth as a Destabilizing Force," *Journal of Economic History*, XXIII (Dec. 1963), pp. 529–552.

7. It might be supposed that even the desire for stable interpersonal relationships can be subsumed under the economic mode of analysis, thereby allowing a clear delineation of a single, comprehensive ideal. The society must trade off stable group relationships with the other things it wants, and accordingly needs some conception of an "ideal compromise." Unfortunately, the economist's tools of thought are not well adapted to dealing with situations in which different individuals' wants are highly interdependent (as they are when they cherish given group relationships) and economists have not usually studied this aspect of reality. Thus, in practice, there is perhaps still a need to keep both of the distinct disciplinary ideals in mind.

7

Personality and Politics:
Problems of Evidence, Inference,
and Conceptualization

FRED I. GREENSTEIN

The original title of this chapter was "Psychology and the Study of Politics." From a perspective of Olympian abstraction it is possible, if somewhat empty, to set forth the following account of the relationships between psychology and political science. Let us think not in terms of the extremely varied activities that scholars with different guild memberships actually engage in, but rather in terms of what the general purposes and preoccupations of the disciplines seem to be.

Psychology, like sociology, evidently aspires to advance general propositions about human behavior. There seem to be two axes along which these basic disciplines divide Gaul: (1) Psychology, as Inkeles puts it, deals with the personal system, sociology with the social system.[1] (2) Psychology is concerned with those determinants of behavior that arise from within individuals, sociology with the effects of the environment, especially the human environment, on individuals' behavior. By this showing, the interests of psychology and sociology are mutually exclusive and exhaustive. Political science (like economics) then proves to be a subdivision of the two basic disciplines, specializing in behavior occurring in the polity, an institution of such great substantive importance and interest that it calls forth the intensive attention of a large community of investigators. It follows that all valid propositions from psychology and sociology may prove to be relevant to political science and other institution-specific social sciences, and that, as Simon says of economics, any "verified generalizations about human" political "behavior must have a place in the more general theories of human behavior to which psychology and sociology aspire."[2]

Suppose, however, that we shift from analytical ideal types to actual disciplines. We promptly discover, of course, that there are few if any "pure" sociologists or psychologists who meet our abstract disciplinary definitional criteria, even though the criteria do suggest the centers of gravity of interests in these fields. Real-world sociologists often study individuals and intrapsychic variables (e.g. attitudes). Real-world psychologists are interested in groups and (as the ubiquity of the term "stimulus" makes clear) the environment.

The abstract conception of political science's relation to the two general disciplines also fails to withstand contact with reality. We all know of the lack of integration of political science with psychology and sociology, as well as the heterogeneity of approach within all three fields. Therefore, although from the Olympian vantage point we can see the possibility for integrating a large number of the major concerns of psychology with those of political science (learning, perception, cognition, motivation, to name a few standard problem areas of psychology; all have important manifestations in politics), at the terrestrial level the bridges between the two fields are few and difficult to build. In fact, for reasons I shall suggest below, as political science has begun to reach out to other disciplines, the connections with sociology have been much richer and more rewarding than those with psychology (whether the academic psychologies, the various clinical psychologies, or the various psychological approaches to anthropology).

For the remainder of this chapter, I shall consider ways in which the study of politics can draw upon simply one of the concerns of psychology —personality. "Personality and politics" is perhaps the area in which the greatest number of self-conscious efforts have been made to connect the two disciplines. And, interestingly, it is an area of inquiry that is notoriously vexed and controversial in its methodological and conceptual status. Although personality and politics writings have appeared with some persistence for several decades, the work in this area has not gained the confidence of the great bulk of practitioners in the parent disciplines, and has been limited in its influence.

This then is a highly selective and rather idiosyncratic traveler's report on the "personality and politics" literature, drawing on, synthesizing, and reconstructing various portions of it, on the basis of my reading of many such studies and a variety of cognate literature.[3] I shall make a number of conceptual distinctions and observations about research strategy. My purpose is to help place this controversial, methodologically gnarled literature on a firmer evidential and inferential basis.

An initial indicator of the messy state of affairs is the difficulty psychologists have had in defining the key term "personality." A standard discussion by Allport lists a full 50 *types* of definitions.[4] For the present purposes, rather than offering still another detailed stipulative definition of "personality," it will be better simply to note typical research and theorizing that falls under the "personality and politics" rubric, and then make a few general remarks about the different meanings this term has had in the literature I am discussing.

Much of the personality and politics literature can be grouped into three rough categories: psychological *case histories of single political* actors, psychological studies of *types of political actors*, and *aggregative* accounts of the collective effects of the distribution of individual political actors and types of actors on the functioning of political institutions (ranging from face-to-face groups through interaction among nations).

The case study literature includes "in-depth" studies of members of the general population by investigators such as Lane[5] and Smith, Bruner, and White.[6] It also includes psychological biographies of public figures.[7] I am using "typological" to refer to all classifications of political actors in psychological terms—ranging from the mere classification of an aggregate population in terms of the categories of some variable, through complex typologies identifying syndromes of interrelated attributes.

The best known and best developed (and possibly most controversial) of the typological literatures is that on "authoritarianism."[8] Other politically relevant categorizations are in terms of "dogmatism"(Rokeach),[9] "misanthropy" (Rosenberg),[10] "Machiavellianism" (Christie),[11] "tradition –inner–other directedness" (Riesman),[12] as well as the various psychological classifications of actual political role incumbents, such as Lasswell's agitator–administrator–theorist classification[13] and Barber's spectator–advertiser–reluctant-lawmaker.[14] Finally, aggregative accounts of personality and politics are the most vexed and controversial of all: here, for example, we find the very extensive corpus of writings on "national character" and the numerous speculations connecting intrapersonal emotional "tension" with conflict among nations.[15]

It is, as my reluctance to offer a formal definition suggests, difficult to pin down with any precision what the term "personality" means when it is used to summarize these various enterprises. And, in fact, later when we consider the various objections to personality explanations of politics, we shall see that the term has had a number of quite different referents. Very generally, it is clear that students of "personality and politics" are interested in discovering how the human "stuff" of politics affects the conduct of politics—the political consequences of what we are like and how we function as human beings, of individual similarities and differences. This suggests an interest in psychology that goes deeper than the usual rather "thin" use of psychological categories and evidence to characterize the goals of political actors and their cognitive maps. However, a large number of the issues that arise in attempting to clarify the tasks of students of personality and politics relate more generally to the use of any kind of psychological evidence in political analysis. Therefore, I shall by and large use such phrases as "personality and politics" and "political psychology" interchangeably, except at those points (for example in Section III) where there is a specific reason to make distinctions.

To a considerable extent, what makes the personality and politics literature controversial is precisely what makes it intriguing. Much of the extant work has direct or indirect roots in the still empirically problematic theories of psychoanalysis. Psychoanalytic hypotheses, especially those drawing upon the central notions of repression and ego defense, have the merit of offering nonobvious explanations of behavior that otherwise seems obscure and inexplicable, and especially of much of the "irrationality" and emotionalism that abounds in politics. The disadvantages of these explanations are suggested by the large volume of polemical and clarificatory literature on psychoanalysis that pours out.[16] Given the substantial continuing skepticism toward the basic theories and concepts of psychoanalysis, "applied" literatures taking these notions for granted are bound also to be skeptically received.

As a consequence, anyone interested in helping to organize and reconstruct the problems raised in the personality and politics literature is bound to find himself discussing problems that fall under the heading of ego defense. In suggesting methodological standards for this literature, we encounter questions about (for example) how to distinguish political behavior which has ego-defensive sources from the large quantity of political behavior (including "irrational" political behavior) that is plainly *not* ego-defensive in its sources, and how to make it possible for assertions about ego-defensiveness to be consensually validated even in the absence of general agreement on theories and vocabularies such as those of psychoanalysis.

Section I of the paper deals with the need for a systematic personality and politics literature. Section II discusses the reasons why such a literature has not developed, elaborating further on the empirical and methodological difficulties that have bedeviled existing research, and noting a series of formal objections that sometimes have been advanced, denying the usefulness *in principle* of personality and politics research. Section III summarizes a rudimentary conceptual framework providing various distinctions relevant for analyzing personality and politics. Section IV employs the framework to show that the formal objections to personality and politics study, while lacking force as general objections, prove on analysis to point to a variety of useful substantive and methodological observations about political psychology and how it may be fruitfully studied.

In Section V, I offer a very brief and selective series of procedural suggestions about psychological case studies of single actors, typological studies, and aggregative research. For the single-case observations, I take my examples from what is generally recognized to be one of the most satisfactory of the psychological biographies, Alexander and Juliette George's *Woodrow Wilson and Colonel House: A Personality Study*. For the typological discussion, I shall draw mainly on the authoritarianism literature. My remarks on aggregation will be mainly schematic and monitory.

I. The Need for Systematic Study of Political Psychology[17]

Fifty-some years ago, Walter Lippmann observed that "to talk about politics without reference to human beings . . . is just the deepest error in our political thinking."[18] That is would be unfortunate to attempt political explanation without attention to the personal psychology of political actors seems on the face of it an unassailable, even a platitudinous, assertion. Such an assertion seems to hold no matter which of the two standard approaches to defining politics we use. We can treat as "political" all of the activities that go on within the formal structures of government, plus the informal, extragovernmental activities impinging upon government, such as political parties, interest groups, political socialization, and political communication. Or we can, in Lasswell's term, define politics "functionally"[19] to refer to some distinctive pattern of behavior that may manifest itself in any of the conventionally designated institutional settings (ranging from families and other face-to-face groups to international interaction). This pattern of behavior might, for example, be the exercise of power and influence, or it might be the processes of negotiation, accommodation, and bargaining that accompany conflict resolution, or it might be "the authoritative allocation of values."

"Politics," by both of these definitional tacks, is a matter of human behavior, and behavior—in the familiar formulation of Lewin and others —is a function of both the environmental situations in which actors find themselves and the personal psychological predispositions they bring to those situations. As Lazarus puts it:

> The sources of man's behavior (his observable action) and his subjective experience (such as thoughts, feelings, and wishes) are twofold: the external stimuli that impinge on him and the internal dispositions that result from the interaction between inherited physiological characteristics and experience with the world. When we focus on the former, we note that a person acts in such-and-such a way because of certain qualities in a situation. For example, he attacks a friend because the friend insulted him, or he loses interest in a lecture because the teacher is dull or un-informed, or he fails in his program of study because the necessity of supporting himself through school leaves insufficient time for studying. It is evident that a man's behavior varies greatly from moment to moment, from circumstance to circumstance, changing with the changing conditions to which he is exposed.
>
> Still, even as we recognize the dependency of behavior on outside stimuli, we are also aware that it cannot be accounted for on the basis of the external situation alone, but that in fact it must arise partly from personal characteristics.[20]

It would not be difficult to proliferate examples of political events that were critically dependent upon the personal characteristics of key actors, or of actors in the aggregate. Take Republican politics in 1964. An account of the main determinants of the Republican nomination that year, and of the nature of the subsequent election campaign, would have to include much more than descriptions of the personal characteristics of the party leaders and members. But any account would be incomplete that did not acknowledge the impact of such factors as the willingness of one of the strongest contenders for the nomination to divorce his wife and marry a divorced woman; the indecision of one of the party's elder statesmen; a politically damaging outburst of temper in a news conference (two years earlier) by the man who had been the party's 1960 presidential candidate; the self-defeating political style of the man who received the 1964 nomination (his unwillingness to placate his opponents within the party, his propensity to remind voters of the issues on which he was most vulnerable). Not to mention aggregate psychological phenomena bearing, for example, on the behavior of voters in the Republican primaries of that year and the actions of delegates to the national conventions.

Attempts to explain the outcomes of adversary relationships often place in particularly clear relief the need for psychological data. For example, the overwhelming defeat in 1967 of numerically superior, better equipped Arab armies by Israel quite obviously was a function of gross discrepancies between the levels of skill and motivation of the two sides, both among leaders and subordinates. A further example, which lays out with a rather grim clarity the possible life-or-death policy relevance of reliable knowledge of the inner tendencies of political actors, is provided by the 1962 Cuban missile crisis.

Clearly each phase of the Kennedy Administration's (and the Soviet Union's) strategic decision-making during that confrontation was intimately dependent upon assumptions about the psychological dispositions of the adversary, as can be seen from an exchange of correspondence by several scholars in the *New York Times* shortly after the initial success of Kennedy's blockade in reversing the Soviet missile-bearing ships, but before the withdrawal of the additional missiles that had already been installed in Cuba.[21] One group of correspondents argued that it was of the utmost importance for the Administration not to assert its demands on the Soviet Union in aggressively uncompromising terms. The Russians, their letter suggested, must be provided with face-saving means of acceding to American demands, lest they conclude that they had no recourse but to fight. In reply, another writer (Bernard Brodie, a RAND Corporation strategic theorist) drew on the special theory of the psychology of Communist leadership developed by Nathan Leites in his controversial *A Study of Bolshevism*. For the Communist leader, Leites suggests, it is an imperative that any sign of capitalist weakness be exploited for maximum advantage. But if the Communist advance meets determined resistance by an opponent capable of inflicting serious damage, retreat is not only possible but *necessary*. And to allow oneself to be influenced by considerations of prestige and provocativeness would be the worst kind of sentimentality. Thus the second correspondent, drawing upon diametrically opposed assumptions about the psychology of Soviet leadership, contended that an uncompromising American stance would make it *easier* rather than more difficult for the Russians to give in, and would decrease rather than increase the likelihood that miscalculations would lead to war.[22]

My concern at the moment, of course, is not to offer substantive hypotheses about the psychological questions raised by the foregoing examples, but rather to point out that there is a pressing need for what we presently have very little of: systematic attention to questions that lie in the overlapping territories of psychology and political science. And the last of my examples should suggest why this need exists in the arena of politics as well as in the literatures of the social sciences.

II. Why has Political Psychology Been Slow To Develop?

An answer to why political psychology is not a well-developed field, but rather is in questionable repute, may be found partly in the sociology of inquiry and partly in its vicissitudes. A full account would draw upon the following points:

1. Systematic empirical study of politics has had a rather brief history.

2. For much of this history, political analysis has seemed to proceed in a quite acceptable fashion without making its psychological assumptions explicit. If one is studying "normal" actors in a familiar culture, it is often convenient simply to look at variations in the setting of politics, or merely to deal with the portion of the actor's psychological characteristics that relate to his social position (socio-economic status, age, and sex, for example).

3. Implicit, common-sense psychological assumptions become less satisfactory when one attempts to explain (a) actors in one's own culture whose behavior deviates from expectations, or (b) actors from a different culture. (An example of the first is Woodrow Wilson's determined unwillingness, under certain circumstances, to follow the American politician's practice of compromising with one's adversaries, as described by George and George;[23] an example of the second is the possible applicability of Leites's theory of Bolshevik leadership to the Cuban missile crisis.) But when the political scientist does sense the importance of making explicit his assumptions about psychological aspects of politics, he is put off by the state of psychology. Rather than finding *a* psychological science on which to draw for insight, he finds a congeries of more or less competing models and frames of reference, with imperfect agreement on the

nature of man's inner dispositions, the appropriate terms for characterizing them, and the methodologies for observation.

4. If the political scientist persists in his determination to make systematic use of psychology, he is likely to experience further discouragement. Much of the research and theory he encounters will seem singularly irrelevant to explaining the kind of complex behavior which interests him. And where psychological writers do address themselves to his subject matter, their political observations often seem naïve and uninformed. Psychologists' insights seem irrelevant to political scientists, for the good reason that many psychologists do not conceive of their science as one which *should* attempt to explain concrete instances of social behavior, but rather as a means of understanding general principles underlying that behavior. A deliberate attempt is made, as one psychologist puts it, to treat psychology as "socially indifferent"—to strip away the elements that are specific, say, to behavior on a congressional committee, or at a political party convention.

> When colleagues in other disciplines (mainly sociology, anthropology, political science, and economics) turn to psychology for help they are disappointed, and, indeed, often aggrieved. What they begin to read with enthusiasm they put down with depression. What seemed promising turns out to be sterile, palpably trivial, or false and, in any case, a waste of time ... Psychologists do study and must study things and activities possessing social content. There is no other way. ... It is only that psychology has been a science that abstracts out of all these content-characterized behaviors the concepts which form the jargons of its subdisciplines. ...

The writer goes on to suggest why it is that when psychologists *do* pronounce on problems of politics and society, their observations so often strike politically knowledgeable readers as dubious.

> I am impressed with how naïve and conventional my colleagues [in psychology] and I are when confronted with most social phenomena. We are ignorant of the historical dimensions of most social activity, we do not see the complex interweaving of institutions and arrangements ... In general, psychologists tend to be like laymen when they confront social phenomena, particularly those that involve large scale patterns. And the reason for all of this is that the main areas of social activity are only the *place* where psychologists study interesting sorts of things, rather than being the *focus of inquiry*.[24]

5. A final, and perhaps the most important, deterrent to a systematic political psychology has paradoxically been that a literature already existed—namely, the mare's-nest of research, theory, and controversy on "personality and politics." Objections have been raised to this literature on empirical, on methodological, and on what might be called formal grounds.

Empirically, critics have pointed to the weakness and instability of the correlations that have been reported between various measures of personality and politics, for example, in the "trait correlation" studies of the 1930's, which sought to relate personality scales to attitude scales.[25] The failure to find relationships has suggested to many observers that the relationships are not there to be found, even under more favorable observational conditions.

In the instance of single-case psychological analysis, the empirical and the methodological difficulties are inseparable. For example, it has been pointed out that psychological biographies of political figures and, in general, case histories of single individuals, often seem to be arbitrary in their interpretations, incapable of replication, and more disposed to catalogue personal pathology than to illuminate adaptation. Quantitative, typological studies based on questionnaire data have encountered formidable difficulties in developing reliable and valid measures of personality and its political correlates, an example being the problems of response-set artifact which plagued the authoritarian personality studies of the 1950's.[26] And attempts at psychological explanation of aggregate phenomena— "national character," "international tensions," the functioning of various political institutions—have been most controversial of all. The standard label for the fallacy of explaining (say) Germany in terms of the typical German is "reductionism."[27] All three types of studies have seemed insensitive to historical and social determinants of political behavior.

In addition to the various empirical and methodological objections to personality and politics studies, there have been a number of suggestions that such investigation is *in principle* not promising. These formal objections are of great interest, because on careful examination they do not seem to provide valid reasons for avoiding the study of personality and politics, yet, nevertheless, they point to important insights for investigators in this area. The objections are susceptible of being rephrased positively in ways that help clarify the tasks that can be usefully performed by students of personality (in several senses of the term) and politics. These objections are most conveniently listed in detail after introducing a rudimentary frame of reference consisting of a schematic statement of the types of variables that are likely to be relevant to personality and politics research, and the ways these variables interact. They are formal objections to the study of personality and politics based on the allegedly greater explanatory power of "social characteristics" over "personality characteristics," the relative impact of "situation" and personality, the significance of ego-defensiveness in everyday action, and the impact of individual actors on events.

III. Conceptual Distinctions Relevant to Analyzing Personality and Politics: A "Map"

Figure 1 is reproduced from M. Brewster Smith's "A Map for the Analysis of Personality and Politics."[28] For a full exposition of this formulation, the reader is referred to Smith's lucid paper. I shall emphasize the following aspects of Smith's map, which is essentially a heuristic device for reminding us of the complex interdependency of different classes of social and psychological determinants of political (and other) behavior. Smith's statement introduces little that is new, but it economically lays out a number of familiar distinctions that are of great importance, with due attention to the complexity of their contextual connections.

The figure graphically reminds us that political behavior (panel V of Figure 1) results, directly or indirectly, from the interaction of psychological variables with three classes of social variables: (1) the immediate situation (panel IV) within which the behavior occurs, (2) the immediate social environment (panel II) extending from birth through adult life, within which the actor's personality develops and his attitudes form, and (3) the "distal" social environment (panel I) which the individual does not experience directly, but which shapes his immediate environment (the distal environment includes the overarching features of the contemporary social and political system, and the historical antecedents of these features). And the map indicates the reciprocal effect of behavior on its psychological and social determinants.

Within the central psychological portion of his map (panel III), Smith outlines a conceptualization of personality expanded from his work with Bruner and White on the "functions" of opinions.[29] He makes the analytic distinction between attitudes and the ordinarily more enduring and deeply-rooted personality processes in which attitudes have their bases.

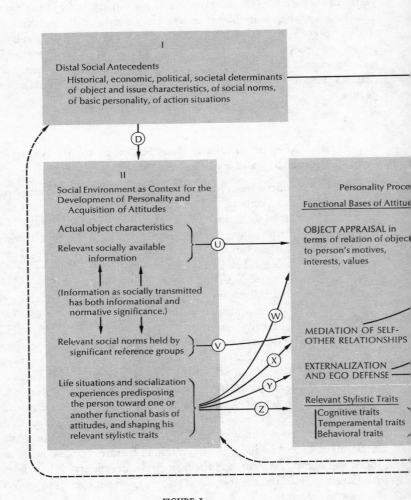

FIGURE I

Types of Variables Relevant to the Study of Personality and Politics

Source: M. Brewster Smith, "A Map for the Analysis of Personality and Politics," *Journal of Social Issues*, 24 (1968), p. 26. (*Publisher's Note*: We are grateful to Professor M. Brewster Smith and the *Journal of Social Issues* for permission to republish the map here.)

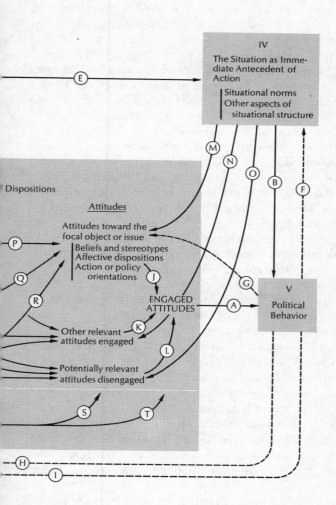

It is the interaction of attitudes and situational stimuli that one looks at first, in order to explain behavior. But to understand the conditions of attitude formation, arousal, stability, and change, one must turn to the underlying personality processes.

One fundamental personality process (or structure) which may be more or less well developed in any individual is specialized toward screening reality and assessing and adapting to the environment. To the degree that an attitude, say an importer's belief in the desirability of low tariffs, has its basis in the need to establish such means-ends relationships, it is said to serve the function of *object appraisal*.

A second fundamental personality process (again, one which varies in its importance from individual to individual) serves to cope with and respond to internal conflict, especially the deeper, anxiety-producing conflicts that have their source in the repression of unacceptable primitive desires and impulses. When an attitude[30] is influenced by the need to accommodate to inner conflicts—when it "externalizes" these internal tensions—it is said to serve the function of ego defense. The relationships between inner needs and such attitudes may run the gamut of mechanisms of defense—projections, displacement, splitting, etc.

A third set of processes that may influence political attitudes consists of the various and ubiquitous psychological tendencies toward identification with others and toward orientation of the self to reference groups and examplars. To the degree that attitudes and behavior result from needs to be like or unlike significant others in one's immediate or distant environment, the function of *mediation of self-other relations* (referred to less aptly in *Opinions and Personality* as "social adjustment") is being peformed.[31] Any single attitude or item of behavior might, in psychoanalytic jargon, be "over-determined," having its basis in more than one of these processes. But frequently it is possible to say that a particular attitude serves one or another predominant function for an individual. And if the same attitude has a different functional basis for different individuals, the same technique will not be appropriate to arouse, reinforce, or change the attitude.[32]

As partial as this summary is, it helps clarify a number of the formal objections to the study of personality and politics, some of which result from the slipperiness of the basic vocabulary for discussing these problems, and others from the complexity of the phenomena themselves—the kinds of variables that need to be observed, the difficulty of measuring them, and the intricacy of their interconnections.

IV. The Positive Implications of Certain Objections to the Study of Personality and Politics

I begin with an objection that is clarified by the sharp distinction Smith makes between personality and its social antecedents (panels III and II of Figure 1), move on to an objection that bears on the interconnections among personality processes and dispositions (panel III), situations (panel IV), and behavior (panel V); then consider an objection to which the distinctions among types of personality processes (panel III) is relevant; and conclude with two objections that prove on examination not to be addressed to psychological issues at all.

"SOCIAL CHARACTERISTICS" VERSUS "PERSONALITY CHARACTERISTICS"

One standard objection to the study of personality and politics which we can clarify by referring to Smith's map runs as follows:

> Personality characteristics of individuals are less important than their social characteristics in influencing behavior. This makes it unpromising to concentrate research energies on studying the impact of personality.[33]

This appears to be an objection posing a pseudo-problem that needs to be dissolved conceptually, rather than resolved empirically. Consider the referents of "social characteristics" and "personality characteristics." By the latter we refer to inner dispositions of the individual (panel III). The term "characteristic" indicates a state of the organism. By the former, however, we usually have in mind ways of characterizing the individual in terms of his social setting, past and present (panel II). The term "characteristics," in other words, refers in this instance not to states of the organism, but to states of its environment. (This is made particularly clear by the common usage "*objective* social characteristics.") It follows that social and personality characteristics are in no way mutually exclusive. They do not compete as candidates for explanations of social behavior, but rather are complementary. Social "characteristics" can *cause* psychological "characteristics." They are not substitutes that can in some way be more important than personality characteristics.

The confusion resulting from failing to take account of the complementarity of "personality processes and dispositions" and the social "context for the development of personality and acquisition of attitudes" is one that easily arises under certain research conditions. Ideally, personality and attitude ought to be measured by various psychological instruments designed to observe the individual's current mental functioning. And the social determinants of personality and attitude ought also to be more or less directly observed—longitudinally and by procedures independent of the respondent's report of his environmental circumstances, past and present. But frequently our only option is to gather evidence both of current personality and attitudes and of social background by interviewing the respondent and by interpreting some of the things he tells us as measures of his environment, and others as measures of the traces that environment (and genetic constitution) have left upon him.

In relating the various measures of respondents' "characteristics" that we have at our disposal to some dependent variable, it is important that we make explicit which of the independent variables have social referents and which have psychological referents. Otherwise the standard research procedures employing partial correlations and other control devices for detecting spurious relationships encourage us to fall into the fallacy of simply *reducing* an association between personality and behavior to its social determinants—of failing, in Herbert Hyman's phrase, to distinguish between "developmental sequences" and "problems of spuriousness."

For an example of how this problem arises, we can consider the very interesting research report by Urie Bronfenbrenner entitled "Personality and Participation: The Case of the Vanishing Variable." Bronfenbrenner reports a study in which it was found that measures of personality were associated with participation in community affairs. However, as he notes, "it is a well-established fact that extent of participation varies with social class, with the lower classes participating the least." Therefore he proceeds to establish the relationship between personality and participation, controlling for social class (and certain other factors). The result: "Most of the earlier . . . significant relationships between personality measures now disappear, leaving only two significant correlations, both of them quite low."[34]

One common interpretation of such a finding would be that Bronfenbrenner had shown the irrelevance of personality to participation. Hyman suggests why this interpretation would be unsatisfactory, when he points out that "the concept of spuriousness cannot logically be intended to apply to antecedent conditions which are associated with . . . [an] independent variable as part of a developmental sequence. . . . [A]n explanatory factor that is *psychological* and a control factor that is *sociological* can be

conceived as two different levels of description, i.e., one might regard . . .
an objective position in society as leading to psychological processes. . . . " [35]

In the Bronfenbrenner example, then, an individual's "objective" socio-economic background (as opposed to such subjective concomitants as his sense of class consciousness) needs to be analyzed as a possible social determinant of the psychological concomitants of participation.

The general import of our consideration of this objection, in the light of Smith's map, is to point to the desirability of distinguishing personality processes from their social antecedents and, so far as possible, obtaining independent observations of both personality and social background. As we shall see in discussing single-case and typological analyses, it is feasible to study personality determinants of political behavior without raising developmental questions about social background, but in fact questions about personality functioning lead logically and empirically to questions about background experience.

SITUATIONAL DETERMINANTS VERSUS PERSONALITY DETERMINANTS

A second standard objection, also one that is illustrated by Smith's formulation, takes this form:

> Personality is not an important determinant of political behavior, because individuals with varying personality characteristics will tend to behave similarly when placed in common situations. And it is not useful to study personal variation, if the ways in which people vary do not affect their behavior.

Easton illustrates this objection with the example of political party leaders who differ in their personality characteristics and who are "confronted with the existence of powerful groups making demands upon their parties." Their "decisions and actions," he points out, will tend "to converge." [36]

But, as Easton's use of tendency language brings out, their decisions are still likely to reflect *some* personal variability. [37] Furthermore, under certain circumstances the personal characteristics of the leaders would be more likely to have an impact than under others. This suggests that the second objection can be rephrased in the following conditional form and that we can (as various commentators have) advance propositions about the circumstances under which it obtains.

Under what circumstances do actors with differing personal characteristics (placed in common situations) vary in their behavior and under
what circumstances is their behavior uniform?

The portion of Smith's map that encompasses the familiar equation of
"situation (IV)→personality and predisposition (III)→behavior (V)"
helps us to isolate the contingencies that make it more or less likely that
behavior will be a function of personality variations.[38] Each of the three
elements in this equation can vary in ways that enhance or dampen the
effects of personal variability.

Since the objection emphasizes the tendency of situations (including
norms, roles, etc.) to reduce the effects of personal variability, it seems
logical to begin by pointing to types of situations that actually *encourage*
the expression of personal differences in behavior. As is often pointed out,
ambiguous situations tend to leave room for personal variability to have an
impact. Ambiguity is to be found in *new* situations, in *complex* situations,
and in *contradictory* situations, among others. Another class of situation in
which the expression of personal variations is fostered is that in which there
are *no sanctions* attached to the alternative courses of behavior.

Paralleling the situational determinants of the expression of personal
variability are psychological determinants. For example, if political actors
lack *mental sets* which might lead them to structure their perceptions and
resolve situational ambiguities, their inner dispositions are more likely to
be reflected in their behavior. If political actors have *intense* dispositions
(other than the disposition to conform!), they are more likely to ignore
environmental sanctions and to behave consistently with their varying
dispositions.

Turning finally to behavior itself, the kind of behavior we choose to
observe as our dependent variable will affect the likelihood of observing
personal variations. For example, variation is much greater in peripheral
than in central aspects of action. (That is, it is much greater, for example,
in the *zealousness* of performance of actions and the *style* of performance
than in the mere fact that a particular kind of action—such as voting, or
writing a Congressman—is performed.) And to the degree that an act is
demanding and not just a conventionally expected performance, it is more
likely to exhibit personal variability.

Thus a general upshot of rephrasing the objection and considering it in
the contextual perspective provided by the map is to sensitize us to circumstances under which situational and other considerations are more or less

likely to bring out or suppress the expression of personal variability. This provides clues to where and when it is especially desirable to engage in analyses of the personal dispositions of individual political actors, and of types of actors.

We have seen that although situational determinants of behavior are sometimes discussed as if they invariably served to weaken the effects of personality on behavior, certain types of situations *enhance* the effects of personality. In fact, careful, theoretically sensitive attention to the situations within which behavior occurs often may be the key to discovering strong personality effects, as can be seen from the important and ingenious research of Browning and Jacob.[39]

Browning and Jacob administered McClelland TATs (measuring levels of need for achievement, power, and affiliation) to matched samples of politicians and non-politicians in the northern city of "Eastport" and to samples of politicians in two Louisiana parishes, "Casino" and "Christian." The most striking impression left by their findings, when considered independently of situational factors, was the lack of aggregate motivational difference between the politicians and non-politicians, and the extreme heterogeneity of the politicians on the McClelland measures. However, once controls were introduced for situational factors, particularly the actual (as opposed to the formal) norms and expectations connected with various political offices in the three communities, distinct motivational profiles began to emerge. Politicians fitting into a syndrome, which Browning has identified operationally in terms of high scores in the needs for achievement and power and low scores in the need for affiliation, were found in some political contexts and not in others.

In the Eastport political system, Browning and Jacob find that on the one hand "expectations are prevalent that it is possible to go to state legislative office or higher" and, on the other, alternative nonpolitical options for achievement in business are limited. In Louisiana "there is no consensus that the important decisions are to be made in the political process" and "opportunities for power and achievement abound in the commercial and industrial life of the area." The Eastport politicians are generally higher on the high-power-and-achievement, low-affiliation syndrome than those in Louisiana. Secondly, the same pattern of differences is systematically exhibited *within* each of the communities between the occupants of offices which provide possibilities for power and achievement and offices which do not (for example, sinecures). Browning and Jacob show special attention to the subtleties of situational variables in their classification of offices in terms of actual community expectations rather than their formal requirements: thus the office of Justice of the Peace is coded as high on power potential in Casino Parish, Louisiana, where this official plays an important role in the relations between gamblers and parish authorities; in Christian Parish, which has no gambling, Justice of the Peace is coded as low in power.

In the course of locating actor motivations in situational contexts, Browning and Jacob are in effect characterizing situations (community contexts and roles) in terms both of actual practices ("Does a particular local political office lead to higher office in community X?") and of what Smith (panel II) calls "situational norms" ("What is the consensual expectation in community X of the consequences of running for a particular office?"). Clearly an actor's *own* expectations (which may not be consistent with community expectations, assuming that there *is* a community consensus) also will be a key intervening variable mediating between his motivational processes and the situation. Browning shows this in his report elsewhere[40] of certain Eastport findings not alluded to in the paper with Jacob: a group of active, striving businessmen who took a leading part in redevelopment in Eastport were found to have the same motivational pattern as the high-power-and-achievement, low-affiliation politicians. But the businessmen came from apolitical families and evidently did not acquire a set of expectations and values that would legitimize partisan politics as a motivational outlet.[41]

THE IMPORTANCE OF EGO-DEFENSIVE DETERMINANTS OF BEHAVIOR

The objection we have just considered—that situations leave little room for personal variability to have an effect on behavior—implies a content-free definition of "personality." "Personality" equals the ways that persons vary. To the degree that one's definition of "personality" refers to some subset of the package of psychological dispositions, it is possible to advance the objection that "personality" as so defined is not sufficiently relevant to political behavior for personality and politics research to be of interest. Many commentators have in mind a conception of personality that places special emphasis on ego-defense when they deprecate the importance of personality for politics. As I have pointed out, the deep motivational variables which are identified through the lenses of psychoanalytic theory and its descendents play a prominent role in the existing personality and politics literature. Depth psychology is central to such benchmark works as Lasswell's *Psychopathology and Politics*, Fromm's *Escape from Freedom*, and *The Authoritarian Personality*.[42]

Thus it is sometimes said that "personality" does not have an important impact on politics because mechanisms of ego-defense, while they may be important in the pathological behavior of disturbed individuals, do not come significantly into play in the daily behavior of normal people. Here again is an assertion that can be rephrased conditionally:

Under what circumstances are ego-defensive needs likely to manifest themselves in behavior?

In general, all of the circumstances that permit personal variability to be exhibited also leave room for particular aspects of personal variability, such as degrees and types of ego-defensiveness. However, certain circumstances probably make the expression of ego-defensive needs likely and not merely possible, and these can be located in terms of the "situation→ predispositions→behavior" formula.

(1) Certain types of stituational stimuli undoubtedly have a greater "resonance" with the deeper layers of the personality than do others. These are stimuli which politicians learn to be wary of—for example, such issues as capital punishment, cruelty to animals, and, in recent years, fluoridation of drinking water. One element in these sensitive issues, Lane and Sears suggest, is that they touch upon "topics dealing with material commonly repressed by individuals. . . ."[43]

(2) The likelihood that ego-defensive needs will affect political behavior is also related to the degree to which actors "have" ego-defensive needs.

(3) Finally, certain types of response undoubtedly provide greater occasion for deep personality needs to find outlet than do others—for example, such responses as affirmations of loyalty in connection with the rallying activities of mass movements led by charismatic leaders, and the various other types of response deliberately designed to channel affect into politics.

Again, by rephrasing the objection in contingent form, and stating the circumstances under which it holds, we can mark off certain portions of the political landscape as promising hunting grounds for the political psychologist, and suggest where he might make most effective use of certain kinds of hypotheses and concepts—in this case, those of depth psychology.

Smith's formulation of personality (panel III) distinguishes three kinds of motivational processes. In addition to the defensive processes, he stresses the ego's constructive coping with the environment and the processes through which self–other relations are mediated. This formulation suggests the importance of developing techniques for classifying individuals in terms of the relative importance of these processes in their psychic economies. We begin to sense certain of the necessary theoretical and methodological refinements appropriate for distinguishing the often elusive but nevertheless important connections between personality and politics. Just as certain relationships are revealed only by virtue of a very careful characterization of the situations within which actors of diverse personal characteristics are to be found, there are relationships which seem to be detectable only if the appropriate personality categorizations are employed as intervening constructs.

A standard problem is the failure to distinguish behavior and orientations rooted in ego defense from object-appraisal-based behavior. These difficulties arise frequently in the political literature because hypotheses drawing upon ego-defense mechanisms often seem well suited to deal with the kinds of irrationality that political psychologists frequently seek to explain. But irrationality (choice of means that are inappropriate for the ends-in-view) also—perhaps most often—may have nonpathological roots; for example, in imperfect information.

The authors of *The Authoritarian Personality* interpreted certain responses to the F-scale and to various projective tests as indicators of unconscious needs—for example, acceptance of pessimistic statements about human nature, and the belief that "wild and dangerous things go on in the world." These needs, according to the theory presented in *The Authoritarian Personality*, are part of a personality pattern in which repressed hostility is displaced to the weak and subordinate; and repression has a variety of further indirect consequences for the personality, such as the tendency to project one's aggressive and sexual impulses onto others. Hyman and Sheatsley, however, were able to point out that some of the responses used to indicate ego-defensive authoritarianism were in fact the "normal" responses and stereotypes prevalent in lower class subcultures, and that socio-economic rather than psychodynamic differences were probably being tapped in some of the research on authoritarianism.[44]

Hence the importance of obviating such confusions by using appropriate techniques for assessing ego-defensiveness, and by observing the differential behavior of individuals who vary in their degree of ego-defensive need. Quite relevant to students of personality and politics is the work along these lines of Daniel Katz and his associates, reported in papers such as "The Measurement of Ego-Defense as Related to Attitude Change."[45] Katz, McClintock, and Sarnoff used devices such as the paranoia scale of the Minnesota Multiphasic Personality Inventory in order to classify subjects by level of ego-defensiveness. Using attitude change techniques that are especially designed to penetrate moderate ego defenses, but are inappropriate for individuals who do not have strong ego defensive needs and too weak for strong ego defenders, they were able correctly to predict that attitude change would occur in the middle ego-defense category. As in the Browning and Jacob research, the finding of a personality effect was possible only when the appropriate categories of respondents were considered, and this in turn was dependent upon sensitivity to distinctions of the sort made in Smith's "map."[46]

THE IMPACT OF ACTORS ON OUTCOMES

Finally, we may note two instructive objections to the study of the impact of "personality" on politics which raise questions about social processes rather than intrapersonal processes. These objections are located by the dotted feedback arrow lettered (I) on Smith's map, which indicates the impact of individual political behavior on "distal social antecedents" of behavior (panel I), including the political system itself. They thus point to the various issues I have summarized under the heading of "aggregation."

1. Sometimes, especially in certain kinds of sociological writings that take a strict Durkheimian approach to analyzing social phenomena "at the social level," one encounters the objection that:

Personality characteristics tend to be randomly distributed in institutional roles. Personality therefore "cancels out" and can be ignored by analysts of political and other social phenomena.

The assumption underlying this objective seems, as Alex Inkeles points out, to be that "in 'real' groups and situations, the accidents of life history and factors other than personality which are responsible for recruitment [into institutional roles] will 'randomize' personality distribution in the major social statuses sufficiently so that taking systematic account of the influence of personality composition is unnecessary." But, as Inkeles easily shows, this assumption is false on two grounds.

First, "even if the personality composition of any group is randomly determined, random assortment would not in fact guarantee the same personality composition in the membership of all institutions of a given type. On the contrary, the very fact of randomness implies that the outcome would approximate a normal distribution. Consequently, some of the groups would by chance have a personality composition profoundly different from others, with possibly marked effects on the functioning of the institutions involved." Secondly,

> There is no convincing evidence that randomness does consistently describe the assignment of personality types to major social statuses. On the contrary, there is a great deal of evidence to indicate that particular statuses often attract, or recruit preponderantly for, one or another personality characteristic, and that fact has a substantial effect on individual adjustment to roles and the general quality of institutional functioning.[47]

The objection turns out therefore to be based on unwarranted empirical assumptions. It proves not to be an obstacle to research, but rather—once it is examined—an opening gambit for identifying a crucial topic of investigation for the political psychologist: How are personality types distributed in social roles and with what consequences?

2. Sometimes, on grounds smacking of the nineteenth-century debates over social determinism, it is argued that:

> Personality is not of interest to political and other social analysts, because individual actors (personalities) are severely limited in the impact they can have on events.

Here again we have an assertion that can be reworded contingently, since the degree to which individuals' actions can have significant impact is clearly variable. The reworded formulation becomes: Under what circumstances are the actions of single individuals likely to have a greater or lesser effect on the course of events?

One determinant of the degree to which individual actors can have an impact on events (for example, political outcomes such as the output of a legislature or the advent of a war) is the degree to which the environment admits of restructuring. Technically speaking, we might describe situations or sequences of events in which modest interventions can produce disproportionately large results as "unstable." They are in precarious equilibrium. Some physical analogies are: massive rock formations at the side of a mountain which can be dislodged by the motion of a single keystone, or highly explosive compounds such as nitroglycerine. The situation (or chain of events) which does not admit of restructuring is usually one in which a variety of factors conspire to produce the same outcome. Hook, in *The Hero and History*,[48] offers the outbreak of World War I and of the February Revolution as instances of historical sequences which, if not "inevitable," probably could not have been averted by the actions of any single individual. On the other hand, Hook attempts to show in detail that, without the specific actions of Lenin, the October Revolution might well not have occurred.

Secondly, the likelihood of personal impact varies with the actor's location in the environment. Normally, of course, it is the positions of formal leadership that provide the greatest leverage for affecting events, but Crozier[49] describes examples of French organizations in which certain insulated roles at lower hierarchical levels offer greater decision-making potentialities than higher roles.

Thirdly, the likelihood of personal impact varies with the personal strengths and weaknesses of the actor.

Earlier we saw certain of the contingencies surrounding the degree to which variations in personality characteristics are likely to affect individual behavior, a phenomenon which I have elsewhere called "actor dispensability."[50] Now we see that the degree to which the actions of individuals affect larger outcomes—what might be called "action dispensability"—is also contingent on various preconditions.

Actor dispensability and action dispensability are logically independent. Actors can behave in highly idiosyncratic ways, but their behavior may be of little significance for whatever phenomenon the political analyst happens to be interested in. And actors may behave in ways that are crucial (necessary, or even sufficient) for political outcomes that interest us, but the acts they perform may be ones that any similarly placed actor might be expected to perform. However, as a matter of investigative strategy, the greater the degree that the action is crucial (say, a presidential order releasing intercontinental ballistic missiles), the greater is the likelihood that we will be interested in the actor's idiosyncracies, even if their effect on his behavior is only peripheral rather than central.

In politics there are frequent examples of individual actions which have macro-consequences. I have already alluded to the well-known potency of American Presidents. Tucker has discussed at some length the probably even greater potential impact on outcomes of totalitarian leaders.[51] Because individual actors can have such great political consequences, psychological case histories of their personalities and behavior—if these can be conducted in an appropriately disciplined fashion—ought to have an important place in political studies. The possibly substantial impact of the individual under certain circumstances is also one of the factors that needs to be considered in our discussion of aggregative political accounts.

V. Three Varieties of Personality and Politics Research: Individual Case Studies, Typological Studies, Aggregative Accounts

Even though any single contribution to the literature may contain more than one of the three kinds of analysis, there is a rough, unfolding logic making it reasonable to organize the issues that arise in personality and politics research in a sequence running from single-case analysis, through typological analysis, to aggregate analysis. Each of the three kinds of investigation poses its own problems, but one tends to lead to another. Frequently, for example, it is our inability to explain why some single political actor—such as Woodrow Wilson—has behaved in a fashion that does not seem consistent with our normal expectations for behavior in comparable situations that initially turns our attention to political personality. In the course of inferring the personality structures that account for the idiosyncrasies of our subject's behavior, we then may come to suspect that in important respects *our* actor resembles certain other political actors, and if we pursue the resemblances, we find ourselves moving inductively in the direction of creating a typology.

There is, however, a two-way trade between analyses of individuals and of types: it also is possible that the actor will in some respects fit an already existing typology, perhaps one with which there is associated a body of theory and empirical evidence relevant to making predictions about our biographical subject and identifying ways in which his behavior is patterned. Thus, for example, George and George were able to make use of the clinical literature on compulsive types in their treatment of Woodrow Wilson.[52]

And there is a three-way linking of individual, typological, and aggregative analyses. There are numerous theories about the relevance for systems —for example, Weimar Germany—of the distribution of individual types in the system.[53] And we have seen that it is possible—and perhaps more so in the political than in other spheres of life—that especially well-placed individuals, such as Presidents of the United States and totalitarian leaders, can have drastic effects on the aggregate system. On George and George's showing, Woodrow Wilson's key role in the failure of the United States to ratify the Paris Treaty and enter the League of Nations is a case in point. We have a long, if checkered, tradition of culture-and-personality (and social structure-and-personality) inquiry to remind us that the causal arrow also points in the opposite direction—that systems have impacts on the individuals and types of individuals that compose them.

PSYCHOLOGICAL CASE STUDIES OF INDIVIDUAL POLITICAL ACTORS

If a case study of a single actor is presented mainly as an illustrative exercise or an occasion for theoretical speculation, and these seem to be the purposes behind many of the case studies of actors from the general population that have been reported, there is likely to be little felt need to perfect standards of evidence and inference for characterizing the actor. Consequently questions of accuracy of diagnosis arise mainly in biographies of public figures. Biographers often are interested in demonstrating that some action of their protagonist has been responsible for a particular outcome (i.e. that his actions have not been dispensable), and under these circumstances it is important to know if any of the variance is a function of the actor's personal idiosyncracies. The analysis of the actor's personality becomes a crucial linchpin in a larger argument.

We cannot expect psychological case studies to achieve the degree of standardization and precision that is appropriate for quantitative studies in which "objective" instruments designed to classify individuals into types are used, and in which it is possible to characterize the reliability of the instrument statistically and to perfect its validity through correlational study. But it *should* be possible to work toward more adequate, more explicit standards for single-case analysis than presently obtain—in other words, to reduce the degree to which psychological biographies are arbitrary literary exercises, wholly dependent upon the whims of the biographer and subject to no consensual standards of evaluation.

There are a number of reasons why it presently is difficult to assess biographical reports, apart from the more mundane problems with sources and their use that inhere in any historical research. First, in most biographies it is unclear what the basis was for the necessary acts of selection through which certain portions of the biographical record are discussed and emphasized, and others are not. Secondly, it often is not clear what interpretive inferences are being made, what if any hypotheses about the subject of the biography have been rejected, and on what grounds.

Interpretation is often implicit rather than explicit, and when it is explicit, it often seems "imposed" rather than to flow logically from general principles and specific evidence. Finally, as a particularly important instance of the previous point, the psychoanalytically inspired biographies in the personality and politics literature often seem (especially to the psychoanalytically uninitiated) to impose peculiarly unverifiable kinds of interpretations on the actor's behavior—interpretations in terms of ego-defensive motivation. Sometimes these interpretations seem to reduce the protagonist to his ego defenses and to be insensitive to the possibility that he may be reacting to the situations he encounters, in terms of the goals and cognitive assumptions he has acquired from his environment, in a more or less straightforward manner.

In asking what makes one single-actor psychological case study more convincing than another, I have found it convenient to reflect on the explicit and implicit practices employed by Alexander and Juliette George in their *Woodrow Wilson and Colonel House*, particularly their treatment of Wilson. Since a number of commentators[54] view this as one of the more satisfactory psychological biographies of political actors, we can turn to it for examples of appropriate technique (as well as assuming that whetever difficulties this work exhibits are likely to be fundamental difficulties with the methodology of such biographies, rather than examples of imperfect craftsmanship). Further, although George and George adopted the strategy of narrative exposition, addressing themselves only to a necessary minimum of methodological issues in the text of the book, the work clearly is guided by a very high degree of methodological (and theoretical) self-consciousness, and many of its methodological premises have been discussed in the appendix to the book and in a number of papers by one or both of the authors.[55]

Very generally, there seem to be two broad classes of reasons for the success of the Georges' study. The first set of reasons involves aspects of the logic of discovery—for example, their long-standing immersion in the details of Wilson's life, including extensive examination of the abundant and often highly revealing primary source material on Wilson; the depth and subtlety of the authors' familiarity with psychoanalytic theory; the long period of time they allowed themselves to develop, test, and reframe their hypothesis about Wilson. These factors, although vital, are not my present concern.[56] The other set of factors relates to the logic of demonstration. Even though George and George refer only briefly to such matters in their explicit remarks in the text of the study, it is evident that they paid far more than the customary amount of attention to developing assertions that were sound, from the standpoint of demonstration. Self-conscious attention to demonstration in psychological case studies seems to involve such elements as:

(1) Being explicit in formulating provisional hypotheses about the subject's personality (these may only be hypotheses about the adult phenomenology of the subject's personality, but analysis of an individual's "presenting characteristics" usually leads to developmental hypotheses about how he came to acquire these characteristics: at any rate, the explicit statement of the hypothesis serves to provide criteria for what to include in the biographical account).

(2) Distinguishing, as far as possible, between the observational data (on current functioning and past development) upon which the hypotheses are based and the interpretive hypotheses themselves.

(3) Establishing specific operational criteria for distinguishing observations that will be accepted in support of the hypothetical statements and those that will lead to rejection or modification of the hypotheses.

(4) At a minimum, ascertaining the reliability of the observational data, including the observations that serve as indicators of the terms used in the hypotheses.

(5) As far as possible, attempting to establish validity by assessing the standing in the relevant clinical literature of the "covering laws" upon which the inferential steps are based.

Space does not permit a detailed discussion of how all of these elements figure in the George and George account of Wilson. We may conclude these schematic remarks on the psychological case study simply by illustrating how several of them appear in the more complex and controversial of the authors' interpretations, those that deal with ego-defensiveness.

The Georges employ psychodynamic notions in the hypotheses they advance about a number of aspects of Wilson's personal and political style and of his development. Among them are the hypotheses addressed to Wilson's stubborn, unyielding intractability and unwillingness to compromise under certain circumstances, which the Georges interpret as evidence of the compensatory needs that were fulfilled for Wilson by refusing to share power in areas with which he felt he was particularly competent to deal. Wilson's refusal to compromise was especially evident in the graduate-school controversy that marked the final period of his presidency of Princeton, and in the closely parallel controversy during his unsuccessful effort to obtain Senate approval of the Paris Treaty, as well as in his dealings as Governor of New Jersey with the 1912 session of the state legislature (an episode the Georges deal with only briefly) and his conduct of peace negotiations in Paris.

For each of the circumstances in which Wilson showed extreme unwillingness to compromise, it is possible that an interpretation not suggesting that his behavior was a function of ego defense might be in order. A non-ego-defensive interpretation would be furthered if it could be shown that his responses to these situations (including those of his actions that molded the situations themselves) were responses that could normally be expected of political actors placed in comparable circumstances (with similar opportunities, restraints, and provocations), or if it could be shown that Wilson's consciously held attitudes were consistent with avoiding compromises under any circumstances. In fact, George and George, by analyzing these political encounters in very great detail, make it clear that Wilson had in each instance very great opportunities to attain his ostensible ends. He had only to admit other actors into the decision-making process and to make relatively slight accommodations and compromises. In other words, his actions did *not* seem to have been constrained mainly by the requirements of the situation.

Nor did they seem constrained by the requirements of Wilson's own values. George and George are able to present examples of explicit statements by Wilson[57] extolling precisely the kinds of compromises he adamantly resisted during the graduate-school and League of Nations controversies. The Georges also point to Wilson's extraordinary flexibility and adaptability under certain other circumstances—namely, those of seeking power, as opposed to exercising power. This provides a further indication that his behavior was not mainly a function of his ideological precepts.

In addition, the authors were able to point to the *recurrent pattern* of Wilson's experience. If an actor is found repeatedly to thrust himself into quite similar encounters, it becomes increasingly appropriate to assume that it is his own more or less deep-seated personality dispositions, rather than environmental factors, that are accounting for the regularities.

Finally, George and George make explicit use of the clinical literature on compulsive personalities in order to help explain the juxtaposition of a variety of traits and behavior patterns in Wilson, and drawing on that literature they specify operational indicators of such terms as "low self-estimates" and "compensation," terms which appear in the hypothesis that Wilson's pursuit of power served compensatory functions. For example, they were able to predict circumstances under which—if their basic diagnosis is correct—Wilson should be expected to experience "euphoric" feelings in connection with the pursuit and exercise of power, and they were fortunate enough to have a sufficiently detailed body of historical data to detect evidence of such feelings.[58]

The foregoing—and other—self-conscious efforts at building up a rigorously probative argument are woven into the text of the Georges' narrative. It is therefore not surprising that the argument has "rung true" to readers in ways that other psychological biographies have not.

ANALYSES OF TYPES OF POLITICAL ACTORS

By far the largest single cluster of political or politically relevant inquiry by psychologists is the massive body of literature on "authoritarianism." *Woodrow Wilson and Colonel House* displays exemplary methodological rigor and theoretical sophistication in an investigative mode that admits of a rather low degree of exactness. The authoritarianism studies, on the other hand, are executed in a research tradition that is highly developed methodologically. But authoritarianism inquiries—both the monumental original "Berkeley study"[59] and the countless subsequent studies—have been plagued with formidable problems of evidence, inference, and conceptualization. Within four years after the publication of *The Authoritarian Personality*, an entire volume of critical essays on that work and its immediate progeny had appeared.[60] Within eight years, a review article summarized 260 research reports on authoritarianism, many of them concerned with unraveling the controversial issues pointed up in the volume of critical essays.[61] And all of this preceded the elaborate methodological snarl that developed in the later 1950's over the finding that "response set" (the automatic tendency to respond positively or negatively to questionnaire items, independent of their content) seemed to have contributed to certain of the initial findings in the literature.

One of the more conspicuous difficulties with the original authoritarianism research was the failure to anticipate the complexity of the linkages between political attitudes and underlying personality processes: there was a tendency to equate authoritarian personality structure with right-wing political attitudes, and a failure to appreciate the possibility that the same personality needs could find alternative outlets, or that (because of the low cathexis of politics for many individuals) personality might not be expressed at all in political attitudes.[62]

A second difficulty bore on the problem of distinguishing ego-defensive from non-ego-defensive personality processes. The original theory guiding the Berkeley research was heavily psychodynamic. Subsequent reinterpretations of the findings suggested that high scores on the standard measure of authoritarianism might in some cases simply reflect the typical sub-cultural orientations toward topics referred to on the F-scale, by individuals of low educational attainment. Hyman and Sheatsley suggested this possibility in their contribution to the volume of critical essays on *The Authoritarian Personality*[63] by analyzing the content of the questionnaire items. The work several years later on response set pointed to the same possibility.[64]

In addition, it was pointed out that the inferences and assumptions in the original work about the relationship of psychological dispositions (personality and attitudes) to behavior were deficient, as were the sociological assumptions about the likely aggregate consequences of differing distributions of "authoritarians" in populations.[65]

In general, the issues raised by the literature had been inadequately conceptualized, and far too much theoretically vacuous data-gathering had been stimulated by the easy availability of the F-scale. The remedy, which in its general strategy is much the same as the prescriptions noted above for single-case analyses, is suggested by the diagnosis. There needs to be more extensive attention to explicit formulation of theories and hypotheses; greater clarity in distinguishing evidence from inference; more in the way of self-conscious attention both to distinguishing among the types of variables summarized in Figure 1 and to the possible interactions among such variables. Here in skeletal form is a sketch of an approach to reconstructing this literature, in order to isolate important research issues.[66]

1. *Phenomenology.* Under this heading, it is possible to summarize all of the psychological characteristics composing a type that are readily observable with a minimum of interpretation; these are, in effect, the "presenting symptoms" of the type. For the purpose of political studies, the crucial presenting characteristic referred to in the authoritarianism literature is the pair of traits that in the original volume were labeled "authoritarian aggression" and "authoritarian submission"—the tendency of the authoritarian to abase himself before those who stand above him hierarchically, and to dominate whomever he senses to be weak, sub-

ordinate, or inferior. Other more or less directly politically relevant traits that seem to be present in this syndrome are the authoritarian's tendency to think in power terms (to be acutely sensitive to questions of who rules whom); his preference for order; his perceptual rigidity ("intolerance of ambiguity"); his use of stereotypes; and his dependence upon "external agencies" for guidance.

The above-mentioned traits "hang together" in a fairly intuitively convincing manner. In addition, the literature suggests that a whole series of less obvious traits are a part of this syndrome: superstitiousness, "exaggerated assertion of strength and toughness," pessimism about human nature, "concern with sexual 'goings-on,' " "impatience with and opposition to the subjective and the tender-minded." It is these rather exotic additional concomitants that lead us beyond phenomenology to the psychoanalytically based theory of the dynamics of "ego-defensive authoritarianism."

The basic research implication of explicitly stating the phenomenological aspects of authoritarian personality theory, however, is to lay out a first-order set of research questions that are potentially more answerable than the knotty issues that arise in explaining why personality traits cluster as they do and what life experiences are responsible for the clustering. At the phenomenological level, one can identify a set of research tasks that can be performed in ways that should elicit agreement about the findings by investigators of quite different theoretical persuasions.[67]

2. *Dynamics.* Under this heading we can summarize our hypotheses about the processes underlying the observable. How are the observable features related to each other? What ties them together? As we have seen, the theory of dynamics on which the original research was based emphasizes ego defense.

> The authoritarian, it is argued, is an individual with strong, but ambivalent, dispositions toward figures of authority. Denial of the negative side of these feelings is central to such an individual's functioning. The authoritarian is able to conceal from himself his rage toward those in authority only by the massive defense procedure of reaction formation, involving a total repression of critical and other unacceptable impulses toward authority and a bending over backwards in excessive praise of it. But repression has its costs and side-effects, and repressed impulses seek alternative outlets. Hostility not only is rechannelled toward whoever is perceived as weak and unauthoritative, but also has a more diffuse effect on the authoritarian's generally negative views of man and his

works, as well as contributing to his need to scan his environment for signs of authority relationships, his tendency (via projection) to see the world as full of dangerous things and people, and his desire to punish others, for example, sex offenders, who have surrendered to their impulses. Feelings of personal weakness are covered by a facade of toughness. A side-effect of channeling enormous energy into repression and reaction formation is that the authoritarian's emotional capacities and even certain of his cognitive capacities are stunted. He is unable to face the prospect of canvassing his own psyche—for fear of what such introspection may yield—and therefore becomes highly dependent upon external sources of guidance.[68]

As we have also seen, other investigators and findings suggest that the phenomenology of authoritarianism can arise without having psychodynamic roots. In the language of Figure 1, authoritarianism may have its basis in needs for object appraisal as well as in externalization and ego defense. At the dynamic level, the research task becomes one of measuring and classifying different patterns of personality needs. Such investigations point in two directions: back to phenomenology (it seems likely that various phenomenological subtypes can be identified, some of which are related to ego-defensive needs and some of which are not), and on to developmental analysis.

3. *Development.* Questions of dynamics lead logically to questions of development. From asking how individuals with different "presenting symptoms' function, it is logical to proceed to questions about how they came to be the way they are. To the degree that research on dynamics points to two general types of authoritarianism (we can loosely refer to them as ego-defensive and cognitive authoritarianism), we would expect to find two quite different typical patterns of genesis.

4. *Distinguishing deeper personality processes from attitudes.* Figure 1 indicates the analytical distinction that can be made between attitudes and the personality processes in which they may have their sources. At some points in this essay it has been sufficient to treat "personality" and "psychological" as synonymous, implying that all of what is entailed by the latter, including attitudes and beliefs, is summarized by the term "personality." For the kinds of tasks that concerned the authors of *The Authoritarian Personality*, the analytic distinction between underlying personality organization and attitudes needs to be sharply maintained. This contributes to avoiding difficulties such as the automatic equating of authoritarianism with political conservatism and ethnic prejudice, and encourages in-

vestigators to anticipate and observe the rather complex contingent associations that seem to exist between beliefs and inner needs.

5. *Analyzing the interplay of personality and attitudes with situations.* It is often pointed out that psychological dispositions may be imperfectly correlated with action, because due to situational restraints and opportunities, people may fail to act upon their impulses. It is well appreciated that situational stimuli may even produce behavior that is quite *in*consistent with underlying dispositions, making it utterly inappropriate to attempt to anticipate behavior from psychological data alone. For example, Katz and Benjamin found in research on the behavior of northern white college undergraduates toward Negro co-workers that authoritarians were actually more deferential toward Negroes than nonauthoritarians, a finding which they felt was "due to the authoritarian's fear of revealing anti-Negro attitudes in a potentially punitive environment."[69]

ANALYSES OF AGGREGATION[70]

Political scientists are typically interested in those ancient preoccupations of Plato and Aristotle—political *systems*. What are their forms? Under what conditions are different forms found? How do they differ in performance? What leads them to be stable or to change? Studies of individual behavior and, pushing back in the causal chain, studies of the motivational bases of behavior, are undertaken by students of politics to a considerable extent not for their intrinsic interest but out of a concern with the collective effects of individual actors.

As Singer[71] points out, problems of moving from parts to wholes are endemic in a variety of fields. And as Smelser[72] points out, "We do not at present have the methodological capacity to argue causally from a mixture of aggregated states of individual members of a system to a global characteristic of a system." The simple extrapolation from impressionistic accounts of "national character" to equally impressionistic observations on system functioning, which characterized the literature of two decades ago, is justifiably passé.[73] There appear to be a variety of possible approaches, depending upon the data at one's disposal and one's theoretical concerns, to treating problems of aggregation in a disciplined fashion.

1. The prescription, stated at various points above, that actors be observed in their social situations, in effect means that studies of individual political actors tend automatically to shade into aggregate accounts of institutional functioning, at least at the small group level. And in the case

of elite actors, as we have seen, the analysis of individuals may clarify the control mechanisms of large systems. The George and George treatment of Wilson's dealings with Lloyd George and Clemenceau at Paris, and with Lodge during the confirmation fight, takes into account both the dispositions of actors and the relationships among their roles. In effect we are provided with the beginnings of general accounts of some of the possible states of the social system of the international conference and of executive-legislative relations. The recent work on "compositional" or "structural" effects suggests ways that individual and group data can be combined in quantitative inquiries.[74]

2. Modern survey techniques now make it possible to obtain systematic "censuses" of the psychological disposition of populations of very large social systems. Thus it becomes possible to avoid the circularities that frequently have been noted in personality and culture research—the tendencies to infer individual characteristics from system properties or cultural products and then to explain the latter in terms of the former. In recent voting literature, very sophisticated individual data-based theories of a non-obvious sort have been advanced to explain such phenomena as the regular loss of congressional seats by the presidential party in the off-year elections, and the far greater stability of party voting from election to election in the United States than in France.[75]

3. But often it will not do simply to aggregate individual characteristics additively, in order to explain the aggregate. To use Singer's analogy: "We can pour pellets of steel into a container until it is full, with little qualitative change in the aggregate; it merely becomes larger. But if we do the same thing with pellets of enriched uranium under appropriate conditions, we will eventually arrive at the 'critical mass' threshold, with important qualitative changes in the aggregate as a result."[76] Thus the consequences of the difference between a 50 versus a 60 per cent authoritarian-personality composition of a population may be disproportionately greater than the consequences of a 40 versus a 50 per cent difference. Very little is presently known about such matters.[77]

In addition, as Ackley[78] puts it, "aggregation is a legitimate procedure when behavior of the individual units subject to aggregation is basically similar." This is certainly not the case with political actors. Rather than simple addition we need, in a figure of speech of Hyman's, ways of "weighting the sums" to account for the greater impact of the dispositions of actors in key roles.[79]

4. A way of approaching the problem of weighting for role incumb-

ency is to make explicit our models of political systems and subsystems, stipulating the roles and their requirements in order to observe the fit between role and the personal dispositions of role incumbents. Lasswell in his essay on "Democratic Character"[80] followed the strategy of making explicit the behavioral requirements of an ideal-typical "democratic community" and theorizing about the personality types necessary (and permissible) for its functioning. Browning's efforts at modeling and simulation of community political recruitment processes can be interpreted as serving the same purposes—with a commendable degree of precision.[81]

VI. Summary and Conclusions

There is need for systematic inquiry into the ways political actors' personal psychological characteristics affect their behavior. But a satisfactory personality and politics literature has been slow to develop. The reasons for this are, I have suggested, partly in the sociology of knowledge and partly in the vexed methodological and conceptual state of the existing literature on personality and politics. To this a further answer might be added: the phenomena that need to be explained by political psychologists are enormously complicated and not easily observed.

What has preceded is a far too condensed sketch of a discussion designed to suggest ways of placing the study of personality and politics on a sounder methodological basis. My remarks have largely, in Smelser's phrase, been "methodological in a theoretical rather than an empirical sense."[82] Drawing upon the careful formulation put forth by Smith, I have suggested conceptual distinctions appropriate for reasoning about personality and politics, and attempted to use the distinctions to suggest how a variety of the formal objections to personality explanations of political behavior can be reconstructed in ways that point to the tasks and tacks appropriate for building up a more convincing literature in this area. Finally, I have attempted to suggest how three standard kinds of tasks for the personality and politics analyst—the psychological case study, typological inquiry, and aggregative analysis—relate to one another, and how each of these tasks can be pursued in a more satisfactory manner.

Riesman and Glazer once wryly commented that the field of culture-and-personality research (within which much of the personality and politics literature falls) has "more critics than practitioners."[83] Unfortunately, much of the critical activity has not contributed creatively to placing personality and politics investigations on a sounder evidential basis. Undoubtedly the progress that can be made in this direction is limited, and certainly "personality" is not the magic key to explaining all that hitherto has been puzzling about political behavior. Nevertheless, the need to know more about how the peculiar strengths and weaknesses of our species contribute to political outcomes seems sufficiently great to justify somewhat larger colonies of investigators than presently occupy the boundary territory between political science and the various branches of psychology, including personality psychology.

Notes

1. Alex Inkeles, "Sociology and Psychology," in Sigmund Koch, ed., *Psychology: A Study of a Science*, VI (New York: McGraw-Hill, 1963), pp. 318–319.
2. Herbert A. Simon, "Theories of Decision-Making in Economics and Behavioral Science," *American Economic Review*, IL (1959), p. 253. Also his "Economics and Psychology," in Koch, *Psychology*, p. 686.
3. Typical examples of work falling specifically under the "personality and politics" heading are cited below. Among the great many cognate literatures that address themselves to related issues are: philosophy of science (e.g. discussions of "reduction" of theories); research technology (e.g. the recent work on causal inference); and theory of history ("methodological individualism").
4. Gordon Allport, *Personality* (New York: Holt, 1937), pp. 24–54.
5. Robert E. Lane, *Political Ideology* (New York: Free Press, 1962).
6. M. Brewster Smith, Jerome Bruner, and Robert White, *Opinions and Personality* (New York: Wiley, 1956).
7. For example, Alexander L. George and Juliette L. George, *Woodrow Wilson and Colonel House: A Personality Study* (New York: John Day, 1956; paperback edition with new preface, New York: Dover, 1964); Lewis J. Edinger, *Kurt Schumacher: A Study in Personality and Political Behavior* (Stanford: Stanford University Press, 1965); Arnold Rogow, *James Forrestal: A Study of Personality, Politics, and Policy* (New York: Macmillan, 1963); E. Victor Wolfenstein, *The Revolutionary Personality: Lenin, Trotsky, Gandhi* (Princeton: Princeton University Press, 1967).
8. Theodor W. Adorno, Else Frenkel-Brunswik, Daniel J. Levinson, and R. Nevitt Sanford, *The Authoritarian Personality* (New York: Harper, 1950); Richard Christie and Marie Jahoda, eds., *Studies in the Scope and Method of "The Authoritarian Personality"* (Glencoe, Ill.: Free Press, 1954).
9. Milton Rokeach, *The Open and Closed Mind* (New York: Basic Books, 1960).
10. Morris Rosenberg, "Misanthropy and Political Ideology," *American Sociological Review*, XXI (1956), pp. 690–695.

11. See the forthcoming volume by Christie and others.

12. David Riesman, with Nathan Glazer and Reuel Denney, *The Lonely Crowd* (New Haven: Yale University Press, 1950).

13. Harold D. Lasswell, *Psychopathology and Politics* (Chicago, University of Chicago Press, 1930; paperback with afterthoughts by the author, 1960).

14. James D. Barber, *The Lawmakers* (New Haven: Yale University Press, 1965).

15. For example, Geoffrey Gorer, "Burmese Personality," (New York: Institute of Intercultural Studies [mimeo], 1943); Ruth Benedict, *The Chrysanthemum and the Sword* (Boston: Houghton Mifflin, 1946); Geoffrey Gorer, *The American People* (New York: Norton, 1948); Otto Klineberg, *Tensions Affecting International Understanding* (New York: Social Science Research Council Bulletin 62, 1950); Leon Bramson and George W. Goethals, *War: Studies from Psychology, Sociology, Anthropology* (New York: Basic Books, 1964).

16. For a representative slice of the polemical issues, see the symposium edited by Sidney Hook entitled *Psychoanalysis: Scientific Method and Philosophy* (New York: New York University Press, 1959). Among the more interesting clarificatory efforts are B. A. Farrell, "The Status of Psychoanalytic Theory," *Inquiry*, VII (1964), pp. 104–123; Peter Madison, *Freud's Concept of Repression and Defense: Its Theoretical and Observational Language* (Minneapolis: University of Minnesota Press, 1961).

17. Substantial portions of Sections I–III draw on my "The Need for Systematic Inquiry into Personality and Politics: Introductory and Overview," *Journal of Social Issues*, 24 (1968), pp. 1–14. That article introduces and summarizes a symposium on "Personality and Politics: Methodological and Theoretical Issues."

18. Walter Lippmann, *Preface to Politics* (New York: Mitchell Kennerly, 1913), p. 2.

19. Lasswell seems first to have introduced the distinction between functional and conventional definitions of politics in Lasswell, *Psychopathology and Politics*, Chap. 4.

20. Richard S. Lazarus, *Personality and Adjustment* (Englewood Cliffs, N.J.: Prentice-Hall, 1963), pp. 27–28.

21. *New York Times*, Oct. 28 and Nov. 13, 1962.

22. Nathan Leites, *The Operational Code of the Politburo* (New York: McGraw-Hill, 1951) and *A Study of Bolshevism* (Glencoe, Ill.: Free Press, 1953). For a later formulation by Leites, taking account of the missile crisis, see his "Kremlin Thoughts: Yielding, Rebuffing, Provoking, Retreating," RAND Corporation Memorandum RM–31618–ISA, May, 1963. These alternative theories of the psychological assumptions underlying policy options in the missile crisis are presented for illustrative purposes, and do not purport to deal adequately with the psychological and strategic issues raised by that sequence of events. Cf. Alexander L. George, "Presidential Control of Force: The Korean War and

the Cuban Missile Crisis," paper presented at the 1967 Annual Meeting of the American Sociological Association.

23. George and George, *Woodrow Wilson*, pp. 290–291.

24. Richard A. Littman, "Psychology: The Socially Indifferent Science," *American Psychologist*, XVI (1961), pp. 232–236.

25. The phrase "trait-correlational" is used by Smith, Bruner, and White in *Opinions and Personality*. For a discussion of the relevant literature, see Chap. 2 of that work.

26. For representative examples of research in the aftermath of the response-set controversy, see Martha T. Mednick and Sarnoff A. Mednick, *Research in Personality* (New York: Holt, Rinehart and Winston, 1963). The work of Herbert McClosky is exemplary in its sophisticated attention to instrument validation. See, for example, his "Conservatism and Personality," *American Political Science Review*, LII (1958), pp. 27–45, and "Psychological Dimensions of Anomie" (with John H. Schaar), *American Sociological Review*, (1965), pp. 14–40.

27. Theodore Abel, "Is a Psychiatric Interpretation of the German Enigma Necessary?" *American Sociological Review*, X (1945), pp. 457–464; Reinhard Bendix, "Compliant Behavior and Individual Personality," *American Journal of Sociology*, LVIII (1962), pp. 292–303.

28. M. Brewster Smith, "A Map for the Analysis of Personality and Politics," *Journal of Social Issues*, 24 (1968), pp. 15–28.

29. Smith, Bruner, and White, *Opinions and Personality*.

30. Or, for that matter, an action that is not mediated by much attitudinal activity.

31. A more or less residual category of less dynamic determinants of attitudes is "relevant stylistic traits," such as cognitive style. For example, Smith, Bruner, and White found that one of their case-study subjects—Charles Lanlin—perceived political objects in a highly fragmented manner that seemed mainly to be a simple extension of a basic cognitive style which showed little capacity for abstraction.

32. The classical example is race prejudice, which may be held for any of the foregoing reasons. The provision of new information may be appropriate to eliminate prejudices that have their origin in object appraisal, but the same technique may actually stiffen the attitudes of ego-defenders for whom prejudice may be a vital prop against intrapsychic perils. For the latter, some more or less psychotherapeutic technique is appropriate. But neither technique will reach the individual whose prejudice mainly performs the function of relating himself to others in his environment.

33. The remainder of this section draws very heavily upon (and in a few instances directly incorporates the text of) my "The Impact of Personality on Politics: An Attempt to Clear Away Underbrush," *American Political Science Review*, LXI (1967), pp. 629–641. Most of the assertions made here are substantially expanded in that essay.

34. Urie Bronfenbrenner, "Personality and Participation: The Case of the Vanishing Variables," *Journal of Social Issues*, XVI (1960), pp. 54–63. For an alternative, and I think, more useful, approach to analyzing the determinants of participation, see David Horton Smith, "A Psychological Model of Individual Participation in Formal Voluntary Organizations: Applications to Some Chilean Data," *American Journal of Sociology*, LXXII (1966), pp. 249–266.

35. Herbert Hyman, *Survey Design and Analysis* (Glencoe: Free Press, 1955), pp. 254–257.

36. David Easton, *The Political System* (New York: Knopf, 1953), p. 196.

37. In this objection, the implicit meaning of the term "personality" is "personal variability."

38. The importance of considering the interaction of psychological and situational determinants of political behavior is emphasized in James Davies, *Human Nature in Politics* (New York: Wiley, 1963).

39. Rufus P. Browning and Herbert Jacob, "Power Motivation and the Political Personality," *Public Opinion Quarterly*, XXVIII (1964), pp. 75–90.

40. Rufus P. Browning, "The Interaction of Personality and Political System in Decisions to Run for Office: Some Data and a Simulation Technique," *Journal of Social Issues*, 24, (1968), pp. 93–110.

41. The observations on the interplay of personality and situation in Browning and Jacob's work more than vindicate a strategy first proposed by Lasswell in *Psychopathology and Politics*, of isolating "functionally comparable" processes and phenomena for study in order to eliminate the high degree of "noise" and heterogeneity one finds when one examines personality concomitants of roles that are formally but not actually similar (such as in the Justice of Peace office in the two Louisiana parishes). Browning and Jacob's careful isolation of comparable situational opportunities for the exercise of power is a counterpart of Lasswell's strategy in devising his "political type" construct: individuals fitting into Lasswell's "political" (or power-centered) type seek out situations that are comparable in that they permit the exercise of power. These situations may or may not be a part of the formal political process. As Lasswell puts it, "the simple fact that a role is performed that is conventionally perceived as political . . . does not warrant classifying a person among the political personalities nor, conversely, does failure to play a conventionally recognized political role necessarily imply that the person is not power-oriented. Obviously the comprehensive appraisal of any social context must sample *all* value shaping and sharing processes, as they are *conventionally* understood, if the political personalities in the functional sense are to be identified. The point is implied, when, as is sometimes the case, it is said that during the rapid growth phase of a private capitalist economy the most power-centered persons engage in 'business'." Harold D. Lasswell, "A Note on 'Types' of Political Personality: Nuclear, Corelational, Developmental," *Journal of Social Issues*, 24 (1968), pp. 81–92.

42. Lasswell, *Psychopathology and Politics*; Erich Fromm, *Escape from Freedom* (New York: Holt, Rinehart and Winston, 1941); Adorno *et al.*, *The Authoritarian Personality*.

43. Robert E. Lane and David O. Sears, *Public Opinion* (Englewood Cliffs, N.J.: Prentice-Hall, 1964), p. 76.

44. Herbert Hyman and Paul B. Sheatsley, " 'The Authoritarian Personality'— A Methodological Critique," in Richard Christie and Marie Jahoda, eds., *Studies in the Scope and Method of "The Authoritarian Personality,"* pp. 50–122.

45. Daniel Katz, Charles McClintock, and Irving Sarnoff, "The Measurement of Ego-Defense as Related to Attitude Change," *Journal of Personality*, XXV (1957), pp. 465–474.

46. The attitude change procedure used by Katz and his associates was an "insight" technique, designed to introduce awareness of the role of defense mechanisms in producing one's attitudes. For the present purposes, which are largely illustrative, I shall ignore a number of thorny questions about whether Katz *et al.* were actually successful in measuring ego-defensiveness and reducing defensive barriers to attitude change.

47. Alex Inkeles, "Sociology and Psychology," p. 354.

48. Sidney Hook, *The Hero in History* (Boston: Beacon Press, 1943).

49. Michel Crozier, *The Bureaucratic Phenomenon* (Chicago: University of Chicago Press, 1964), p. 192.

50. This distinction is discussed at much greater length in my "The Impact of Personality on Politics: An Attempt to Clear Away Underbrush."

51. Robert C. Tucker, "The Dictator and Totalitarianism," *World Politics*, XVII (1965), pp. 555–584.

52. Alexander L. George, "Some Uses of Dynamic Psychology in Political Biography," unpublished paper, 1960.

53. See Fromm's well-known account in *Escape from Freedom*. For an attempt to deal more systematically with aggregate effects of individual psychological characteristics, see Harry Eckstein, *A Theory of Stable Democracy*, Princeton University Center of International Studies, Research Monograph No. 10 (April, 1961).

54. The most extended appreciation of the George and George volume is by Bernard Brodie: "A Psychoanalytical Interpretation of Woodrow Wilson," Bruce Mazlish, ed., *Psychoanalysis and History* (Englewood Cliffs, N.J.: Prentice-Hall, 1963), pp. 115–123. For a brief set of critical remarks that are, I think, poorly taken, but illustrative of the lack of general awareness of the possibilities for rigorous reasoning in single-case psychological analysis, see Page Smith, *The Historian and History* (New York: Knopf, 1964), pp. 125–126.

55. George and George, *Woodrow Wilson*, "Research Note," pp. 217–221; Alexander L. George and Juliette L. George, "Woodrow Wilson: Personality and Political Behavior," paper presented at the 1956 Annual Meeting of the American Political Science Association; Alexander George, see note 52;

Alexander George, "Power as a Compensatory Value for Political Leaders," *Journal of Social Issues*, 24 (1968), pp. 29–50.

56. Cf. the Preface to the Dover edition of *Woodrow Wilson and Colonel House.*

57. *Woodrow Wilson and Colonel House*, pp. 290–291.

58. See in particular George's paper cited in note 52, and his "Power as a Compensatory Value for Political Leaders."

59. Adorno *et al.*, *The Authoritarian Personality.*

60. Christie and Jahoda, *Studies in the Scope and Method of the Authoritarian Personality.*

61. Richard Christie and Peggy Cook, "A Guide to Published Literature Relating to the Authoritarian Personality through 1956," *Journal of Psychology*, XLV (1958), pp. 171–199. For a recent literature review, see John P. Kirscht and Ronald C. Dillehay, *Dimensions of Authoritarianism* (Lexington: University of Kentucky Press, 1967).

62. Edward Shils, "Authoritarianism: 'Right' and 'Left,' " in Christie and Jahoda, pp. 24–49.

63. H. H. Hyman and P. B. Sheatsley, "Authoritarianism Re-examined," in Christie and Jahoda, *Studies in the Scope and Method of the Authoritarian Personality*, pp. 123–196.

64. See the articles reprinted in Chap. 6 of Mednick and Mednick, *Research in Personality.*

65. See Note 61.

66. These remarks are substantially expanded upon in my "Personality and Political Socialization: The Theories of Authoritarian and Democratic Character," *Annals of the American Academy of Political and Social Science*, CCCLXI (1965), pp. 81–95. The statements in quotation marks are from *The Authoritarian Personality*, unless otherwise indicated; for further documentation see "Personality and Political Socialization." In addition, portions of the passages tht follow are adapted from my "The Need for Systematic Study of Personality and Politics."

67. M. Brewster Smith has reported a technique that does not rely upon the overused F-scale for identifying individuals exhibiting the characteristics of the authoritarian type. See the description of Q-Sort analyses of psychiatric interview data in his "An Analysis of Two Measures of 'Authoritarianism' Among Peace Corps Teachers," *Journal of Personality*, XXXIII (1965), pp. 513–535.

68. Greenstein, "Personality and Political Socialization," p. 87.

69. Irwin Katz and Lawrence Benjamin, "Effects of White Authoritarianism in Biracial Work Groups," *Journal of Abnormal and Social Psychology*, LXI (1960), pp. 448–456.

70. What follows is based on my "The Need for Systematic Study of Personality and Politics."

71. J. David Singer, "Man and World Politics: The Psychological Interface," *Journal of Social Issues*, 24 (1968), pp. 127–156.

72. Neil J. Smelser, "Personality and the Explanation of Political Phenomena at the Social-System Level: A Methodological Statement," *Journal of Social Issues*, 24 (1968), pp. 111–126.

73. Alex Inkeles and Daniel J. Levinson, "National Character: The Study of Modal Personality and Sociocultural Systems," in Gardner Lindzey, ed., *Handbook of Social Psychology*, II (Cambridge, Mass.: Addison-Wesley, 1954), pp. 977–1020.

74. Peter M. Blau, "Structural Effects," *American Sociological Review*, XXV (1960), pp. 178–193; James A. Davis, Joe L. Spaeth, and Carolyn Huson, "A Technique for Analyzing the Effects of Group Composition," *American Sociological Review*, XXVI, (1961), pp. 215–225.

75. Angus Campbell, Phillip E. Converse, Warren E. Miller, and Donald E. Stokes, *Elections and the Political Order* (New York: Wiley, 1966). See especially Campbell's chapter on "surge and decline" (pp. 400–462) and the discussion by Converse and Dupeux of "politicization" in France and the United States (pp. 269–291).

76. J. David Singer, "Man and World Politics," p. 143.

77. For methodological suggestions, see Hayward R. Alker, Jr., "The Long Road to International Relations Theory: Problems of Statistical Nonadditivity," *World Politics*, XVIII (1966), pp. 623–655.

78. Gardner Ackley, *Macroeconomic Theory* (New York: Macmillan, 1961), p. 573.

79. Herbert Hyman, "The Modification of a Personality-Centered Conceptual System when the Project is Translated from a National to a Cross-National Study," in Bjorn Christiansen, Herbert Hyman, and Ragnar Rommetveit, *Cross-National Social Research* (Oslo: International Seminar, Institute for Social Research, 1951, mimeograph).

80. Harold D. Lasswell, "Democratic Character," in *Political Writings of Harold D. Lasswell* (Glencoe: Free Press, 1951), pp. 465–525. See also the gloss on this essay in my "Harold D. Lasswell's Concept of Democratic Character," *Journal of Politics*, xxx (1968), pp. 696–709.

81. Rufus Browning, "The Interaction of Personality and Political System."

82. Neil J. Smelser, "Personality and the Explanation of Political Phenomena."

83. David Riesman and Nathan Glazer, "The Lonely Crowd: A Reconsideration in 1960," in Seymour M. Lipset and Leo Lowenthal, eds., *Culture and Social Character* (New York: Free Press, 1961) p. 437.

8

Psychiatry and Political Science: Some Reflections and Prospects

ARNOLD A. ROGOW

Despite the long and obvious relationship between theories of human nature and theories of politics—Aristotle, Hobbes, Locke, Rousseau come easily to mind—despite, too, the pioneering explorations of political psychodynamics in our own time, I think it is fair to say that the marriage of psychiatry and political science has never been properly consummated, or at least not to the point at which healthy offspring can be expected. In this chapter I should like to deal with some reasons why this is so, and also to suggest possibly productive collaborations in the future between psychiatrists (and psychologists) and political scientists.

Of the reasons that may be advanced for the failure of political scientists to respond to psychiatry, three in particular stand out. The first is the long and tenacious tradition within political science of conceiving of the discipline as consanguinely related to law, history, and philosophy rather than to behavioral science. Emphasizing the study of constitutions and enactments, approaching the state and other political entities descriptively rather than analytically, treating the history of normative political ideas as the sum and essence of political theory, political science for a very long period has eschewed a dynamic interpretation of political life. The Founding Fathers of American political science, many of whom did graduate work in German and British universities, could not conceive of the personality dimension as relevant to political science; most of them,

This chapter is a shorter version of "Psychiatry, History, and Political Science: Notes on an Emergent Synthesis," in Judd Marmor, ed., *Modern Psychoanalysis* (New York: Basic Books, 1968).

at the beginning of the present century, were unhappy with efforts to view the political process as a function of groups competing and bargaining for power, much less the outcome of individual and group interrelations influenced in part by unconscious motivations. Even today, it is worth noting, political science in Europe and elsewhere remains steeped in legalistic, historical, and philosophical exegesis, although there are exceptions and indubitably modernizing trends are underway.

A second cause of resistance to psychoanalysis is the challenge posed by Freudian principles to the heuristic rational and superstructural models which, for a very long time, constituted nuclear political science. Freud's belief that metal processes are essentially unconscious appeared to undermine the Enlightenment view, incorporated into political science, that man was a reasoning calculator of his own self-interest whose judgment of what would benefit himself and society would improve with increasing education and diffusion of knowledge. The conviction of Freud that culture itself was the result of a fragile tension between constructive and destructive tendencies in man, with the latter frequently in ascendancy, threatened the very root structure of the belief in progress and its corollary liberal doctrine of change and perfectability of human nature. Psychoanalysis, insofar as it was understood by political scientists, seemed to be saying, finally, that the entire political superstructure—conservative and radical parties, ideologies, voting, the state itself —could be "explained" in terms of childhood traumas, oedipus complexes, father figures, castration fears, libido diversion, and the like. Freud, it appeared, like Marx before him, was suggesting that political institutions were essentially a facade, a veneer, a gloss to mask the real interests and motivations of man, and much of the treatment accorded Freud was similar to that accorded Marx and other demolishers of the superstructure: disbelief, disdain, disinterest. There are also those in the political science profession, the moral views of which have always been closer to Calvin than to Casanova, who shared the opinion of the Dean of the University of Toronto in 1910 that Freud was an advocate "of free love, removal of all restraints, and a relapse into savagery,"[1] in short, a dirty old man. After Freud, as, from another perspective, after Hitler and the national insanity of Naziism, it could no longer be maintained that man was cast in the image of God, or if not God, at least Thomas Jefferson or John Stuart Mill.

A third source of estrangement between psychiatry and political science, and one that constitutes a major threat to continuing possibilities for collaboration, has to do with methodological developments in both disciplines. Since World War II, political scientists have been increasingly concerned with the discipline's methodological lag behind the other social and behavioral sciences. Doctoral candidates in political science, unlike those in economics and sociology, knew no mathematics or statistics; hence their models and paradigms were verbal constructs, and there was little agreement even within the profession about the words used, especially such words as power, influence, consent, coalition, authority, and so forth. Few political scientists were skilled in techniques of quantitative and qualitative measurement; therefore they were unable to process aggregate data such as that produced in sample surveys, or to undertake multivariate analysis. One major consequence of this technological lag was that certain research areas, notably research in public opinion formation and voting behavior, were transferred, as it were, from political science to sociology and psychology. Another result was that studies undertaken by political scientists—for example, studies of interest groups, or local governments, or decision-making processes—tended to be, however illuminating, subjective and frequently idiosyncratic. They were difficult, often impossible to replicate, were not susceptible to proof or disproof, and hence were of little utility in that slow and painful construction process by which a discipline transforms itself into a science.

While this is not the occasion to discuss all the motivations for change, it may be noted in passing that a professional inferiority complex, especially among younger practitioners, has played an important role, as have a number of foundations whose funds are seemingly available without limit for "hard" research. The impact of the Center for Advanced Study in the Behavioral Sciences, where political scientists and historians have been welcomed since operations began in 1954, should not be overlooked; shifts of emphasis within the Social Science Research Council and National Science Foundation have also been important.

The contributions of psychoanalysis and psychiatry to our understanding of politics, on the other hand, are limited by the inordinate "softness," that is, lack of methodological rigor, of much psychiatric research. While in psychiatry, too, there is growing dissatisfaction with traditional methods, what has been said about methodological lag in political science applies with even greater force to psychiatry. Whether or not it is overstatement to suggest that "psychology can be of use to the social sciences *only* if its use can be reduced to a technique which is verifiable, teachable, and can be corrected or changed in the face of new evidence,"[2] it is plausible to suggest that the limitations of much psychiatric research—for example, the lack of standardization in the concepts and measures employed by psychiatrists, the proneness to generalize findings that are based on a highly selective, nonrepresentative, middle-class population sample, the tendency to minimize the importance of variables found to be significant by political scientists, such as social class, income, education, and religious affiliation—all constitute a severe restriction of its utility.

While it is evident that many psychiatrists are more interested than ever before in interdisciplinary methodologies and research efforts, it is far from clear, at least to an outsider, what the effects will be, on the one hand, of the increasing separation between clinicians and researchers, and, on the other hand, of the growing interest in biochemical and engineering approaches to mental illness. No doubt it is too early—it may be totally in error—to say that the most imaginative and competent psychiatrists are gradually abandoning clinical practice for research, instead of engaging in both; the implications of such a development, especially implications for interdisciplinary training programs that include political scientists and historians, are not all of them happy ones. Similarly, it may be wrong, or at least premature, to conclude that the interest in biochemistry and psychophysiological research will draw psychiatry back toward medicine and the natural sciences, which is where Kenneth M. Colby and others feel it belongs,[3] and further away from the social sciences. In psychiatry, as in all other branches of knowledge at the present time, there are conflicting trends; the only certain thing is the necessity of continuing discussions and analysis of trends.

But assuming, once again, that psychiatry and political science are drawing closer together rather than further apart, what does psychiatry have most to contribute to political science? What can political science offer psychiatry? Where are the interdisciplinary frontiers and "cutting-edge" areas, and the richest possibilities for innovative developments?

The research contributions of psychiatry to political science and history can be roughly classified under the headings of methods, emphasis, and insight. In terms of methodology, Freud's most significant achievement was undoubtedly the unstructured, free-associational interview. Depending as it does on observational techniques that require special interpretational skills on the part of the investigator, the free-association interview has not been fully exploited by political scientists interested in contemporary affairs and the recent past. Yet it would appear that the psychoanalytic-type interview is an indispensable tool for intensively exploring and theoretically charting areas of political behavior that are not amenable to other methods of inquiry.

For example, much research by political scientists into the etiology of right-wing extremism suggests that members of organizations like the John Birch Society are plagued by high levels of anxiety, low self-esteem, strong needs for inviolacy, and hostile and misanthropic orientations toward the social order. Many of them belong to the discontinued classes of society—that is, they are the older residents of burgeoning towns and cities, the proprietors of neighborhood stores and small business threatened by the huge chains and shopping centers, the elderly retired who are made apprehensive by small children, non-whites, noise, traffic, and tax increases —and these drop-out citizens are attracted to subcultures of despair such as the Birch Society. Unfortunately, they are much less likely to cooperate with social investigators using survey research and other "hard" instruments of research than individuals who are more sanguine in both personality and outlook. Hence, studies positing a relationship between, say, alienation and extremism are characterized by a high refusal rate for requested interviews and questionnaire returns, and a consequent failure to demonstrate that the relationship holds at levels of statistical significance. In fact, we know very little altogether about those who consistently refuse to participate in survey studies, whatever their nature. Surely, here is a collaborative area that would benefit from a merger of the "soft" technique of the clinician with the "hard" techniques currently used in political science.

Even less developed than the free-association interview is the application of free-association to the analysis of documents, letters, diaries, and written records of all sorts. Although the historian frequently deals with hand-written accounts, almost no effort has been made to analyze changes of handwriting, including sudden changes in the way one signs letters, that are known to occur under conditions of great internal as well as external stress. Hence we are uninformed about the relationship of such changes to life and career experiences. While handwriting, to a great and growing extent, has been replaced by the telephone, the typewriter, and the tape recorder, it is by no means impossible to search typewritten and spoken messages for clues to traumatic events. Much could be learned, for example, by approaching taped political interviews, speeches, press conferences, and so forth, in a fashion similar to that employed in the analysis of taped psychiatric interviews and group therapy sessions.

Related to the free-association interview is Freud's emphasis on the "latent, unconscious, irrational, and archaic aspect" of behavior, and the stress he placed "on the formatic influence of early childhood, of dreams and of phantasies."[4] Little of this emphasis has penetrated research in political science, although efforts are now underway, in political science, to study the processes by which children become interested, involved, and partisan in politics.[5] So far as is known, no attempt has been made to collect and interpret the dreams and phantasies of political figures. No doubt this is due in part to the fact that what we know of living individuals is by and large what they want us to know, and what we know of the dead is by and large what their families and their posterity permit us to discover. But it is also true that special skills are required for the analysis of inferred motivations as opposed to those that are manifest; lacking such skills, political scientists tend to confine themselves to that which is conscious, declared, and easily observable. Thus the latent, underlying motivations of both individuals and institutions, in the concealment or disguise of which all advanced societies excel, may be totally overlooked by the political behaviorist.

The third or insight component of Freud's contribution to political science is that large body of psychoanalytic and psychiatric literature that deals with politics and history. The term "insight" is used because such literature is designed to provide an analysis in depth, based on psychoanalytic and psychiatric theory, of phenomena that are only partly explored or understood by political scientists and historians. Most of this literature, for reasons already discussed, has originated with psychiatrists themselves, but an increasing amount is being published by psychoanalytically inclined social scientists.

Broadly speaking, the history of insight literature is, like other histories, a history of changing times, interests, and intellectual styles. Someone once remarked, in an effort to explain a Supreme Court decision, that the "Supreme Court reads the headlines." In a similar vein it may be observed that psychiatrists read the headlines and are affected by them, at least insofar as their insight writings are concerned. Thus, during the "long twilight" that glowed over Europe between the Franco–Prussian War and 1914, Freud and his colleagues wrote very little outside the area of primary concern—the origins, symptoms, and treatment of neuroses and psychoses. While Freud early demonstrated an interest in literary and artistic themes —his essays "The Theme of the Three Caskets" and "The Moses of Michaelangelo" appeared in 1913 and 1914 respectively—he did not turn his attention to problems of war and peace until 1915 when he published

"Thoughts for the Times on War and Death." His preface, "Psycho-analysis and War Neuroses," appeared in 1919. During the relatively peaceful 1920's he wrote little on the subject, but in 1930 his *Civilization and Its Discontents* was perhaps more prophetic than anything else that year of the approaching end of tranquility or, in Harding's coined phrase, "normalcy." The Freud–Einstein exchange of letters, "Why War?" was published in 1933 (although the letters were written late in 1932), on the eve of the Nazi long march.[6]

The psychiatric interest in the conditions of war and peace, it need hardly be said, had no cause to diminish since Freud observed in his letter to Einstein "that owing to the perfection of instruments of destruction a future war might involve the extermination of one or perhaps both of the antagonists. All this is true, and so incontestably true that one can only feel astonished that the waging of war has not yet been unanimously repudiated."[7]

During and immediately after World War II, the writings of Alexander,[8] G. Brock Chisholm,[9] Trigant Burrow,[10] and others argued that war is not inevitable from a psychiatric point of view, although it does serve as a release for frustrations and conflicts of all sorts. Much of the literature of this period built less on Freud's conception of the place of Thanatos in human affairs than on the sequential "frustration and aggression" theme developed by John Dollard and his associates in 1939.[11]

With the founding of the Group for the Advancement of Psychiatry in 1946, usually referred to as GAP, the attention of psychiatrists was specifically drawn to the problem of war and related problems that beset the national and world communities. Since 1960 the writings of Jerome D. Frank[12] and Judd Marmor,[13] some of which are addressed to lay audiences, have been influential, and in 1964 GAP itself published a widely read report titled *Psychiatric Aspects of the Prevention of Nuclear War*.[14] Citing as difficulties in the way of nonviolent solutions such factors as psychological defense mechanisms, "primitivising effects of extreme fear or panic," increasing dehumanization, ethnocentric perceptual distortion, and other factors that contribute to the psychological escalation of aggression, the GAP study nevertheless insisted that other ways could be found "of conducting conflict between groups of people, or between nations, that can serve these psychological needs more adaptively in our modern world." War, concluded the report, "is a social institution; it is not inevitably rooted in the nature of man."

A second area of interest between the two world wars and for some

years after 1945, although perhaps rather more developed by psychoanalysts than psychiatrists, was the concept of dimensions of national
character, especially the character of Germany. That Germany received
focal attention is understandable in view of the fact that the disruptions
attributable to German-provoked wars and, above all, to Nationalist
Socialism, included the persecution and forced migration of a large
number of psychoanalysts including—in addition to Freud himself—
Rank, Adler, Stekel, Fromm, Fromm-Reichman, Alexander, Horney,
Reich, Erikson, and Reik. Almost all of these prominent exiles from Nazi-
occupied territory were of Jewish extraction; paralleling the interest in the
psychopathology of German national character was a deep concern,
personal as well as professional, about the possible spread of virulent anti-
Semitism. To be sure, the Germans were not the only ones to receive
attention. A survey of the relevant literature reveals numerous articles and
a few books dealing with the American, British, Russian, Chinese,
Japanese, and even Norwegian so-called national character. But in books
such as Richard M. Brickner's *Is Germany Incurable?*[15] and Wilhelm
Reich's *The Mass Psychology of Fascism*,[16] in articles such as Erik H.
Erikson's "Hitler's Imagery and German Youth,"[17] and Fritz Moellenhoff's "The Price of Individuality: Speculations about German National
Characteristics,"[18] German national character and Naziism, its most
virulent expression, were subjected to a psychoanalysis more searching
than that accorded any topic or theme in the social sciences. Much of this
analysis was devoted to an explication of paranoid tendencies in German
history and thought and the means by which these tendencies could be
abolished or at least reduced after the war; but there were also efforts, as
in the writings of Erich Fromm, to gaze at Germany and the general
problem of authoritarianism through spectacles, the right lens of which
had been contributed by Freud, and the left donated by Marx.[19] Since 1950,
interest in Nazi Germany has very largely been confined to historians,
some of whom have attempted to apply psychoanalytic categories, while
the study of national character as such is not now a central interest in either
psychiatry or the social sciences.

Ethnic group prejudice, on the other hand, is a continuing concern.
There have been shifts of emphasis, however, reflecting changing problems
and research needs. A vast literature dealing with anti-Semitism, to which
psychoanalysts and psychiatrists have made influential contributions, has
succeeded in exposing the roots of anti-Semitism, although precise boundaries are not fixed as between religious, historical, social, economic and

psychopathological causal explanations. Since publication of *The Authoritarian Personality*,[20] the most significant effort made to link anti-Semitism to a variety of individual and social disorders, most work on anti-Semitism has been in the form of surveys that attempt to measure the distribution of opinions among a given population.

After 1954, the year of the momentous school desegregation decision of the Supreme Court, interest conspicuously shifted to problems in white–Negro relations and related civil rights activities. Prior to the *Brown vs. Board of Education* decision of a unanimous Court in 1954, American psychiatry, like American society itself, did not demonstrate much concern for Negroes apart from an occasional article dealing with race riots or with the high incidence of mental illness in predominantly Negro communities. Perhaps this neglect owed something to the relatively small position that Negroes occupy in psychiatry, either as doctors or as private patients. Whatever the explanation, not much was known about the psychiatric aspects of either segregation or desegregation prior to a 1956 roundtable on the subject sponsored by the American Orthopsychiatric Society. In 1957 a GAP publication *Psychiatric Aspects of School Desegregation*[21] was an important contribution to the small body of literature on the subject, and since then race relations themes have been dealt with in a number of articles published by psychiatrists. It remains broadly true, however, that psychiatry, much less psychoanalysis, has not given to the civil rights area the attention it has given to other problems in the social psychiatry field, or the attention that civil rights problems deserve. Partly for this reason, there is as yet no published work as substantial as *The Authoritarian Personality*; indeed, the most significant book on race relations is still Gunnar Myrdal's *An American Dilemma* of 1944,[22] and Myrdal was neither an American nor a psychiatrist, nor yet a political scientist or historian, but a combined economist–sociologist of Swedish nationality.

A fourth dimension of psychiatric insight literature, and one closely related to research on ethnic group relations, has been concerned with democratic and nondemocratic modal personality types. Most psychiatrists who have written on social issues have had something to say about contrasting authoritarian and nonauthoritarian character structures, although it is fair to comment that their work, like that of political scientists with similar interests, is given more to implication than explication, especially with regard to the nonauthoritarian character structure. Much of what has been published is also vulnerable to a criticism similar to that leveled at *The Authoritarian Personality*, namely, that the nuclear concept excludes left wing behavior. While efforts have been made to study individual Communists, the personality type occasionally referred to as the authoritarian liberal remains elusive, at least in research terms.

Insofar as authoritarian and nonauthoritarian modal types can be extrapolated from the diverse body of literature which describe certain essentials of democracy and dictatorship, it would appear that the authoritarian type, from a psychiatric point of view, is a coercive, anxious, suspicious, and id-rejecting individual who is oriented toward power and extremely limited in his capacity to give and receive affection. Demanding from others either dominance or submission, the authoritarian type tends to be the total leader in one kind of situation, and the total rebel in another. "Intolerant of ambiguity," in Frenkel-Brunswik's phrase, his problem-solving methods are rigid, quick, and direct, and his preferred solution is always simplistic. He prefers his wife passive, his children submissive, his home life undemanding, his friends deferential, and his employees docile. He is frequently skilled in masking his basic hostility behind a facade of spurious warmth and friendliness, and he is often a master in the art of dissimulation. Enjoying the delusion of rectitudinous grandeur, he may see himself as an honest man who has not been discovered by Diogenes, or as an unappreciated Nehru who has every right to burn since Rome does nothing but fiddle. If he is conservative as well as authoritarian, phrases and words such as Communist, socialist, Stevenson, one world, Medicare, and beatnik may engender spontaneous combustion. If he is liberal as well as authoritarian, the inflammable terms are capitalism, Wall Street, Hoover (both Herbert and J. Edgar), CIA, military–industrial complex, and Catholic hierarchy.

The democratic type, by contrast, is a persuasive, secure, trustful, and id-accepting individual for whom power is only one of a number of values. Able to give and receive affection, his relations with others are characterized, in Erikson's working, by "mutuality." Lacking the desire to be either the absolute leader or absolute follower, the democrat as husband, father, and employer does not demand that others strip their own egos in order to clothe his own; his role may require that he be *primus inter pares* in decision-making situations, but he is supportive in such a role and he takes others into account. He can accept criticism, understand frailty in others as well as himself, and limit his hostile and aggressive impulses or discharge them harmlessly. Politically he may lean to either side, but whether a conservative or a liberal, he rejects devil theories of politics and controls his emotional reaction to manipulations of symbols irrespective of their plus or minus value in his belief system.

Clearly these characterological types should be of immense importance in the study of political behavior, and yet political scientists have made very little use of them. Some reasons for this have already been noted—the "hard" approach infatuation of many political scientists, for example—but in addition, many students of political behavior feel that the authoritarian and democratic personality models are too vague and imprecise to be of research utility. Some critics go so far as to suggest that such models are more imaginative then descriptive, arguing that the key concepts are not dichotomized terminals between which a given population distributes itself, but points on a personality continuum within individuals. The same person, they maintain, will be authoritarian in one situation, and democratic in another, in accordance with his role perceptions. They also express doubts that the authoritarian subculture, assuming one exists, plays a significant role in American life, or that it is increasing in size and importance.

These reservations and criticisms may or may not be legitimate; what is certain is that they will not be resolved unless "hard" and "soft" methods are joined in a collaboration between psychiatrists and political scientists. From psychiatry, for example, we need much more specifically with regard to the interpersonal (family, school, workplace) environments that nourish democratic and authoritarian personalities, and recommended measures for strengthening democratic as opposed to authoritarian tendencies in society. From history, we need more information about economic, social, and political conditions which have given rise to authoritarian subcultures and paranoid pseudo-communities within democratic societies. From political science, we need to know more about the extent to which authoritarian tendencies in political life can be modified by role settings and expectations, by interaction between authoritarians and democrats, by enlightenment, and, finally, by restriction and confinement in the larger social environment. These demands made upon the several disciplines hardly exhaust the research needs and opportunities with reference to possible linkages between personality types and political behavior.

It is indeed difficult to think of any insight area in social psychiatry, or any research in political and historical behavior, that would not benefit from collaboration between the three disciplines. The study of voting behavior, for example, a "hard" research field in social science if ever there was one, would become more exciting and significant if voting motivation and intention underwent psychological scrutiny in depth; adaptations of the psychiatric interview would add an important dimension to research into the behavior of bureaucrats, congressmen, state legislators, city councilmen, and the like. While psychiatrists have gradually become aware of correlations between socio-economic variables and mental illness (and the treatment thereof), more research is needed on the national cultural aspects of mental health and illness. If biographies are to serve as the rich tapestries of entire lives and not merely pale sketches of names, dates, and places, biographers will have to acquire some skills from psycho-analysis in making inferences, reconstructions, and interpretations.

The frontier areas of these disciplines, however, require less an exchange of methods and insights than their merger into a comprehensive science of social behavior. In this development the psychiatrist would find himself working in tandem not just with medical specialists but with social scientists who shared with him a common interest in man's fate. The merger of methods and insights in the future may even extend to practices, treatments, and therapies. It requires little imagination to foresee the time when there are psychiatry members of Political Science Departments, and when political scientists are attached to hospital and clinic staffs.

The emergent science of social behavior will not lack for challenging research areas; indeed the problem will be to assess priorities among problems that demand attention. But by any test, one urgent problem is bound to be the problem of defining democracy in terms that are meaning-ful in a twentieth-century world of nuclear weapons, super-powers, gross inequalities of wealth, racial tensions, and, in the so-called advanced portions, giant organizations that transform men into pigmy automatons and ant-like robots. Put another way, the problem is how to make the world safe for democratic character development, and unsafe for those authoritarian and destructive tendencies that threaten an end of the human experience. In short, the most urgent question facing the emergent science is the question of man's survival itself.

A collaborative approach to the question of survival might initially focus on those institutions and behavioral patterns, national and international, that create or contribute to neurosis and psychosis. Reference here is not to the concept of "society as the patient," as useful in certain circumstances as that concept may be, but to the belief that a good deal of disturbed behavior, both social and individual, is rooted in societal conditions. While efforts have been made to identify these conditions and relate them to deviant behaviors, much remains to be known about the nature and treatment of such relationships.

It is fairly well established, for example, that the distribution of mental illnesses is inversely related to class and income, that, to take one case, proportionately more of the poor than the rich suffer from schizophrenia and other illnesses. There is also evidence that Americans in general worry more about financial insecurity than about any other problem in their lives. Clearly, the unhappiness of a great many, and the psychoses of some Americans, is to some extent a reflection of the economic and social environment in which they find themselves. It follows that the environment needs changing, and gradually—all too gradually—it is being changed, in some respects. But for the short run, at least, much could be accomplished if we could account for the fact that not everyone in a poverty culture becomes schizophrenic or otherwise mentally ill, and not all Americans are equally worried about financial insecurity. What factors, then, *in addition to environment*, determine whether one does or does not become ill or markedly insecure? Here, surely, is a collaborative area, the exploration of which would save many more from crippling illnesses than are now helped by conventional treatment methods.

Another neglected area of research, and one of equal challenge, is the relationship between sexual and social behavior. While it is a truism, since Freud, to declare that psychosexual disturbances in the individual are a prime cause of neurosis, very little research has been done on the extent to which the sexual aspects of culture promote as well as reflect disturbed behavior in political and social arenas as well as individual lives. Many of those who work with young people are persuaded that they especially suffer from the strains and tensions that are built-in features of American sexual culture—although, again, we cannot discriminate with any precision among the factors that predispose some to suffer more than others. But not only young people. There is evidence that adults also suffer from what Sullivan called the "lurid twilight" of sexuality in America, a "twilight" made up of unrestricted stimulation, on the one hand, and restricted response, on the other. No doubt Sullivan had in mind some sections of the mass media which, quite apart from their catering to voyeuristic tastes, parade before us a thousand inviting male and female images, although the mores make us do with one husband or wife at a time, inviting or otherwise. Despite sporadic protests, New York is now publishing books banned in almost all other Western countries, and Hollywood is making movies for popular consumption that were formerly reserved for stag evenings at American Legion halls. The unprecedented rise of *Playboy*, the only magazine in its price class ever to reach a 5,000,000 per month circulation, is a related phenomenon, as is the appearance of the bare-bosomed waitress.

If our sexual mores had changed *as much* as the books and magazines, there would be fewer problems arising from the supercharged erotic atmosphere. The mores, however, while they have undoubtedly changed, still do not endorse premarital or extra-marital sexual intercourse, nor are they tolerant of deviant sexual practices. The frequent result of the visual do's and verbal don't's is a psychic state inimical to either physical or mental health. Yet there have been few efforts to study the "lurid twilight" in terms of its relationship to political extremism, delinquency, violence, ethnic group tension, and other problems.

A third important and somewhat neglected research area is the relation-ship between personality and political leadership. The psychodynamics of political leadership is largely unexplored territory, despite the efforts of some political scientists and historians to make limited and not always successful use of psychiatric insights in particular cases. For reasons not entirely clear, psychiatrists and psychoanalysts have written relatively little about political leaders; apparently they have preferred to deal with cultural and religious figures. As a consequence, we know relatively little about the role of personality factors in opinion formation and in the shaping of political career patterns. We are even less informed about the influence of physical and mental illness on decision-making processes, although the list of sick statesmen is a long one. Thoroughly international, it may also be significant for an understanding of certain key decisions that have had a strategic effect on world history.[23]

It is fascinating to think what might be accomplished by systematic research and discussion of the role of personality variables in the decisions to drop the Bomb on Hiroshima, or to intervene in Korea and Vietnam. Much could be accomplished if most of the 318 psychiatrists in the District of Columbia were willing to collaborate with political scientists in studying the consequences for decision-making of stress, tension, and illness. As it is, neither psychiatrists nor political scientists can say much about the factors that predispose particular individuals to tolerate successfully stress in decision-making situations. We simply do not know who breaks down, and why, and what the effect has been in policy terms. Practically nothing is known about the influence of tranquilizers and related drugs; for that matter, nothing reliable is known about the role of psychiatry itself in the nation's capital, apart from the fact that Washington, D.C. is a leader in the ratio of psychiatrists to population. Here, again, collaboration between the disciplines could have only the most beneficial results in terms of both public welfare values and research frontiersmanship.

The stability of the democratic community may also be threatened by the impact of automation in areas that have always been characterized by warm, face-to-face interpersonal relations. In medicine the day is not far off when diagnosis and treatment will be carried out by computers, and in psychiatry there are those who believe that in the future many varieties of mental illness will be diagnosed and prescribed for by tape-fed machines rather sophisticated in processing somatic data. Within ten years or less the average patient, without leaving his hospital bed much less his room, will be able to feed and bathe himself, administer certain medications, take his temperature and have it recorded, and even undergo surgery. Clearly the need for confrontations with doctors, nurses, technicians, orderlies, nurses' aides, and other hospital personnel will be sharply reduced.

The automated university is hardly further away than the hospital. Much of the teaching now done by professors will be done by teaching machines, closed-circuit television, tape recorders, and other devices. Perhaps the day will come when the student, like the patient, need never leave his room to obtain the benefits he had paid for. Students already complain that they rarely see their professors; in the future, at a great many universities, they will *never* see their professors.

All this signifies that in medicine and education, not to mention the factory and office, there will be a marked decrease in interpersonal contacts and face-to-face relationships, in short, a decrease in opportunities for rewarding human relationships. What will be the consequences for mental health? Family life? Our economic and political institutions?

If these questions are to be answered in a positive and hopeful fashion, and before the full consequences of technology are upon us, collaboration between the social and humanistic sciences may have to go beyond research into the practice areas themselves. If it be assumed, for example, that the technological revolution will be accompanied by a rising incidence of psychiatric disorders, notwithstanding the material benefits conferred by technological development, then it is clear that something more is needed than a collaborative research orientation and the conventional treatment methods now in effect in psychiatry. Perhaps what is required is collaboration to broaden and deepen the concept of the therapeutic community to make it apply, not to the mental hospital and psychiatric clinic,[24] but to any subculture of society that directly or indirectly promotes mental health and democratic citizenship. In this sense, a therapeutic community is one that not only treats those who are ill; it seeks to prevent illness by establishing an environment that is supportive of health, rationality, and creativity. Oriented toward the whole man and not merely one of his roles or functions, a therapeutic community would help develop in everyone the potential for neurosis-free behavior in both the personal and social setting.

One such therapeutic community, in this sense, is the university, although it is rarely thought of that way. For four years or more in the lives of millions of persons, the university constitutes a distinct subculture of society providing not only education but moral instruction, social life and companionship, physical activity, and esthetic uplift. Education in terms of formal classroom instruction is perhaps the least important aspect of university life, at least as regards time. Each week the average student will spend between twelve and fifteen hours in class, and the average professor will devote between six and twelve hours to teaching. The remainder of the student's time is spent in the library, dorm or fraternity house, dining room, union, dating, and attending sports events. Professors devote much of their time to reading and writing, department meetings, committee work, advising students, answering mail, and so forth. Evenings and weekends are generally given over to the family, but on many campuses even family life is campus-related: the dinner party guests will be drawn mainly from the faculty, and the children's friends are likely to be the children of colleagues.

Clearly the structure and function of this subculture, the extent to which it satisfies basic needs, are important in considering such campus problems as suicides (the second-ranking cause of death among college students), nervous breakdowns, drugs and alcoholism, theft, sexual promiscuity, failures and dropouts; needless to remark, the faculty, too, has its share of these problems, and it is a share that is increasing. Yet within the university these problems are rarely discussed as societal problems, that is, as problems generated by stresses, strains, and tensions in the academic community as such. And when they are discussed, it is comparatively rare for administrators to draw on the specialized knowledge of either behavioral or humanistic scientists. Psychiatrists and political scientists are usually consulted less than other behavioral experts such as electrical engineers, biochemists, and deans of the business and law schools. The problems mentioned are invariably approached as administrative problems which, by definition, are problems that can be solved by a new rule or disciplinary action.

But the university is only one type of organization rarely thought of as a therapeutic community. While universities lag far behind corporations and law firms in developing the equivalent of executive health programs, the latter do not yet see themselves as therapeutic communities in which there is a central concern for mental as well as physical health. Existing health programs too often focus on the maximization of productivity, commonly defined in terms of output, job-performance, or some other crude measure of efficiency. It therefore is no surprise that many of these programs function at the expense of health, rationality, and creativity rather than in support of these values.

If the concept of the therapeutic community is to be successfully re-defined, there will have to be significant changes in the training of behavioral and humanistic scientists and in the role played by them in society. Since the supply of clinicians is extremely limited, clinical training must be provided for all those whose occupational positions require them to serve as teachers, counsellors, advisors, and social planners—in short, for all those who occupy important posts in the therapeutic community. In the university, for example, the larger part of the guidance function is performed by the professors with whom students are in frequent contact; in effect, the professors are called upon by students to act as clinicians, irrespective of whether they have any clinical training or vocation for clinical practice. Moreover, if the university is to be successfully trans-formed from a learning factory into a therapeutic community, those who plan and direct the transformation must be familiar with psychiatric methods and insights. Decisions about curricular and degree require-ments, the design of buildings and physical settings to provide the necessary amounts of privacy and collegiality, rules and regulations, students and faculty housing arrangements, and much else—these decisions require more than the part-time consultative services of a social psychi-atrist or clinical psychologist. Ideally those who make these decisions will be generalists, not specialists, and as generalists they will be participant-observers in therapeutic processes that draw on the whole range of the behavioral and humanistic sciences.

The challenge presented by and to the therapeutic community is a formidable one, to be sure. But if the challenge is very great, so, too, is the opportunity thereby presented to increase the potential—individual and social, national and international—for health, rationality, and creativity.

Insofar as these values of the therapeutic community are realizable only in a world that has abolished war, peace itself would not be least among the outcomes of a fruitful collaboration between psychiatrists and political scientists.

But it would be naïve to imagine that collaboration will be either easy or immediately productive, for innovative, "breakthrough" thinking is not the foremost characteristic of either the clinic or the academy. At least twice in his life, Freud observed that there were three "impossible" professions: educating, healing, and governing. He has not yet been proven wrong.

Notes

1. Ernest Jones, *The Life and Work of Sigmund Freud*. New York: Basic Books, 1955. Vol. 2, p. 57.

2. Abram Kardiner, *The Psychological Frontiers of Society*. New York: Columbia University Press, 1945, p. 23. Italics added.

3. Kenneth M. Colby, *An Introduction to Psychoanalytic Research*. New York: Basic Books, 1960.

4. Else Frenkel-Brunswik, "Interaction of Psychological and Sociological Factors in Political Behavior," *American Political Science Review*, 46 (1952), 44–65.

5. Fred Greenstein, "The Benevolent Leader: Children's Images of Political Authority," *American Political Science Review*, 54 (1960) 934–943; and his *Children and Politics*. New Haven: Yale University Press, 1965. See also, David Easton and Robert D. Hess, "The Child's Changing Image of the President," *Public Opinion Quarterly*, 24 (1960), 632–644, and "The Child's Political World", *Midwest Journal of Political Science*, 6 (1962), 236–247.

6. Sigmund Freud, *Civilization and Its Discontents*. London: Hogarth Press, 1930; "Thoughts for the Times on War and Death," (1915) in *Collected Papers*, IV, 288–317. London: Hogarth Press, 1949; and "Why War?" (1932) in *Collected Papers*, V, 272–287. London: Hogarth Press, 1950.

7. Freud, *Collected Papers*, V, 285.

8. Franz Alexander, *Our Age of Unreason*. Philadelphia: Lippincott, 1942; and "Aggressiveness—Individual and Collective," in *The March of Medicine*. New York: Columbia University Press, 1943, pp. 83–99.

9. G. Brock Chisholm, "The Psychiatry of Enduring Peace and Social Progress," *Psychiatry*, 9 (1946).

10. Trigant Burrow, "Neurosis and War: A Problem of Human Behavior," *Journal of Psychology*, 12 (1941), 235–249.

11. John Dollard *et al.*, *Frustration and Aggression*. New Haven: Yale University Press, 1939.

12. Jerome D. Frank, "Breaking the Thought Barrier: Psychological Challenges of the Nuclear Age," *Psychiatry*, 23 (1960), 245–266.

13. Judd Marmor, "War, Violence, and Human Nature," *Bulletin of Atomic Scientists* (March, 1964), 19–22.

14. *Psychiatric Aspects of the Prevention of Nuclear War*, Report No. 57, September, 1964.

15. *Is Germany Incurable?* Philadelphia: Lippincott, 1943.

16. *The Mass Psychology of Fascism*. New York: Orgone Institute Press, 1946.

17. Erik Erikson, "Hitler's Imagery and German Youth," *Psychiatry*, 5, (1942), 475–493; and "Wholeness and Totality," in C. J. Friedrich (Ed.), *Totalitarianism*. Cambridge: Harvard University Press, 1954.

18. Fritz Moellenhoff, "The Price of Individuality: Speculations About German National Characteristics," *American Imago*, 4 (1947), 33–60.

19. Erich Fromm, *Escape from Freedom*. New York: Rinehart, 1941.

20. T. W. Adorno *et al.*, *The Authoritarian Personality*. New York: Harper and Bros., 1950.

21. *Psychiatric Aspects of School Desegregation*, Report No. 37, May, 1957.

22. Hugh L'Etang, "The Health of Statesmen," *The Practitioner* (January, 1958); and Arnold A. Rogow, "Disability in High Office," *Medical Opinion and Review*, I (April, 1966), 16–19.

23. Gunnar Myrdal, *An American Dilemma*. New York: Harper and Bros., 1944.

24. Maxwell Jones, *The Therapeutic Community*. New York: Basic Books, 1953. See also his *Beyond the Therapeutic Community*. New Haven: Yale University Press, 1968.

9

American Election Analysis:
A Case History of Methodological
Innovation and Diffusion

RICHARD JENSEN

Since World War Two the space filled by behavioral articles in the *American Political Science Review* has rocketed from 16 to 59 per cent of the total. The transition from traditional or institutional approaches to politics to behavioralism constitutes a central episode in the history of American political science.[1] This chapter traces the erratic development of probably the most important contributor to that transition, the analysis of election statistics. The focus will not be the hypotheses generated to explain voting behavior, but rather the origins, advancement, and transmission of the relevant methodological paradigms inside and among the disciplines of journalism, statistics, geography, history, sociology, and political science. The story begins early, and is still unfolding, but emphasis here will be on developments before World War Two—in fact, before 1932.

The divination of the meaning of election returns has always been a valued art among working politicians and journalists. Perhaps the earliest published voting analysis explained and justified the costly decision of Massachusetts' Governor James Bowdoin to suppress Shays' Rebellion in 1787. Bowdoin's vigorous countermeasures led to his defeat at the hands of the popular hero, John Hancock. Shortly after the election an "Impartial Observer" released to the press a list "as accurate as could be obtained" of the "number and division of the votes, among the different classes of citizens in [Boston]":

This is a slightly revised version of a paper read at the American Political Science Association Convention, September, 1967. The author is grateful to the many men mentioned in the Notes who provided information and reminiscences.

	For Mr. B	*For* Mr. H
Physicians.	19	2
Clergymen.	2	0
Lawyers.	17	3
Independent Gentlemen.	50	0
Merchants and Traders.	295	21
Printers.	8	4
Tradesmen.	328	299
Labourers, servants, &c.	5	446
Total	724	775

The methods of voting analysis have never been firmly established; two researchers can derive startlingly different conclusions about the same events. Thus three days later a Hancock man lamented the "very great error in the arrangement of the votes last Monday," and gleefully presented the "authentick" breakdown[2]:

	For Mr. B	*For* Mr. H
Usurers,	28	0
Speculators in Publick Securities,	576	0
Stockholders and directors of the M—tts B—k,	81	0
Persons under British influence,	17	0
Merchants, tradesmen, and other worthy members of society,	21	448
Friends to the Revolution,	0	327
Wizards,	1	0
	724	775

This pioneer newspaper duel displayed the eagerness of politicians to bolster the prestige of their cause and to denigrate the opposition by exposing the patterns of voting behavior. While the use of social science for partisan purposes has always been uncommon in this country, the curiosity of the politicians about their sources of strength, coupled with the pride and power of the winning candidates, led to the extensive publication of raw returns in newspapers, almanacs, and official state year-books, beginning in the 1830's.[3]

Of the thousands of series of almanacs published in the nineteenth century, the *Tribune Almanac* (1838–1914) stands out as the most reliable and complete collection of county returns in presidential and gubernatorial races. Horace Greeley, whose *New York Tribune* published the *Almanac*, included election statistics in the 1860 Republican "campaign textbook," thus inaugurating the G.O.P.'s unbroken concern with election statistics. New York Democrats, however, published the first notable set of com-prehensive historical returns, giving the ward vote in all major New York City elections since 1822 in the *Manual of the Corporation of the City of New York* (1871 and previous years). The 1871 edition included the first tabulation of the percentage breakdown of the vote, giving the Democratic percentage in each ward for every year from 1840 to 1869. Indeed, only one other compilation of percentage breakdowns appeared before World War Two, in the *Blue Book of . . . Wisconsin* (1897). Politicians and journalists evidently thought in terms of pluralities not percentages. Concerned with the raw aggregate totals, that is, with who won and who lost, they rarely pondered subtle percentages.

The most statistically oriented political party in American history was the Prohibitionists. The well-educated Protestant clergymen and laymen who led the party labored for years to demonstrate a statistical causality between drinking and poverty, venality, disease, and social deterioration. Although they failed to use the sophisticated mathematical techniques discovered by British statisticians, the Prohibitionists educated generations of Americans in the use (and misuse) of dazzling arrays of "scientifically ascertained" numbers. Save in coalition with a major party, the Pro-hibitionists rarely enjoyed the sweet pleasure of carrying a precinct any-where in the United States. The party adjusted to its size by expanding its pretensions, and claimed it represented the "balance of power" in American politics. In its almanac, the *Political Prohibitionist* (1887, 1888, 1889), comprehensive tabulations of percentage gains, losses and share of the vote, by cities, states and regions, exhibited the drys' threat to wet politicians, and indicated new ways of tabulating and presenting election statistics. Remote was the county and lopsided the election in which the Prohibitionists did not claim the "balance of power," and their legacy survives in this century in the similar claims made frequently by various groups supposedly concerned with only a single salient issue.

Less directly an influence on modern methodology, but more fascinating than compilations of returns, was the development of polling techniques in the last quarter of the nineteenth century. Political clubs have always canvassed the voting intentions of their wards and neighborhoods, but comprehensive, systematic polling began around 1874, probably first in the fiercely contested swing states of Indiana and New York. By 1888, Democrats could report to President Grover Cleveland that his Hoosier supporters "have maps of counties made out by sections and the names and parties of each and every voter living on each section of land."[4] In 1880 senatorial candidate Benjamin Harrison commissioned a poll of every Union veteran in Indiana, and was doubtless pleased to discover that 69 per cent of his 26,000 comrades in the state voted Republican.[5] In 1892 a national Democratic leader explained that the Midwestern states were polled thoroughly in order "to get down to bed-rock facts on which to base our calculations and efforts."[6]

Not everyone approved of these new-fangled polls. One outraged Indianapolis man thought they were designed to spot hospitable recipients of corruption money. "Polling the voters before the election," he charged, "is an infamous contemptible conspiracy in this glorious free republic."[7] Nevertheless polling reached a climax in the intense campaign of 1896. The Democrats spent much of their scanty funds on polls, while Mark Hanna spent a small fortune on them. The G.O.P. that year convassed every voter in Chicago three times before election day. Soon everyone from college clubs to breakfast food companies joined in the fun and conducted straw polls. The *Chicago Tribune* sent teams of reporters across Illinois to poll some 14,000 factory hands and railway workers with secret ballots (over 80 per cent preferred McKinley).[8]

By far the most elaborate and expensive poll conducted in the nineteenth century was the enterprise of an independent Chicago newspaper, *The Record*. In 1896 the newspaper spent upwards of $60,000 to mail postcard ballots to what it hoped was a random sample of one voter out of every eight in twelve Midwestern states. An additional 328,000 cards went to each registered voter in Chicago. By the end of October, when a quarter million returns had been tabulated, the *Record* employed a team of eminent mathematicians to interpret the results, and predicted that McKinley would win 57.95 per cent of the Chicago vote (he won 57.91 per cent).[9]

The Democrats feared the *Record* poll was a Republican trick, and warned Bryanites that the postcards would go to ruthless Hanna. The biased response made the job of interpretation especially difficult, even

when the mathematicians tried to control for the respondents' 1892 vote
and the actual 1892 results. Outside Chicago the adjusted results still
showed a McKinley landslide of grossly exaggerated proportions. The
Democratic National Committee finally denounced the poll publicly:

> The whole scheme is one of fraud and debauchery, and may be taken
> as the first step in a conspiracy to do away with popular elections under
> the law, and place the molding of public opinion in the hands of million-
> aires and corporations.[10]

After 1896 party polls fell rapidly into disuse. Not until the *Literary Digest*
and advertising agencies coupled opinion polls with sales tactics in the
1920's and radio market research began in the 1930's did polling revive.[11]

The first scholarly, nonjournalistic study of elections grew out of the
new techniques of statistical cartography pioneered by geographers and
statisticians in the U.S. Census Bureau. Francis Walker, the superintendent
of the 1870 and 1880 censuses, revealed the power of graphic presentation
in his *Statistical Atlas of the United States* (1874) based on the 1870 census.
The maps for the 1880 census (drawn by geographer Henry Gannett)
appeared in the magnificent *Scribner's Statistical Atlas of the United States*
(1883). The *Scribner's Atlas* was a triumph in the history of American
statistics, cartography, and bookmaking. Its beautiful multi-hued folio
maps displayed the variation from county to county of scores of demographic, social, economic, cultural, and political indices. It demonstrated
the power of maps to reduce great quantities of statistics into compre-
hensible format. Plates 7 to 10 gave multicolored maps of the states for
every presidential election, using the different hues to represent the
percentage strength of the leading candidate. Plate 11 represented the
birth and the most brilliant advance of scientific election analysis. It was a
folio-size map with twelve shades of red and blue clearly representing the
percentage strength of the leading candidate in every county in 1880.
The underlying percentages were not separately reported, but contained
a few errors. In 1888 and 1890, Scribner's published shorter atlases
designed primarily for election analysis. They included folio maps for the
1884 and 1888 elections, as well as similar maps showing the distribution
of different immigrant groups, and must be judged the most accurate,
attractive, and complete election maps ever published.[12]

The Census Bureau attracted the services of several men interested in
election statistics. Edward Stanwood, a Boston journalist and Census
official, wrote *A History of Presidential Elections* (1884) which, in numerous

editions for half a century, furnished the best compendium of statewide returns, convention proceedings and roll calls, platforms and campaign highlights. But he largely ignored the voting patterns of the various segments of the electorate. Another Census official, Thomas Campbell-Copeland, gathered county returns for all presidential races from 1872 through 1888, computed the leader's plurality in each county, and published the results in the 1888 edition of *Appleton's Annual Cyclopedia* (1889). The 1896 edition of the *Cyclopedia* furnished excellent statistical analyses of the county voting patterns in the McKinley–Bryan contest, written by Campbell-Copeland and Oscar Austin, a free-lance statistician on the staff of the Republican National Committee.[13]

The cartographic achievements of the Census Bureau might have been neglected had not the Johns Hopkins University (founded in 1876) emphasized the value of maps in the social sciences. Hopkins President Daniel Coit Gilman, a friend and fellow geographer of Walker, stressed the empirical study of human behavior, especially as it is affected by the physical environment.[14] Thanks to Gilman's familiarity with German research, Hopkins scholars in history, economics, and political science enjoyed the use of a "Statistical Bureau" and a "Geographical Bureau," two research rooms stocked with maps, atlases, almanacs, statistical reports, census publications, and other data sources. Gilman found a powerful and energetic historian, Herbert Baxter Adams, to supervise the study of the social sciences. Adams made extensive use of the bureaus in training students, for as he explained, "physical and historical geography are made the basis of instruction in historical and political science."[15]

In 1885 one of the most promising young historians at Hopkins, J. Franklin Jameson, proclaimed the new orientation Gilman and Adams had given to political and historical analysis:

> The true history of our nation will not be written until we obtain a correct and exhaustive knowledge of the history of public opinion upon politics, the history of the political views and actions of the ordinary voter. If we are attempting to discover the causes which gave this or that issue to a recent presidential election even, we do not think of being satisfied with an explanation expressed, so to speak, in terms of national politics only; we ask ourselves: What influences worked upon the mind of the average voter in Ohio, leading him, with whom the decision rested, to decide thus? What combination of circumstances so affected the political molecules in Massachusetts or in Virginia as to give a new complexion to the political tissue?[16]

Jameson's manifesto sounds like a modern introduction to a panel study of voting behavior in a particular community—or perhaps like the application for a foundation grant to make such a study. And in a sense it was both. Jameson did important research on turnout rates in the late eighteenth century, and his colleagues at Hopkins studied suffrage and election procedures in colonial and early American history.

Another influence on election studies at Hopkins was interest in the social conflict theories of Ludwig Gumplowicz and especially of Gustav Ratzenhofer. Albion Small, who taught history at Hopkins for a while before founding the sociology department at Chicago, was particularly concerned with the sociology of conflict, and the idea that interest groups were the basis of society and of the political struggles for power in society. Arthur Bentley became interested in conflict sociology, either at Hopkins or during his studies in Germany, and developed the interest group theory of politics in his seminal book, *The Process of Government* (1908).[17]

Combined with the Hopkins tradition of empirical studies of political behavior, the sociology of interest group conflict provided the basis for the analysis of American party struggles. However, statistical analysis of American voting patterns quickly leads to a de-emphasis on economic conflict, and a realization of the primacy of party loyalty and long-run stability of geographical and ethnic voting patterns.[18] Thus the economic conflict approach either is abandoned, or else empirical statistical analysis is abandoned.[19]

The most fruitful long-run impact of the Census and Hopkins styles of election analysis emerged in the school of quantitative historiography founded by Frederick Jackson Turner. Turner learned something of elections, polls, and censuses from his father, Andrew Jackson Turner, a Republican politician, newspaper editor, and Wisconsin supervisor for the 1890 census. At Johns Hopkins, Turner worked with Adams, Jameson, Small, Woodrow Wilson, and others, learning not only their theories but also coming to appreciate the utility of statistical cartography. In the great maps of *Scribner's Atlas*, Turner spotted the movement of the frontier, and the changes it brought in economic, social, and political conditions in the different sections of the nation. He found the election maps of special interest, and determined to devote his career to the geographical analysis of American development, using statistical cartography as his most powerful descriptive and analytic tool.[20]

Although best known for his frontier hypothesis, Turner directed most of his own and his students' research to the sectional patterns of American political, economic, and social history. As professor of history at Wisconsin (1885 to 1910) and at Harvard (1910 to 1924), he trained hundreds of historians and political scientists in his methodology. The first doctoral thesis Turner directed was Orin G. Libby's brilliant analysis of *The Geographical Distribution of the Vote of the Thirteen States on the Federal Constitution, 1787–8* (Madison, 1894). Libby mapped the constituencies of the supporters and opponents of the Constitution and correlated visually the sentiments of the delegates to state conventions with the ecological characteristics of their constituencies. He interpreted the controversy over ratification in terms of the group conflict theory of political process, emphasizing economic conflict between farmers and merchants.

Libby worked vigorously in the field of political statistics for the next two decades. He often emphasized the need to study the geographical distribution of public opinion, and was the first scholar to make careful studies of legislative roll calls. Before his departure to the University of North Dakota in 1902, Libby worked closely with Turner in the rapidly expanding Wisconsin history department, and in 1897–98 he taught a pioneering course on "American Sectionalism" that studied "the geographical distribution of political parties with especial reference to the votes in Congress and in state legislatures."[21]

Meanwhile Turner made numerous maps of election returns (by counties) and compared the sectional patterns that emerged with all the geographical and ecological data he could find. He recommended that his students:

> make in selected areas, detailed study of the correlations between party votes, by precincts, wards, etc., soils, nationalities and state-origins of the voter, assessment rolls, denominational groups, illiteracy, etc. What kind of people tend to be Whigs, what Democrats or Abolitionists, or Prohibitionists, etc.[22]

As an example of the sophistication even Turner's undergraduate students achieved, consider the unpublished senior thesis written by William Dickinson in 1901.[23] Under the supervision of Libby and Turner, Dickinson classified all the members of the Wisconsin state legislatures of 1850, 1860, and 1870 according to party, nativity, occupation, personal assessed wealth, and average assessed wealth of their constituencies. After analyzing the resulting distributions, the young scholar took nine important roll-callvotes and classified the ayes and nays according to the same categories. Dickinson got excellent results for his painstaking work, but he never followed up the study, and aside from Libby and Turner, no one ever heard of it.

Unfortunately Turner did not equip his students with the statistical techniques necessary to handle the data they were working with, such as measures of dispersion and association, correlation coefficients, graphing techniques, and time series trending. Instead he relied wholly upon visual correlation of maps, which rapidly becomes confusing and misleading when great quantities of data are involved. Nevertheless the maps were a powerful device for relating data, revealing patterns, and suggesting hypotheses. One of Turner's students recalled:

> One lasting impression which the student carried away from Turner's classes and from his workshop was that of countless maps, jigsaw in appearance, because they represented the plotting of votes by counties. Such graphic representation revealed sectional interests, the force of habit, the persistence of viewpoint carried by the migrants from older areas into newer ones. When thrown against geological survey maps, racial maps, or cultural maps of various kinds, they added something to the American story not to be found elsewhere. Turner gave the United States census maps a new place in the historian's equipment.[24]

Turner's influence spread beyond the confines of the historical profession. He read his most important papers before conventions of political scientists, geographers, and sociologists to proselytize his views. The warmest response came from political science, a field with traditionally strong ties to history (most political science students minor in history). Among his students were Frederick Ogg (specialist on national politics and the Jacksonian period), Charles McCarthy (who switched from history to political science), Paul Reinsch (legislative procedure), Arthur Holcombe (national parties), Wilfred Binkley (national party history), and William Schaper (who also switched from history).

The Turnerians directed scholarly attention away from the constitutional, institutional, and metaphysical dimensions of history, emphasizing instead the interaction between political behavior and social, economic, and physical environment. Instead of treating politics from the viewpoint of grand historical trends, or petty backstage maneuvering, the Turnerians stressed voting patterns, campaign strategy, and the responses of the political system to the demands of constituents.[25] Thus the empirical study of human behavior became central to their work, and the behavioral approach spread outward from history into geography and political science, where it encountered another wave of behavioralism radiating from psychology and sociology.

The Turnerian tradition in history, or the Turnerian paradigm as it were, did not outlive the master, whose death in 1932 marks the end of an era in American social science. Already in the 1920's young historians began turning away from difficult statistical research and inclined instead to biography and diplomatic history. In the 1930's the frontier thesis fell into disrepute, and historians paid more attention to urban and labor history. The influence of Charles Beard, Arthur Schlesinger Sr., and Vernon Parrington from the late 1920's down to the late 1940's diverted historians from using Turnerian techniques to trace the complex interplay of numerous economic, social, cultural, and geographical factors; instead historians thought more in terms of simple economic determinism.

The demise of the Turnerian school can be traced to a basic flaw in its communications system. In the first quarter of this century the Turnerians totally dominated virtually all of American historical scholarship. But by failing to provide an adequate training in statistical methods, Turner left his students vulnerable to frustration and the enticement of a simpler paradigm, economic determinism. By not establishing a journal to publish its research, and by neglecting methodological publications or special training programs, the school failed to standardize and disseminate its technical advances. By the middle 1920's the internal flaws of the school's structure had doomed it.

Turner's efforts to proselytize political science scored numerous successes. Most of the knowledge of American political history used by the political scientists came from books by Beard, Holcombe,[26] E. E. Robinson,[27] and Wilfred Binkley,[28] all of whom relied heavily upon Turnerian studies. The historical accounts of elections helped the political scientists jump from discussions of ballot length and registration laws to a concern with voting behavior. Equally influential in shaping the style of election analysis undertaken by political scientists was the stream of behavioral methodology emanating from sociologists (and psychologists) at Columbia and Chicago.

Inspired by sociologist Franklin Giddings, the Columbia departments of sociology, government, psychology, and history stressed the value of statistics in social science research.[29] In the early years of this century a second generation of Columbia scholars, especially Charles Beard, Charles Merriam, William Ogburn, and Stuart Rice, developed the methods of election analysis that set the pace in the field between the world wars.

Charles Beard's influence among historians, political scientists, and laymen was enormous. He built his widely read study *An Economic Interpretation of the Constitution* (1913) upon Libby's research on ratification and Turner's suggestions about the importance of economic factors. In *Economic Origins of Jeffersonian Democracy* (1915), *Contemporary American History* (1914), *The American Party Battle* (1928), and especially in his monumental *The Rise of American Civilization* (1927), Beard examined, or exposed, the economic foundation of all of American politics. Scholars influenced by Beard developed a cynical view of the American political process, and more and more neglected the analysis of elections in favor of exposés of the supposed control of politics by business. Howard Beale, a student of Turner and disciple of Beard, finally concluded that "claptrap" so obscured the "real" (i.e. economic) issues in elections that voting behavior analysis was practically irrelevant.[30] The tendency to debunk the claptrap of the politicians climaxed in Matthew Josephson's popular history of party warfare, *The Politicos: 1865–1896* (1938).

Beard's economic determinism proved less fruitful for election analysis than the mathematical model-building of Ogburn and Rice. Both men tried to measure the "consciousness of kind" that Giddings said bound men together into parties and voting groups. Ogburn used sophisticated new tools of time series curve fitting, and Pearson product-moment coefficients of correlation (both simple and partial), to study the interplay of numerous demographic, ecological, and electoral statistics. At Columbia (1919–27) and Chicago (1927–51), Ogburn trained scores of sociologists in quantitative techniques, and wrote numerous articles on voting patterns and cycles.[31]

Rice shared the concern of his mentors Giddings and Ogburn for liberal-left political reform, and also for quantitative methods to handle the problems of society and scholarship. Rice applied his fertile imagination and statistical virtuosity to the measurement of political attitudes and influence, and to spatial and temporal distributions of attitudes. His dissertation, *Farmers and Workers in American Politics* (1924), remains well worth reading, although most of his technical innovations are summarized in the most influential methodological work in the field, his *Quantitative Methods in Politics* (1928). Neither Ogburn nor Rice primarily devoted himself to election statistics, and they both eventually lost interest in the subject. Since most of their students were sociologists, their impact on election analysis was primarily through their writings.

Although several sociology departments, especially the one at Chicago, were strong in urban ecology, using mapping techniques and environmental hypotheses closely resembling the Turnerian paradigm, the urban sociologists almost entirely ignored voting patterns. One sociologist who tried reported that election results were "accidental" and "but a momentary phase of unstable equilibrium among contending forces."[32] But one statistically minded urban sociologist, Calvin Schmid, drew elaborate ecological maps of elections in Minneapolis, St. Paul, and Seattle. Perhaps Schmid acquired an interest in voting data from his association with a heterogeneous group of scholars at Minnesota who had come to election studies from several fields. At one time or another between the wars, election experts at Minnesota included sociologists F. Stuart Chapin, Pitirim Sorokin, and George Lundberg (a student of Libby); political scientists William Schaper, Williams Anderson (both Turner students), and Herman Beyle (a student of Gosnell); historians George Stephenson and Solon J. Buck (both students of Turner); and undergraduates Elmo Roper, Richard Scammon, and Malcolm Moos (who became president of the university in 1967).

No department comprised of Charles Merriam, Quincy Wright, Leonard White, Harold Gosnell, and Harold Lasswell is in jeopardy of being ignored by a historian of American political science. The Chicago group of the 1920's and 1930's spun so many fresh ideas, explored so much new territory, and trained so many able students (V. O. Key, David Truman, Gabriel Almond, Avery Leiserson, Roy Peel, Herbert Simon, and on and on) that it represented a watershed in the history of the discipline.

Chicago's greatest achievement was the true interdisciplinary cooperation it achieved in the social sciences. Political scientists trained there knew something of psychology, history, sociology, and statistics, and perhaps some economics, philosophy and law as well. Chairman Charles Merriam was the spark-plug for some ideas, the motive force for others (and the radiator for all). His entrepreneurship ranks high in the annals of academia —besides organizing the Chicago department he founded the Social Science Research Council and became one of the key Washington planners in the 1930's. Except for Merriam's concern for psychology and nonvoting (he was also a major Chicago politician), his interests were not reflected in election studies. Intellectually more important was the work of a junior member of the Chicago department, Harold Gosnell.

Gosnell worked on several studies of Chicago politics, (*Machine Politics* [1937], *Negro Politicians* [1935]), nonvoting (*Non-Voting*, with

Merriam [1924]) and the psychology of leadership (the brilliant *Boss Platt and His New York Machine* [1924]), but his heart was with statistics. In numerous articles in the 1930's, Gosnell explored the application of statistical concepts to political science, especially to voting analysis.[33] His research and teaching revolutionized election analysis, bringing it back to political reality and the historical context without sacrificing the statistical splendor of the techniques, such as factor analysis, that had been developed by statisticians, economists, sociologists, and psychologists.

Gosnell had an excellent grasp of the literature of voting analysis, both American and European. His study of *Why Europe Votes* (1930) was probably the best piece of comparative statistical political science since A. Lawrence Lowell's "Oscillations in Politics," a pioneer gem of election analysis that appeared in 1898.[34] Gosnell influenced two other men who organized studies of American and German elections, James Pollock and Rudolph Heberle. Pollock had studied with Turner and Holcombe at Harvard, but stressed to his students at Michigan (including Samuel Eldersveld, Edward Litchfield, and Richard Scammon) the value of Gosnell's work. Heberle was a German, the son-in-law of Ferdinand Tönnies, and was led to election analysis by Merriam and Gosnell. They recommended to him André Siegfried's *Tableau politique de la France de l'Ouest sous la troisième République* (Paris, 1913), whose maps and general approach were strongly suggestive of the Turnerian school. Heberle also developed some of the ideas of the urban ecologists into what he termed "political ecology," and applied the technique to Louisiana and German elections.[35]

During the Roosevelt years, the Chicago department turned more and more to problems of government planning. Public administration began to overshadow voting analysis. During the war the Budget Bureau and the Department of Agriculture provided Washington posts for many election experts turned administrators. (Gosnell, Rice, V. O. Key, Louis Bean, Paul David, Avery Leiserson, Earl Latham, and others were in the Budget Bureau but did not discuss elections there.) Scholarly interest in elections faded everywhere during the 1930's.[36] For example one effort at Columbia to begin publishing election statistics on a large scale (comparable to Scammon's *America Votes* series) foundered for lack of money.[37]

After 1930 concern with voting patterns fell more and more into the hands of the pollsters. The *Literary Digest* had begun nationwide samplings of opinion with studies of sentiment toward prohibition (the publisher was, of course, a Prohibitionist), and the Gallup, Roper, and Crossley polls brought more or less scientific techniques to bear on political attitudes in the mid 1930's.

In the 1940's the psychologists and sociologists had their turn at dominating the electoral stage. Publication of *The People's Choice* (1944),[38] *Voting* (1954),[39] and *The Voter Decides* (1954)[40] helped shift scholarly concern from the political and historical dimensions of elections to the psychological questions of when and why a voter makes up his mind to vote. By the late 1950's and early 1960's, a reaction had set in against ignoring the significant political and historical questions that voting patterns raise. Thus in several of the essays in *Elections and the Political Order* (1966)[41] written at the Inter-University Consortium for Political Research, extensive use was made of historical statistics that the Consortium has been systematically collecting.

Election analysis (as opposed to voting studies) recovered from the doldrums slowly in the 1940's. A review of some 800 research projects underway in 75 political science departments in 1950 revealed that only 24 appeared to use election statistics; nonetheless those projects constituted the bulk of the research using quantitative methods.[42]

The postwar revival of election studies was the achievement primarily, though not entirely, of V. O. Key. His teaching and research at Johns Hopkins, Alabama, Yale, and Harvard attracted a small stream of students to the study of elections and the cognate field of roll-call analysis. Key's impressive textbook, *Politics, Parties and Pressure Groups* (1942, 1947, 1952, 1958, 1964), went beyond excellent reviews of the current literature to indications of the fertile areas of new research. His classic study of *Southern Politics* (1949) familiarized the profession anew with Turnerian techniques (especially maps), and in *A Primer of Statistics for Political Scientists* (1954) Key disclosed enough of the secrets of the trade to guide scores, perhaps hundreds of students and senior scholars through masses of aggregate data.

Election analysis received further boosts from the publication, in a dozen and a half states, of compilations of county returns. The first and most elegant was *Presidential Politics in Kentucky, 1824–1948* (1950) by Jasper Shannon and Ruth McQuown. Shannon not only provided the county returns, but also provided Turnerian maps and analyses for each contest. E. E. Robinson's much used *The Presidential Vote: 1896–1932* (1934), one of the finest products of the Turnerian school, provided the model for W. Dean Burnham, *Presidential Ballots: 1836–1892* (1955). More recently Richard Scammon has edited a series of county and ward returns in *America Votes* (1956, 1958, 1960, 1962, 1964, 1966, 1968), and a retrospective volume, *America at the Polls: 1920–1964* (1966). Soon the Consortium plans to issue ten volumes of county returns covering every major race since 1824, based on its collection of returns already on computer tape.

In the last dozen years historians have re-entered the field of statistical election analysis. The impetus came not from a rediscovery of the forgotten Turnerian paradigm, but rather from interdisciplinary contact with the work of political scientists, sociologists, and even psychologists. Most projects remain unpublished, but the pioneer work of Lee Benson in emphasizing the need to study the occurrence and causes of changes in patterns, and his perceptive analysis of grass-roots voting patterns in early New York deserve special mention.[43]

With many historians in a mood for interdisciplinary cooperation in the social sciences, it appears the largely untapped reservoirs of election and census statistics will become major sources of data for the analysis of general models or theories of political behavior. Perhaps the rich heritage of research and cooperation already shared by history, political science, sociology, and psychology will stimulate and legitimize further work, and prevent another breakdown in interdisciplinary communication and awareness.

Notes

1. For more general reviews of the rise of behavioralism, see Albert Somit and Joseph Tanenhaus, *The Development of American Political Science: From Burgess to Behavioralism* (Boston, 1967), esp. p. 192; Robert Dahl, "The Behavioral Approach in Political Science: Epitaph for a Monument to a Successful Protest," *American Political Science Review* (cited as *APSR*) (1961) 55: 763–72; and the important theoretical article by David Truman, "Disillusion and Regeneration: The Quest for a Discipline," *APSR* (1965) 59: 865–73. For a different interpretation, see the author's chapter, "History and the Political Scientist," above.

2. [Boston] *Massachusetts Centinal*, April 4 and 7, 1787.

3. For a brief guide see W. Dean Burnham, "Sources of Historical Election Data; A Preliminary Bibliography," (East Lansing, 1963), and his chapter in Stein Rokkan and J. Meyriat (eds.), *International Guide to Electoral Statistics* (Paris, 1969).

4. C. M. Anderson to Grover Cleveland, October 26, 1888; copy in Grover Cleveland Papers, Library of Congress microfilm, series 2, reel 65.

5. "The Number of Ex-Union Soldiers in Indiana and Their Politics in 1880," unsigned manuscript giving the exact figures by county, in the Benjamin Harrison Papers, Library of Congress microfilm, series 14, reel 143.

6. Don Dickinson, quoted in *New York Times*, September 7, 1892.

7. W. G. Wreythaler, letter to Indianapolis *Sentinel*, Jan. 2, 1889.

8. See the Chicago *Tribune*, September 21, 1896, for detailed results.

9. See the Chicago *Record*, Oct. 24, 31, 1896; and Charles Dennis, *Victor Lawson* (Chicago, 1935), pp. 169, 171, 177.

10. Quoted in Omaha *World-Herald*, October 14, 1896.

11. On other aspects of the early history of polling, see Claude Robinson, *Straw Votes* (New York, 1932).

12. See Fletcher Hewes (ed.), *Citizen's Atlas of American Politics: 1789–1888* (New York, 1888), and *Scribner's Historical Atlas of American Progress* (New York, 1890); for background see Fulmer Mood, "The Rise of Official Statistical Cartography in Austria, Prussia, and the United States, 1855–1872," *Agricultural History* (1946) 20: 209–225.

13. From time to time the Census Bureau used election turnout figures to estimate population growth, and in 1946 it issued a handy *Compendium of Votes Cast in Presidential and Congressional Elections, 1928–1944*, the first such collection of county returns in the twentieth century that included the percentage distribution of the vote. Although many election experts have served as advisors and high officials in the Bureau, its role in election studies has been unimportant.

14. See John K. Wright, *Human Nature and Geography* (New York, 1966), pp. 168–87, and Hugh Hawkins, *Pioneer: A History of the Johns Hopkins University, 1874–1889* (Baltimore, 1960).

15. Herbert Baxter Adams, "Methods of Historical Study," *Johns Hopkins University Series in History and Political Science* (1884) 2: 129; see also pp. 79–81, 130, 137.

16. J. Franklin Jameson, "An Introduction to the Study of the Constitutional and Political History of the States," in *Hopkins Series* (1886) 4: 190–91.

17. See the edition by Peter Odegard (Cambridge, 1967); on conflict sociology see Albion Small, *General Sociology* (Chicago, 1905), Ch. 22.

18. For a recent summary of the evidence see Robert Dahl, "The American Opposition," in Robert Dahl (ed.), *Political Opposition in Western Democracies* (New Haven, 1966), pp. 34–69.

19. But Bentley did use Pearson product-moment correlations to analyze precinct voting patterns in Chicago; see *Process of Government*, pp. 487–92. He was thus far in advance of all the other social scientists in the country. Incidentally, Bentley joined the news staff of the Chicago *Record* about the time it was tabulating its great 1896 poll.

20. The literature on Turner is extensive. For an excellent summary see Ray Billington, *America's Frontier Heritage* (New York, 1966), pp. 6–22.

21. Quoted in Fulmer Mood, "The Development of Frederick Jackson Turner as

a Historical Thinker," in *Transactions of the Colonial Society of Massachusetts* (Boston, 1943) 34: 341; see pp. 328–51 for a discussion of Turner's teaching at Wisconsin. Libby's most important articles are: "A Plea for the Study of Votes in Congress," in American Historical Association, *Annual Report for 1896* (Washington, 1897) 1: 321–34, and "Political Factions in Washington's Administrations," *The Quarterly Journal* [of the University of North Dakota] (1913) 3: 291–318.

22. Quoted from class notes by Joseph Schafer, "The Microscopic Method Applied to History," *Minnesota History Bulletin* (1921) 4: 19.

23. William F. Dickinson, "The Personnel of the Wisconsin Legislature for the Years 1850, 1860, and 1870," B. L. thesis, University of Wisconsin, 1901, typescript in the University of Wisconsin Library.

24. Avery Craven, "Frederick Jackson Turner," in William Hutchinson (ed.), *The Marcus W. Jernegan Essays in American Historiography* (Chicago, 1937), p. 265.

25. Among the Turnerian historians of elections were: E. E. Robinson, Theodore C. Smith, U. B. Phillips, William O. Lynch, Joseph Schafer, Arthur C. Cole, Louis Pelzer, Dixon Ryan Fox, Charles O. Paullin, Solon J. Buck, Theodore C. Pease, George M. Stephenson, Fred Haynes, Carl Russell Fish, Carl Becker, Homer C. Hockett, Charles H. Ambler, William Dodd, William A. Robinson, John Hicks, George Knoles, R. Carlyle Buley, Emerson Fite, John D. Barnhart, James Malin, Ray Allen Billington, Merle Curti, and Manning Dauer, as well as geographer John K. Wright.

26. See his *The Political Parties of Today* (New York, 1924), and *The Middle Classes in American Politics* (Cambridge, 1940).

27. See his *The Evolution of American Political Parties* (New York, 1924), *The Presidential Vote: 1896–1932* (Stanford, 1934), and *They Voted for Roosevelt* (Stanford, 1947).

28. See especially his *American Political Parties* (New York, 1943, 1945, 1958, 1962).

29. See R. G. Hoxie (ed.), *History of the Faculty of Political Science* (New York, 1955); and *A Bibliography of the Faculty of Political Science of Columbia University, 1880–1930* (New York, 1931).

30. Howard K. Beale, *Critical Year* (New York, 1930, 1958 ed.), pp. ix–x, 140–41.

31. See especially W. F. Ogburn and N. S. Talbot, "A Measurement of the Factors in the Presidential Election of 1928," *Social Forces* (1929) 8: 175–83 (which used partial correlations, not Thurstone's factor analysis); and his fascinating essays in *On Culture and Social Change* (Chicago, 1964, ed. Otis Dudley Duncan), esp. pp. 221–85. See also Rice's essay on Ogburn's methods in Stuart Rice (ed.), *Methods in Social Science* (Chicago, 1931), pp. 586–613.

32. Roderick McKenzie, "Community Forces," *Social Forces* (1924) 2: 564.

33. See his "The Techniques of Measurement" in T. V. Smith and Leonard White (eds.), Chicago: *An Experiment in Social Science Research* (Chicago, 1929) pp. 90–112; this is a key book in understanding work at Chicago in the 1920's.

Gosnell's "Statisticians and Political Scientists," *APSR* (1933) 27: 392–403, was an excellent review of the literature; his *Grass Roots Politics* (Washington, 1942), and "Factorial and Correlational Analysis of the 1934 Vote in Chicago," with M. J. Schmidt, *Journal of the American Statistical Association* (1936) 31: 507–18, are dazzling statistical displays, with a new apologetic note for statistics in the 1942 book.

34. *Annals of the American Academy* (1898) 13: 69–97. For European election analysis see Rokkan and Meyriat (eds.), *International Guide to Electoral Statistics*, and Sten Nilson, *Histoire et Sciences Politiques* (Bergen, 1950).

35. See Rudolph Heberle, *Social Movements* (New York, 1951).

36. Somit and Tanenhaus date the decline of quantitative political science to 1930, *Development of American Political Science*, pp. 98–100, 128.

37. See Idella Swisher, "Election Statistics in the United States," *APSR* (1933) 27: 422–32. Under the direction of Clifford Lord, a Turnerian historian, the W.P.A. in New York and New Jersey compiled and mapped tens of thousands of Congressional roll-call votes, but only published one volume of *The Atlas of Congressional Roll Calls* (Cooperstown, N.Y., 1943) out of a projected 42 volumes.

38. By Paul Lazarsfeld, Bernard Berelson, and Hazel Gaudet.

39. By Bernard Berelson, Paul Lazarsfeld, and William McPhee.

40. By Angus Campbell, Gerald Gurin and Warren Miller. For discussions of the survey studies see Eugene Burdick and Arthur J. Brodbeck, *American Voting Behavior* (Glencoe, 1959), especially the essay by Peter Rossi, pp. 5–54; and see the hostile view by Walter Berns in Herbert Storing (ed.), *Essays on the Scientific Study of Politics* (New York, 1962), pp. 1–62. Important syntheses of the psychological and sociological studies are S. M. Lipset *et al.* "The Psychology of Voting," in Gardner Lindzey (ed.), *Handbook of Social Psychology* (Cambridge, 1954) 2: 1124–75; Robert Lane, *Political Life* (Glencoe, 1959); and Lester Milbraith, *Political Participation* (Chicago, 1965).

41. By Angus Campbell, Phillip Converse, Warren Miller, and Donald Stokes dedicated to the memory of V. O. Key. See the same authors' important *The American Voter* (New York, 1960).

42. Claude Hawley and Lewis Dexter, "Recent Political Science Research in American Universities," *APSR* (1952) 46: 470–85.

43. See his "Research Problems in American Political Historiography," in Mira Komarovsky (ed.), *Common Frontiers of the Social Sciences* (Glencoe, 1957), pp. 113–241; and his *The Concept of Jacksonian Democracy* (Princeton, 1961).

10

Statistics and Politics:
The Need for Causal Data Analysis

HAYWARD R. ALKER, JR.

> Sir Francis Bacon ... has made a judicious parallel in many particulars,
> between the Body Natural and the Body Politic, and between the arts
> of preserving both in health and strength: and as its anatomy is the
> best foundation of one, so also of the other: ... to practice upon the
> politic, without knowing the symmetry, fabric, and proportion of it,
> is as casual as the practice of old women and empirics.
>
> Sir William Petty
> *Political Anatomy of Ireland* (1672)

As the historical relationship between statistics and politics is an especially
close one—the terms at one point had overlapping meanings—I would
like briefly to retell this history. The suggestion follows that the main
contemporary contribution of statistics to politics should be to aid in
causal data analysis. By the "causal data analysis" of political phenomena
I mean both the deriving from data of causally suggestive political
"anatomies" and the data-based measurement of the causes and effects of

Most of these ideas were developed in a seminar on Mathematical Political Analysis
held at the University of Michigan in the summer of 1966 and jointly sponsored by
the Inter-University Consortium for Political Research and the Mathematical Social
Science Board. A first draft was prepared for the September 1967 meetings of the
American Political Science Association with partial assistance from the Office for
Advanced Political Studies and the Computer Center at Yale University. The final
draft was prepared under the aegis of the Center for Advanced Study in the Behavioral Sciences with support from National Science Foundation Grant 65-1979.
Many helpful suggestions and criticisms cannot be acknowledged individually. But
communications with M. Takabatake and R. MacDonald about model alternatives
require special mention; so do the specific alterations suggested by Neil Henry,
Duncan MacRae, and Edward Tufte.

political life. Such analyses require that political data be interpreted in terms of a mixture of causal statistical models and determinative political hypotheses. The body of this chapter will review a variety of statistical procedures from this perspective and will conclude with some comparative remarks about the correspondence of their modeling assumptions with political reality.

I. The Political Roots of Modern Statistics[1]

Following Meitzen, Paul Lazarsfeld has described the two seventeenth-century "roots" of modern statistics—"political arithmetic" introduced in England by William Petty (1623–87), and "university statistics" fathered at about the same time by Hermann Conring (1606–82), a German professor. Both were concerned with the political problems of their day—state-building and state-preservation—and both were concerned with achieving empirical foundations for their political ideas. Thus an eighteenth-century definition shows a commonly accepted meaning of "statistics" as the exposition of the noteworthy aspects of the state

> ... that branch of political knowledge, which has for its object the actual and relative power of the several modern states, the power arising from their natural advantages, the industry and civilization of their inhabitants, and the wisdom of their governments, has been formed, chiefly by German writers, into a separate science ... distinguished by the new-coined name of *statistics*.[2]

Both having had medical training, the two writers were interested in the classificatory problems of political anatomy and political pathology, and they both sought effective ways to preserve the health and strength of the body politic. Using available fragmentary evidence, Petty and the political arithmeticians compared states as to their demographic basis of power, and they sought to explain how social structure might also contribute to good government. In Lazarsfeld's words, Petty looked for "causal relationships between quantitative variables" because of the intellectual climate of the Baconian era, the rational spirit of English capitalism, the need in larger states for a more abstract basis of public administration, and the mercantilist's belief that "size of population was a crucial factor in the power and wealth of the state."[3]

Conring and subsequent "university statisticians," on the other hand, lived amidst 300 small German principalities in a precarious era of civic reconstruction. He looked for a theoretical system which would make facts about the complex international situation easier to remember, to teach, and to be used by men in government. Treating the state as an acting unit, he derived categories of description and explanation explicitly from within the framework of Aristotelian causation. Classifications of states in terms of their "formal causes"—their constitutions and laws—were presented along with descriptions of "material causes," such as economic and demographic resources. More important from the states-men's view, perhaps, were the "final causes" or goals of states and their "efficient causes"—various elite activities, including informal admini-strative practices. Despite its theoretical background and policy-orienta-tion, however, this tradition of analysis remained largely descriptive and qualitatively comparative.[4]

Subsequently, "political arithmetic" developed into modern quantita-tive statistics, while "university statistics" dissolved into nineteenth-century German political science. The reasons for, and causes of, divergence from an early similarity of viewpoints remain in the provinces of the sociologist of knowledge and the historian of scientific ideas and methods. An equally intriguing, analogous problem would be the rise in twentieth-century America of a wedding of theoretical concerns and analytical practices in many ways similar to the empirical orientations of the political arithmeticians and university statisticians.[5] What seems more relevant here in a contemporary assessment of the relationship between political science and statistics is a discussion of the primary purposes for marrying these two disciplines, and the fruitfulness of such a marriage from the political scientist's point of view.

In retrospect, the qualitative, concrete, taxonomic, classificatory tendencies of the German school dominated their interest in causal explanations of a state's success or failure. Conversely, the English approach to description became an increasingly quantitative one, with a corresponding shift towards more abstract, causal explanatory investiga-tion. If one were to try and resynthesize the contributions of both roots of statistics, it is clear that both *descriptive* and *explanatory* emphases would be appropriate. The former emphasis would include both qualitative classi-ficatory descriptions and quantitative measurements; the latter would provide explanatory methods using both qualitative and quantitative attributes. Moreover, *a unifying concern with causal data analysis could be discerned: first, in the search for the best descriptive characterizations of the fundamental attributes, variables, or predispositions tending to effect political actions; secondly, in the search for the politically decisive explanations of these attributes, variables, predispositions, actions, and their consequences.*[6]

II. The Contribution of Multivariate Statistical Theory

In their classic statistics textbook, Yule and Kendall state:

> By *Statistics*, we mean [qualitative and] quantitative data affected to a marked extent by a multiplicity of causes.
>
> By *Statistical Methods*, we mean methods specially adapted to the elucidation of [qualitative and] quantitative data affected by a multiplicity of causes.
>
> By *Theory of Statistics* or, more briefly, *Statistics*, we mean the exposition of statistical methods.[7]

Now the recognition that various forms of political causation underlie all data sets on political behavior does not logically imply that the causal description of data interdependencies and the causal explanation of variable dependencies are the only goals of political statistics. Indeed, with the generalization of statistical methods and theories to other areas of substantive application, and the growing recognition by statisticians that their model assumptions do not adequately represent the working principles of complicated underlying social and behavioral mechanisms, a number of less ambitious goals have been espoused. As implicitly recognized by Yule and Kendall, the discovery of patterns, the estimation of properties, the classification of cases, the calculation of risks of inductive generalization, and the making of reasonably accurate predictions regardless of the appropriate causal theory have become accepted statistical tasks of data "elucidation" or "analysis." Similarly, the "exposition" of statistical methods and models can and does involve considerable skill in the recognition and definition of noncausal statistical problems, and the discovery of feasible and potentially novel methods relevant to them; so does the comparison and evaluation of such methods in terms of criteria of efficiency and appropriateness short of causal significance.[8]

Nonetheless, the thrust of the earlier statistical concern with causally describing and explaining political data, and the more recent development by geneticists, econometricians, and sociometricians of quasi-experimental statistical methods that substantiate Yule and Kendall's earlier theoretical commitment, combine to suggest a more powerful role for political statistics. The urgency of theoretical and practical political concerns argues for the realization of these possibilities.

As originators, expositors, appliers, and critics of mathematical models of influence processes underlying political data, political statisticians can significantly advance political science. Even if the role of the modern "polimetrician" is less grand than that of a "political arithmetician" or "university statistician" in the classical sense, he can serve to mediate the interaction of experience, coded as data, and theory, formulated in a potentially operational manner. Being well aware of the ambiguous theoretical significance of most complex accumulations of political data, he can try to increase our theoretical understanding of political experience by proposing, rationalizing, comparing, and empirically justifying methods of data analysis, giving them a causal interpretation whenever possible and appropriate.[9]

At the risk of slighting, by implication, several statistical topics of interest to political scientists—such as theories of the nature of rational decision-making in uncertain situations, and alternative methods of experimental design and time series analysis[10]—I shall now briefly review, illustrate, and compare a number of causally suggestive or interpretable, nonexperimental multivariate data analysis techniques. Such a discussion will help concretize the kind of contribution that "polimetrics" can make to the topics raised by contemporary political scientists. I have in mind some of the questions asked by a policy-relevant political science not unlike that proposed by William Petty or Herman Conring.

III. Methods and Models for Causal Explanation

Presuming some familiarity with at least the elementary modes of causal modeling, I should like first to review, interpret causally, illustrate, and comment on a number of approaches to multivariate statistical explanation.[11] In rough ascending order of complexity, they are linear regression analysis, analysis of variance and covariance, nonlinear regression analysis, stepwise regression analysis, interaction-seeking stepwise procedures, "hierarchically" and "reciprocally" interdependent regression systems, and nonlinear extensions of the same. Although these forms of "dependence" analysis go more to the heart of politics than many of the less conclusive measurement techniques, familiarity with most of the former is necessary before a causally understandable discussion of anatomical or dispositional measurement procedures is possible.

A. ANALYSIS OF VARIANCE AND COVARIANCE

Even though it is the subject of some extended statistical treatises, the analysis of variance and covariance is not inordinately complex. In fact, it forms the basis for frequent interpretations of regression equations in terms such as "percentage of variance explained."

1. *Analysis of variance*. But a more important reason for discussing this kind of data analysis here is its close association with the development of experimental design and scientific causal inquiry. Thus, agricultural scientists might randomly or nonrandomly assign a variety of seed, fertilizer, and soil mixes to experimental plant beds in trying to produce better crops. Or international relations simulators might study which combinations of experimentally induced surprise, time pressure, and value threat are most likely to cause dangerous crisis decision-making syndromes of behavior.

In either case, despite the great difference in substantive material, the policy-relevant, causal question is very similar in form: What are the separate "main effects" (e.g. of fertilizer and surprise)? What are the higher order or "interaction effects" (such as increases in irrationality due to the *simultaneous combination* of value threat, surprise, and time pressure, but not attributable to any or all of these factors acting separately)? And what are hopefully uncorrelated "error effects" (due to variables not conscientiously incorporated into an experiment, such as shaded plots or excited experimenters)?

Given the problem of distinguishing these effects, a statistician might suggest data analysis in terms of the following model:[12]

$$y_{ijkl} = \alpha_i + \beta_j + \gamma_k + \sigma_{ij} + \varepsilon_{ik} + \mu_{jk} + \kappa_{ijk} + u_{ijkl} \tag{1}$$

Here, y_{ijkl} indicates the dependent value (productivity, "irrationality") of the lth object "treated to" amounts or types i, j, and k of the three independent variables which we shall call A, B, and C. The model assumes three "main effects" associated with these treatments, three first-order interaction effects associated with pairs of these treatments (e.g. value threat and time pressure acting jointly), one second-order interaction effect (κ_{ijk}) associated with the joint action of all three causal factors, and a random error effect (u_{ijkl}) specific to each object of investigation.[13]

From a causal modeling point of view, Equation (1) represents an *additive model of additive and nonadditive causes.* The explanatory variables are assumed to be nominally or ordinally measured, while the dependent variable must be an interval scale. To apply the model, additional distributional assumptions (homoscedasticity, normality) have also to be assumed. But the important points to note from a causal perspective are the *unidirectional, additive, independent-to-dependent causal assumptions; the absence of direct causal relationships among the (separately manipulated) independent variables;* and the presumed *lack of any immediate "feedbacks"* from the dependent to the independent variables.

2. *Covariance analysis.* When one or more "independent variables" is measured on an interval scale, then interaction effects among these and other, categorical variables can be defined in a slightly different way. The analysis of covariance focuses on how the effects of nominal or ordinal "control" variables on the covariance of other, interval scale independent and dependent variables. Thus, a "catalytic" or "threshold" model like Equation (2) is assumed:

$$y_{ij} = \alpha_i + \beta_i X_{ij} + u_{ij} \tag{2}$$

Here, y_{ij} refers to observation j of variable y in control category i; α_i is an additive effect associated with each different category or "region" of the control variable; and $\beta_i X_{ij}$ represents a multiplicative interaction term. Those effects undisturbed by the control variable are assumed to be independent of it causally.

An example of a simple covariance analysis is the following. Let y_{ij} be the per capita "death from domestic group violence" rate for contemporary nations. And use i values of 1 or 2 to refer to "European" and "non-European culture," which are expected, respectively, to deflate or enhance the violent consequences of land inequality (X_{ij}). Elsewhere[14] I have shown that such a covariance model significantly accounts for 22 per cent of the contemporary variance in natural violence rates (y) if the α_i and β_i are assumed to be equal, that allowing two different values of α_i adds 38 per cent more variance explained, and that allowing β_i also to differ among cultures brings explained variance in violence levels up to about 62 per cent of the total variance.

Obviously, the idea of modeling covariance effects may be incorporated into a generalized analysis of variance and covariance model. As with analysis of variance studies, estimation of the various effects with averages and sums of squared deviations is relatively straightforward: we shall not repeat the usual treatments here.

Causally, however, it is worth geometrically representing the alternate mechanisms just discussed. These representations will facilitate further comparative remarks. In Figure 1b, note how we have used the symbol "⊕" to indicate an interactional "threshold" or "catalytic effect." From a modeling point of view, the figure helps clarify the *additive and multiplicative treatment of additive and nonadditive effects characteristic of covariance analysis. In both models, causes of the independent variables are not represented, and nonmodeled influences on the dependent variable (the u's) are assumed to vary independently of the other explanatory variables.*

3. *Variance components models.* A third interesting kind of variance analysis is well exemplified in the work of Donald Stokes. In discussing a variance components model of political effects,[15] Stokes uses an equation like the following:

$$y_{dst} = \underbrace{D_{dst} + S_{st} + C_t}_{\substack{\text{district state country} \\ \text{time-specific effects}}} + \underbrace{\delta_{ds} + \sigma_s + \gamma}_{\substack{\text{district state country} \\ \text{time-independent effects}}} \tag{3}$$

y_{dst} refers to one party's percentage of the two party vote, or total turnout, in congressional district d in state s in election year t. Using rather complex estimation procedures, Stokes finds that for the 1952–60 period in the United States, country-wide factors have the greatest effect on turnout, but that state and local factors account for more than half of the differences in inter-party voting support (an important argument against a national power elite, at least one not interested in different partisan effects in different states). Historical comparisons of this sort would clearly be fascinating in other historical time periods and other multilevel political systems.

Without further substantive comment, we turn to some of the causal modeling implications of this approach. First of all, ignoring sampling considerations (which Stokes does not), we can show plausible ways of disentangling these various effects and their variances. Equations (4) suggest "estimates" of the "independent" variables:

$$\hat{D}_{dst} = [(Y_{dst} - Y_{\cdot st}) - (Y_{ds\cdot} - Y_{\cdot s\cdot})]_i \quad \hat{\delta}_{ds} = (Y_{ds\cdot} - Y_{\cdot s\cdot})$$
$$\hat{S}_{st} = [(Y_{\cdot st} - Y_{\cdot t}) - (Y_{\cdot s\cdot} - Y_{\cdot\cdot})] \; ; \quad \hat{\sigma}_s = (Y_{\cdot s\cdot} - Y_{\cdot\cdot})$$
$$\hat{C}_t = [(Y_{\cdot t} - Y_{\cdot\cdot})] \qquad\qquad ; \quad \hat{\gamma} = (Y_{\cdot\cdot}) \tag{4}$$

The "dot" subscripts indicate averages calculated over the omitted subscript. Note the way "timeless" effects are estimated using averages of the

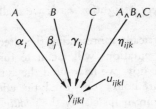

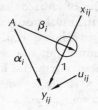

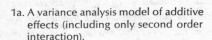

1a. A variance analysis model of additive
effects (including only second order
interaction).

1b. A simple covariance analysis model
with interaction effects.

FIGURE I

Arrow Diagrams of Simple Variance and Covariance Models

"time-specific" ones; see also how adding up all these terms makes Equation (3) tautologically true. Since all these terms have averages of zero and the timeless terms are constant, it is easy to derive a variance and covariance components breakdown for the variance of y (Var y_{dst}):

$$\text{Var } y_{dst} = \text{Var } D_{dst} + \text{Var } S_{st} + \text{Var } C_t$$
$$+ 2\left[\text{Cov}(D_{dst}, S_{st}) + \text{Cov}(D_{dst}, C_t) + \text{Cov}(S_{st}, C_t)\right] \quad (5)$$

Because Stokes found empirical "cross-level" covariance or "interaction" terms not very different from what could be expected on a statistically random basis, he was able to summarize his findings in terms of variance components alone. The radical simplification of research results thus obtained is evidenced by the pictorial representation in Figure 2 of the "multilevel effects" model of Equation (3) and the variance components model of Equation (5).

Figure 2a shows the *logical* interrelationships among the explanatory variables in Equation (3), symbolized by equality-like, double-headed arrows; the existence of ambiguous empirical causal links is signified by the thinner double-headed arrows. Note also how we have labeled the district, state, and country effects with their magnitudes, and the corresponding causal arrows with unities. Because the logical interrelationships of Equations (4) and Figure 2a have negligible effects on the covariance terms of Equation (5) and Figure 2b, talking separately of district, state, and country "effects" and "variance components" is not statistically misleading. *But the absence of error terms, the insignificance of cross-level interactions, and the existence of logical interrelationships among explanatory and*

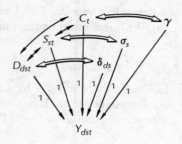

2a. A multilevel effects model.

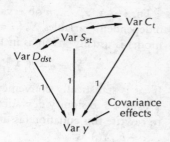

2b. A derived variance components model.

FIGURE 2

Arrow Diagrams of a Multilevel Effects Model and
a Related Variance Components Formula

dependent variables represent complicating assumptions of additive, multilevel models of political effects.

B. REGRESSION ANALYSIS

Regression analysis may be thought of as an extension of simple, non-interactional variance analysis to the case of interval scale independent and dependent variables. But it too can be used to investigate nonlinearities in, and interactions among, independent variables if the investigator is concerned with such possibilities.

1. *Linear multiple regression.* Multiple regression analysis is widely used in political data analysis to explain citizens' and representatives' voting behavior, levels of political development, violence levels, propensities to international transaction, etc. Often results are discussed as if they were causal explanations; sometimes, only relational or predictive findings are claimed. Available options include "probit analysis" of dichotomized dependent variables, the use of nominal scales broken up into dichotomized independent "dummy" variables, standardized and unstandardized coefficients, weighting standardized coefficients by deviations from natural zero points to measure net influence, and logarithmic transformations that, in effect, allow the interpretation of standardized or unstandardized regression coefficients as analogous to economic elasticities.[16]

For $i = 1, 2, \ldots, n$ observations on one dependent variable Y and on m independent variables X_j ($j = 1, 2, \ldots, m$), the linear multiple regression model is usually given as in Equation (6):

$$Y_i = \alpha + \beta_1 X_{1i} + \ldots + \beta_j X_{ji} \ldots + \beta_m X_{mi} + u_i \tag{6}$$

If, as is statistically convenient, we replace capital X's and Y's by small x's and y's to signify deviations about their respective means, it is possible to rewrite this equation (assuming, as can be shown, that $\alpha = \bar{Y} - \beta_1 \bar{X}_1 - \ldots - \beta_m \bar{X}_m$) as:

$$y_i = \sum_{j=1}^{m} \beta_j x_{ji} + u_i$$

Relevant modeling assumptions, which are easily stated from a causal modeling perspective, can be discerned from the usual procedures for β estimates. They parallel rather closely those of the analysis of variance model, without interaction: *the dependent variable depends linearly and additively on measured and nonmeasured causes; the implicit nonmeasured causes are assumed to be random variables that are not correlated with, or causes of, the independent variables. The measured independent variables are assumed to be causally independent or, at worst, to be imperfectly correlated, and not to be influenced by the dependent variable.*

Turning now to graphic representations, we see in the first four cases of Figure 3 some of the strength and weaknesses of causally interpreting β coefficients. Only in the case of uncorrelated causes—analogous to the experimentally manipulated, randomized treatments of the analysis of variance approach—do we correctly assess direct *and* indirect causal effects. In this case, of course, there are no indirect causal effects, by which is meant causes acting through several links, as occurs with x_1 and x_m in case 3 of the figure. When, as is more often the case, we fail to specify causal interpretations for observed correlations (denoted by two-headed arrows) among the independent variables, then indirect causal impacts cannot be adequately assessed. Assuming that measurements are accurate enough to distinguish such relationships, the only way out of situations in which either the independent variables are causally interdependent (case 3) or dependent on nonrandom error variables (case 4) is to measure the variables concerned and assess their direct and indirect effects using multi-equation regression methods.[17]

2. *Nonlinear and interaction seeking regression models.* The form of the general regression model of Equation (6) is such that x_2 could be defined

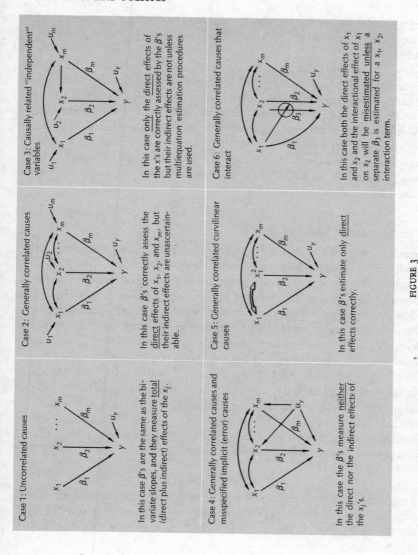

FIGURE 3

Six Differing Causal Interpretations of Regression Analysis Results

as x_i^2 or x_3 defined as $x_1 x_2$ without violating the requirements that there be no exact *linear* correlations or causal ties among the explanatory variables.

Some of the causal implications of curvilinear or generally nonlinear regressions of this sort are suggested in cases 5 and 6 of the figure. If, as is too rarely the case, a political scientist were to *look for interaction* of the covariance sort using multiplicative terms in multiple regression programs, he would probably correctly discover whether or not it existed. If he did not investigate that possibility, he might be lucky and come to no seriously wrong conclusions. But as case 6 suggests, even the direct effects of interacting independent variables will be misassessed by naïve—noninteraction testing—linear regression models.

C. STEPWISE REGRESSION ANALYSIS

Something of a halfway house between multiple regression analysis and full-blown multiequation causal models is the automated data analysis procedure known as stepwise regression. Of the several varieties of this approach, which tends to be written up at computer centers more than in statistical textbooks, I shall describe the one most closely related to the automatic interaction detection technique procedures to be described below. What all these methods of analysis have in common is a special way of building up orderings of the explanatory variables.

The procedure can be easily programmed; it works something like the following. First, select m explanatory variables and a dependent variable and standardize them so that they all have equal or, better, unit variances. Then calculate and compare all the *first order, bivariate* regression slope estimates, that is, $\hat{\beta}$'s or b's. Pick the x_j with the highest magnitude—call it x_1^*—and enter it in an explanatory model of the form

$$y = b_{y1} x_1^* + u_1 \qquad (7')$$

and calculate the residual u_1. Then find among the remaining variables the one (x_j) with the highest *second-order, partial regression slope*, estimated by either b_{yu} or $b_{y2.1}$. Call this variable x_2^* and enter it into Equation (7'), with a second-order $\beta_{yj.1}$:

$$y = b_{y1} x_1^* + b_{y2.1} x_2^* + u_2 \qquad (7'')$$

It should be noted that, except when $r_{12} = 0$, $b_{yu} \neq b_{y2.1}$ and gives therefore a biased estimate of $\beta_{y2.1}$ despite its ease of computation. Keep repeating this procedure, checking to see whether the increment in explanatory power (as measured by the squared multiple correlation) due to the latest additional explanatory variable is statistically indistinguishable from a random effect. The resulting final equation looks like

$$y = b_{y1}x_1^* + b_{y2\cdot1}x_2^* + b_{y3\cdot12}x_3^* + \ldots + u \qquad (7)$$

Does this procedure have a causal interpretation? Or is it only to be thought of as a parsimonious way to narrow down and "order" in some sense the set of independent variables in an ordinary multiple regression equation? I believe it does have a causal interpretation, which may well have influenced attempts to interpret its results in causal language. The key interpretive ideas appear to be the *assumption that the ordering ascertained by the automatic stepwise procedure is a causal one, and that the various partial regression slopes measure direct effects.*

Consider Figure 4 as a hierarchically ordered causal model with error variables omitted. By means of procedures to be described more fully below, we could estimate direct causal links with y by the $\hat{\beta}$ coefficients given there; for the last variable included in the figure at any one time, we would find that its $\hat{\beta}$ correctly estimates its direct causal effect. Unfortunately, however, when each new variable is added, the model changes and the earlier $\hat{\beta}$'s are no longer unbiased estimates.

Interpreting regression results in these terms seems at least as suggestive to development conscious political scientsts as does the additive model of multiple regression analysis. Thus Ted Gurr has used stepwise regression procedures for a first test of a causal model of civil violence.[18] Although he does not report standardized $\hat{\beta}$ coefficients like those indicated in Figure 4, one might expect some correspondence between the pattern of these coefficients and the development sequences suggested by his model:

FIGURE 4

A Causal Model Similar to the Stepwise Regression Procedure

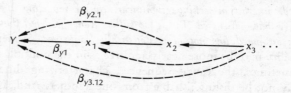

discrepancy between value expectations and capabilities→discontent→ consideration of collective responses→increased likelihood and magnitude of civil violence.

But an important caveat is needed at this point. Even if the model assumptions of Figure 4 are *necessary* for a causal labeling of new stepwise regression coefficients, *the application of the procedure is in no way a sufficient test of this interpretation. Other causal models seem always to be consistent with such empirical findings.*[19]

D. INTERACTION-SEEKING STEPWISE PROCEDURES

When fewer variables explain more variance, models seem to fit the data better and, *perhaps*, thus to be better representations of underlying causal processes. Following up on the intuitively attractive appeal of stepwise analysis procedures and looking also for a way to increase variance explained by taking interaction effects into account, several years ago, Morgan and Sonquist developed an interaction-seeking stepwise computer program for "Automatic Interaction Detection" (AID). They were also hopeful of coming closer to causal interpretations with their procedures, as reference to Sewall Wright's early causal modeling work in the original article indicates.[20]

AID uses nominal scale explanatory variables, which may be derived from particular ranges of interval or ordinal variables. It seeks to maximize the correlation ratio, E^2, by finding the dichotomization of any one of a set of m independent variables that explains the greatest (additional) fraction of variance in y. Within each of the inductively defined groups, it looks for further dichotomizations on the basis of previously unused categorizations. This allows interactions where one explanatory variable helps further discriminate among one subgroup, but not so among others. Moreover, the free determination of how to split up categories allows one to detect curvilinear effects.

By creating population subgroups describable in terms of different developmental causal orderings of maximally dichotomized variables, AID comes closer to automated, interaction-seeking, nonlinear causal modeling than all other procedures we have discussed. But it too suffers from the defect that the causal pattern thus estimated has not been statistically confirmed. Sometimes, for instance, reality may be more nearly additive as in the multiple regression model; sometimes, the causal sequences, characterizing different subgroups, may not be distinguishable from one another. And, as we have already noted, models with only one dependent variable do not allow any of the explanatory variables to depend on it.

Nonetheless, the approach on some modified versions of it remains attractive and suggestive as a preliminary data analysis procedure. Morgan and Sonquist, for example, doubled the explanatory power of dummy variable multiple regression models for explaining family income levels by using AID. Subcultures seem to exist where some conditioning variables appear to have different effects on poverty levels. The substantive particulars certainly seem worth exploring further.

Figure 5 illustrates the graphical "tree" suggested by another AID analysis of survey data, this time on political efficacy among American Negroes. We see that political knowledge appears to have the largest, most immediate effect on efficacy. Then vote history of some participation for those low in knowledge and perfect possible participation for those higher in knowledge is next most important and immediate. Major interactions are indicated by the apparent impact of mass media attentiveness on efficacy for extreme vote history and political knowledge types, but *not* for those with mixed patterns of political knowledge and vote history.

The figure raises almost as many questions as it answers. Why does media participation seem to have a greater effect on the extremely efficacious or unefficacious? Doesn't something else—perhaps even political efficacy, the dependent variable—cause or facilitate active voting histories and political knowledge? The need for further specification and testing of the causal relations involved is apparent.

E. HIERARCHICAL CAUSAL MODELING

The most exciting aspects of hierarchical causal models—I prefer this term as more politically suggestive and debatable than the equivalent mathematical term "recursive"—are *the ways in which they encourage one to synthesize, compare, and test empirical political theories.* First of all, they allow more than one dependent variable to be studied at a time, thus truly focusing on the causal *interdependencies* so characteristic of the political realm. Moreover, multiple equation models express multiple sets of propositions, whose theoretical power may well exceed that of any or all of the propositions taken singularly. And the absence or presence or hypothesized magnitude of causal links within any particular causal ordering of variables and equations can be tested for, thus allowing us to

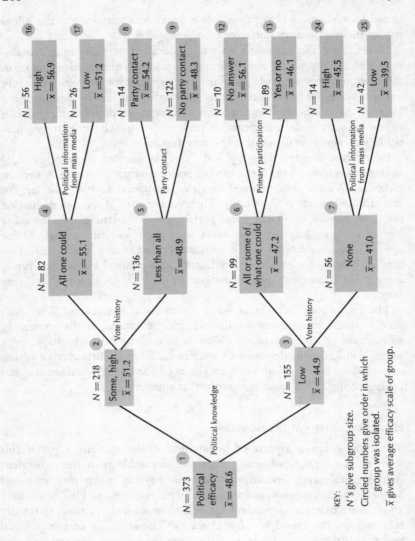

Figure 5
An Interaction-Seeking Stepwise Analysis of Survey Data
on Negro Political Efficacy
Source: J. Aberbach, with revisions.

choose among a variety of explanatory theories by rejecting some of the assumptions of either the stepwise regression model or of an ordinary multiple regression model. This feature alone establishes the superiority of the approach over any of those we have yet discussed.

The basic, clearly metaphysical, assumption of the approach is that given a pattern of correlational interdependencies, there exists a true hierarchical ordering of variables which, if discovered, will account for the manifested correlations. *Thus unreal or "spurious" correlations will disappear when,* ceteris paribus *prior causes are taken into account.* Statistically, this has usually meant that regression slopes or partial correlations will disappear for superfluous links, when effects of causally prior variables are estimated by multiple regression techniques.

Mathematically, the causal ordering idea associated with the Simon-Blalock approach is expressed in terms of a hierarchical arrangement on nonzero coefficients. For the four-variable case in which x_1 is the "first cause" and x_4 is the "fourth" totally dependent variable, the general set of equations associated with a causal diagram like that of Figure 4 (but with different subscripts) is:

$$
\begin{aligned}
x_1 &= u_1 \\
a_{21}x_1 + x_2 &= u_2 \\
a_{31}x_1 + a_{32}x_2 + x_3 &= u_3 \\
a_{41}x_1 + \alpha_{42}x_2 + \alpha_{43}x_3 + x_4 &= u_4
\end{aligned}
\tag{8a}
$$

Ceteris paribus assumptions are more explicitly stated than in most verbal discussions. Thus, the random or implicit causes of x_1 through x_4 (u_1, ... u_4 respectively) are assumed uncorrelated with each other. For variables with zero means, this is equivalent to:

$$
\Sigma u_i u_j = 0 \quad (i \neq j; \quad i, j = 1, 2, 3, 4)
\tag{8b}
$$

If the causal ordering is indeed correct, and the *ceteris paribus* assumptions also valid, then Wold and others have shown that ordinary multiple regression analysis of each separate causal equation is an efficient estimation procedure. Hence, only the last stepwise $\hat{\beta}$ in Equation 7 is correct *if* Figure 4 is correct; note that the stepwise procedure provides no way to estimate links like that from x_3 to x_1.) *When certain a coefficients in this equation set are not significantly different from zero, we have in a sense tested and corroborated those theories saying such a link does not exist, and rejected those theories that claimed otherwise.* More elaborate procedures for *a priori* hypotheses concerning nonzero a's are conveniently summarized in Christ's *Econometric Models and Methods*.

An interesting six-variable example of such a recursive or hierarchical causal model is given in Figure 6. Standardized β estimates are placed along the appropriate paths, only the solid ones of which are statistically significant. With this model, Arthur Goldberg has measured the relative importance of various influences on the presidential voting choices of a sample of American party identifiers.[21] The mediating or encapsulating role of partisan attitudes—the usual Michigan set of questions summarized in a single index—and of party identification are also compared. The influence of partisan attitudes is apparently stronger than party identification, and it is more independent of the index of sociological characteristics. Goldberg has also suggested a more dynamic model in which attitudes and party identifications slowly change their voting effects in response to new events.

As usually applied by Goldberg, myself, and others, there are a number of limitations to this data analysis approach, powerful as it may be. First of all, as with regression analysis, *interactions and non-linearities are only detected when they are looked for.* And the necessity of a hierarchical causal ordering makes *the possibility of simultaneous reciprocal causation untestable and unmeasurable using this approach.* Moreover, although any alternative model within the same causal order can be rejected by testing for the randomness or nonrandomness of the relevant regression coefficients, *other causal models from different causal orders may also be consistent with the one so obtained.* Finally, ceteris paribus *assumptions that implicit "error variables" do not affect both independent variables cannot be adequately tested for and must remain a question of empirical judgment.* Of course, every one of the nonexperimental techniques we have discussed—and even, to a degree, the experimental ones, as Blalock has argued—suffers from all or most of these same limitations.

F. RECIPROCAL CAUSAL MODELING

Although they are no panaceas, a number of alternative modeling approaches are available that in some way modify the assumptions of the simpler hierarchical approach.[22] The simplest case of reciprocal (or "non-recursive") causation, for example, would be

$$x_1 \rightleftarrows x_2$$

where one could consider x_1 the U.S. defense budget and x_2 that of the Soviet Union. Thus formulated, the model is "underidentified" and causally indeterminate. But if, on the basis of outside theoretical knowledge, one can find variables y_1 and y_2 known individually and separately to affect x_1 and x_2 respectively, the magnitude of each reciprocal link can then be satisfactorily estimated.

Disentangling procedures for interpreting results in this case, represented

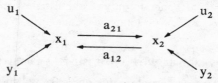

below both graphically and by Equations (9), are not widely known among political scientists, so we shall spell one out here.

$$x_1 + a_{12}x_2 + b_{11}y_1 \qquad \doteq u_1$$
$$a_{21}x_1 + \quad x_2 \qquad + b_{22}y_2 = u_2 \tag{9}$$

The essential statistical reason why the predetermined or "exogenous" y variables have been included in Equations (9) is so as to allow one to identify accurately the a_{12} and a_{21} coefficients. Thus we do not make any assumptions about what the y's are caused by. Rather, in a frequently used "indirect least squares" approach, one solves for a restated causal system in which the x's each hierarchically depend on the y's. Ordinary least squares techniques can then be satisfactorily applied and the a's calculated from these results.[23]

Thus substituting the first and second of Equations (9) into each other gives:

$$x_2 = \underbrace{\left(\frac{a_{21}b_{11}}{1-a_{21}a_{12}}\right)}_{c_1} y_1 \underbrace{\left(\frac{-b_{22}}{1-a_{21}a_{12}}\right)}_{c_2} y_2 + \underbrace{\left(\frac{u_2 - a_{21}u_1}{1-a_{21}a_{12}}\right)}_{u'_2}$$

$$x_1 = \underbrace{\left(\frac{-b_{11}}{1-a_{21}a_{12}}\right)}_{c_3} y_1 + \underbrace{\left(\frac{a_{12}b_{22}}{1-a_{12}a_{21}}\right)}_{c_4} y_2 + \underbrace{\left(u_1 - a_{12}u_2\right)}_{u'_2} \tag{10}$$

Since the relationships of x_1 and x_2 are now ones of direct dependence on y_1 and y_2, ordinary least squares estimation of c_1, c_2, c_3, and c_4 gives acceptable results. At this stage one could assume either that u_1 and u_2 are uncorrelated or, less restrictively, that they do not affect y_1 or y_2. Solving Equations (10) for a_{12} and a_{21} in terms of c estimates gives numbers resolving the ambiguities of reciprocal interdependence:

$$a_{12} = \frac{-c_4}{c_2}; \quad a_{21} = \frac{-c_1}{c_3} \tag{11}$$

The calculations clearly degenerate only in the cases where x_2 ceases to depend directly on y_2, and x_1 no longer depends on y_1 ($c_2 = c_3 = 0$).

G. NONLINEAR CAUSAL MODELS WITH UNMEASURED VARIABLES

A final example of a more complex, interactive causal model involving definite causal relations among the residual terms is given in the bottom half of Figure 6. The arrow diagram slightly oversimplifies one of a class of models suggested by Gerald Kramer for explaining changes in the Democratic (or Republican) percentage of the American two party Congressional vote (V) over roughly the last 50 or 60 years. As in the Goldberg models, a partisan identification variable P, this time not explicitly measured, is assumed to change from election to election (rather than from generation to generation). Economic interests, such as changes in real national income (ΔI), are also thought to affect the national vote directly and indirectly, with a time delay, through the vote's effect on the partisanship level. A most interesting complication of the Kramer time-series model is a dichotomous in-or-out-of-office dummy variable OH, which has a direct effect α on V, as well as an intensifying or diminishing effect of magnitude β on the impact of income changes on voting percentages (the advantages or disadvantages of being in office during an economic boom or depression, even if one's party is not causing the boom or depression). Using periodic time subscripts, the appropriate equations look something like

$$\begin{aligned} V_t &= P_t + OH_t[\alpha + \beta\Delta I_t] + u_t \\ P_t &= \lambda V_{t-1} + (1 - \lambda) P_{t-1} \end{aligned} \tag{12}$$

Without discussing the estimation problems involved nor the related substantive discoveries, we can conclude that a number of reinterpretations of political history are likely to come from such explicit theory-relevant causal investigations, vastly more suggestive than ordinary multiple regression analyses.

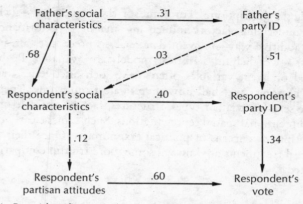

A. Party identification as voter preference encapsulation (Goldberg)

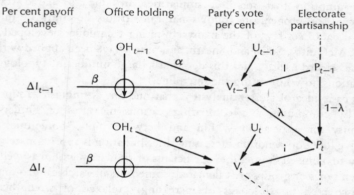

B. Electorate partisanship as experience encapsulation (Kramer)

FIGURE 6

Two Complex Causal Models of Voting Behavior

IV. Some Procedures for Causal Description

Consistent with a concern to analyze data in terms of political causation, there are a number of measurement questions about the underlying causes or dispositional properties of political action. Such concerns we have labeled "causal description." For some of these questions—such as the quest for underlying factors influencing manifest performances in a linear and additive way—relevant data analysis precedures already exist. For others, fewer helpful statistical models are available. Problems of unmeasured or latent variables often make such discoveries statistically difficult. The topics we shall now investigate from a causal perspective include the search for latent types, structures, factors, variable orderings, and multidimensional spatial representations. Such topics clearly comprise major descriptive concerns of political taxonomists. Once their different mathematical treatments are known, some more fruitful comparisons can be attempted.

A. THE SEARCH FOR LATENT TYPES: CLUSTER ANALYSIS

The assumption that manifest similarities are due to shared traits, tendencies, or progenitors follows naturally from the study of much political data. Yet few of the many clustering techniques developed by Tyron, McQuitty, Sokal and Sneath, and others have been applied within political science itself,[24] and this despite the large number of typological speculations now informing the discipline.

The basic idea of cluster analysis is that one can distinguish groups or types by computing and comparing various measures of similarity, proximity, or association within and between units. Sometimes an objective function denoting increasing discrimination is approximately or exactly maximized; sometimes coefficients of similarity within as well as between types or groups are calculated; sometimes hierarchical groupings are discovered on the basis of increasingly relaxed or strengthened membership criteria; and sometimes joint information as to cluster memberships and typical related variable characteristics are retained. Usually not all of these options are concurrently available, nor is a statistical rationale of inference from the manifest to underlying dispositions always well developed in correlational or causal terms.

Our particular example of cluster analysis will be a relatively unsophisticated computational procedure that is susceptible to an unusual causal interpretation and is tied to an intriguing problem in contemporary political theory: that of typologizing types of political development taking into account the influences of prior or parent political systems and the stages or crises that form part of the collective history of particular system types. The cross-sectional procedure I shall use is one derived from the literature on biological evolution, and has been corroborated successfully for at least one species against longitudinal fossil evidence.

The results of any such value-laden assessments are bound to be disputed. My main aspiration is to show how causally suggestive statistical procedures can help explicate and modify the content of the normative and empirical questions and answers involved.[25]

For illustrative purposes we shall assume that political development involves greater popular participation in politics (as through elections of *either* the British *or* the Soviet variety), a *greater* degree of oppositional legitimacy and organized competition, *decreasing* problems of territorial integration (sectionalism), *greater* interest articulation by associational groups and *less* by institutional groups, *more* rationalized, achievement-oriented bureaucracy, *less* uninstitutionalized conflict (riots), and *less* anticonsensual revolutionary violence.[26] *Evolutionary steps are assumed to be discrete and irreversible* (the opposite metahypothesis is of course equally interesting to investigate, *but no more plausible*). The "primitive" state of a particular characteristic will be denoted by a zero; it will be assumed that the characteristic can evolve by integral jumps in either the positive or negative direction. The original data for our analysis, derived largely from earlier classifications by Banks and Textor, are given in Table 1.

The procedure we shall use in trying to find the evolutionary"tree" generating the data configuration of Table 1 is based on the powerful assumption of *evolutionary parsimony: nature has undergone as few evolutionary steps as possible in producing (or causing) the variety of state characteristics that now exist.* When we think in terms of shared developmental stages, *one evolutionary step can be defined as a change in a particular characteristic affecting all countries further down the same branch of an evolutionary tree.*

From Table 1 we see that about half of the characteristics there have undergone up to two evolutionary steps (from 0), while half of them allow only one measurable improvement.

After forming a matrix of shared evolutionary steps, clustering states in terms of the number of such steps should suggest some notion of their evolutionary proximity. Ordering the resulting matrix so that nation pairs with the highest number of shared steps are near the diagonal suggests an evolutionary order and a simple evolutionary tree. The higher the number of shared steps, the more shared branching choices for the pair and the higher they have climbed together on it. Thus, for example, Table 1 suggests that the United States and the United Kingdom may have shared up to

19 evolutionary "increments" in common while Tanganyika and Spain had at most three common advancements in their ancestors.

Does such a way of deriving an "evolutionary tree" give a most parsimonious tree? No, because further manipulations of the evolutionary tree suggested by such a matrix of shared evolutionary steps reduces the number of evolutionary steps required to explain the original data configuration from 43 to 35 (the number of positive "bars" and negative

TABLE I

Contemporary Stages of Development of
Eight Characteristics Twelve Countries on

	COUNTRY												
Characteristic	U.S.	U.K.	France	Spain	Greece	Turkey	U.S.S.R.	Poland	Mexico	Paraguay	S. Africa	Tanganyika (c. 1960)	Minimum possible evolutionary steps
1) Vote participation	1	1	1	0	1	1	−1	−1	0	0	0	0	2
6) Oppositional competition	2	2	1	0	1	1	0	0	1	1	1	0	2
9) Sectionalism	1	1	1	0	1	1	1	−1	0	0	0	0	1
10) Associational articulation	1	2	1	0	1	2	1	2	1	0	0	1	2
11) Institutional articulation	1	2	1	1	0	0	2	0	1	0	1	1	2
18) Modernized bureaucracy	1	1	0	1	0	0	1	1	1	0	1	0	1
28) Riots	1	1	0	1	1	1	1	0	1	1	0	1	1
34) Revolutionary violence	2	2	2	2	1	2	2	1	1	0	0	1	2
Total of developmental scores (absolute values)	10	12	7	5	6	8	9	5	6	2	3	4	13

"crosses" in Figure 7). No further readjustment of branches seems to reduce the extent of original evolution required. Thus if the principle of "evolutionary parsimony" is valid for political systems we would expect Figure 7 to be historically accurate.

Let us speculate for a while on the interpretability of Figure 7's developmental reconstruction. Clearly, relaxing or reversing some of our assumptions would have a marked effect and might be of heuristic value. Moreover, the rankings of states seem intuitively plausible to a certain kind of comparative analysis. The U.S., U.K., and to a lesser extent France here shared the largest number of evolutionary branches and steps

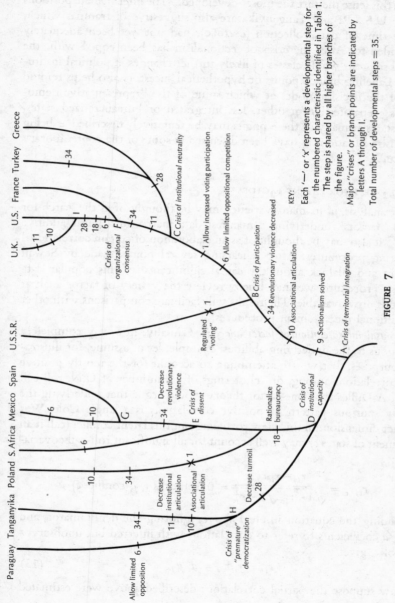

FIGURE 7

A Parsimonious Clustering of Polities in Terms of their Mutually Shared Stages of Political Development

and in this sense they are the most "developed." The intermediate positions of the U.S.S.R. and Tanganyika are also suggestive of traumas which, at the time of data collection (c. 1960), had not yet been adequately responded to. After the crisis of sectionalism has been coped with, the model suggests whole classes of likely further changes in political institutions. Labeling branch points or hypothetical ancestors also helps remind one of the decision nodes at which some of the "representative democracies" separated from other, less integrated or bureaucratized states. Thus states at many of these points may be tentatively described as being at "crisis" situations as have been discussed in some of the contemporary literature.

B. THE QUEST FOR LATENT FACTORS

Factor analysis, in its many varieties, may be thought of as the search for causal "factors" underlying a manifest data matrix in a linear additive way.[27] It also may be thought of as an elaboration of certain correlational clustering procedures. After rehearsing several points made by Sewall Wright and Blalock about the causal significance of this popular data analysis procedure, we shall briefly review the variety of factor analysis methods now available. The results will facilitate comparisons with other dispositional measurement procedures.

A causal interpretation of factor analysis. Causally, in a way completely analogous to the underlying abilities example, let us assume, for illustrative purposes, that we are attempting to account for the mostly positive intercorrelations among, or "clusterings of," a number of U.N. roll-call votes. A Dulles type one-factor theory would argue that underlying the largely spurious pattern of positive correlations is a single Cold War conflict dimension. In this view partialing out this latent conflict (call it an alignment of states c) may well account for all significant roll-call covariations:

$$r_{ij \cdot c} = \frac{r_{ij} - r_{ic}r_{jc}}{\sqrt{1 - r_{ic}^2}\sqrt{1 - r_{jc}^2}} = 0 \text{ (roll calls } i, j, \text{ conflict } c)$$

Expanding the equation implied above, ignoring the denominator, and using a coefficients to refer to correlations with inferred but unobserved variables, gives

$$r_{ij} = r_{ic}r_{jc} = a_{ic}a_{jc} \tag{13}$$

Now suppose the partial correlations described above were estimated and found not to be all zero. A Krishna Menon type theory, to over-characterize some political views once again, might be that a Cold War and an anticolonial conflict alignment (c_1 and c_2) underlay the manifest roll-call intercorrelations. These two dimensions are assumed uncorrelated with each other. Then

$$r_{ij} = a_{ic_1}a_{jc_1} + a_{ic_2}a_{jc_2} \tag{14}$$

follows from

$$r_{ij \cdot c_1 c_2} = 0 \quad (\text{roll calls } i, j, \ i \neq j, \text{ conflicts } c_1, c_2)$$

as before.

A further argument, suggested in more detail below, is that four or five major voting alignments are discernible in a similar manner.

If we interpret r_{ii} as explained variance in i (or the "communality of i") equal to $a^2_{ic1} + a^2_{ic2}$, we can generalize Equations (13) or (14). In compact matrix form an equation for m variables assumed to be caused by n underlying conflicts is

$$\underset{(m \times m)}{\mathbf{R}^+} = \underset{(m \times n)\,(n \times m)}{\mathbf{A}\mathbf{A}'} \tag{15}$$

Here $\mathbf{R}^+$ is an $m \times m$ matrix of r_{ij}'s with r_{ii}'s on the diagonal, and $\mathbf{A}$ is assumed to be a $m \times n$ matrix of factor "loadings," that is, correlations with underlying conflict variables. Equation (15) is known as the fundamental equation of factor analysis.

Also suggested by the partial correlation coefficients above is the idea that a linear model will explain manifest variables as caused by combinations of latent ones. It is easy to show that an appropriate "factor model" of responses is nothing more than

$$X_{jl} = \sum_{k=1}^{n} a_{jk}c_{kl} + u_{jl} \quad (j = 1, .., m; l = 1, .., N) \tag{16}$$

where j represents one of m variables, l indicates one of N individuals, and u_{jl} is a random error term. Thus, assuming the x_{jl}'s to be standardized scores, and the "principal conflict components" c_{kl} to be uncorrelated with each other, the factor model of Equation (16) will generate the fundamental equation of factor analysis, Equation (15).

The principal estimation problem in factor analysis is deriving the c's and the a's. Unfortunately this cannot be done without further restrictions, the most common of which is that in a stepwise sense we look for those few uncorrelated factors which most parsimoniously explain manifest correlations. The main step in estimating the latent variables is the calculation of eigen vectors and values of either the adjusted $\mathbf{R}^+$ or the ordinary correlation matrix with unities on the diagonals. The eigen vector equations look like

$$\mathbf{R}^+\mathbf{a}_k = \lambda_k\mathbf{a}_k \qquad (17)$$

Resulting eigen vectors a_k (with corresponding values λ_k) can after normalization, be considered column vectors of factor loadings. But many psychologists and others argue that the resulting a's are not the most causally correct, that the real links will be found by rotating the axes of the matrix of factor loadings until a "simple structure" of high positive, zero, and/or high negative loading coefficients is found. As Tukey has argued, the causal validity of even the simple structure idea is, however, a debatable question.

Causal assumptions of unilateral, linear, additive effects on otherwise uncorrelated variables strike a doubtful chord in many applications, although for the U.N. the idea that resolutions additively evoke mixes of underlying conflict predispositions does have some causal appeal, if a lot of vote trading does not occur. If these assumptions seem debatable, interpretations of factor analyses must retreat to merely correlational language such as considering factors to be merely "variance rescaling" devices. Quite a useful half-way house interpretation in such cases is that *factors* help separate *clusters* of relatively highly interdependent variables from each other. Note, however, that there can be *clusters* of highly positive factor loadings or intermediate size loadings (for variables with low communalities) or highly negative roll-call loadings all along a single factor *dimension*. Thus the measurement concept "factor dimension" may be seen to be more general than that of "similarity" or "correlational cluster."

Alternate versions of factor analysis. Since an extended factor analysis of U.N. voting is discussed in a later section of this paper, we shall mention here a growing variety of modified factor analysis procedures that are worth considering as dispositional measurement techniques. First of all, it is possible (Q analysis) to correlate individuals over a number of characteristics, as well as *vice versa* (R analysis, as previously discussed). And we may relax the uncorrelated factors assumption in order to show "oblique" factor axes, where intercorrelations may be of interest. "Second-order factor analyses" of interfactor correlations may then be calculated. (Finding an East–West and North configuration underlying the Cold

War, anticolonialism, Moslem, and supranationalism factors in the U.N. might be such an example.)

A somewhat different kind of data analysis, "direct factor analysis" tries to discover row and column vectors **u** and **v** which can respectively be considered eigen vectors of R and Q type covariance matrices which both multiply the raw data matrix **X** to give the other, and which simultaneously give quantitative information as to the clustering or dimensioning of the row *and* column variables being studied.

$$\mathbf{X v'} = \mathbf{u}; \qquad \mathbf{u' X} = \mathbf{v} \tag{17a}$$

$$\mathbf{X X' u} = \lambda \mathbf{u}; \qquad \mathbf{v X' X} = \lambda \mathbf{v} \tag{17b}$$

Using dichotomous data on friendship patterns, MacRae has applied this technique to cluster givers and receivers of such choices using the **u** and **v** vectors respectively. The similarity of Equations (17) and (17b) is of course striking: eigen values are given by λs and $\mathbf{R} = \frac{1}{N}\mathbf{X X'}$ if the **X**'s are standard scores with zero means and unit variances. This technique closely resembles the approach of quantification scaling to be discussed below, and with modifications could be given a spatial interpretation.[28]

Fourthly, as Richard Stone and others have done, one can "factor" a matrix of quasi-Euclidean distances giving results that may approximate more orthodox multidimensional scaling procedures. But if underlying dimensions with attractive "distance" properties are desired, using multidimensional scaling techniques discussed below would seem more appropriate.

Finally, there have been various nonadditive extensions of the factor model to include three coefficients in each term ("three mode factor analysis"), or other nonlinearities ("nonlinear factor analysis"). These approaches tend to merge with latent structure analysis, also to be discussed below.

C. THE SEARCH FOR UNDERLYING ORDERS: UNIDIMENSIONAL SCALE ANALYSIS[29]

Causal descriptions treat observable data as manifestations of underlying regularities, such as evolutionary principles or progenitors, and factor structures. A distinguishing characteristic of a number of qualitative unidimensional scaling procedures is a search for an underlying spatial positioning of actors or item categories. Moreover, the ordering principle

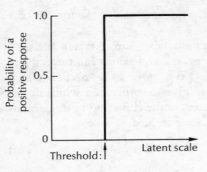

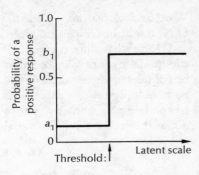

A. A perfect cumulative item   B. An approximate cumulative item

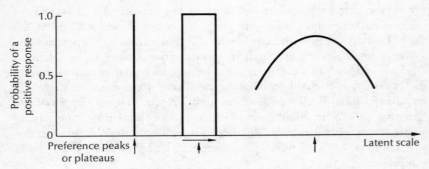

C. Perfect point, perfect interval, and approximate point items

FIGURE 8

Trace Line Representations of Response Probabilities Evoked
by Various Cumulative, Point, and Interval Questionnaire Items

governing a particular positioning of actors or items is likely to provide a
key to a special conception of dispositional relationships. We shall here
briefly discuss cumulative scales, point scales, simplices, and circumplexes
from this point of view.

"Trace lines" have been used by Lazarsfeld and others to relate underlying dispositions to manifest responses. They usually represent the probabilities associated with positive responses to a particular item in terms
of an assumed position on some underlying continuum. Figure 8 shows

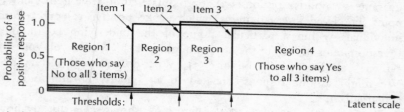

A. A cumulative scale (Guttman Scale)

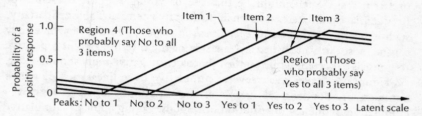

B. A point scale with reversed items (prob. Yes + prob. No = 1)

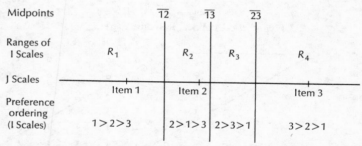

C. An unfolded J Scale— Ordering 3>1>2 is impossible if scale is correct

FIGURE 9

Joint Preference Spaces of Actors and Alternatives According to the Cumulative Scale Model, the Point Scale Model with Reversed Items, and the Coombsian Unfolding Model (3 or 6 items)

three of the most common kinds of items: 1) perfect cumulative items involving a kind of threshold which, for anyone above that threshold, guarantees a positive response; 2) approximate cumulative items; and 3) point (or closed interval) items which evoke positive responses from individuals within a particular range of the underlying continuum. Question items of each of these types might be: 1) "Would you vote for Nixon?" 2) "Do you like Nixon?" 3) "What do you think of Nixon?" We might assume responses related to an underlying dimension of conservatism.

The Guttman or cumulative scale. Figure 9A shows schematically how several cumulative items might be ordered along an ideological continuum or latent scale. Such might be the case of voting support by states for Presidential candidates, as shown in the first five items of Table 2. Spatially, such items imply that items *have threshold points* by means of which they can be most easily identified: to one side of the threshold point a positive response is expected, while on the other side a negative reply should occur. As Figure 9A makes clear, several cumulative trace lines, each of which cumulates respondents above a certain threshold, together suggest a cumulative frequency distribution of responses along a line of cumulative items. Such a cumulative pattern is evidence for the existence of a "Guttman scale."

TABLE 2

A Hypothetical Political Response Pattern

Actor	Item	1a	2a	3a	4a	5a	1b	2b	3b	4b	5b
Mississippi		I	I	I	I	I	o	o	o	o	o
Arizona		o	I	I	I	I	I	o	o	o	o
California		o	o	I	I	I	I	I	o	o	o
Michigan		o	o	o	I	I	I	I	I	o	o
New York		o	o	o	o	I	I	I	I	I	o
Massachusetts		o	o	o	o	o	I	I	I	I	I

| | Yes to | | | | | No to | | | | |

Cumulative
interpretation   Gold. Reagan Nixon Romney Rock.   Gold. Reagan Nixon Romney Rock.

Yes to

Gold. Reagan Nixon Jackson LBJ Humphrey Romney Rockefeller Kennedy Fulbright
Point
interpretation

Another point of interest suggested by Figure 9A is that the latent scale there orders both items and individuals. The *respondents* are located within various open-ended *regions* delineated by *item threshold points.*

Point scales. Consider Figure 8C once again. It is clear that a number of point or interval items, possibly overlapping in their ranges of high probability positive responses, might also reflect an underlying scale. Although political scientists accustomed to looking for Guttman scales rarely think of unstructured response categories in terms of such a hypothesis, on reflection it seems quite a plausible alternative. In fact, the well-known literature on single peaked preference curves over a range of political alternatives assumes the existence of point scales rather than of cumulative items and scales.

Now recall that the Guttman scale in Table 2 was presented in parallelogram form, with items 1b–5b, reversed or opposite versions of items 1a–5a, tacked on rather redundantly at the end of the scale. If we consider each of these items to be a cumulative item, then some kind of contradiction in assumptions occurs in those scale ranges where both an item and its opposite are supposed to have perfect probabilities of a positive response. At best some kind of interval of positive response, corresponding to the 1's in the appropriate column of Table 2, would be roughly consistent with such a representation.

A much more felicitous expression of this possibility is suggested by the parallelogram itself. Why not consider each item (of the *a* or *b* type) to have a trace line approximating one of the point or interval items from Figure 8C? For each actor, a range of items seems to evoke positive responses; if the actors and items are ordered in terms of their ideological extremeness, these ranges will have approximately the shape of a parallelogram. Looking at the bottom of Table 2, the option of treating items 1b–5b not as reversals of earlier items, but as separate candidate possibilities represents a more extreme version of a point scale interpretation. And looking now at Figure 9B, we see that treating positive items and their reversals as approximate point scales can generate trace lines strikingly like cumulative scales within the ranges of attitudinal predispositions being measured. Here two item preference peaks, with positive response thresholds occurring gradually in between them, serve to locate a response item, while respondents again fit into various open-ended regions.

I and J scales. A related Coombsian scaling procedure, unfolding analysis, is suggested by Figure 9C. In an ordinal, nonprobabilistic fashion, it too is based on the assumption of single peaked preferences; items again act like point items. Assuming individual "I scale" information on the comparative attractiveness of various alternatives is at hand, Coombs postulates the existence of "J scales" representing a joint space or continuum along which *item points* and *individual ideal points* coexist. Preferences are assumed to be derivable from the relative closeness of various items to individual preference peaks. Although individuals cannot be distinguished within certain ranges, the consistency of preference orderings with the underlying hypothesized continuum allows us to predict that individuals with certain preference orderings (for example, $1 < 2 > 3$ in the one-dimensional case) will not occur.

Radex analysis. Up to this point we have examined a number of possible ordering principles and variables underlying manifest data regularities. In developing his ideas of radex analysis, Guttman has tried to generalize these notions and come up with different ordering principles, in particular the "simplex" and the "circumplex" hypotheses. After briefly reviewing how the "simplex" notion generalizes the unidimensional ordering notions we have been discussing, we shall investigate some empirically determined approximate circumplexes.

If we were to correlate the first five items in Table 2, in the order given there, the resulting 5×5 correlation matrix would be clearly patterned. Items close to each other would be highly correlated, those farther away less so; items 1 and 5 would positively correlate around 0.20. The correlation matrix would have high entries near the main upper left-lower right diagonal, and smaller ones off the diagonals. Now if we were to treat all ten items in Table 2 as point items along the same continuum, a similar pattern would occur, but extreme items would lead to negative correlations far off the main diagonal. Correlating individual preference orderings (I scales) drawn sequentially from an unfolded J scale such as the one in Figure 9C would lead to similar results. So would a developmental causal chain like $X_1 \rightarrow X_2 \rightarrow X_3 \rightarrow X_4 \rightarrow X_5$. Guttman calls a set of ordered items that produce a high set of near diagonal correlations, with regularly decreasing magnitudes as one moves along any row or column away from the diagonal, a "simplex." Looking for simplices in data matrices can be suggestive of a variety of intriguing causal phenomena.

Are there any other such simple correlational patternings suggestive of underlying causal ordering principles? Of course, a one-factor model will lead to an ordering of U.N. roll-calls in terms of decreasing factor loadings (which square to give communalities). Consider also a more complex, but fascinating correlational patterning suggested by radex theory and evidenced in Table 3 below. Except for the bracketed correlations we see a general progression in correlations along a column or row of the table from high to low to high again. In this sense somehow there appears to

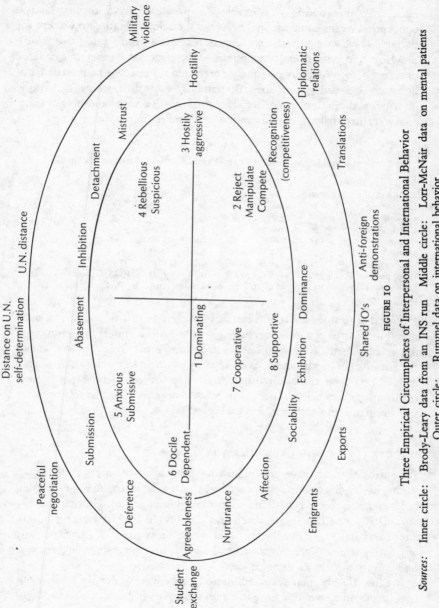

FIGURE 10

Three Empirical Circumplexes of Interpersonal and International Behavior

Sources: Inner circle: Brody-Leary data from an INS run   Middle circle: Lorr-McNair data on mental patients
                Outer circle: Rummel data on international behavior

be a circular ordering of variables, as predicted by Timothy Leary's conception of the interpersonal behavioral circle. In Figure 10, except for variable 1, we see a circular configuration derived from Table 3 that is very much in line with these conceptions. Moreover, two other rather large data sets—Lorr-McNair obliquely correlated dimensions of interpersonal behavior derived from mental patients, and dimensions of dyadic international relations as collected by Professor Rummel and his associates —give rather striking corroboration of this circumplex patterning.

TABLE 3

Ordinal Correlations among Leary-Brody Content Analysis Categories*

	1.	2.	3.	4.	5.	6.	7.	8.
1. Dominating	1.00							
2. Rejecting	0.32	1.00						
3. Hostile	0.28	0.59	1.00					
4. Rebellious	[0.50]	0.44	0.57	1.00				
5. Anxious	0.45	0.02	0.10	0.24	1.00			
6. Docile	0.52	0.12	−0.04	0.21	0.53	1.00		
7. Cooperative	0.72	0.40	0.14	0.31	0.56	0.57	1.00	
8. Supportive	[0.69]	0.39	0.12	0.21	0.43	[0.37]	0.83	1.00

* Derived from content analyses of an Inter-Nation Simulation by Richard Brody.

Whether or not such results can be interpreted causally remains an open question. Guttman and others have suggested some underlying circularizing mechanisms (or component structures) that might have causal significance. Note also that a circular array of imperfect point items would generate a correlational circumplex. Clearly some underlying structural relationships are being reflected in such a situation, but which ones are valid remains an unanswered causal question.

D. GUTTMAN-HAYASHI QUANTIFICATION SCALING

An extremely attractive generalization of some of the ideas in Guttman scaling and radex analysis is a procedure that appears to have been invented independently by Hayashi and Guttman, specialized by Guttman to the cumulative scale case, generalized and interpreted by Hayashi, Kyogoku, and Takabatake in a number of Japanese publications.[30] *It provides a way of spatially representing, in a meaningful way, a joint plot of actors and response categories, each treated as single points.*

Because the mathematical estimation procedure is already spelled out in an Appendix, we shall here focus on a simple illustration. The problem

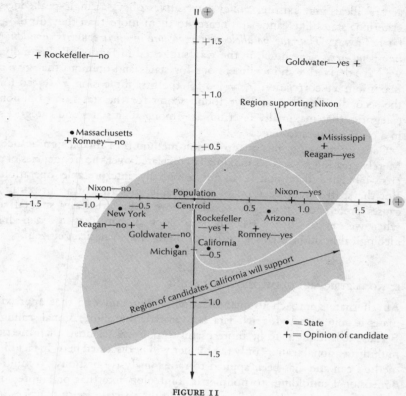

FIGURE 11

A Joint Metric Representation of 80 Per Cent of the Information
in a Guttman Scale of Hypothetical Political Preferences

Source: Table 2.

investigated in the Appendix is how best to quantify the qualitative
information about states and their opinions of candidates as they appear in
Table 2. *It turns out that an ordinal Guttman scale can lead to interval scale
numbers for each row respondent and column category in a multidimensional
representation of a unidimensional scale.*

A number of points about the Guttman–Hayashi procedure are suggested
by Figure 11. First of all we see how a joint spatial treatment of both

actors' ideals and existing policy alternatives obeys a single-peakedness criterion: states like candidates nearer to them more than they do those farther away. *Thus the parallelogram procedure in effect converts cumulative into point items* very much in the way suggested in Figure 9B. Secondly, we have derived x and y dimensions for states and opinions that give a maximum xy correlation ($r^2 = .60$ for the first dimension, $r^2 = .20$ for the second). Thirdly, we have found scores for the states and opinion categories that maximally discriminate among such states and categories in a correlation ratio sense.

Causally speaking, this quantification method is of mixed significance. Merely creating x's and y's maximally correlated over the frequencies of a cross-tabulated data matrix is not a causally interpretable operation. But the spatial interpretation of these results in terms of a "proximity causes preference" principle is much more voluntaristically suggestive when we can say "Rockefeller is more popular than Reagan *because* his ideological position is closer to that of the typical American citizen."

E. NONMETRIC MULTIDIMENSIONAL SCALING

An alternate approach to quantification scaling, and one that approximates it quite closely for rich data, is nonmetric multidimensional scaling. Because it is thought to be more useful to political scientists than metric multidimensional scaling, only the former will be discussed here. In fact this method can and has been applied to radex analysis questions, to multidimensional unfolding, to nonmetric joint plots like that of Figure 11, and to nonmetric factor analysis, including the special case of matrices of Euclidean distances.[31] As such it logically includes all the dispositional measurement procedures we have so far discussed.

The basic idea of the approach is to construct the smallest spatial representation of data interpreted as distances or proximities. The nonmetric relaxation of measurement assumptions comes in the use of only the *ranks* of these proximities or distances. For the Guttman–Lingoes version of this approach, smallest space analysis (or GL(SSA)), a least-squares derivation suggests an iterative eigen vector procedure for approximating spatially interpretable coordinates that tend parsimoniously to reproduce the original data. Assuming an $n \times N$ matrix, it minimizes:

$$\sum_{i=1}^{n} \sum_{j=1}^{N} (\rho_{ij} - d_{ij})^2$$

Here ρ_{ij} is a quasi-distance measure derived from the original data matrix, for example, $1 - r_{ij}$ for correlation coefficients. Because results are only expected to correspond in an ordinal way with the original ρ_{ij}'s, one can calculate the extent to which "stress" has been reduced by a particular spatial representation in terms of a normalized phi:

$$\text{stress } \phi = \frac{\sum_i \sum_j (d_{ij} - d_{ij}^*)^2}{2 \sum_i \sum_j d_{ij}^2} \tag{18}$$

where d_{ij}^* is the same data as the d_{ij}'s, but permuted to give a better data fit while still preserving the rank order of the ρ_{ij}'s.

Applications of GL(SSA) methods to square matrices, for which only orderings of rows are desired, are computed with programs of the SSA series: SSA-I was used to calculate the Brody-Leary circumplex, for example. Figure 12 shows an application of SSA-II, designed for assymetric matrices, to a preprocessed trade matrix for the North Atlantic area. The figure shows how the major geographic and political groupings of the area do tend to determine trading patterns, particularly for a cohesive Common Market and a not so cohesive EFTA. Comparisons through time are also interesting: there seems to be a very slow shift of the United Kingdom toward the Common Market.

When a joint plot is desired, programs of the SSAR series are available. Their results would be directly analogous to those of quantification scaling or direct factor analysis of asymmetric matrices. Multidimensional unfolding of a matrix of preference ranks is also possible when only the *ranks in the rows* are approximated, but a sufficient variety of information is necessary to achieve nondegenerate results.

The close fit of these programs with a number of the data analysis problems we have already examined is quite encouraging. Making fewer distributional assumptions, we can still look for causally suggestive models that would reproduce manifested data patterns. But each technique by itself does not *prove* the existence of an underlying causal pattern, it merely assumes it in order that its parameters may be better calculated.

F. LATENT PROFILES AND LATENT STRUCTURES

Latent profile analysis is an extremely general approach to dispositional measurement based on interval scale data. Despite its mathematical

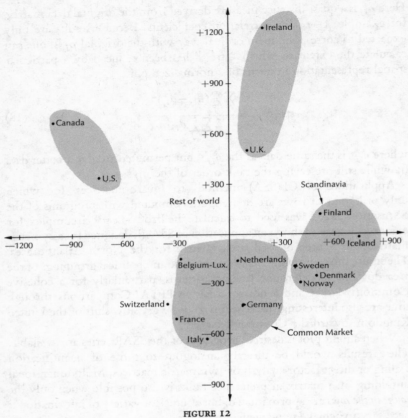

FIGURE 12

A Nonmetric Two-Dimensional Representation of
1959 North Atlantic Area Trading Partnerships

Source: RA coefficients from Alker and Puchala, *op. cit.*, subjected to GL(SSA-II)
analysis.

complexity, a number of special cases have been studied, including
Lazarsfeld's original development of the dichotomous attribute latent
structure case. A further *specialization* of this approach is the latent distance
model, which is nonetheless a *generalization* of ordinary Guttman scaling!
(Recall the probabilistic tracelines of Figure 8B.)

The fundamental equations of the approach are consciously derived from those of factor analysis, but they are interaction-sensitive. The basic idea is that regular bivariate and higher order correlations contain all the information in a set of data. Latent classes or continua are assumed to exist which probabilistically are reflected, via a particular trace line model, in the manifest responses. *It is assumed that manifest triple-product and bivariate correlations can be broken down into vanishing associations within classes and structural or "ecological" correlations among them.*

The rationale is very much like the $r_{ij.c1c2} = 0$ notion in factor analysis, except, additionally, that no interactional differences between the several classes are allowed. Thus both bivariate and interaction-sensitive triple product correlations are assumed to vanish within particular subclasses. For q different subclasses, standardized variables Z_j, Z_k, and Z_l, the fundamental equations of Gibson's latent profile analysis (using suprabars to indicate averages) are:

$$
\begin{aligned}
1 &= P_1 + P_2 + \ldots + P_q \; [P\text{'s are proportions}] \\
0 &= P_1 Z_{1j} + P_2 Z_{2j} + \ldots + P_q Z_{qj} \\
r_{jk} &= P_1 Z_{1j} Z_{1k} + \ldots + P_q Z_{qj} Z_{qk} \\
r_{jkl} &= P_1 Z_{1j} Z_{1k} Z_{1l} + \ldots + P_q Z_{qj} Z_{qk} Z_{ql}, \text{ etc.}
\end{aligned}
\tag{19}
$$

A hypothetical example of the simpler latent distance case will illustrate some of the power of the approach. Assume we are trying to measure the particularistic element in the political culture of a developing country. Although questions like "Do you think one ought to report a friend who reused old postage stamps? buys on the black market? cheated on his civil service exams? is fomenting sedition?" might be very roughly scalable in a Guttman sense, the fit would probably be too rough to satisfy the usual reproducibility requirements. *By assuming the items involved have tracelines like those of Figure 9B, with probabilities of Yes and No that are neither one nor zero, we can estimate these probabilities and place individuals in a proper ordering of particularistic loyalty.* Cross-national comparisons with equivalent items could then be made.[34]

In some senses latent profile analysis represents the most powerful procedure for causal description that we have reviewed. It explicitly relates manifest properties and latent traits; adding some ordering assumptions gives results very much like Guttman scaling or factor analysis. The causal hypothesis of "local independence" within subclasses is explicit and powerful. Unfortunately, however, as with nonlinear factor analysis, estimation problems mean that only small sets of data can easily be treated in such a manner.

V. Choosing Among Data Analysis Procedures

Given the variety of causal data and noncausal analysis procedures suggested in the previous two sections, one needs to develop better rationales for choosing among such methodologies. This means choosing one or several procedures on the bases of the substantive problems involved, the modeling assumptions implied by the methods, and the appropriateness of these assumptions to the empirical problem.

Such choices may show certain methods to be complementary or contradictory. Presenting two somewhat extended and comparative data analyses simultaneously involving several methodologies should serve to highlight some of their similarities and differences and the analytical choices involved. Some concluding remarks will attempt to generalize such insights.

A. THE MILLER–STOKES REPRESENTATIONAL PARADIGM

A major theoretical problem of the Miller–Stokes representation study is to determine the causal importance and the influence pathways of constituency opinions relating to Congressional roll-call voting behavior.[35] Correlations among average district opinions (D), Congressional perceptions of these (P), Congressional attitudes (A), and Guttman scaled roll-call votes in the civil rights issue area (R), are as follows:

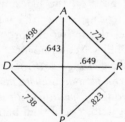

As we shall see, the interpretations we make of these data depend crucially on the causal modeling assumptions consistent with the various interpretive methods we might use. Unfortunately, the different techniques lead to rather different conclusions.

Thus, were the "generally correlated additive causes" assumptions of Figure 3, case 2, deemed plausible and a multiple regression equation estimated, it would show that

$$R = .34D - .04P + .68A + u$$

and would explain about 75 per cent of the variance in R. Indicating Congressional attitudes to be the dominant influence on R, this equation also shows a considerable effect traceable to district opinions.

But if, as Cnudde and McCrone argue, perceptions mediate or funnel district influences, and they influence attitudes but not *vice versa*, the multiple regression model short-changes these indirect effects. Moreover, it seems theoretically unlikely that a direct causal link exists between the district and roll-call voting without being reflected in the measured Congressional attitudes or perceptions. Thus, the causal model portrayed in case 1 of Figure 13 is intuitively more plausible than the additive causes case.

This perceptual mediation model is further supported by derivations from the assumptions that $b_{AD.P} = 0$ and $b_{RD.AP} = 0$, from which follows $r_{AD.P} = 0$ and $r_{RD.AP} = 0$. Comparisons of actual and derived results are:

Derived Relation	*Actual vs. Derived Results*	*Discrepancy*
$r_{AD} = r_{PD} \cdot r_{AP}$		
$r_{RD} = r_{RA}\, r_{DA} +$		
$\dfrac{(r_{PD} - r_{PA\ DA})(r_{RP} - r_{RA\ PA})}{1 - r^2{}_{PA}}$	.498 vs. .47	0.03
	.649 vs. .62	0.03

A number of problems exist, however, concerning the perceptual mediation model of Cnudde and McCrone. In particular, other equally plausible models, suggested by Forbes and Tufte, also fit the data. Case 3 of Figure 13 suggests the hypothesis that reported attitudes are primarily vote rationalizations. Here attitudes have *no* independent causal effects! Again we see a Blalock type test that corroborates this very different "rationalization model."

Model "Derivation"	*Predicted vs. Actual Results*	*Discrepancy*
$r_{DA} = r_{DP} r_{PR} r_{RA}$	.498 vs. 44	0.06
$r_{DR} = r_{DP} r_{PR}$	.649 vs. 61	0.05

If this interpretation is correct, then the Cnudde–McCrone finding and Miller and Stokes' paradigm are seriously in need of revision. Moreover, the multiple regression analysis results are extremely misleading as to the "independent" importance of Congressional attitudes.

Trying stepwise regression procedures would cast further doubt on these conclusions, suggesting but not proving the validity of an alternative model. From the correlation data it is clear that P would be found to be

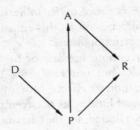

Case 1: Perceptual mediation

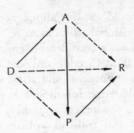

Case 2: Stepwise regression

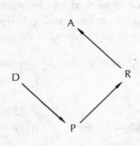

Case 3: Vote rationalization

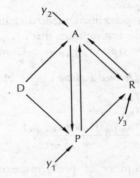

Case 4: Reciprocal reinforcement

FIGURE 13

Four Causal Models of the Miller-Stokes Representational Paradigms
(D = District opinion; P = Representative perception; A = Representative
attitude; R = related Representative roll-call voting position)

causally most proximate to R. Comparing the two relevant second-order
b's as to the correct next step suggests that attitudes are the next most
proximal cause of voting positions. Recalling the representation of stepwise regression results in Figure 4, a stepwise analysis would then find or
assure a fourth modeling interpretation, case 2 in Figure 13. Here a basic
$D \rightarrow A \rightarrow P \rightarrow R$ sequence suggests that Congressional attitudes tend to
distort Congressmen's perceptions of constituency preferences!

As a general rule of thumb, *it appears that when several different causal
orderings of explanatory variables are plausible* (as with cases 1, 3, and perhaps
2 in Fig. 13), *simultaneous, reciprocal interdependence is a highly plausible*

theoretical alternative. In fact, Miller and Stokes originally *assumed reciprocal* Perception ⇄ Attitude *links and derived results as to the importance of links through perceptions on the basis of that assumption*. Certainly *recursive* causal modeling cannot *test* for reciprocal reinforcements of the sort in case 4 of the figure, because *such relationships are assumed not to occur*. In this sense, finding *either* that $P \rightarrow A$ is basic (as Cnudde and McCrone argue) *or* that $A \rightarrow P$ link dominates, as Dexter and others might argue, is a Pyrrhic victory—when reciprocal reinforcement, a plausible alternative, is not being considered.

How do we get out of this host of dilemmas? On the basis of theoretical judgments of plausibility, the gathering of additional data, and the methodology of reciprocal causal modeling. Thus extra variables with causal impacts like those of y_1, y_2, and y_3 in Figure 13, case 4, must be found in order to disentangle the reciprocal influence pathways involved, in fact to *test* the *assumptions* of the various hierarchical modeling approaches. Methods like the previously illustrated indirect least squares procedure would then be appropriate.

B. ACTORS AND ALTERNATIVES IN THE INTERNATIONAL ARENA

More complementary usage of causal data analysis procedures may also be achieved. Our example concerns a causal description problem pre-occupying a number of roll-call analysts: how can we measure the preferences of various actors for various alternatives? A spatial representation of actors' preference curves, mountains or valleys and policy alternatives would ideally be a joint plot in the same space: both ideal points and legislative items would be given point representations. Distances in the same space would differentiate both legislators and roll-calls; proximity of an actor and an alternative would mean a strong preference relation. Regions in such spaces might signify the range of support each legislator is likely to offer with the more uncompromising respondents being those with preferences that are more "peaked." Resolution-writing and coalition-building strategies should be readily apparent.

How far does factor analysis go to meet such needs? Table 4 gives a rotated factor matrix from a previous orthogonal factor analysis of 70 important roll-calls in the 16th U.N. General Assembly.[36] Relatively clear substantive meanings for the first four factors can be suggested: Factor I is anticolonial and economic-development oriented, or "self-determination"; Factor II evidences small power plus allies' attempts to increase the economic and peace-keeping role of the U.N., or "U.N. supranational-ism"; Factor III is obviously a "Cold War" factor, specialized to "member-ship" issues. Finally, Factor IV combines Indonesian–West Irian and Palestine issues, topics with mixed responses among the anticolonial states; a "Moslem support" label might be appropriate. There are considerable advantages to the causal insight that, when bargaining is infrequent, roll-calls can be thought of as stimuli differentially activating underlying voting predispositions.

Although these distinctions are clearly useful ones, and a plot of factor scores reveals significant regional-political groupings in positions on the above-mentioned factors, a number of problems remain if a preferential perspective on the data is desired. First of all, the factor loadings do not give ideologically meaningful spatial plots of roll-call issues. Strongly anticolonial resolutions can have the same communality as much weaker ones; low magnitude loadings reveal other underlying issues at work, but not that some highly anticolonial states may have supported the resolution because of its striking "self-determination" flavor. The absence of a joint plot of nations and roll-calls—factor scores exist in spaces where factors represent axes, not points—prevents discussions of the relative ideological heterogeneity of a roll-call's supporters, preference priorities, or potential coalition partners. And factor scores, although they appear to be interval scale numbers, are in fact just weighted ordinal indices. An especially troublesome problem, that multidimensional scaling procedures cannot handle either, is our reliance on *post influence* data in trying to estimate "true factor positions" or "ideal points."

Working with a U.N. roll-call correlation matrix previously interpreted in factor analysis terms (Table 4), we might proceed to get "preference spaces" as follows. Quantification scaling would be possible for 101 countries and 70 roll-calls with some kind of positive integer vote scores. But this method's dependence on metric assumptions when ours is rank order data (Yes > Abstain > No) leads us to prefer a nonmetric scaling procedure to the extent possible. Unfortunately, the appropriate SSAR programs of the Guttman–Lingoes variety do not handle data matrices nearly as large as 70 × 101, and revising them to do so would be prohibi-tively expensive. But a smallest space analysis of ordinal versions of the correlations among 70 roll-calls is possible using G-L (SSA = 1).

The results, taking around 20 minutes of IBM 7094 computer time, are given in Figure 14 (ignore the national groups there for a moment). A four-dimensional spatial representation gives a stress coefficient below

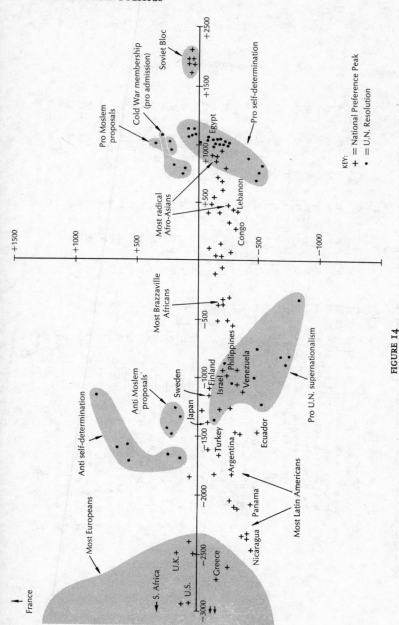

FIGURE 14

A Single Peaked Preferential Map of Nation States and Resolutions in the 1961 U.N. General Assembly

TABLE 4

Dimensions of United Nations Conflict: A Rotated Factor Matrix for 70 Important Roll Calls at the 16th General Assembly

Roll Call	I	II	III	IV	Factor V	VI	VII	VIII	IX
1. Censure South Africa	.77	.02	.00	.17	.16	.08	-.11	.03	-.09
2. Sanction South Africa	.88	-.10	.19	.13	.05	-.11	.03	-.03	-.11
3. Security Council & S. Africa	.91	-.06	.25	.16	.06	-.07	.06	-.06	-.00
4. No arms to South Africa	.82	-.12	.28	.08	-.05	-.15	.14	-.15	-.11
5. No petroleum to S. Africa	.84	-.14	.24	.11	-.02	-.20	.11	-.13	-.14
6. Oman self-determination	.67	-.19	.15	.51	.17	.06	.09	-.07	.02
7. Reconstitute Pal. Con. Com.	.24	-.08	.09	.19	-.01	-.85	-.02	-.03	.03
8. Reconstitute Pal. Con. Com.	.43	-.12	.19	.65	.08	-.33	-.06	-.02	-.13
9. Protect Arab refugees	.45	-.12	.23	.71	.03	-.22	-.03	-.07	-.08
10. U.N.R.W.A.	-.33	.28	-.18	-.67	.18	-.18	-.18	-.01	.09
11. U.S. Palestine Resolution	-.38	.32	-.21	-.65	.13	-.21	-.10	.06	.01
12. Czech Res. on S.C.E.A.R.	.60	-.25	.40	.30	-.14	-.03	-.01	-.04	.06
13. Czech Res. important	-.64	.25	-.44	-.33	-.05	-.02	.05	-.01	.00
14. Admit Mauritania	-.37	.28	-.40	-.59	-.08	.13	-.18	.02	.03
15. China question important?	-.22	.20	-.83	-.30	-.10	.05	0.01	.15	.09
16. China Declaration	.34	.13	.86	.12	.00	.03	.15	-.09	.00
17. Seat People's Rep. of China	.33	.16	.84	.08	-.09	-.01	.11	-.09	.01
18. Representation of China	.33	-.17	.87	.12	-.01	-.03	.01	-.11	-.01
19. Stop 50 megaton bomb	-.22	.79	-.21	-.16	-.12	.04	.30	.20	.06
20. General & Complete Disarm.	.69	-.16	.42	.33	-.18	.01	-.01	-.10	-.08
21. Regrets tests; need treaty	.24	.76	-.04	-.02	.25	.20	.17	-.13	-.23
22. Regrets rejection of US-UK	-.26	.59	-.51	-.32	-.09	.00	.12	.01	.05
23. De-nuclearize Africa	.31	-.03	.48	.42	.05	.01	.11	-.52	-.10
24. Nuclear vs. humanity	.85	-.02	.29	.17	.07	.01	.04	-.19	-.09
25. Non-nuclear club	.31	.00	.47	.38	.09	.06	.01	-.53	-.19
26. Question of Algeria	.35	.07	.46	.36	.05	-.00	.02	-.58	-.12
27. P.D.R. & UNCURK	-.29	.37	-.67	-.32	-.04	.07	.15	.05	.14
28. Report of UNCURK	-.47	.35	-.58	-.43	-.03	-.04	.11	.12	-.05
29. Deplores Hungary	-.72	.31	-.47	-.22	.07	-.00	.07	.08	.03
30. Non-interference (Cuba)	.48	-.17	.57	.49	.03	-.13	-.01	-.07	-.02
31. Friendly relations with Cuba	.67	-.15	.54	.29	-.04	-.17	.02	-.09	-.08
32. Trade conference	.83	-.06	.31	.19	-.11	-.11	.07	-.23	-.04

33.	Primary commodities	.44	.11	.11	.03	.67	−.04	.11	−.25	−.19
34.	Study trade conference	−.34	.48	−.41	−.45	−.09	.07	.14	.03	.12
35.	Special int. devel. agency	.67	.06	−.09	.30	−.43	−.05	−.08	.13	−.20
36.	Conference on patents	−.60	.05	.03	−.38	−.51	−.10	.09	−.14	.01
37.	Capital & technical assist.	.06	.78	−.07	−.10	.12	.02	.18	.26	.03
38.	Population & econ. devel.	.23	−.16	.51	.05	.02	−.26	.07	−.43	.25
39.	Tibet on agenda	−.49	−.43	−.47	−.39	.05	.05	.01	−.04	−.12
40.	Resolution on Tibet	−.32	.48	−.56	−.49	.03	−.01	.03	−.02	−.10
41.	Absentee marriage	.01	−.38	−.08	−.18	−.01	−.03	−.74	.12	−.14
42.	"Hatred and hostility"	.82	−.13	.22	.13	.06	−.03	−.08	.13	.02
43.	Safeguard right of reply	.45	−.26	.23	.40	−.39	−.03	.01	−.27	.09
44.	Algerian prisoners	.69	.01	.35	.09	−.01	−.05	.17	−.44	−.13
45.	1962 end of colonialism	.72	−.30	.45	.19	−.04	−.11	−.07	−.13	−.05
46.	W. Irian self-determination	−.32	.16	−.35	−.65	−.12	−.08	−.07	−.13	−.10
47.	Commission on W. Irian	−.36	.16	−.38	−.63	.10	.20	−.06	.22	−.06
48.	Indian res. on W. Irian	.37	−.09	.35	.61	.23	.18	.03	.20	−.06
49.	Regrets Port non-compliance	−.85	.05	−.20	−.15	−.12	−.05	−.02	−.33	−.03
50.	Renew CINSGT	.04	.84	−.11	−.11	.06	−.12	−.11	.14	−.02
51.	Swedish res. on S. Africa	−.84	.19	−.21	−.10	.08	.07	.23	.02	−.24
52.	Ask SC 17: S. Rhodesia SGT?	.91	−.04	.16	.21	−.10	−.05	.08	−.09	−.04
53.	S. Rhodesia on agenda	.90	−.00	.13	.22	.09	−.06	.06	−.07	−.06
54.	"1 man 1 vote" S. Rhodesia	.86	−.07	.23	.20	.06	−.06	.02	−.12	−.04
55.	Regret UK on S. Rhodesia	.82	.05	.02	.23	−.07	−.04	.09	−.15	−.05
56.	Condemn Portugal	.76	−.21	.40	.25	.18	.04	.01	−.12	−.16
57.	Report on Angola	.65	−.17	.37	.24	.23	−.05	−.07	−.12	−.04
58.	Angola & SC 17	.77	−.09	.31	.34	.10	−.12	−.07	−.10	.10
59.	Burundi Prime Minister	−.85	.06	−.22	−.30	.06	−.05	−.06	−.11	.10
60.	Rwanda & Burundi sovereign	−.58	.14	−.49	−.30	−.07	.04	.00	.09	.02
61.	Evacuate R. & B. by 1 Jul. 62	−.75	−.20	.42	.31	−.05	.00	.11	.14	−.01
62.	Rwanda & Burundi Evacuation	.30	.19	.09	.10	−.03	−.11	−.08	−.15	−.14
63.	Rwanda & Burundi Evacuation	−.05	.70	−.14	−.09	.12	.04	−.15	−.13	.02
64.	$2 million to S.G. for R. & B.	.01	.75	−.04	−.11	.16	−.08	.26	.15	−.81
65.	5 Secretariat members/country	.64	.41	.21	.28	−.35	−.01	.10	−.03	−.44
66.	Congo expenses and I.C.J.	−.51	.61	−.32	−.20	−.10	−.01	.24	.04	−.14
67.	Congo cost	−.28	.83	−.01	−.00	.11	−.02	−.13	−.10	.03
68.	U.N.E.F. expenses	−.36	.76	.02	−.11	.07	.01	−.30	−.08	−.01
69.	Budget for year 1962	−.12	.76	−.03	−.29	.07	.06	−.29	−.06	.17
70.	Conf. on consular relations	.65	−.23	.56	.29	−.10	−.04	−.27	−.13	.23

0.05, with the first axis alone accounting for more variance in the resulting space than the other three put together. Looking at Figure 14, we see a general approximate circumplex pattern not unlike the hypothetical quantification scale of state-candidate preferences in Figure 11. Substantially, the first two axes of these results seem to describe the same North–South and East–West dimensions found in the factor matrix in the original source. (But a plot of the unrotated factor loadings, for which the distance interpretation of Figure 14 does not hold, shows a number of differences.) Without interpreting the results causally, we can use the previous rotated factor analysis—or any other clustering type procedure—to find issue subgroups or classes. When plotted on the figure, the results are highly suggestive as to relationships among "factor clusters" such as "Cold War" or "supranationalism" issues, in terms of their relative cohesiveness, their proximity to each other, and their East–West or North–South position. But if we want to give more meaning to "self-determination" clusters (Factor I), "supranationalism" issues, or the other major factors of Table 4 (Cold War membership controversies, "Moslem questions" concerning Palestine and West Irian), we need to locate 101 national representatives in this space to see who has generally supported the various proposals before the Assembly.

For this purpose, a variant of the quantification method, using newly derived metric distances from the SSA analysis and tentative quantifications of roll-call responses, was developed (see the Appendix, Case 3). Fortunately, distances among roll-calls were already meaningful, so that only distances between national actors and roll-calls had to be considered. The results, quite evocative of a number of substantial points, are the national locations given in the figure.

In commenting on the patterns there, first we mention that using 1, 0, −1 scores for "Yes," "Abstain," and "No" shows about nine states—South Africa, France, and Belgium among them—with stronger tendencies to say "No" than to say "Yes" in the General Assembly. In these cases, peaks of preference curves are not discovered by the quantification procedure. Rather, the bottoms of preference valleys are limned. Such actors have "no place to hide" in a conventional coalition-building sense and according to the model would prefer to be as distant as possible from the U.N. policy arena, perhaps to leave the organization. Weighting "Yes" votes more strongly gives a more conventional plot (Figure 14) of most favored ideological positions. As could not be suggested by factor scores or loadings, we see what our experience suggests, that a quantification of American and European most preferred positions—as distinguished from the watered-down compromises they reluctantly support—puts many of these states further West than their most conservative proposals.

Further comparisons of the relative height and steepness of various preference peaks (or valleys) would also be illuminating. We would thus rank states as to the degree of their toleration of, or support for, non-ideal policy alternatives. Plotting ellipses in this space could visually delimit these regions of support, which would also be useful for assessing the accuracy of a two-dimensional preference space. Although no such curves have been drawn in the figure, they tend to include about 85 per cent of the "Yes" or "Yes" plus "Abstain" votes.

Given a theoretical concern with preference spaces, the superiority of multidimensional quantification and scaling data analysis techniques seems incontrovertible. But we were also able to use our earlier factor analyses in a noncausal way, generating six suggestive roll-call clusters from four orthogonal factors.

C. SOME PRIORITIES IN DATA ANALYSIS

At the risk of being both too elliptical and too dogmatic, let me highlight some of the main emphases of the comparative discussions above in a prescriptive way. A clear underlying theme is the belief that too many contemporary researchers have become overcommitted to a single methodology. Surely principles preferable to what Kaplan has called the "law of the instrument" (given a hammer everything becomes a nail) can be practiced. Consider, as antithetical, the *principle of least automation*: the more one understands the assumptions of a wider range of available data analysis procedures, the greater the probability of achieving more realistic problem definitions and choosing substantively appropriate methods of data analysis for solving them. In other words, the greater the knowledgeable uncertainty in a researcher's mind when first confronted with a data analysis problem, the more freedom he has in determining an appropriate response. Paradoxically, as a matter of practice, the principle of least automation entails greater rather than less reliance upon computerized data processing, because the range of analysis possibilities is greatly extended when more, sometimes harder procedures are easily available as computer programs; but it also requires greater flexibility—more "control card options"—in the choice of methods appropriate to a set of data and the questions provisionally being raised about it.

An obvious case of where I could have benefited from the invocation of this law would have been in the choice of U.N. roll-call analysis procedures. Given my substantive interests in "preference spaces" as more basic than a search for "underlying voting components or factors," had I known of the existence of, and had access to, programs for implementing quantification scaling or nonmetric multidimensional scaling procedures, I would not have chosen first to factor analyze my U.N. data. Similarly, one wonders how many additive one-equation regressions or stepwise regression analyses would be repeated (or published) once their original employers could easily employ multiequation, nonadditive causal models such as used by Boudon and Kramer.

Another general principle clearly implicit in our discussions has to do with capitalizing on the repertoire of multivariate data analysis techniques that might be occasioned by adherence to the law of least automation. The many situation-specific complexities in the definition of an "appropriate" method of analysis of course preclude any one's offering an unambiguous norm, but explicit attention to the *principle of causal correspondence* seems called for. This notion, categorically stated, means that the researcher should try to match the deterministic assumptions of his data analyses procedures with his substantive questions about the political data he is looking at. Hopefully his substantive problems will include the discovery of politically determinative influence relations in the data, as a strong form of the above principle suggests. But it is also likely that causal awareness will breed analytical humility when it becomes clearer that the assumptions of almost any "canned" analysis procedure are not directly testable nor necessarily appropriate to an empirical context. Thus factor analysis can only be correctly causally interpreted when its causal assumptions are met in a particular data set.

A strong case of poor causal correspondence was the hypothetical application of one-equation methods in the Miller-Stokes representation data. Even though the results might appear plausible, the assumptions of the procedure were inappropriate for the data. Only slightly less problematic was the attempt to use methods assuming unilateral causation to untangle what were hypothesized to be reciprocal interdependencies. Here, reciprocal causal modeling, perhaps with interaction terms, comes closest to meeting the injunction of the causal correspondence principle.

A similar argument holds concerning my own work on the U.N. General Assembly. The more one watches its changing patterns of issue definition and voting coalition, the greater the desire to model the process in terms of its underlying influence relationships. This entails introducing bargaining and unilateral influence processes explicitly into the data analysis, and allowing for pre-influence "preference peaks" not necessarily coincident with those manifested in the data. Causally speaking, an empirically corroborated computer simulation model of parliamentary diplomacy would do more justice to the data (and would require a lot more data collection as well) than either more multidimensional factoring or scaling, although these procedures may well be helpful in such an enterprise.[37]

In some ways an acceptable retreat from these problems, which require more detailed, expensive, and piecemeal investigation of modeling assumptions, is not to be causal at all, thus not violating a weaker form of the causal correspondence principle. But even when merely interested in "finding correlational patterns" or predicting trends without theoretically understanding them, one must still apply principles of problem-assumption correspondence. Thus MacRae has shown how to find scales by clustering matrices of Yule's Q's, but looking for clusters with unidimensional scaling procedures will not work in a nonscalable universe. Factor analyses of unadjusted roll-call correlations do not generate scales; smallest space analysis of the same matrix will do so.

Barely submerged in these discussions is another principle, the *principle of minimal statistical constraint*: in testing or searching for empirical generalizations, try to use a procedure that imposes the fewest modeling constraints in formalizing substantive relationships; if costs are too high, add only those constraints that seem likely not be be seriously violated. Thus, *ceteris paribus*, nonlinear factor analysis is in general to be preferred to linear factor analysis because the linearity assumptions of the ordinary factor model can be tested with the former procedure, but not the latter. And interaction seeking procedures such as the analysis of variance, AID, or nonadditive causal modeling are in practice to be preferred to linear or stepwise regression approaches, not so as to violate parsimony but so as to discover when simpler linear assumptions are in fact valid. This principle does not mean that transforming data so as to meet linearity assumptions is inappropriate: in fact it calls for an investigation of the appropriateness and significance of such transformations. From the same perspective, probabilistic latent distance analysis, unfolding analysis, and nonmetric multidimensional scaling have advantages over metric multidimensional scaling procedures that may outweigh the costs of attempting such procedures. If we do not have to assume the interval nature of our data, and there are reasons to believe such specifications to be seriously in error, why do so when nonmetric procedures are available? Or if we are accustomed to opinion items which don't have perfect cumulative trace lines, why not try to use procedures like latent structure analysis, nonlinear factor analysis, or quantification scaling combined with "preference ellipsoids" that may suggest new, less constrained insights? Fewer abortive falsifications of significant verbal hypotheses might result because of their too crude formalizations.[38]

William Petty urged his peers and successors as political arithmeticians to be good taxonomists, measuring the phenomena of politics and searching for their causal explanations. He also cautioned against blind empiricism. I have assumed that increased methodological awareness of the theoretical assumptions behind various multivariate measurement techniques will lead to increased substantive understanding of the political process. It is to be hoped that the present exercise will help decrease the costs of such awareness. But the possibility of getting bogged down in methodological controversy should be avoided; it violates the dominating principle of political statistics, that of increasing political understanding.

Notes

1. In this section, I shall rely extensively on Paul F. Lazarsfeld's fascinating "Notes on the History of Quantification in Sociology—Trends, Sources and Problems," in H. Woolf (ed.), *Quantification: A History of the Meaning in the Natural and Social Sciences* (Indianapolis: Bobbs-Merrill, 1961), pp. 147–203. For the sources of the introductory quote, see ibid. pp. 151–155. A somewhat related discussion going back to Aristotelian political analysis is given in my *Mathematics and Politics* (New York: Macmillan, 1965), Chapter 1.

2. A quotation from E. A. W. Zimmermann, a German at Conring's university writing in English in his *A Political Survey of the Present State of Europe*, 1787. Quoted, along with similar citations, in G. U. Yule and M. G. Kendall, *An Introduction to the Theory of Statistics*, 14th edition, (New York: Hafner, 1958), pp. xvi–xviii, at p. xvii.

3. Lazarsfeld, *op. cit.*, p. 153, p. 149.

4. Ibid., pp. 154–161.

5. The bibliography on such a topic is, of course, enormous. I have discussed some of the arguments particularly relevant to statistics and international politics in "The Long Road to International Relations Theory: Problems of

Statistical Nonadditivity," *World Politics*, Vol. 23, No. 4 (July 1966), pp. 623–655.

6. The historical hypothesis implicit here is that a concern with causal measurement and causal explanation underlay the invention of many experimental and nonexperimental statistical procedures. Also implied is an associated interest in biological, psychological, social, and political problems. Spearman's efforts with factor analysis to uncover *the* basic dimension of human intelligence that causes positive correlations among test items would be a case in point (as discussed by Louis Guttman in his article "The Radex: A New Approach to Factor Analysis" in Lazarsfeld (ed.), *Mathematical Thinking in the Social Sciences*, The Free Press of Glencoe, 1955). So would the development by Pearson and Yule of "panel" type applications of multiple regression analysis, viz. the amazingly timely G. Udny Yule, "An Investigation into the Causes of Changes in Pauperism in England, Chiefly During the Last Two Intercensal Decades," Part I, *Journal of the Royal Statistical Society*, LVII (1899), pp. 249–286 (as cited by Hanan C. Selvin, p. 116 n., in R. A. Nisbet, *Emile Durkheim*, Englewood Cliffs, N.J.: Prentice-Hall, 1965). Multiequation regression systems as studied by economists Frisch and Tinbergen, and the experimentally linked development of analysis of variance and covariance easily fit the same generalizations.

7. Yule and Kendall, *Introduction to the Theory of Statistics*, p. xvi. I have added the bracketed "qualitative" references to the text to do justice to the widely used treatment of statistical relationships among qualitative attributes in the first several chapters of that volume.

8. These categories are adapted from J. W. Tukey, "The Future of Data Analysis," *The Annals of Mathematical Statistics*, Vol. 33, No. 1 (March 1962), pp. 1–67 at p. 7. See also his "Statistical and Quantitative Methodology" in D. P. Ray (ed.), *Trends in Social Sciences* (New York: Philosophical Library, 1961). Tukey's rebellious, reality-oriented emphasis on statistics as an empirical science in which problem recognition and approximate solutions are higher priority items of business than mathematical elegance at the price of empirical irrelevance should ring a bell for political scientists. His eclectic approach to the choice of *appropriate* analytical techniques is also refreshing and has, I hope, influenced the subsequent discussion at a number of points.

9. I know of no better statements on the central role of human causal relationships in empirical political theory than Herbert Simon's *Models of Man* (New York: Wiley, 1957), Part I; and R. A. Dahl, "Cause and Effect in the Study of Politics" and "Discussion," pp. 75–98 in D. Lerner (ed.), *Cause and Effect* (New York: Free Press, 1965). Some of the relevant objections to this approach are treated in my "Causal Inference and Political Analysis" in J. Bernd (ed.), *Mathematical Applications in Political Science*, II, (Dallas: Southern Methodist University Press, 1966).

10. A better idea of the topics not covered here could be gained by looking through

M. G. Kendall and A. Stuart, *The Advanced Theory of Statistics*, Vol. 1: *Distribution Theory*; Vol. 2: *Inference and Relationship*; Vol. 3: *Design and Analysis, and Time Series* (London: Charles Griffin, 1958–66). Interesting shorter introductions are the chapters on statistics and data analysis in both the old and the forthcoming *Handbook of Social Psychology*. The recent chapter by Mosteller and Tukey is especially useful as an introduction to the literature on Bayesian inference, which we, for reasons of space, will not discuss here.

11. A useful bibliography of social science and life science treatments of multivariate statistical analysis would certainly include the following:

H. M. Blalock, Jr., *Social Statistics* (New York: McGraw-Hill, 1960); and his *Causal Inferences in Non-experimental Research* (Chapel Hill: University of North Carolina Press, 1964), which is the best introductory statement of the causal orientation in social science research;

R. Boudon, *L'Analyse mathematique des faits sociaux*, (Paris: Librairie Plon, 1967), broadens and deepens Blalock's concern and parallels this paper in a number of respects;

C. F. Christ, *Econometric Models and Methods* (New York: Wiley, 1966), has excellent chapters on ways of estimating and validating causal models beyond those discussed by Blalock or Boudon;

C. H. Coombs, *A Theory of Data* (New York: Wiley, 1966), is especially instructive concerning preferential data;

F. M. Fisher, *The Identification Problem in Econometrics* (New York: McGraw-Hill, 1966), is most instructive concerning alternate ways of specifying and testing *ceteris paribus* assumptions;

W. L. Hays, *Statistics for Psychologists* (New York: Holt, Rinehart and Winston, 1963), is especially clear on causal interpretations of analysis of variance models used experimentally by psychologists;

P. Horst, *Factor Analysis of Data Matrices* (New York: Holt, Rinehart and Winston, 1965), covers a great variety of widely used factor analytic procedures;

E. Malinvaud, *Statistical Methods of Econometrics* (Chicago: Rand-McNally, 1966), is extremely thorough and a standard reference;

H. L. Seal, *Multivariate Statistical Analysis for Biologists* (New York: Wiley, 1964), suggestively differs in content from econometrics texts;

R. R. Sokal and P. H. A. Sneath, *Principles of Numerical Taxonomy* (San Francisco: Freeman and Company, 1963), covers a great variety of clustering procedures;

S. A. Stouffer, L. Guttman, E. A. Suchman, P. F. Lazarsfeld, *et al.*, *Measurement and Prediction* (New York: Wiley, 1966, originally Princeton University Press, 1950), is a classic study;

W. S. Torgerson, *Theory and Methods of Scaling* (New York: Wiley, 1958), is a standard review of scaling theory and includes many procedures profitably employable by political statisticians.

Note also the range of applications in *Quality and Quantity: European Journal of Methodology*, Vol. 1, No. 1-2 (January 1967), entire issue, published by Marsilio Editori, Via S. Eufemia 5, Padova, Italy.

12. In Equation (1) I have used the Greek letters to signify "true" or "underlying" characteristics and Roman letters for sample specific variables (y, u). A good relatively introductory treatment of these kinds of models is given in Hays's *Statistics for Psychologists*. A more synthetic statement is J. Fennessey, "The General Linear Model: A New Perspective on some Familiar Topics," *American Journal of Sociology*, Vol. 74, No. 1 (July 1968), pp. 1-27. Unfortunately, Blalock's *Social Statistics* does not state or emphasize underlying model equations in its treatment of analysis of variance and covariance. Whereas Blalock talks of sampling error, Hays talks of measurement error and underlying probabilistic distributions. A combination of these treatments of error seems appropriate to much of political data analysis.

13. The example of a second-order interaction effect is adapted from a forthcoming book by Charles Hermann (incidentally, in this case, *only* interaction effects were found to be statistically significant). An example of an insightful use of an analysis of variance model, but without any interaction terms, in making tentative causal inferences from nonexperimental data is Thomas A. Flinn, "Party Responsibility in the States: Some Causal Factors," *American Political Science Review*, Vol. 58, No. 1 (March 1964), pp. 60-71. A sophisticated use of analysis of variance techniques to show that most vote-predisposing factors, except for party identification, do have additive independent effects is contained in Pool, Abelson, and Popkin, *Candidates, Issues, and Strategies* (Cambridge: M.I.T. Press, 1965).

14. *Mathematics and Politics*, pp. 107-111. The results are striking in that a previous five variable linear regression model without region-specific α's and β's, when applied to analogous data, explained only about 50% in the variance of y. An interesting partial attempt at detecting and accounting for "control group" direct and interaction effects is T. Gurr's *The Conditions of Civil Violence: First Tests of a Causal Model* (with C. Rittenberg), Research Monograph #28, Center of International Studies, Princeton University, subsequently published in an abbreviated form as "Psychological Factors in Civil Violence," *World Politics*, Vol. XX, No. 2 (January 1968), pp. 245-278. Gurr finds cultural and technological control variables greatly affect the potency of various violence-causing factors.

15. "A Variance Components Model of Political Effects," in Claunch (ed.), *Mathematical Applications in Political Science*, I (Dallas: S.M.U. Press, 1965), pp. 61-85. Stokes draws on statistical work by Kish, MacRae and Meldrum, Kempthorne, and others who have used these procedures to investigate, *inter alia*, at what level of the sampling design—state, community, block, or family—most of the variance (or inequality) in opinions, values, possessions, etc., occurs.

As with several of the examples already discussed, these "explanations," of course, cry for further analysis of the *causes* of such *effects*. Unfortunately, "cross-level" causal modeling of such interest to students of federal political systems, has not yet been fully developed as a data analysis procedure.

16. Most relevant applications and citations may be found in various sections of Campbell, Converse, Miller, and Stokes, *The American Voter* (New York: Wiley, 1960); and Russett, Alker, Deutsch, Lasswell, etc., *World Handbook of Political and Social Indicators* (New Haven: Yale University Press, 1964). Blalock's introductory treatment in his *Social Statistics* of the statistical issues involved is particularly informative for the interval scale case, as is Coleman's interaction-sensitive, dynamic equilibrium interpretation of regression models relating dichotomous attributes in his *Introduction to Mathematical Sociology* (New York: Macmillan, 1964), Chapters 4–6. See also D. J. Finney, *Probit Analysis* (New York: Cambridge University Press, 1963).

17. A number of recent papers have raised similar points as to ways in which correlated explanatory variables violate assumptions of their causal and statistical "independence." Thus Blalock, "Correlated Independent Variables: The Problem of Multicollinearity," *Social Forces*, XLII (December 1963), pp. 233–237, emphasizes how estimation procedures are subjected to greatly magnified sampling and measurement errors in cases of high intercorrelations; Evans and Anastasio, "Misuse of Analysis of Covariance When Treatment Effect and Covariate are Confounded," *Psychological Bulletin*, Vol. 69, No. 1 (April 1968), pp. 225–234, show how spurious tests of significance arise when the explanatory variable (X_{ij} in Equation 2) causes some of the group differences in the dependent variable of a covariance analysis scheme (y_{ij} in Equation 2); Gordon, "Issues in Multiple Regression," *American Journal of Sociology*, Vol. 73, No. 5 (March 1968), pp. 592–616, cogently criticizes "the partialling fallacy" of assessing causal importance apart from a theoretical specification of all relevant causal relations, especially when several imperfect indices of the same theoretical concept are used in the same regression equation. D. E. Farrar and R. R. Glauber, "Multicollinearity in Regression Analysis: The Problem Revisited," *Review of Economics and Statistics*, Vol. 49, No. 1 (February 1967), pp. 92–107, suggest a number of related significance tests as well as corrective procedures.

18. Ted Gurr, with C. Rittenberg, *Conditions of Civil Violence*, p. 7, pp. 45–54. From this summarization, I have left out the interactive effects of Gurr's social control and social facilitation variables. Gurr does consider interaction analysis in another context, and finds such effects, but he has not yet incorporated them into a multiequation statement of his theoretical model. The title and footnotes of his original monograph indicate that further developments along these lines are to be expected.

19. This important point should be clear from the simplest case: $\overset{\frown}{y \leftarrow x_1 \leftarrow x_2}$, which we would infer from significant links and $r_{y1} > r_{y2}$. But $\overset{\frown}{y \leftarrow x_2 \leftarrow x_1}$ is also

consistent with $r_{y1} > r_{y2}$. Furthermore, both b_{u2} and $b_{y2 \cdot 1} > 0$ whenever $b_{y2} > b_{y1} b_{12}$. Because these two models are "exactly identified," there appears to be no *a priori* statistical rule for choosing between these two cases. Thus, the total explanatory power of each model is also the same. The only difference, when interactions are ignored, appears to be to which of the explanatory variables goes the credit for the variance in y which either could explain.

Another application of stepwise regression procedures suffering from the same ambiguities is Murphy and Tanenhaus, "Public Opinion and Supreme Court: The Goldwater Campaign," *Public Opinion Quarterly*, Vol. 32 (Spring 1968), pp. 31–50.

20. "Some Problems in the Analysis of Surveys and a Proposal," *Journal of the American Statistical Association*, 1961. See also a more recent University of Michigan monograph, Sonquist and Morgan, *The Detection of Interaction Effects*. Related procedures have been developed by Howard Rosenthal, Gerald Shure, and several others.

I am grateful to Joel Aberbach, from whose dissertation in progress the application of AID in Figure 5 was drawn. More striking interactions than these are seen when the figure is compared with an analogous one for American Whites. For this latter group, the order of explanatory importance is, first, vote histories; second, past political participation levels; third, different levels of attention to political information in the mass media.

21. This example is taken from A. Goldberg, "Discerning a Causal Pattern among Data on Voting Behavior," *American Political Science Review*, Vol. 60, No. 4 (December 1966), pp. 880–898. Goldberg rejects a number of other recursive models in which either partisan attitudes or party identification is the sole channel for sociological influences farther back in the causal funnel. His use of a single index to summarize multidimensional variables such as partisan attitudes or sociological characteristics is a practice needing further analysis.

22. The examples I give here are derived from the work by Sewall Wright—who considered the problem of reciprocal causation some years ago—and by Gerald Kramer in a paper delivered at the September 1967 meeting of the International Political Science Association.

I have developed a nonrecursive causal model of competitive coexistence in the "Causal Inferences" paper previously referred to, which, in combination with any one of the econometric texts by Malinvaud or Christ or Fisher, might serve as an introduction to the subject of nonrecursive causal modeling, estimating and testing.

23. There are other relevant estimation procedures than indirect least squares methods, such as variants of the maximum likelihood procedure, but these will not be discussed here.

24. Duncan MacRae's "Cluster Analysis of Congressional Votes with the BC TRY System," *Western Political Quarterly*, Vol. 19 (December 1966), pp. 631–638,

would be a self-conscious example of cluster-analysis, although MacRae's purpose was looking for Guttman scales using clustering techniques applied to large matrices of Yule's Q's. Rummel, Russett, Banks and Gregg, among others, have used Q-type factor analysis in a similar manner, as cited in A. S. Banks and P. M. Gregg, "Grouping Political Systems: Q-Factor Analysis of a Cross-Polity Survey," *American Behavioral Scientist*, Vol. IX, No. 3 (November 1965), pp. 3–6.

The statistical literature on cluster analysis is itself rather large and not well integrated. Particularly suggestive are: Tyron's *Cluster Analysis*; C. Alexander's *Four Computer Programs for the Hierarchical Decomposition of Systems, Which Have an Associated Linear Graph* (used by Brams to group trading partners on the basis of a matrix of zeros and ones); Sokol and Sneath's *Principles of Numerical Taxonomy* (*op. cit.*); Louis McQuitty's many papers, written originally with the problem of typologizing mental health status, but also of interest because of an increasingly nonmetric inferential orientation that compares and contrasts with some of the above citations, especially "A Mutual Development of Some Typological Theories and Pattern—Analytic Methods," *Educational and Psychological Measurement*, Vol. 27, No. 1 (Spring 1967), pp. 21–46, and a hierarchical interval scale procedure developed with J. A. Clark, "Clusters from Iterative, Intercolumnar Correlation Analysis," mimeographed, 1967. Shorter papers of relevance include Fortier and Solomon, "Clustering Procedures," in P. Krishnaiah (ed.), *Multivariate Analysis: Proceedings of the International Symposium on Multivariate Analysis* (New York: Academic Press, 1966); H. P. Friedman and J. Rubin, "On Some Invariant Criteria for Grouping Data," *Journal of American Statistical Association*, Vol. 62, No. 320 (December 1967), pp. 1159–1178; B. King, "Stepwise Clustering Procedures," *ibid.*, Vol. 62, No. 317 (March 1967), pp. 86–101; and G. H. Ball, "A Comparison of Some Cluster Seeking Techniques," Stanford Research Institute, Menlo Park, California, 1968.

25. For a political scientist, sociologist, or anthropologist, the literature on evolutionary development is full of suggestive and provocative ideas. Taxonomically, a small war has been simmering over whether or not phenetic classifications on the basis of similarities of observed characteristics are, or should be, distinguished from or preferred to phylogenetic or cladistic categorizations, with genetic and/or lineage (i.e. causal) significance. Papers with especially flavorful arguments include those by Mayr; Rubin; Kendrick and Weresub; Sokol and Camin; Sokol, Camin, Rohlf, and Sneath; all within the same three years (1965–67) of *Systematic Zoology*. The method I have used in the present paper, written by some of the leading "pheneticists" in an attempt to meet the phylogenetic aspirations which all zoologists seem to share, is described along with several different approximate computing programs in J. H. Camin and R. R. Sokol, "A Method for Deducing Branching Sequences in Phylogeny," *Evolution*, Vol. 19, No. 3 (September 1965), pp. 311–326; and

R. L. Bartcher, "Fortran IV Program for Estimation of Cladistic Relationships Using the IBM 7040," Computer Contribution #6, State Geological Survey, University of Kansas, Lawrence, 1966; others have developed similar techniques without the "irreversibility" assumption.

The social scientific significance of such topics for quantitative research has been emphasized in such recent works as Joel Cohen's *A Simple Model of Competition* (Cambridge: Harvard University Press, 1966); R. S. Kuzara, M. R. Mead, K. A. Dixon, "Seriation of Anthropological Data: A Computer Program for Matrix-Ordering," *American Anthropologist*, Vol. 68, No. 6 (December 1966), pp. 1442–1455; and Herbert Simon, "The Architecture of Complexity," *General Systems*, X (1965), pp. 63–76.

26. The data bases and sources for these arguments are mostly those discussed in a careful factor analytic study "Aggregate Data and the Study of Political Development" (*Journal of Politics*, forthcoming) by Raymond Hopkins. Where the judgments are controversial, such as Banks's and Texter's coding of Almond's versions of the pattern variables, I have not tried to change them, as one of the values of the present technique is that it provides a sophisticated rationale for detecting anomalies.

27. The literature on factor analysis is enormous. Besides the Horst volume, papers of particular methodological interest include a direct factor analysis by MacRae and Meldrum in "Critical Elections in Illinois: 1888–1958," *American Political Science Review*, Vol. 54, No. 3 (September 1960), pp. 669–683; MacRae, "Direct Factor Analysis of Sociometric Data," *Sociometry*, Vol. 23, No. 4 (December 1960), pp. 360–371; Joseph Levin, "Three-Mode Factor Analysis," *Psychological Bulletin*, Vol. 64, No. 6 (1965), pp. 442–452; and R. Stone, "A Comparison of the Economic Structure of Regions Based on the Concept of Distance," *Journal of Regional Science*, Vol. 2, No. 2 (1960), pp. 1–20. Stone's calculation of eigen vectors of a distance matrix corresponds almost exactly to early multidimensional scaling methods, as described in Torgerson, *op. cit.*, Chapter 11. A monograph pointing to a Lazarsfeld like generalization of the linear factor analysis model is R. P. McDonald, "Nonlinear Factor Analysis," *Psychometric Monograph* #15, 1967. Also of interest to political scientists will be Rummel's forthcoming *Applied Factor Analysis*.

28. Equations (17a and 17b) are so close to Equations (A2, A3, A4, and A7) of the Appendix that I now think it more appropriate to consider direct factor analysis a version of the Guttman-Hayashi method, without its particular rationale. (The equivalence, except for normalization, follows when in 17a and 17b we change u and v to x and y, and X to a.) This result corresponds closely to MacRae's attempts (personal communication) to find XY vector products that give a best least squares fit to a data matrix of cross-tabulated frequencies with direct factor analysis techniques.

29. This section relies heavily on Torgerson, *Theory and Methods of Scaling*, Chapter 12 on "Deterministic Models for Categorical Data," Coombs, *Theory of*

Data, and Guttman's "A New Approach to Factor Analysis: The Radex" in Lazarsfeld (ed.), *op. cit.* Also relevant is Guttman's "Order Analysis of Correlation Matrices," Chapter 14 in Cattell's monumental reference work, the *Handbook of Multivariate Experimental Psychology* (Chicago: Rand McNally, 1966). It should be emphasized that a lot (but not all) of Guttman's work avoids the necessity of inference from manifest to latent dispositions. Nonetheless I shall, as does Lazarsfeld, emphasize latent dispositional interpretations of his work in order to make it as consistent as possible with the focus of the present paper.

30. Hayashi's quantification scaling papers, have had considerable influence in Japan. Many have appeared in English in the *Annals of the Institute of Statistical Mathematics*, published in Tokyo, starting with "On the Quantification of Qualitative Data from the Mathematico-Statistical Point of View," Vol. II, No. 1, 1950. Some more recent improvements in the method are summarized in M. Takabatake's "Application of 'Quantification Scaling' to Socio-Political Data," mimeographed, 1967 (c/o Rikkyo University, Tokyo). Guttman's work is more accessible, either through the Stouffer or Torgerson volumes or the original articles in other sources. One of the nicest applications I know is Takabatake's dynamic, quasi-Downsian graph of two parties moving through a space with 48 states in it, with a period of close correspondence followed in 1964 by one of the parties heading down toward Mississippi.

31. The early literature is well summarized in Torgerson, *Theory and Methods of Scaling*, and Coombs, *Theory of Data*. A number of recent conceptual and computational procedures by Shepard, Kruskal, and Guttman have recently appeared in *Psychometrika*. See also R. Beals, D. H. Krantz, and A. Tversky, "Foundations of Multidimensional Scaling," *Psychological Review*, Vol. 75, No. 2 (1968), pp. 127–142. Leaving to another occasion a detailed comparison of these various methods, I shall concentrate on the Guttman-Lingoes approach for reasons of expositional clarity. See especially J. C. Lingoes, "Recent Computational Advances in Nonmetric Methodology for the Behavioral Sciences," University of Michigan, mimeographed, 1966, and recent *Behavioral Science* computer program reports. In a comparative vein, H. J. Spaeth, "An Evaluation of Nonmetric Techniques for Multidimensional Scaling," Michigan State University, 1966, mimeographed, is quite suggestive of a number of relatively minor differences.

32. Data are RA indices taken from Alker and Puchala, "Trends in Economic Partnership in the North Atlantic Area," in J. D. Singer (ed.), *Quantitative International Politics* (New York: Macmillan, 1968). A good description of the Deutsch-Savage RA index and its statistical rationale is L. A. Goodman, "A Short Computer Program for the Analysis of Transaction Flows," *Behavioral Science*, Vol. 9, No. 2 (April 1964), pp. 176–186. It is of particular interest that Takabatake, *op. cit.*, has achieved very similar results to Figure 13 using quantification scaling of the *raw* data matrix.

33. Lazarsfeld's theory and Gibson's generalization of it are discussed in the previously cited Torgerson and Stouffer volumes, in Lazarsfeld and Henry (eds.), *Readings in Mathematical Social Science* (Chicago: SRA Associates, 1966), and in their *Latent Structure Analysis* (Boston: Houghton Mifflin, 1968).

34. This example derives loosely from Stouffer's "An Empirical Study of Technical Problems in Analysis of Role Obligation," in Parsons and Shils (eds.), *Toward a General Theory of Action* (New York: Harper Torchbook, 1962), pp. 479–496.

35. Warren Miller and Donald Stokes, "Constituency Influence in Congress," *American Political Science Review*, Vol. 57, No. 1 (March 1963). See also C. F. Cnudde and D. J. McCrone, "The Linkage between Constituency Attitudes and Congressional Voting Behavior: A Causal Model," ibid., Vol. IX, No. 1 (March 1966), pp. 66–72.

   In "Some Indirect Evidences of Constituency Pressures on the Senate," *Public Policy* (1967), pp. 253–270, John Jackson begins to investigate a nonrecursive reformulation, an issue also raised in D. Forbes and E. Tufte, "A Note of Caution in Causal Modelling," *American Political Science Review*, Vol. LXII, No. 4 (December 1968), pp. 1258–1264.

   In our discussions we shall ignore the problem of testing for type I and type II statistical errors in our use of Simon–Blalock techniques, not because further refinements along those lines are not desirable but because the original study does not publish enough information about sampling procedures to enable the reader to calculate sampling distributions.

36. H. R. Alker, Jr., "Dimensions of Conflict in the General Assembly," *American Political Science Review*, LVIII (September 1964), pp. 542–557. Table 4 is reprinted with permission.

37. For an outline of such a model, see my "Computer Simulations, Conceptual Frameworks and Coalition Behavior," in Groennings, Kelley, and Leiserson (eds.), *The Study of Coalition Behavior*, forthcoming.

38. Surely one of the advantages of a conscious awareness of model assumptions, such as have been algebraically and geometrically reviewed here, is the increased awareness of convergent approaches. Thus, James McKeon, in "Canonical Analysis: Some Relations Between Canonical Correlation, Factor Analysis, Discriminant Function Analysis, and Scaling Theory," *Psychometric Monograph Number 13*, shows the equivalence of Mahalanobis D^2 analysis and the basic metric versions of multidimensional scaling discussed by Torgerson. And we have noted how direct factor analysis and quantification scaling are formally remarkably similar. Other correspondences include the specializations of smallest space analyses to do unfolding or radex analysis and of latent structure analysis to do Guttman scaling, MacRae's use of cluster analysis of certain associational coefficients (Yule's Q's) to generate Guttman scales, and the near miss of stepwise regression procedures in generating recursive causal models. The more such correspondences are known, the less useless generation of insignificantly different analytical procedures.

Appendix: Some Derivations of Quantification Scaling Procedures*

Case 1: The general method for quantifying attributes.

Let us assume that various actor types have various attributes or opinions, as represented in the table below:

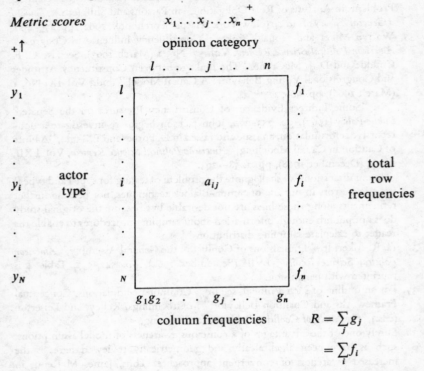

Metric scores $x_1 \ldots x_j \ldots x_n \xrightarrow{+}$

$+\uparrow$ opinion category

Notational conventions should be obvious from the figure. Note especially that a_{ij}'s are frequencies ≥ 0, and that the total number of responses, R, in general is greater than N or n.

* These derivations start from either Guttman, *Measurement and Prediction*, pp. 334–361, or the matrix equation treatment in Takabatake, "Application of 'Quantification Scaling' to Socio-Political Data," or Mosteller's simpler results in Torgerson, pp. 338–345. The procedures involved may be seen in part to parallel Lingoes's discussion of his MAC-11 program (basically the Guttman-Hayashi case), and his modified, nonmetric procedures MSA-I and MSA-II in "The Multivariate Analysis of Qualitative Data," *Multivariate Behavioral Research*, Vol. 3, No. 1 (January 1968), pp. 61–94.

As originally defined, the Guttman-Hayashi procedure seeks to find those interval scale scores x_j and y_i for row and column categories in a frequency table that maximize the squared correlation of x and y. This corresponds to seeking to reorder "actor" and "opinion" categories in the table so that as x and y both increase (as there indicated by arrows), cell frequencies tend to cluster along the lower left-upper right diagonal. Every response in the table is a point in its cell; therefore, we should define the produce-moment r over the total set of R responses.

We derive the x's and y's as follows. It is convenient and not restrictive to assume that x and y have zero means. Then

$$s_x^2 = \frac{1}{R} \sum_j g_j x_j^2; \qquad s_y^2 = \frac{1}{R} \sum_i f_i y_i^2$$

$$s_{xy} = \frac{1}{R} \sum_i \sum_j a_{ij} x_j y_i; \qquad b_{yx} = s_{xy}/s_x^2; \qquad b_{xy} = s_{xy}/s_y^2$$

$$r^2 = \frac{s_{xy}^2}{s_x^2 s_y^2} = \frac{\left(\sum_i \sum_j a_{ij} x_j y_i \right)^2}{\sum_i f_i y_i^2 \sum_j g_j x_j^2} \tag{A1}$$

Differentiating r^2 with respect to x_j and then y_i and setting the results equal to zero gives maximum x's and y's as follows:

$$\frac{\partial r^2}{\partial x_j} = \frac{2 s_x^2 s_y^2 R s_{xy} \sum_i a_{ij} x_j y_i - 2 s_{xy}^2 R s_y^2 g_j x_j}{s_x^4 s_y^4} = 0$$

or

$$\sum_i a_{ij} y_i = \frac{s_{xy}}{s_x^2} g_j x_j = b_{yx} g_j x_j \tag{A2}$$

Similarly,

$$\sum_j a_{ij} x_j = b_{xy} f_i y_i \tag{A3}$$

Now, to solve Equations (A2) and (A3) for x's and y's alone, we substitute one equation into the other and simplify, giving

$$\sum_j \frac{a_{ij}}{g_j} \sum_i a_{ij} y_i = f_i b_{xy} b_{yx} y_i = f_i r^2 y_i$$

$$\sum_i \frac{a_{ij}}{f_i} \sum a_{ij} x_j = g_j r^2 x_j \tag{A4}$$

The above equations are the familiar characteristic equations of principal components analysis, and can be solved by a number of eigen vectoring routines. After the first, trivial eigen value and vector are extracted (corresponding to row and column averages), each subsequent eigen *value* gives the additional r^2 being explained by the eigen *vector's* x scores and the corresponding *y*'s associated with it. (Only the highest variance nontrivial scores have been used here.)

If the solutions to equations (A4) solve the "quantification" problem, we have yet to show that the results are interpretable in a "scaling" sense of providing a joint spatial representation of actors and opinions. This result follows readily from considering the following spatial representation data analysis problem.

We would like to find those x's *and* y's *that minimize along every dimension the distance between those* i's *and* j's *with high corresponding* a_{ij} *frequencies.* In other words, we want actor types and opinion categories to be spatially proximate whenever especially many actors choose these response categories. Formally, this result could be achieved by minimizing the following squared distance expression (along any particular axis):

$$D^2 = \frac{1}{R} \sum_i \sum_j a_{ij}(y_i - x_j)^2$$

$$\text{(A5)}$$

$$= \frac{1}{R} \sum_i \sum_j a_{ij} y_i^2 - \frac{2}{R} \sum_i \sum_j a_{ij} x_j y_i + \frac{1}{R} \sum_i \sum_j a_{ij} x_j^2$$

Now, if we standardize x and y so as to have equal variances, in particular the eigen values λ corresponding to their derivation in Equations (A4), then the above expression immediately simplifies to

$$D^2 = 2\lambda - 2s_{xy} = 2\lambda(1 - s_{xy}/\lambda) = 2\lambda(1 - r) \qquad \text{(A6)}$$

Thus, *maximizing* r *or* r^2 *is equivalent to minimizing* D^2 *whenever* x *and* y *variables are jointly plotted with equal variances.*

Case 2: Quantifying cumulative scales or point scales: the principal components of scale analysis.

Guttman treats a special case of equations (A4) in deriving his metric for cumulative scales. The second and higher score vectors thus achieved, he calls intensity, closure, etc. Mosteller, in simplifying the derivation has shown an equivalent result holds for point scales as well.

For a Guttman scale of m dichotomous items, represented tabularly in parallelogram fashion, $n = 2m$, $f_i =$ a constant number of categories c, $a_{ij} = e_{ij} = 1$ or 0, depending on whether i does or does not check category j. Rewriting equations (A4) with rearranged summations and indices then gives

$$\sum_k \sum_j \frac{e_{ij}e_{kj}}{\sum_k e_{kj}} y_k = cr^2 y_i$$

$$\sum_k \sum_i \frac{e_{ij}e_{ik}}{\sum_k e_{ik}} x_k = g_j r^2 x_j$$

(A7)

These equations, with coefficients on the left that are weighted row and column products, are exactly those Guttman originally published. When dichotomous noncumulative or point scales are used, then a parallelogram representation of items and their opposites is not necessary, the number of items included is only m, and equations (A7) again hold.

Case 3: Plotting actors in a predetermined issue space so as to maximize proximity-preference relationships.

A special problem arises when there are many actors that one would like to plot close to the objects or opinions of their choice, when these opinions have already been given a spatial representation by either a metric or nonmetric procedure. If computing costs for a joint scaling procedure are prohibitive, the following specializations of the quantification scaling approach seem appropriate.

The Takabatake Procedure. Michitoshi Takabatake has suggested that the problem may be solved by using the same equations as in the general quantification method. We shall use slightly different notation. Let $a = 1, 2, \ldots, m$ (the axes involved), and $i = 1, 2, \ldots, n$ (the range of opinions), and $k = 1, 2, \ldots, N$ (the number of countries or subjects). Then x_{ia} would be the (given) scores of opinion i on axis a; $V_{ik} = a$ the quantified expression of support by country k for an opinion i, such as "Yes" $= 1$, "Abstain" $= 0$, "No" $= -1$, and something within this range for absent countries. As with equation (A5), we want to find a positioning of each country k on every axis a, that is a set of Y_{ka}'s, so that d_{ik} is small when V_{ik} is highly positive. This criteria is measurable in terms of a $\theta_{ik} = V_{ik}d_{ik}^2$, which we would like to be small when V_{ik} is positive and large, and negative when V_{ik} is negative.

Therefore let us minimize (A8):

$$\theta.. = \frac{1}{nN} \sum_i^n \sum_k^N V_{ik}d_{ik}^2 = \frac{1}{nN} \sum_i^n \sum_k^N V_{ik} \sum_a^m (x_{ia} - Y_{ka})^2 \qquad (A8)$$

with respect to Y_{ka}, x_{ia}, and V_{ik} being known in advance and fixed. Minimization occurs when first derivatives are zero and second derivatives near the first derivative's solution point are positive.

$$\frac{\partial \theta..}{\partial Y_{ka}} = -\frac{2}{nN} \sum_i^n V_{ik}(x_{ia} - Y_{ka}) = 0$$

$$\frac{\partial^2 \theta..}{\partial Y_{ka}^2} = \frac{2}{nN} \sum_i^n V_{ik} = \frac{2}{N} V._k \quad \text{(independent of } Y_{ka}!\text{)}$$

From these equations, we see that the Takabatake Y estimate, call it $\widehat{TY}$, is given by

$$\widehat{TY}_{ka} = \frac{1}{nV._k} \sum_i^n V_{ik}x_{ia} \qquad (A9)$$

and that these $\widehat{TY}_{ka}$'s will maximize single-peakedness whenever a country's average vote score or support score is greater than zero.

As noted in the text, when $V._k$ for country k is below zero, the country is generally discontented with most opinions or resolutions being proposed. Moreover, in this case, the above mathematics derives not preference peaks, but preference pits. While these latter points have considerable substantive suggestiveness, some reformulation of the above approach should be possible. Within the present framework, perhaps the most appealing alternative would be somehow to rescale the V_{ik}'s on the basis of evidence about intensities or simply with V_{ik}'s greater than 1.0 when a rare "Yes" occurs. As long as $V._k > 0$, a meaningful result, based on particular metric assumptions about the V_{ik}'s, will be found. (For Figure 14, $V(\text{yes}) = 2.0$ was used.)

An Alternative Procedure. Although the formula involved is somewhat more complex, another procedure, derived independently of the former one, appears to give joint country-opinion plots susceptible to proximity = preference interpretations with fewer restrictions on the values of the $V._k$'s. Essentially, it requires that certain averages of the $V._k$'s be greater than zero.

Let us begin by restricting the form of Y_{ka} in the above equation for

$\theta..$ to an *a priori* plausible form: some linear transformation of a $V_{ki}x_{ia}$ average. (Intuitively, the higher opinion i is on axis a, the more k belongs on that side of the a axis when k supports that opinion strongly.) Then the same rationale as above suggests calculating first and second derivatives of $\theta..$ where now

$$Y_{ka} = \frac{C_a}{n} \sum_i V_{ik}x_{ia} + C_a'$$

$$= C_a S_{ka} + C_a' \text{ (for convenience)} \qquad \text{(A10)}$$

Thus

$$\frac{\partial \theta}{\partial C_a} = -\frac{2}{nN} \sum_i \sum_k V_{ik}(x_{ia} - C_a S_{ka} - C_a) S_{ka} = 0$$

$$\frac{\partial^2 \theta}{\partial C_a^2} = \frac{2}{nN} \sum_i \sum_k V_{ik} S_{ka}^2$$

$$\frac{0\theta}{\partial C_a'} = -\frac{2}{nN} \sum_i \sum_k V_{ik}(x_{ia} - C_a S_{ka} - C_a') = 0 \qquad \text{(A11)}$$

$$\frac{\partial^2 \theta}{\partial C_a'^2} = -\frac{2}{nN} \sum_i \sum_k V_{ik} = 2V..$$

We can already see how the minimization conditions—that the second derivatives be greater than zero—are much easier to satisfy.

Solving equations (A11) for C_a' and C_a estimates, we find it convenient to summarize the results as:

$$\hat{C}_a = \frac{KM_a - nNL_aS_{.a}}{KP_a - L_a^2}; \qquad \hat{C}_a' = \frac{nNS_{.a} - C_aL_a}{K}$$

$$\hat{Y}_{ka} = \frac{\hat{C}_a}{n} \sum_j V_{jk}x_{ja} + C_a'$$

where, for double sums always over i and k,

$$K = \sum \sum V_{ik}, \quad L_a = \sum \sum S_{ka}V_{ik}, \quad M_a = \sum \sum S_{ka}V_{ik}x_{ia},$$

$$P_a = \sum_i \sum_k S_{ka}^2 V_{ik}, \quad S_{.a} = \frac{1}{N} \sum_k S_{ka} = \frac{1}{nN} \sum \sum V_{ik}x_{ia}.$$

One could see how different these results are from the Takabatake solution by comparing $\hat{C}_a$ with 1 and $\hat{C}_a'$ with zero: exact correspondence would mean equivalent results. An experimentation with this approach showed, in fact, that $\hat{C}_a =$ and $\hat{C}_a'$ gave very similar results.

Index

Abel, T., 72 n27
Aberbach, J., 258 n20
abolitionists, 233
acephalous societies, 35
Ackley, G., 198
action dispensability, 187
actor dispensability, 187
Adams, H. B., 1, 2, 231, 232
Ademan, I., 39
Adler, A., 214
Adorno, T. W., 165 n8, 183 n2, 193, 215 n20
African states: anthropology of new nations, xii, 40–45; interdisciplinary study of, 33–36; modernization of, 35–36; political development in, 18, 33–36; political science of, 29–30; rioting in, 33–36; social changes in, 33–36
aggregate data, 33
aggregative analysis, 165, 172, 197–99
Alexander, C., 266 n24
Alexander, F., 213, 214
Alford, R. R., 72 n20, 75–76, 84
alienation, 146, 154, 158–59
Alker, H. R., Jr., xvi, 80 n37, 198 n77, 244–307, 245 n105, 246 n5, 250 n14, 253 n16, 284, 289 n36
Allport, F., 5, 7
Allport, G., 5 n3, 165

Allardt, 87 n59
Almond, G., xix, 7, 14 n16, 32, 33 n3, 42 n24, 44 n27, 69, 237, 267 n26
Ambler, C., 234 n25
American Historical Association, 12
American Orthopsychiatric Society, 215
American Political Science Association, xvi, 2, 12, 163, 206, 244
American Populism, 22–23
analysis of covariance, 250–51
analysis of variance, 249–50
Anastasio, 254 n17
Anderson, C. M., 229 n4
Anderson, W., 237
anthropology, vii, 164; and economics, 146; of new nations, 40–44; and political science, 29–48, 57; and sociology, viii, xi, xiii, xvi, xx, 7, 15, 55; techniques of study, 37
anti-behaviorism, 9, 11
Apter, D. E., 33, 34–35, 81 n39, 86 n57
Apthorpe, R., 35 n14
Aristotelian world view, 58, 60, 246
Aristotle, vii, xix, 56, 197, 207
Aron, R., 75, 81

identity crisis, in political science, 2, 11, 12
Industrial Revolution, 51–52, 61
Inkeles, A., 101, 103, 163, 185–86, 197 n73
Institut für Politische Wissenschaft, 65
interaction (statistical), 249–51, 254–56, 258–59, 301
interdisciplinarian, role of, 30–31
interdisciplinary studies, 7, 14, 23; anthropology and political science, 29–48; economics and social science, 137–62; politics and sociology, 65–100; psychiatry and political science, 207–25; sociology and political science, 47–64; statistics and politics, 244–307
international relations, 39–40, 142, 149, 151, 159
International Sociological Association, 65
inter-tribal relations, 39–40
Inter-University Consortium for Political Research, 23–24, 239–40, 244

Jackson, J., 276, 286 n35
Jacksonian politics, 234
Jacob, H., 181–82, 185
Jahoda, M., 165 n8, 184 n44, 193, 194 n62, 194 n63
Jameson, J. F., 231–32
Janowitz, M., 80 n38, 92 n73, 101, 103
Jefferson, T., 208
Jensen, R., x–xi, xii, 1–28, 226–43
Jernegan, M. W., 234 n24
John Birch Society, 211
Johns Hopkins University, x, 2, 232, 239
Johnson, L. B., 276
Jones, E., 208 n1
Jones, M., 222 n24
Josephson, M., 236

journalism: and election analysis, 226ff.; and historians, 15
Jouvenal, B. de, 25
jurimetrics, 8, 24

Kafoglism, M. Z., 11 n18
Kahl, J. A., 81 n40
Kaldor, N., 127
Kaplan, A., 55 n14, 295
Kardiner, A., 209 n2
Katona, G., 117 n27
Katz, D., 185
Katz, I., 197 n69
Kaufmann, H., 113
Kelley, 297 n37
Kempthorne, 251 n15
Kendall, M. G., 245 n2, 247–48
Kendrick, 267 n25
Kennedy, J. F., 169, 276; administration, 169
Key, V. O., Jr., xix, 7, 8 n8, 13–14, 19, 24, 237, 238, 239
Keynes, J. M., 25, 127
Kilson, M., 34
Kirchheimer, O., 23 n24, 25
Kirschen, E. S., 118 n28, 123
Kirscht, J. P., 193 n61
Kish, L., 251 n15
Kleinsorge, P., 111 n18
Klineberg, O., 165 n15
Knoles, G., 234 n25
Koch, S., 163 n1, 164 n2
Kojève, A., 74 n24
Komarovsky, M., 240 n43
Korean War, 15
Kornhauser, W., 101, 103, 106
Kramer, G., 113, 262 n22, 264, 296
Kranz, D. H., 282 n31
Krishnaiah, P., 266 n24
Kuzars, R. S., 267 n25
Kyogker, 280

Labor party, 76, 78, 84
Lane, R. E., 165, 183, 239 n40
Lanlin, C., 176 n31
La Palombara, J., 14 n14